Guide to
Linux Shell Script
Programming

Todd Meadors

THOMSON

™

COURSE TECHNOLOGY

Australia • Canada • Mexico • Singapore • Spain • United Kingdom • United States

THOMSON
———— ✳ ————™
COURSE TECHNOLOGY

Linux Shell Script Programming

Todd Meadors

Product Manager:
Alyssa Pratt

Managing Editor:
Jennifer Muroff

Developmental Editor:
Laurie Brown

Editorial Assistant:
Christy Urban

Production Editor:
Kristen Guevara

Cover Designer:
Steve Deschene

Compositor:
Gex Publishing Services

Manufacturing Coordinator:
Laura Burns

Disclaimer
Course Technology reserves the right to revise this publication and make changes from time to time in its content without notice.

ISBN 0-619-15920-0

BRIEF

Contents

TABLE OF
Contents

Preface

*L*inux Shell Script Programming is designed to provide the intermediate programmer with the tools to create shell scripts that allow for greater flexibility, coherence, and efficiency in the Linux work environment. It would be helpful to have taken at least one programming or programming design theory and logic class. Familiarity with basic Linux or UNIX concepts is essential.

ORGANIZATION AND COVERAGE

Linux Shell Script Programming begins by discussing operating systems in general and the Linux operating system in specific. Basic Linux commands are also covered to help the reader become more familiar with how Linux functions.

After the reader understands some of the basics of the Linux operating system and its commands, the book presents the following:

- An introduction to the Linux file system
- An overview of the shell environment, as well as shell grammar, shell builtin commands, and command types
- Use of redirection, pattern matching, expansion, and quoting in the shell environment
- The basics of shell script programming concepts
- Use of decision structures within shell scripts
- Use of looping structures within shell scripts
- Functions and arrays
- Use of sorting and searching techniques for managing files and scripts
- Use of specific programs to augment scripts such as the arbitrary precision calculator, `grep`, and `sed`
- Use of `awk` to manage data, files, and scripts
- Implementation dialog boxes to create user-friendly scripts
- Design of Web-page scripts to interface with MySQL
- Use of the Revision Control System
- Creation of manual pages for scripts

FEATURES

Linux Shell Script Programming is a superior textbook because it also includes the following features:

- **Read This Before You Begin Page.** This page is consistent with Course Technology's unequaled commitment to helping instructors introduce technology into the classroom. Technical considerations and assumptions about hardware, software, and default settings are listed in one place to help instructors save time.

- **Step-by-Step Methodology.** This unique Course Technology methodology keeps readers on track. They write program code always within the context of solving the problems posed in the chapter. The text constantly guides users and lets them know where they are in the process of solving the problem. The numerous illustrations guide readers in creating useful, working programs.

- **Tips.** These notes provide additional information on Linux commands, programming, and computer performance. For example, they might identify an alternative method for performing a procedure, some background information on a technique, or a warning about a commonly-made error.

- **Summaries.** Following each chapter is a Summary that recaps the programming concepts and commands covered in each section.

- **Review Questions.** Each chapter concludes with meaningful, conceptual Review Questions that test readers' understanding of what they learned in the chapter.

- **Hands-on Projects.** Each chapter concludes with Hands-on Projects that give readers additional practice with the skills and concepts they learned in the chapter. These exercises increase in difficulty and are designed to allow the student to explore the language and programming environment independently.

- **Cases.** Two Cases are included with each chapter. One is a running case that develops as the reader progresses through the book. Each case highlights the concepts covered in each chapter, building on the programming concepts covered in previous chapters.

THE LINUX ENVIRONMENT

This book was written and tested using Red Hat Linux 8.0 installed on a personal computer. Screen shots were captured using Red Hat Linux 8.0, with a few captured using Windows 2000. Although most scripts will run on prior versions of Red Hat 8.0, the output may differ.

TEACHING TOOLS

All the teaching tools for this text are found in the Instructor's Resource Kit CD-ROM, which is also available on Course Technology's Web site. Additional teaching tools, including standardizing naming conventions, can be found on the same Web site.

You should be familiar with the following:

- **Instructor's Manual**. The Instructor's Manual was written by the author of the main text and was thoroughly quality-assurance tested. It is available at *www.course.com*. Call your customer service representative for the specific URL and a password. The Instructor's Manual contains the following items:

  - Answers to all the Review Questions and solutions to all the Hands-on Projects in the book. The files contain instructor's notes about each solution and its expected difficulty level.

  - Teaching notes to help introduce and clarify the material presented in the chapters.

  - Technical notes that include troubleshooting tips.

- **ExamView®**. This textbook is accompanied by ExamView, a powerful testing software package that allows instructors to create and administer printed, LAN-based and Internet exams. ExamView includes hundreds of questions that correspond to the topics covered in this text, enabling students to generate detailed study guides that include page references for further review. The computer-based and Internet testing components allow readers to take exams at their computers and also save the instructor time by automatically grading each exam.

- **Solution Files.** Solution files contain a possible solution to every program readers are asked to create or modify in the chapters' Hands-on Projects and Cases. Each solution contains numerous comments to help explain the code found in the solution file. (Due to the nature of programming, readers' solutions might differ from these solutions and still be correct.)

- **Data Files.** Data files containing all the data that students will use for the chapters and exercises in this textbook are provided through *www.course.com* and on the Instructor's Resource Kit CD-ROM. A Help file includes technical tips for lab management. See the "Read This Before You Begin" page before Chapter 1 for more information on the data files and their organization.

ACKNOWLEDGEMENTS

A book of this scale is not just the work of the author. There are many people along the way who helped complete this project. First, I'd like to thank Laurie Brown, my developmental editor, for her continued support and direction while working on this project. Laurie kept me focused and on track every step of the way.

I'd like to thank Alyssa Pratt for always looking toward the future and keeping an eye on the fast-paced changes and developments of Linux. The end result is a top-notch shell script programming book with the most current operating system Red Hat offers.

Also, thanks to Jennifer Muroff, Managing Editor, for giving me the opportunity to write this book. Without her support, this never would have gotten off the ground.

I would like to thank Nicole Ashton and her Quality Assurance team for the time they spent fine-tuning this book. I'd like to thank the reviewers: Paul F. Almquist, Chippewa Valley Technical College; Tim Chappell, Dona Ana Branch Community College; and Robert Koch, Empire College for their technical comments. Thanks again for helping me strive to make a better book. Saving the best for last, I would like to thank my wife Micki for her steadfast support along the way. I want to dedicate this book to her and our two wonderful children, Zachary and Jessica. Additionally, I'd like to thank my parents, Dr. and Mrs. Lawrence H. Meadors, for the sacrifices they made for my education. Thanks, Mother, for tutoring me so much in the 3rd grade–it continues to pay countless dividends.

Read This Before You Begin

The following information will help you as you prepare to use this textbook.

To the User of the Data Files

In some cases, to complete the steps and projects in this book, you will need data files that have been created specifically for this book. Your instructor will provide the data files to you. You also can obtain the files electronically from the Course Technology Web site by connecting to *www.course.com*, and then searching for this book title. Note that you can use a computer in your school lab or your own computer to complete the Hands-on Projects in this book. The data files for this book are organized such that the examples and exercises are divided into folders named Chapter.*xx*, where *xx* is the chapter number. Compiled solutions appear in the Solutions*xx* folder. Use these precompiled solutions to help you visualize the end result of the steps. You can save the data files anywhere on your system unless specifically indicated otherwise in the chapter.

Using Your Own Computer

To use your own computer to complete the steps and Hands-on Projects, you will need the following:

- **Software.** Although many of the commands and scripts will work with most versions of UNIX and Linux, there are some scripts that may require slight modification if you use them on other versions. To get the most out of the book, you need to install Red Hat Linux 8.0 to successfully complete all of the labs. This book includes a copy of the Publisher's Edition of Red Hat® Linux® from Red Hat, Inc., which you may use in accordance with the license agreement. Official Red Hat® Linux®, which you may purchase from Red Hat, includes the complete Red Hat® Linux® distribution, Red Hat's documentation, and may include technical support for Red Hat® Linux®. You also may purchase technical support from Red Hat. You may purchase Red Hat® Linux® and technical support from Red Hat through the company's Web site (*www.redhat.com*) or its toll-free number 1.888.REDHAT1. There is a sticker on the top of the envelope containing the Red Hat® Linux® CD-ROMs (this sticker may also be on the inside back cover of the text). By ripping this seal, you agree to the terms listed above.

- **Hardware.** A Pentium II–class processor, 450 MHz or higher, personal computer.
- **Data Files.** You will not be able to complete the chapters and projects in this book using your own computer unless you have the data files. You can get the data files from your instructor, or you can obtain the data files electronically from the Course Technology Web site by connecting to *www.course.com* and then searching for this book title.

Basic Installation Guidelines for Red Hat® Linux® 8.0

This book assumes that Red Hat Linux 8.0 is pre-installed on a computer system. Although the complete installation steps are not covered in this book, the general procedure is as follows:

1. Shut down your computer system.
2. Insert the first Red Hat Linux 8.0 installation CD into the CD-ROM drive of your computer system.
3. As the computer is starting and performing the Power On Self Test (POST), press the key that allows you to enter the Basic Input Output System (BIOS) setup. A menu should appear. While the key to enter BIOS can differ for every computer, it is typically the DEL key. Next, you need to search until you find where you can change the start sequence. Again, each BIOS setup is different, so exact steps are not given. Change the start sequence so the CD-ROM starts first. Make sure you save the BIOS setup changes.
4. Now the computer should start from the installation CD. Follow the steps on the screen to complete the installation. For additional information, access the Internet and go to the Red Hat Web site at *www.redhat.com/docs/manuals/linux/RHL-8.0-Manual/installguide/*.
5. Once installation is complete, change your BIOS setup again so the computer starts from the hard drive first.

VISIT OUR WORLD WIDE WEB SITE

Additional materials designed especially for this book might be available for your course. Periodically search *www.course.com* for more details.

A NOTE ON SYNTAX

This book includes many examples of Linux command statements. As the statements in Linux can sometimes become quite long, they may not always fit on a single line for formatting reasons. A command statement that must appear on two lines for formatting reasons will appear with the subsequent line indented below the original line.

1

INTRODUCTION TO THE OPERATING SYSTEM ENVIRONMENT

In this chapter, you will:

♦ Understand operating systems
♦ Define the Unix and Linux operating systems
♦ Understand classifications of software
♦ Understand data
♦ Understand the user roles
♦ Understand basic Linux commands
♦ Create shell scripts

The operating system is a set of software instructions that run the computer. When you write shell script programs, you combine Linux operating system commands and programming logic to create automated tasks. In this chapter, you will learn about the major operating systems as well as features specific to the Linux operating system. You will learn about the types of users in a Linux environment, which will help you determine the type of access and type of scripts individuals need. Some of the common basic Linux commands will be discussed. You can use these commands in scripts to make a user's job easier. Finally, to get you started with shell programming, you will create a few shell scripts.

UNDERSTANDING OPERATING SYSTEMS

Software is a set of instructions that are processed by the computer system. The **operating system** is software that governs computer systems. The components in a computer system are the users, the applications, and the hardware. The operating system acts as a liaison between these components. It is the operating system that allows you to save a file to disk, retrieve a file from disk, run a spreadsheet application, print a file, compile a program, point and click with your mouse, enter text commands, or navigate the graphical user interface (GUI). Think of the operating system as the software "brains" of the computer system. Figure 1-1 highlights the relationship between the operating system and the other components in a computer system.

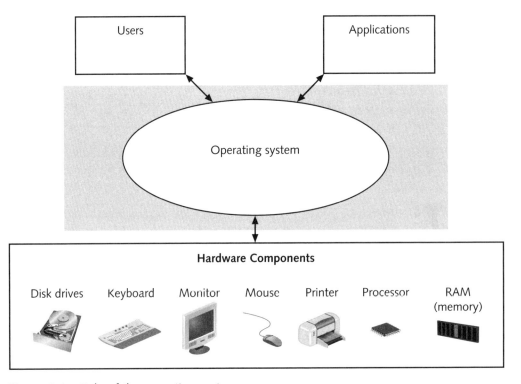

Figure 1-1   Role of the operating system

 The terms "software" and "programs" are synonymous in the computer industry.

There are many different operating systems running many different computer systems both for business and home use. Operating systems run large mainframe computers, server-based networks, PC (personal computer) systems, laptops, and even small handheld devices.

Mainframe operating systems are designed to handle the input/output (I/O), processing, and storage requirements for many users. These operating systems run mainframe computers and are generally used in large corporations. An example of a mainframe operating system is the IBM Multiple Virtual Storage (MVS) system.

Network operating systems allow computers to share resources over a network. A **resource** is a hardware device, a software program, or a file. A printer that can be used by multiple users is an example of a shared resource. In the past a **network** was defined as a group of computers and printers connected by cables. However, with the advent of newer technology, computers and printers can communicate via wireless transmission as well. Network operating systems use **protocol software** to facilitate the communication among computers throughout a network. TCP/IP is the most common protocol used today. **Transmission Control Protocol/Internet Protocol (TCP/IP)** allows you to connect to the Internet and browse Web sites, perform searches, or shop online. Each computer, called a **host**, must have an **IP (Internet Protocol) address** to communicate with other computers on the network. The host may also have a **Domain Name Service (DNS) name** such as Redhat.com. This is sometimes called its "friendly name." The DNS name is used so people won't have to remember the IP address of a host.

In a network, **servers** are computers that allow other computers to connect to the server's shared resources. **Clients** are the computers that use the resources made available by the servers. The **client/server** model is when a server computer handles the requests made by the client computer. There are usually more clients than servers in a network. Because the server has to handle numerous client requests, the server typically has more memory, hard drive space, and processing capability than the clients. Examples of operating systems that run on servers are Novell NetWare, Microsoft Windows NT Server, 2000 Server, and UNIX/Linux. Windows 95, Windows 98, Windows NT Workstation, Windows 2000 Professional, and Windows XP are examples of client operating systems. You can also run UNIX/Linux as a client. Servers and clients must use the same protocol in order to communicate with one another. Even if clients are using different operating systems, the use of a common protocol allows communication to occur. In Figure 1-2, you can see the server and clients in a network environment.

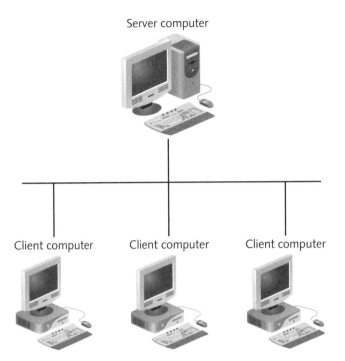

Server computer

Client computer   Client computer   Client computer

Figure 1-2   Client/server model in a network

Defining the Unix and Linux Operating Systems

The UNIX operating system goes back to the 1960s. Several employees working for AT&T developed an operating system based on the C language and called it UNIX. The initial version was called AT&T System Release V. The operating system code was freely distributed to major universities where changes were made to it. So, unlike proprietary operating systems such as Microsoft Windows, Novell, and IBM, a single vendor has not developed UNIX. There have been numerous versions of the initial operating system, and many vendors have customized UNIX to fit their own platforms. IBM has written a version of UNIX called Advanced Interactive Executive (AIX), Sun has written Solaris, and Hewlett-Packard has written HP-UX, and there are many others. Recently, software vendors who have traditionally developed their own operating systems for their own hardware are beginning to use the Linux operating system.

The Linux operating system was developed from another version of UNIX called MINIX. It comes with many built-in features, a full compliment of programming languages, compilers, and system administration tools, and is available at a very reasonable cost. Table 1-1 shows a listing of some of the versions of the Linux operating system and the associated Web sites for researching them. This book focuses on the Linux operating system.

Table 1-1   Versions of Linux and their Web sites

Version	Web Site
Debian	www.debian.org
OpenLinux	www.calderasystems.com
SuSe	www.suse.com
Slackware	www.slackware.com
Mandrake	www.mandrake.com
Red Hat	www.redhat.com

Let's look at some of the features the Linux operating systems offers. They are as follows:

- Multiuser capability
- Portability
- Multitasking
- Ability to use multiple processors
- Multiple modes of operation

Multiuser Capability

A **multiuser** operating system is one capable of handling multiple requests by a variety of users. Many companies run Linux as their mainstay operating system for their business because it provides a multiple user platform. They can install their applications on a Linux server and have client computers access the application on the server over the network. Some operating systems are single-user platforms (only one user can use the computer), such as Windows 95 and 98.

 A platform comprises both the hardware and software combination on which a given system runs. For example, if Linux version 8.0 is the software running on an Intel-based hardware system, then the two combined are called the platform.

Portability

Portability allows you to carry the Linux operating system to another hardware system, recompile it, and run the operating system. Of course, this is always easier said than done because installing an operating system can be an arduous task. Many operating systems are written for a specific processor. Each processor has its own **instruction set**, which is the set of instructions the processor uses to operate. The instruction sets of different processors are typically not compatible. You can think of an instruction set as being the language specific to the processor.

There are two general types of processors. A **complex instruction set computer (CISC)** has a large set of instructions in its instruction set. A **reduced instruction set computer (RISC)** has a reduced number of instructions in its instruction set but relies on hardware to perform the tasks not provided by the instruction set. Because of the enhanced hardware, a RISC processor is faster, yet more expensive, than a CISC processor. The processor in most PCs is a CISC processor. Windows 98 runs only on CISC-based Intel processors. Red Hat Linux can run on both CISC and RISC processors. The portability of the Linux operating system gives you more hardware options on which to run the operating system because you can choose to run Linux on either type of processor.

Multitasking

Multitasking is when the operating system can handle multiple jobs at seemingly the same time. When a program executes, it is known as a job or process. Technically, the operating system performs only one job at a time. However, through time slicing, the operating system gives each job a little bit of time. The jobs take turns being processed in a round-robin manner. Let's look at an example. Assume the operating system gives each job only one minute of CPU time. If a job exceeds the one-minute time slice, it is sent to the swap file. Then the next job in line begins processing. If this job finishes in less than a minute, then the system can retrieve the next job in the process queue or continue processing the first job that was sent to the swap file. This is done for all jobs until there is no more work to be done. The advantage of this is that one large job lasting 15 minutes or so won't slow down the whole system and keep smaller jobs that require less processing time from being completed.

The Linux operating system employs preemptive multitasking as opposed to cooperative multitasking. With **preemptive multitasking**, the operating system has the ability to take control of the system from an application. With **cooperative multitasking**, the application takes control of the system resources. The advantage of preemptive multitasking is that if an application fails, the whole system won't necessarily crash. In cooperative operating systems, a failed application can cause the whole computer to freeze or crash.

Ability to Use Multiple Processors

The ability to have several processors to improve overall throughput, or the amount of work that can be put through the system, is another advantage of the Linux operating system, and Linux can accommodate up to 32 processors. Linux also uses **multithreading** which allows for a program to be split across several processors, with each processor working on a different piece of the program at the same time.

Symmetrical multiprocessing (SMP) facilitates multithreading. SMP greatly enhances throughput because several processors handle one large task instead of a single processor handling the same task alone. SMP is typical on systems with a large number of users where throughput demands are great.

Multiple Modes of Operation

The Linux operating system operates in two modes. They are as follows:

- Graphical user interface (GUI)
- Text

Graphical User Interface (GUI) Mode

The GUI program, called X Windows, offers a Windows look and feel to the Linux environment. What you see on your screen is called the **desktop** because it includes the tools you need to perform daily functions. Some of the tools provided as part of the desktop are a GUI file manager, a Desktop manager and an Internet Web browser. Figure 1-3 shows a screenshot of the Linux Gnome desktop.

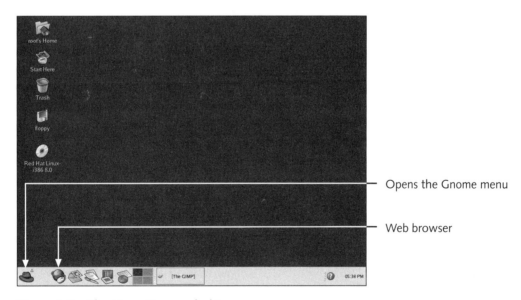

Figure 1-3   The Linux Gnome desktop

 Linux also gives you access to the Internet by utilizing the necessary hardware to run Netscape Communicator, Web browser software, and TCP/IP.

Figure 1–4 shows a screen shot of the Linux file manager open on the desktop.

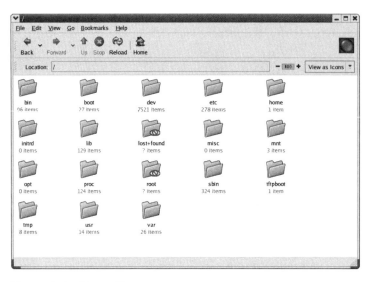

Figure 1-4 Linux file manager

Text Mode

Linux also provides you with a text mode interface. In this interface you use commands to navigate the Linux system and write your shell scripts. You will need to use text or graphical editors to write shell script programs. Figure 1-5 shows a screenshot of the Linux text mode open on the desktop of the GUI.

Figure 1-5 Linux text mode

You access the text mode in the Linux operating system via a shell. Acting as an interpreter, the **shell** accepts commands from the keyboard and either executes the command or displays an error if the command encounters a problem. Technically, the shell is a language, so you must adhere to its syntax, or rules. A few of the shells available on Linux are listed in Table 1-2.

Table 1-2   Various shell interpreters available on Linux

Shell Name	Description
sh	The original shell written by Steven Bourne, also known as the Bourne Shell
bash	Publicly licensed Bourne-Again Shell compatible with the original Bourne Shell; this is the default shell you get at login
csh	C-shell which uses a C-like syntax
ksh	Publicly licensed Korn shell written by David Korn

UNDERSTANDING CLASSIFICATIONS OF SOFTWARE

It is always a good idea to know what software is running on your system. This way, you are better equipped to troubleshoot in case a problem occurs. Also, software can be under a software contract, so you may be able to contact someone if problems arise.

Software is divided into the following categories:

- System software
- Application software

System Software

System software includes the core components of the system that must be present in order for the computer to operate. Examples of system software are:

- The kernel
- Job management software
- Memory management software
- Programming languages
- Device drivers
- Software utilities

The Kernel

The kernel is the "heart" of the operating system. When any computer system boots, a set of program instructions are loaded from the hard drive and kept in memory. Many programs are kept, or cached, in memory for speedy access, but the **kernel** is the core of any operating system that occupies memory as long as the computer remains on. It controls all other software activity. Only the most important and widely used programs are part of the kernel. The kernel calls upon other programs that are held on disk or in other areas of memory by interfacing with other operating system programs with the hardware of the computer system. Most operating systems have a kernel that remains in memory. Examples include Linux, Novell NetWare, Windows NT, Windows 2000, and Windows XP.

 The kernel is cached in memory. Caching means to keep programs in memory for quick access. Because memory access is faster than retrieving files from a hard disk or network, cached programs are retrieved quicker.

Customizing your Linux kernel allows you to give your computer system different capabilities. You can modify your kernel by adding or removing support of different features such as the ones shown in Figure 1-6.

Job Management

It is the function of the operating system to manage processes that are executing. In general, when a program executes it is known as a **job** or **process**.

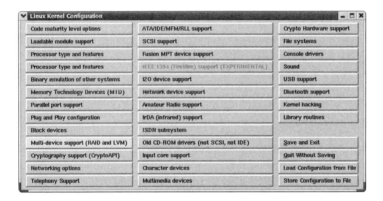

Figure 1-6   Kernel features you can customize

 A daemon is a job that runs in the background waiting for work. Many of the system programs are jobs run as daemons.

Prior to job execution, a job is placed in a job process queue. A **job process queue** is a holding area for the job while it waits its turn for execution. A running process has CPU and memory resources bound to it. The Linux operating system uses **a process tree** to keep track of the processes on the system. When a program or command executes, it is assigned a number, called the **process ID (PID)**. The PID is used for internal purposes by the operating system. The operating system uses the PID when communicating with the process. The process name is much like your own name and the PID is much like your Social Security number.

Each process is created from a parent. Linux uses the term **spawning** to describe one process starting from another. At times, a process may encounter problems causing it to consume excessive CPU time or to become orphaned. For instance, if process A spawns process B, then process A encounters a problem and is killed and removed from the process tree, process B, which is still running, is said to have been "orphaned."

Memory Management

Memory management software allows you to manage all of memory—including both physical memory and virtual memory. **Virtual memory** is the concept of the system utilizing physical memory as well as a section of hard disk space for accommodating multiple processes. The use of virtual memory facilitates the multiuser and multitasking features and capabilities of an operating system.

 The area on the hard disk reserved for virtual memory is sometimes called the page file or swap file. The swap file is created during the installation of the operating system.

Here is how virtual memory works. Programs are loaded into physical memory, also known as **random access memory (RAM)**. Programs are allocated a certain amount of time, called a time slice. When memory utilization reaches a certain threshold or when a process's time is up, the system sends the program and its data to the hard drive. Here the program is in a wait state and is placed temporarily on hold. When the system is ready to process the program and data that is currently on hold, the program's data is sent back to physical memory for main processing.

Mainframe operating systems and some network operating systems, such as Novell NetWare, UNIX, Linux, and Windows platforms, utilize virtual memory. One way to speed up your computer system is to add more memory to it. Another way is to increase the size of your swap file by allocating more disk space to it.

Programming Languages

Software programs are written in languages such as C, C++, Java, Visual BASIC, COBOL, FORTRAN or Assembly. Languages are divided into two major classifications:

- High-level
- Low-level

High-level Programming Languages   High-level programming languages are designed with people in mind. They tend to be similar to English in style and are much easier for the programmer to read and comprehend than low-level programming languages. For example, review the following excerpt of a COBOL programming language statement:

```
IF HOURS > 40 THEN
     PERFORM CALCULATE-OVER-TIME
ELSE
     PERFORM CALCULATE-REGULAR-TIME
END-IF
```

In the example, if the hours exceed 40, then overtime is calculated. If the hours are under and including 40, then regular time is calculated. You can clearly see how this sample COBOL program is very much like English. Examples of high-level programming languages include: Perl, COBOL, C, BASIC, Visual BASIC, and FORTRAN. High-level programming languages must be converted from their human-readable form into computer- or machine-readable form. This conversion can be done through either compiling or interpreting. The compiler or interpreter is software that is written to perform the conversion.

With **compiling**, the entire program is converted into an executable program. Once it is free of errors and compiled, the program is capable of being run or executed. On many systems, it is just a matter of clicking an icon representing the program. Examples of compiled languages are: C, C++, COBOL, and FORTRAN.

In the case of **interpreting**, each line is converted into machine-readable form as it is executed. The statements within the program are still converted into machine-readable form; it's just done line by line. Think of an interpretive language as being one where a minicompile is done for each statement. Some examples of interpretive languages are: Visual BASIC (however you can compile the code), Perl, BASIC, and shell programs.

Low-level Programming Languages   Each processor has its own programming language, often called a low-level programming language. The term "low-level" is used because the language is native to the processor instead of being similar to English. Examples of these are the Assembly language statements that are specific to every computer system. So, you could not take an Assembly language program and run it on just any system. However, you are more likely to take a high-level program and run it on another system with maybe only a few modifications. Take a look at the following excerpt from an Assembly language program:

```
L  1,X
A  1,Y
A  1,Z
ST 1,T
```

The above programming code simply adds up a set of three variables, X, Y, and Z, and stores them in a variable named T. It is not like English, and it greatly differs from the COBOL program example you saw earlier.

Device Drivers

Keep in mind that if you have a piece of hardware, such as a printer or scanner, you must have software that governs it. **Device drivers** are software instructions that manage a particular device. You must configure the correct driver for the type of hardware you install. Unfortunately, it's not uncommon to install a device driver incorrectly. Take a printer driver for example. A possible symptom of an incorrectly installed printer driver is that the printer's output is garbled and unreadable. Another symptom is the printer prints one line on a page and then advances to the next page to print the next line.

 Remember, you must use the device driver that goes with the device. In other words, if you are using a brand X, model Y device, you must use a brand X, model Y device driver or the device will not function properly.

Software Utilities

Software utilities are commands that help augment the functionality of the operating system. They are especially important because they can be used in combination with shell script programming logic to automate certain tasks.

The following are some software utilities:

- Backup and restore
- Compression and uncompression
- Printer management

Backup and Restore One of the most important aspects of any job is backing up your data. Whether you back it up to a floppy disk, CD, hard drive, or tape, you should always back up your data. Although many organizations use redundant servers in case one goes down, or they use redundant disks storage, they still require their personnel to perform backups.

Backups typically occur during off-hours when users are not working with application files. The reason being that if you back up files during business hours, you cannot guarantee the backup has indeed backed up the data that is being processed at that moment by the application. Also, some backup utilities do not backup files that are in use.

The restore process is the copying of the data that was backed up to either its original storage location or another one. The backup and restore processes should be tested to verify they work in case a real emergency ever occurs.

Compression and Uncompression   Most every file has something in it that is repeated. For example, one of the most common words is the word "the," which occurs in many documents and books, such as this one. **Compression** is the process of removing those repeating portions of a file, thereby making a new smaller file. Compression varies based on the amount of data that is duplicated and the compression algorithm that is used. At times, compression can yield between a 75% and 90% savings. You would generally compress a file that is to be downloaded over the Internet. It takes less time to download a compressed file because it is smaller. Another advantage of compression is that it saves disk space because of the reduced file size. However, in order to utilize the file, you must uncompress it first.

Printer Management   The Linux printing system uses the concept of print queues to temporarily hold print jobs. When a user sends a print job to a printer, the print job is spooled to a directory for the printer where it waits.

The term "spool" is an acronym that comes from IBM mainframe terminology. It stands for Simultaneous Peripheral Operations OnLine.

Simply stated, it means the system can send a print job to the printer software concurrent with other system activities. If the printer is busy or not turned on, the print job waits in the print queue until the printer is ready to accept the request. When the printer is ready to print, the print management software looks in the printer's directory, or queue, and prints the next job. It then deletes the print job request from the print queue.

Application Software

Application software is software that assists users in performing typical office work such as writing letters and business proposals, managing numeric information, and organizing large amounts of data. As such, application software is generally divided into these major categories:

- Word processing
- Spreadsheet
- Database

Word-Processing Software

Word-processing software has been around since the early 1980s. Word-processing software allows you to create, modify, delete, save, and print office-quality documents. Word-processing software also includes the enhanced capabilities of spell checker, dictionary, and a thesaurus. Today, Microsoft makes Word and Sun Microsystems offers a word-processing package as part of the Star Office software package suite. Star Office runs on the Linux operating system.

Spreadsheet Software

Also during the early 1980s, a group of students taking an accounting class grew tired of making numerous changes to the accounting sheets when only one number changed. These students eventually started the Lotus Corporation, one of the first companies to create spreadsheet software for PCs. Spreadsheet programs allow you to manage numeric data on a large scale. Spreadsheets hold data in cells, which are much like storage locations. When one cell changes, all cells referencing the original cell also change. Cells are labeled consecutively starting with A1 and continuing as far as your data demands. Letters represent the columns and numbers represent the rows.

Spreadsheet programs are extremely powerful and can include programming logic. They also include built-in functions. **Functions** are miniprograms that do the work when you supply the data, such as performing a mathematical calculation.

You will learn how to use shell script programs to create functions in Chapter 8.

In this spreadsheet example, =AVERAGE(A1:A20), you can see the power of a spreadsheet function. The AVERAGE function is given, or passed, two values—the beginning cell in a cell range, A1, and the ending cell in a cell range, A20. Whatever values are held in any of the 20 cells in column A are included in the average. If a value in any cell in the range changes, the average changes too.

Database Software

Database programs allow you to manipulate and manage data, create tables of data for organization, and join or combine data from multiple tables to create views or subsets of tables. Data held in databases can be accessed quickly via a unique identifier called a key field. Ashton-Tate Corporation developed one of the first database programs on the market for PCs in the 1980s called dBASE. Other companies such as IBM, Microsoft, Oracle, and Sun Microsystems have also developed database software. Linux comes with a database product called MySQL. It allows you to add, delete, and modify data within databases.

UNDERSTANDING DATA

In order to successfully write shell script programs, you must understand what data is as well as the structure of data. **Data** is made up of raw facts that are not much use until they are processed into information. Consider the number 75. This is considered data. You cannot look at the number 75 and tell if it is an exam grade, the outdoor temperature, or someone's age. Only when a program, in conjunction with the computer's processor, processes the number can it become information. The programmer's job is to write program code to turn data into useful information. Think of data as a hierarchy or a pyramid. Figure 1-7 shows the data pyramid.

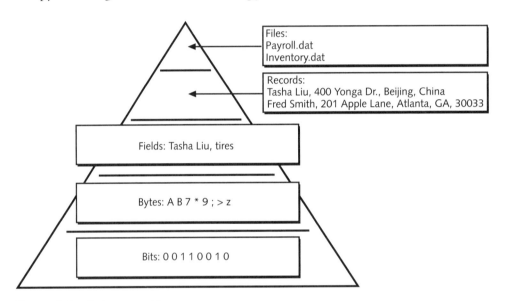

Files:
Payroll.dat
Inventory.dat

Records:
Tasha Liu, 400 Yonga Dr., Beijing, China
Fred Smith, 201 Apple Lane, Atlanta, GA, 30033

Fields: Tasha Liu, tires

Bytes: A B 7 * 9 ; > z

Bits: 0 0 1 1 0 0 1 0

Figure 1-7   Data pyramid

At the lowest level of the data hierarchy are bits. The term bit stands for binary digit and is either a zero (0) or a one (1). Each computer system has a character set that maps all the letters on the keyboard to its appropriate bit sequence. American Standard Code for Information Interchange (ASCII) is a character set common among most computer environments including all Windows operating systems and the Linux operating system. Although you don't typically use anything as small as a bit in your daily dealings with computers, you do need to understand the concept.

In the computer industry, the term **byte** refers to eight bits taken in sequence. Another synonym for the term byte is alphanumeric character. An alphanumeric character is defined as any of the letters A through Z, numbers 0 through 9, and special symbols. Although it is up one notch on the data hierarchy, a character is generally the lowest level of the data hierarchy that people process.

A group of bytes is called a **field**. For example, if you've ever filled out a job or college admission application, or even your 1040 tax forms, you know that you must fill in little boxes or blank lines with your personal data. Each of the boxes or blank lines is entered into an application screen to be processed by a program. These boxes and blank lines are considered fields. Fields are labeled, or given names, so that you may refer to the data contained within them. For instance, a field called NAME, may have the following data: Tasha Lui. If you wanted to print the NAME field, it would print the name Tasha Lui. Notice also that a field is comprised of characters or bytes.

A group of related fields makes up a **record**. For example, consider the employee records containing the field names and data shown in Table 1-3. There are three records with six fields each. In this case, you can think of a record as a row and think of a field as a column.

Table 1-3 Sample employee records

Name	Address	City	State	Zip	Phone
Sarah Togar	214 Scott Way	Concord	NH	03301	555-5550
Xin Chun Liu	428 Aubrey Way	Lilburn	GA	30047	555-5551
Molly Obakin	1027 Michelle Lane	Tulsa	OK	74101	555-5557

In most application systems, there is one unique identifying field in a record called the **primary key field**. This field is used to access the remaining fields in the records. The purpose of the primary key is to locate the data in the record efficiently. When a bank teller asks you for your bank account number, the account number is used as the primary key. Your Social Security number is used as a primary key when you fill out your tax returns or an employment application.

To help you understand the primary key concept, think about how the index in the back of this book works. If you want to look up a term, you go to the index and look through the alphabetical listing until you locate the page number reference for the term. Then, you go to the actual page number that describes the term. The primary key is analogous to the term you seek in the index. In an application, the primary key field is used to locate the record containing the rest of the data.

A grouping of related records is called a **file**. A file has a name and location for where the data is housed. A file can contain two major types of data, executable, or binary data, and nonexecutable data.

Executable or **binary files** are files that have been compiled and perform some type of operation or task. They are written using text editors following the strict syntax of the language and then they are compiled. The compilation process creates the executable code. The commands that you'll use in this book are executable files.

Nonexecutable files are generally data that the executable files operate on. The user runs an application or program that creates data files. Data files can also be created automatically by programs that run without user intervention. Examples of nonexecutable files are text files, word-processing document files, spreadsheet files, database files, or picture files.

UNDERSTANDING USER ROLES

In the Linux computing environment, there are several types of users, each with differing roles. Understanding the role of a user is important because it helps you decide the type of shell scripts that person might need on the job. Additionally, the role governs the type of access the user has to the system. Here is a list of the typical user types:

- Standard user
- System Administrator or root user
- Shell programmer

Standard Users

The **standard user**, sometimes just called "user," is the person who uses the Linux operating system on a daily basis. Users may also have access to commands via the text mode and other programs in the GUI. They also use the system to access applications. The applications they need depend upon their functions in the organization. Consider this example of typical users' needs. An accounting manager may need access to the accounting application, an engineer may need access to a computer aided design/computer aided manufacturing (CAD/CAM) program, an insurance agent may need access to the insurance adjustment application, and a travel agent may need access to the travel booking application.

Users access the Linux system by logging in using a user account. Generally, a computer specialist, such as a System Administrator who has authority to create the accounts, generates the user accounts. The user account should also have a password that is assigned to it. Once the users log in, they usually set their own passwords.

System Administrator

The **System Administrator** is a computer specialist who is responsible for the operations of the computer systems and network. Depending upon the size of the operation, there may be more than one System Administrator in an organization. They are completely responsible for ensuring that the systems, the networks, and the applications are available to the users during the hours needed by the users.

System Administrators perform a variety of tasks including upgrading applications and installing system software, changing user passwords, monitoring the network for bottlenecks, and in some cases, changing printer toner cartridges. Some have to be on call 24 hours a day to provide support for multiple shift operations.

1

System Administrators also maintain security, making sure users have the right access to application files and folders on the computer system. The goal is to give each user just what is needed to do the job, but no more.

At times, a System Administrator may have to log in to a special user account that has the ability to perform system administrative work, such as add a print queue, change another user's password, or backup a system file; standard user accounts don't have the ability to do these things. In Linux, the name of the user with complete administrative capability is called **root**. The root user has access to programs and configuration files that standard users don't.

You must use caution when logging in as the root user because you can delete or modify configuration files and programs that are unrecoverable without completely reinstalling the operating system.

Depending upon the organization, the System Administrator may be responsible for writing shell scripts, or the responsibility could be relegated to a shell programmer.

Shell Programmer

A **shell programmer** is responsible for writing shell scripts. A **shell script** is a program that is written to automate a process in the Linux operating system. A shell programmer writes the script using an editor, tests the script, and when the script passes the tests, makes the script available to users. The shell programmer must have an understanding of programming concepts as well as the Linux commands in order to successfully write scripts. For example, a shell programmer may need to write a script that uses system commands and decision logic for a System Administrator who needs a way to automate the backup process. Or a shell programmer may need to create a menu so several users can run Linux commands without entering the complete syntax of the command. Typically, a shell programmer logs in using a regular user account unless the task requires them to use the root user account.

At times a shell programmer may have to **debug** scripts or remove any syntax or logic error from scripts or programs. A **syntax error** is one that does not conform to the rules of the language. An example of a syntax error is a misspelled command. A compiler or interpreter usually displays an error message when it encounters a syntax error. A script or program can not run until it is syntax-error free. Shell programmers must learn the syntax of the shell to prevent syntax errors.

The term debug was coined in the 1940s when a moth short-circuited electrical components in a mainframe computer system causing a system failure. By removing the moth, the system was "debugged."

A **logic error** is an error that does not meet the requirements of the programming logic as decided upon by the users and management. These are typically more difficult for the shell programmer to identify because the scripts are most likely syntactically correct. The compiler or interpreter does not display a message indicating the error and the program appears to run normally. An example of a logic error would be using a less-than symbol instead of a greater-than symbol in an overtime calculation script. In the following set of COBOL statements, a logic error occurs because the less-than symbol is used in place of the greater-than symbol. In the example, a person working more than 40 hours will have their pay calculated on regular time. The program would run because the use of the less-than symbol is syntactically correct, but the output of the code would be undesirable. Compare this example to the earlier COBOL example where use of the greater-than symbol (> 40) is logically correct.

```
IF HOURS < 40 THEN
      PERFORM CALCULATE-OVER-TIME
ELSE
      PERFORM CALCULATE-REGULAR-TIME
END-IF
```

UNDERSTANDING BASIC LINUX COMMANDS

The Linux operating system contains numerous commands. Some are only available to System Administrators and not to standard users, while other commands are available to everyone. You need to learn about the commands that are available to all users because they may also be used in shell scripts.

Logging In and Logging Out

One of the first things you need to know is how to log in to the Linux system. You need a username and password. (To complete the activities and projects in this book, you may need to ask your instructor for your username and password.)

There are two ways of logging in to a Linux system. First, you can physically sit in front of the system and enter you username and password. Second, you can use the `telnet` command to log in to the Linux system. This requires the host to have an IP address or DNS name.

Next you will log in using the second method just discussed. You will use the `ping` command to verify the Linux computer is accessible on the network and the `telnet` command to connect to it if it is. You will access the Linux system from a Windows-based system that is running TCP/IP.

To verify the Linux host is accessible and connect to the Linux system if it is:

1. Start Windows on your computer (any version of Windows will work).

2. Click the **Start** button, and then click **Run**. The Run dialog box opens.

3. Type **command**, and then click **OK**. The Windows command prompt opens.

1

4. Type **ping *hostname/hostaddress***, and then press **Enter**. Be sure to substitute your correct host's name or IP address. If the command succeeded, you should see a "Reply from" message. If so, proceed to Step 6.

5. If you received an error, such as "Request timed out," it means the host is inaccessible. See your instructor. Do not go to the next step.

6. Type **telnet *hostname/hostaddress***, and then press **Enter**. Be sure to substitute your correct host's name or IP address. The Linux login prompt appears. Figure 1-8 includes the logging-in process to the Linux system from the Windows command prompt.

7. Type your **username**, and then press **Enter**. Your username appears on the screen, and you are prompted for a password.

8. Type your **password**, and then press **Enter**. Your password will not appear on the screen for security reasons. You have now successfully logged in and have access to the Linux system.

9. To log out, type **logout**, and then press **Enter**. Your connection to the Linux host is terminated, and you return to the Windows command prompt.

 Another way to log out is to press Ctrl+D instead of typing `logout`.

```
F:\WINNT\System32\cmd.exe - telnet 160.100.100.1
Red Hat Linux release 8.0 (Psyche)
Kernel 2.4.18-14 on an i686
login: root
Password:
Last login: Wed Oct  9 17:47:14 from 160.100.100.20
You have mail.
[root@s1 root]#
```

Figure 1-8   Logging in to a Linux system from a Windows-based PC

The `cal` Command

Once you've successfully logged in to the Linux system, you can use other Linux commands. The `cal` command displays the current calendar month. However, you can use the `cal` command to display a variety of months and years. Here is the general format of the command:

```
cal month year
```

The *month* is an optional number between one and 12 representing the numeric number for the month. You can only display the month if you include the *year* option. The *year* is an optional number between one and 9999 reflecting the year. So, for example, if you want to display the current month's calendar, you would run this command: `cal`. To display the calendar for the whole year, you would run the `cal` command with the year only. For example, the following statement displays the calendar for the first nine months for the year 2004.

```
cal 2004
```

Figure 1-9 shows the partial calendar for the year 2004.

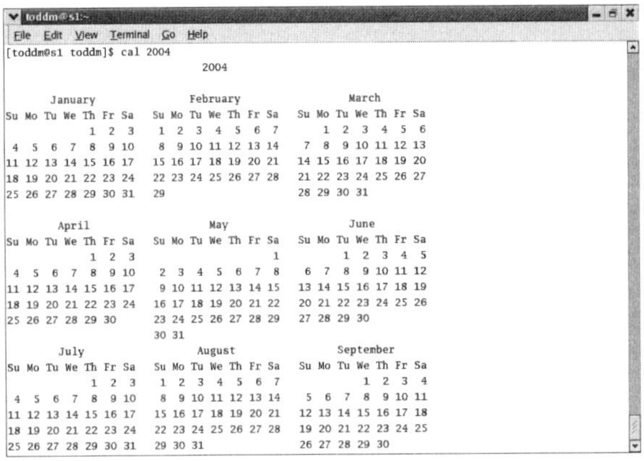

Figure 1-9   The results of the `cal 2004` command

The cat Command

The `cat` command allows you to display the contents of text files very easily. You simply type in the command followed by the filename; the text displays on your screen. After the command completes its task, your prompt returns.

The `cat` command is derived from the term concatenate which means to join or fuse together. The `cat` command concatenates the contents of a file on your disk with the screen. The command takes the following form:

```
cat option filename
```

Here is an example that displays the contents of the sales file:

```
cat sales
```

The `cat` command not only allows you to display text on the screen, but also allows you to create a file. To do this you use the greater-than redirection operator, >. At this point, all you need to understand is that the output of the `cat` command is redirected to a file instead of your screen. This results in the creation of a new file.

The concept of redirection will be fully discussed in Chapter 4.

Next you will create a file using the `cat` command and the redirection operator, and then display the file's contents.

To redirect text to a file using the `cat` command:

1. Log in to the Linux system as a user.

2. Right-click a blank area of the desktop, and then click **New Terminal**. The Terminal emulation program window appears with your prompt.

3. Type `cat > file2.txt`, and then press **Enter**. Notice that the cursor moves to the beginning of the next line and that there is no prompt on that line.

4. Type the following code exactly as it is shown, being sure to press **Enter** at the completion of each line:

   ```
   Shell Programming will help me on the job.
   Linux is fun!
   ```

When creating a file with the `cat` command, once you've pressed Enter at the end of a line, you cannot go back to that line and edit it. Creating a file using the `cat` command is for quick tasks. To edit the file, you need to use one of the editors discussed later in this chapter.

5. Press **Ctrl+D** to send an end-of-file (EOF) character to the `cat` command. The cursor moves to the next line and your prompt returns.

6. To display the contents of the file, type `cat file2.txt`, and then press **Enter**. Figure 1-10 shows the contents of the file you just created as well as your creation of that file.

7. To exit the window, type `exit`, and then press **Enter**.

8. Log out.

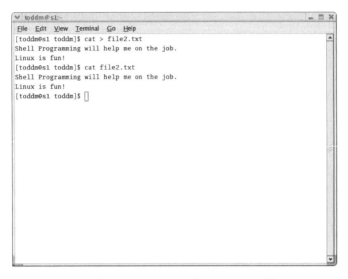

Figure 1-10   The cat command to create a file

The date Command

The **date** command displays or sets the system date and time. Here is the general syntax of the command:

    date option +format

Table 1-4 provides a listing of available formats for the **date** command.

Table 1-4   Options for the date command

Option	Description	Example
%D	Displays the date in MM/DD/YY format; this is where MM is the two-digit month, DD is the two-digit day, and YY is the last two digits of the year	date +%D
%d	Displays the two-digit day	date +%d
%Y	Displays the four-digit year	date +%Y
%H	Displays the two-digit hour	date +%H
%h	Displays the three-letter month	date +%h
%T	Displays the time	date +%T
%j	Displays the numeric day from 001 to 366; this is sometimes called the Julian date	date +%j
%m	Displays the two-digit month	date +%m

Figure 1-11 shows a screenshot of the **date** command run using various formats shown in Table 1-4.

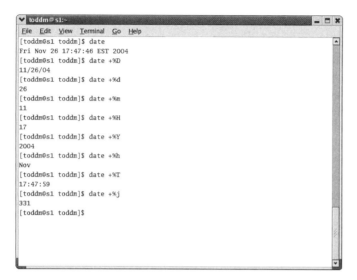

Figure 1-11   The **date** command run with different formats

The echo Command

You use the **echo** command to display text on the screen. As such, the **echo** command is a very useful debugging tool that can help you troubleshoot shell script programs. The **echo** command takes the form of the following:

```
echo "Text to display"
```

While not required on all versions of Linux, on some versions you do need the quotes. However, it is good practice to enclose text that includes spaces in quotes. You will learn more about use of quotes in Chapter 3. Consider this example:

```
echo "How are you doing?"
```

You can use the **echo** command to create a file. However, using the **echo** command to do this is only recommended when you only need a small file consisting of just a few lines. To do this you use the greater-than operator, **>**, to redirect the output from the screen to a file. Redirection will be discussed in Chapter 4.

In the following example, the output of the **echo** statement is sent to a file called sales:

```
echo "March sales exceed projections for the Houston Branch
office." > sales
```

Next you will use the **echo** command to redirect text to the sales file, and then use the **cat** command to display the contents of the file.

To redirect text to a file using the echo command:

1. Log in to the Linux system as a user.

2. Right-click a blank area of the desktop, and then click **New Terminal**. The Terminal emulation program window appears with your prompt.

3. To redirect the output to a file named sales, type the following code, and then press **Enter**:

   ```
   echo "March sales exceed projections for the Houston Branch
   office." > sales
   ```

   The command executes but returns no output to the screen because the output is redirected to the sales file.

4. To display the contents of the sales file to your screen type `cat sales`. Figure 1-12 shows a screenshot of the creation of the sales file using the `echo` command and it's displayed using the `cat` command.

5. To exit the window, type `exit`.

6. Log out.

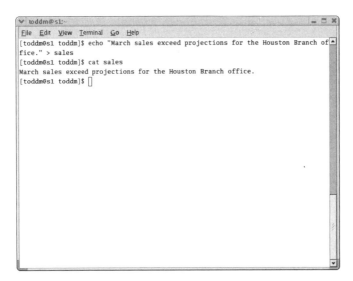

Figure 1-12 The echo command used to create the sales file

The `history` Command

If you want to see the commands you've already entered, you can run the `history` command. This command is useful for saving keystrokes. You can use your up and down arrows to go up and down through your history list to locate a command you previously entered. Once you locate the command you can use the backspace key to modify it, or you can press Enter to rerun the command as is.

Here is the general format of the command `history`:

```
history option
```

If you enter the `history` command without any options, it displays the last 1,000 commands you've entered. Used without any options, it can provide you with more information than you may be prepared to deal with. Here are a few ways you can use the `history` command.

The `history` command feature allows you to enter a recently executed command by placing the ! operator prior to the command. So, to rerun the most recently executed `cal` command, enter:

```
!cal
```

 You don't have to enter the complete command when using the ! operator. For example, if you entered, !da, the most recently executed command that begins with the letters "da" is executed. If the `date` command was the most recently executed command, then it would be rerun.

The `history` command displays numbers to the left of each command in its list. If you see a command in the history list that you want to rerun, you can enter the ! operator followed by the number of the command in the list. So, to rerun the 1031st command in the list, enter:

```
!1031
```

Figure 1-13 shows a screenshot of running the `history` command using the ! operator.

```
toddm@s1:~                                         _ □ ✕
File  Edit  View  Terminal  Go  Help
 1025  clear
 1026  history
 1027  clear
 1028  history
 1029  date
 1030  clear
 1031  cal 12 2004
 1032  clear
 1033  pwd
 1034  history
[toddm@s1 toddm]$ !1031
cal 12 2004
     December 2004
Su Mo Tu We Th Fr Sa
          1  2  3  4
 5  6  7  8  9 10 11
12 13 14 15 16 17 18
19 20 21 22 23 24 25
26 27 28 29 30 31

[toddm@s1 toddm]$ !da
date
Fri Nov 26 17:52:16 EST 2004
[toddm@s1 toddm]$ █
```

Figure 1-13   The `history` command using the ! operator

The `lpr` Command

The `lpr` command places a file in the print queue for printing. You use this command to send a document to the printer.

The format of the command `lpr` is:

```
lpr option filename
```

To print the sales file you created in an earlier exercise, you enter the following code:

```
lpr sales
```

Although the `lpr` command prints to the default printer set up by the System Administrator, it can also be used to print to a specific printer using the –P option. For example, to print the sales file to a printer named LinuxPrinter, enter `lpr –P LinuxPrinter sales`.

 Most commands allow you to enter options. However, because each command has a different function, the formats of their options are usually different. For the most part, an option is preceded by either one or two dashes, as in `-t`.

The `man` Command

The `man` command allows you to display the manual, or help, pages for a command. You run this command to see a description of a command and its options, if it has any. The general form is:

```
man command
```

To use the `man` command to display the manual pages for the `echo` command, enter `man echo`. Figure 1-14 shows a screenshot of the man pages for the `echo` command.

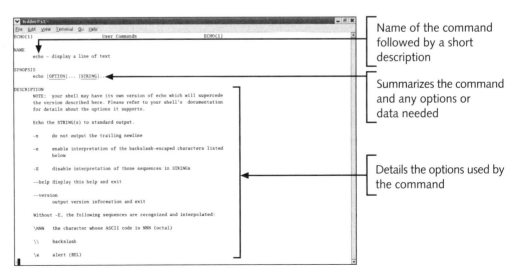

Figure 1-14   The man echo command

The `touch` Command

The main purpose of the `touch` command is to update the modification date and time stamp of a file. This is particularly useful when writing shell script programs. For example, if you had a shell script program that ran overnight or anytime when you weren't available to check on it, you can ensure the script ran or the file was updated by running the `touch` command for the file. The `touch` command takes the following form:

    touch *filename*

You can also use the `touch` command to create an empty file and set the modification date and time on that file using the same form.

The `who` Command

The `who` command allows you to display the list of users who are currently logged on to the Linux system. The form of the command is as follows:

    who *options*

You can also display a count of the total number of users logged in using the **-q** option. Figure 1-15 shows a sample screenshot of both the `who` and `who` **-q** commands.

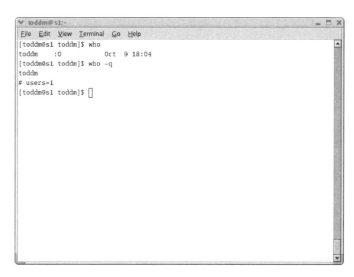

Figure 1-15   The who and who -q commands

Refer to Table 1-5 for a listing of the common basic Linux commands.

Table 1-5 Basic Linux commands

Command	Description
cal	Displays a calendar
cat	Displays the contents of a file
clear	Clears the screen
date	Displays or sets the date and time
echo	Displays text
history	Displays previously entered commands
login and logout	Allows you to log in and log out
lpr	Prints a file
man	Displays manual (help) pages for a command
ping	Determines if another TCP/IP system is available
telnet	Connects to a TCP/IP computer
touch	Updates the modification date and time of a file
who	Displays the currently logged on users

CREATING SHELL SCRIPTS

Because the shell is a command interpreter that makes use of programming capabilities, it allows you to use traditional programming concepts. Here are some of the traditional programming concepts the shell allows you to perform with scripts:

- Make decisions based upon conditions
- Perform arithmetic operations
- Create a menu using looping statements
- Use functions to perform very specific tasks
- Manipulate data using an array

 The terms "script" and "program" are synonymous.

A shell script performs one other function that traditional programming languages do not typically support; the shell script runs operating system commands. Like other programming languages, you write your shell script, and then you execute it. Next you will create a simple shell script.

To create and execute a simple shell script:

1. Log in to the Linux system as a user.

2. Right-click a blank area of the desktop, and then click **New Terminal**. The Terminal emulation program window appears with your prompt.

3. Type **cat > script1**, and then press **Enter** to create a file called script1.

4. Type the following code to add text to script1:

   ```
   echo "Welcome to my shell script."
   echo "This is one of my first shell scripts!"
   echo "Shell script programming is a tool for helping users
    automate their tasks."
   ```

5. Press **Crl+D** to terminate the line. Your prompt returns.

6. To execute the script, type **bash script1**, and then press **Enter**. Your screen should look like Figure 1-16 which shows the script you have input as well as the resulting output.

7. To exit the Terminal emulation program, type **exit**, and then press **Enter**.

8. Log out.

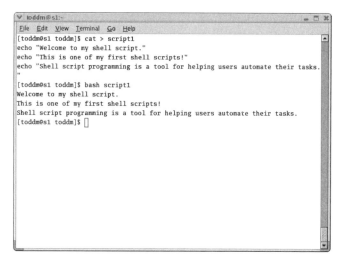

Figure 1-16   script1 and resulting output

To reinforce what you've already learned about using commands and creating shell scripts, next you will create a shell script that displays the calendar for the current month, the current time on the screen, and the usernames of the users currently logged in.

To create a shell script which displays the calendar, the current time, and the usernames of those users currently logged in:

1. Log in to the Linux system as a user.

2. Right-click a blank area of the desktop, and then click **New Terminal**. The Terminal emulation program window appears with your prompt.

3. Type **cat > script2**, and then press **Enter** to create a new file named script2.

4. Type **cal**, and then press **Enter** to include the current calendar.

5. Type **date**, and then press **Enter** to include the current date.

6. Type **who**, and then press **Enter** to display the users that are currently logged in. Press **Crl+D** to terminate the line. The prompt returns.

7. To execute the script, type **bash script2**, and then press **Enter**. Your screen should look like Figure 1-17 which displays the script you have input as well as the resulting output.

8. Record the output.

9. To exit the Terminal emulation program, type **exit**, and then press **Enter**.

10. Log out.

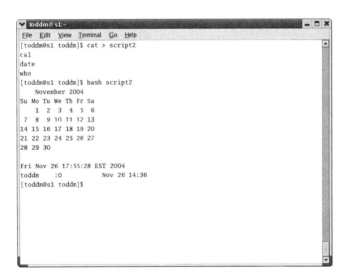

Figure 1-17 script2 and resulting output

CHAPTER SUMMARY

❐ The operating system is the software "brains" that manage the computer system. The operating system interacts with users, the applications, and the hardware. All computer systems must have an operating system in order for the system to run.

❐ The Linux operating system is a portable, multiuser, multitasking, and multiprocessing system. Linux supports both a graphical user interface (through the use of X Windows) or a text mode interface. There are numerous versions of Linux in the marketplace. The Linux shell interprets shell scripts.

❐ Software can be classified into systems software and application software. System software includes the kernel, job management software, memory management software, and device drivers. System utilities include backup and restore software, compression and uncompression software, file system management software, and printer management software. The kernel is the nucleus of the operating system. It remains in memory and controls other software components.

❐ Data is made up of raw facts. Information is processed data. A bit is either a binary zero or one. A byte is a group of eight bits. A field is a group of bytes. A record is a group of fields. A primary key field is a special field that allows you to quickly access a record in a file. A file is a group of records. There are two types of files: executable, or binary, and nonexecutable. Examples of executable files are commands and programs. Examples of nonexecutable files are picture files or text files.

❐ It is important to understand the user roles in a Linux environment so you can create appropriate scripts and access to the system for the user. A standard user is a person who uses the application and system on a daily basis to perform a certain job function such as payroll, accounting, marketing, finance, or engineering. A System Administrator is responsible for maintaining, monitoring, upgrading, and troubleshooting the system and network so users can do their jobs. A shell programmer writes shell programs for users. Shell programmers apply their knowledge of programming logic and Linux commands to create scripts for users.

❐ Linux allows you to interact with the operating system via commands. There are literally hundreds of commands. Most have multiple options that augment the command in some way. You use the manual pages for the command you want to learn more about.

❐ Shell script programming combines programming logic structures with operating system commands to automate routine tasks. The shell runs commands in the shell program.

REVIEW QUESTIONS

1. _____ is the software that remains in memory and controls other activity.

   a. Kernel

   b. Software utilities

   c. Backup software

   d. Job management software

2. Shell script programs usually run in the _____ mode of Linux.

   a. X Windows

   b. MS Windows

   c. graphical

   d. text

3. Which of the following is an interpreted language?

   a. COBOL

   b. C

   c. C++

   d. Bourne-Again Shell (bash)

4. A spreadsheet is an example of _____ software.

   a. backup

   b. application

   c. print management

   d. assembly language

5. A group of fields is also known as a _____.

   a. byte

   b. character

   c. record

   d. table

6. How many bits are in a byte?

   a. 1

   b. 2

   c. 4

   d. 8

7. What company first developed UNIX?

   a. Microsoft

   b. Linux

   c. Red Hat

   d. AT&T

8. _____ is another name for a process.

   a. Job

   b. Disk drive

   c. Folder

   d. X Windows

9. Which command allows you to display the manual pages for a command?

   a. `man`

   b. `pages`

   c. `who`

   d. `lpr`

10. When was UNIX developed?

   a. 1960s

   b. 1970s

   c. 1980s

   d. 1990s

11. Which command allows you to display the two-digit day?

   a. `date +%Y`

   b. `date +%T`

   c. `date +%d`

   d. `date +%D`

12. _____ is raw facts?

   a. Information

   b. Job

   c. Data

   d. Daemon

13. _____ is a background job.

    a. Information

    b. Job

    c. Data

    d. Daemon

14. The _____ command sends a document to the printer.

    a. `lpr`

    b. `printit`

    c. `date`

    d. `echo "Hi" > file4.txt`

15. A _____ is a group of related records.

    a. field

    b. file

    c. bit

    d. character

16. A _____ is a person who uses the system on a daily basis to do his specific job, such as manufacturing, accounting, or payroll.

    a. System Administrator

    b. standard user

    c. shell programmer

    d. daemon

17. A _____ is a person responsible for making sure the systems and net-works are available to the users when needed.

    a. System Administrator

    b. standard user

    c. shell programmer

    d. job

18. A picture file is an example of a _____ file.

    a. binary

    b. executable

    c. nonexecutable

    d. job management

19. A command is an example of a _____ file.
    a. binary
    b. nonexecutable
    c. print queue
    d. X Windows
20. A _____ is a person who writes scripts as his or her main job function.
    a. System Administrator
    b. standard user
    c. shell programmer
    d. print queue

HANDS-ON PROJECTS

Project 1-1

In this project, you will visit an organization that uses the Linux operating system and discuss the type of hardware and software it uses. You'll also record if the organization uses any scripts, and if so, for what purpose.

1. Locate an organization that uses the Linux operating system as the main operating system for their organization.
2. Record the name of the organization.
3. Interview one of the System Administrators or other persons responsible for the computer system. Record the type of hardware used.
4. Record the version of Linux used.
5. Record the application software used.
6. Record the shell interpreter used by their users.

Project 1-2

In this project, you will visit various Linux vendor Web sites and record your findings. To complete this project, you will need Internet access.

1. Open your Web browser, then go to the **redhat.com** Web site.
2. Spend some time browsing this Web site.
3. Record information about cost, hardware requirements, software version, and product offerings of the Red Hat version of Linux.

4. Change the address location to the **calderasystems.com** Web site.

5. Spend some time browsing this Web site.

6. Record information about cost, hardware requirements, software version, and product offerings of the Linux version offered by Caldera.

7. Change the address location to the **mandrake.com** Web site.

8. Spend some time browsing this Web site.

9. Record information about cost, hardware requirements, software version, and product offerings of the Linux version offered by Mandrake.

Project 1-3

In this project, you will execute basic Linux commands to help you understand how to interact with the operating system shell.

1. Log in to the Linux system as a user.

2. Open a Terminal emulation window.

3. Type **who**, and then record the output.

4. Type **cal**, and then record the output.

5. Type **date**, and then record the output.

6. Type **history**, and then record the output.

7. Type **!#** where **#** is a number in the history list of a command you want to execute.

8. Record the command that was used.

9. Use the up and down arrow keys to scroll back and forth in the history list of recently executed commands, and press **Enter** to execute a command.

10. Record the command.

11. To exit the Terminal emulation program, type **exit**.

12. Log out.

Project 1-4

In this project, you will execute different variations of the commands to help you understand how to run commands using different options.

1. Log in to the Linux system as a user.

2. Open a Terminal emulation window.

3. Type **date +%h**, and then record the output.

4. Type **date +%T**, and then record the output.

5. Type **date +%m**, and then record the output.

6. Type **who -q**, and then record the output.

1

7. Type **cal *month year*** where *month* is your two-digit birth month and *year* is your four-year birth year, and then record the day of the week you were born on.

8. To exit the Terminal emulation program, type **exit**.

9. Log out.

Project 1-5

In this project, you will write a small shell script to display text on the screen.

1. Log in to the Linux system as a user.

2. Open a Terminal emulation window.

3. Type **cat > Project1-5**.

4. Type the following code to insert text into the Project1-5 script:

```
echo "Welcome to my shell script."
echo "This is one of my first shell scripts."
echo "Shell script programming is a tool for helping System
Administrators."
```

5. Send an end-of-file (EOF) character to the **cat** command.

6. To execute the script, type **bash Project1-5**.

7. To print your script to the default printer, type **lpr Project1-5**. If you don't have access to a printer, record what displays on the screen on a separate sheet of paper.

8. To exit the Terminal emulation program, type **exit**.

9. Log out.

Project 1-6

In this project, you will write a shell script to display the current Julian date and the number of users currently logged in.

1. Log in to the Linux system as a user.

2. Open a Terminal emulation window.

3. Type **cat > Project1-6**.

4. Type **date +%j**.

5. Type **who -q**.

6. Send an end-of-file (EOF) character to the **cat** command.

7. To execute the script, type **bash Project1-6**.

8. Record the output.

9. To print your script to a specific printer, type **lpr -P *printer-name* Project1-6** where ***printer-name*** is the name of the printer. You may have to get the printer name from your instructor.

10. Close your Terminal emulation window.

11. Log out.

Project 1-7

In this project, you will use the manual pages to help you locate a particular option.

1. Log in to the Linux system as a user, and then open a Terminal emulation window.

2. Type **man cat**.

3. Locate the option to number all output lines, and then record the letter for that option.

4. To use the option, type **cat** *—option* **Project1-6** where *option* is the letter you recorded in the previous step. (Line numbers display to the left of the commands in the previous script for the previous project.)

5. Type **man lpr**.

6. Read through the man pages and find a new option for the **lpr** command that has not been discussed in this chapter, and then record the option and its description.

7. Type **man touch**.

8. Read through the man pages and find an option for the **touch** command, and then record the option and its description.

9. Run the command using the option you chose, and then record the command and the option you chose.

10. Close your Terminal emulation window.

11. Log out.

Project 1-8

In this project, you will create a script containing three statements. You will insert different versions of the **date** command using various options.

1. Log in to the Linux system as a user, and then open a Terminal emulation window.

2. Use the **cat** command to create a file named **Project1-8**. (*Hint:* You need to use the redirection symbol.)

3. Using the correct option from Table 1-4, insert the **date** command so it displays the date in MM/DD/YY format.

4. Using the correct option from Table 1-4, insert the **date** command so it only displays the current time.

5. Send an end-of-file (EOF) character to the **cat** command.

6. Display the contents of the Project1-8 script, using the **cat** command.

7. Record the contents of the script.

8. Execute the script using the **bash** command.

9. Print your script. If you do not have access to a printer, record what displays on your screen on a separate sheet of paper.

10. Record the command needed to print the script.

11. Close the Terminal emulation window.

12. Log out.

CASE PROJECTS

Case 1-1

TMI Corporation is currently running mainframe computers in a distributed environment. There are about 25 users connecting via dumb terminals to the main office, located in Lawrenceville, Georgia. They use manufacturing, inventory, and personnel applications written in COBOL. Their programmers are willing to learn other languages but have not yet had the chance because they've been too busy maintaining the current applications. The company has outgrown its computing resources. It is in the process of selecting an entirely new computer system—from hardware to software.

Write a proposal to the company's chief information officer (CIO) convincing her to choose the Linux operating system. Include specifications for the TMI Corporation, accounting for enough computers to service the current number of users, two servers, and five printers. Indicate the programming language the new applications should be written in and support your decision. Include a rationale for sending two System Administrators to attend Linux administration classes.

Case 1-2

The Daisy Mae Woo Haberdashery Corporation currently is running a proprietary UNIX operating system from the XYZ Corporation vendor. The XYZ Corporation is going out of business because of a downturn in the economy. The Daisy Mae Woo Haberdashery's business is thriving, but they are worried about the potential lack of support in the future. The Daisy Mae Woo Haberdashery has five remote offices located within 10 miles of its main office. The Daisy Mae Woo Haberdashery has financial applications running in C and many of the System Administration tools are written in the Bourne Shell. Many times, the software locks up the computer system causing it to halt. So, a new operating system is needed. The current version of UNIX is compatible with versions of MINIX.

The Daisy Mae Woo Haberdashery Corporation has decided to go with a new vendor, the Alpha Firm, for consulting services. Write a proposal to The Daisy Mae Woo Haberdashery Corporation as if you were a vice president for the Alpha Firm. Include in your proposal which version of Linux you would recommend, the shell you would support, and how you would go about migrating the current programs to the new system. Defend your decision on paper.

2

UNDERSTANDING THE LINUX FILE SYSTEM

In this chapter, you will:

♦ Understand the Linux tree hierarchy
♦ Navigate the tree hierarchy
♦ Understand directory management commands
♦ Use editing commands
♦ Understand file management commands

In this chapter, you will gain an understanding of the Linux file system. You will learn its purpose and how to navigate and manipulate it. You will also learn about some editors you can use to accomplish a variety of tasks, as well as various Linux commands you need to accomplish these goals.

UNDERSTANDING THE LINUX TREE HIERARCHY

The Linux file system is based upon a tree hierarchy. Like other hierarchies, an order exists within the tree. There is a top level with other sublevels branching beneath it. The tree hierarchy offers storage and quick access.

Storage

Storage within the Linux file system is accomplished with two main elements: directories and files. **Directories** are considered holding areas or containers. From a user's standpoint, directories can contain files and other directories, sometimes called subdirectories. Files contain data—text, binary information, picture images, and other types of information. Files are stored in directories. Typically, files that are alike are stored within one directory. While a directory can contain multiple directories and files, files themselves cannot contain directories or other files.

The Linux operating system treats every storage component such as a directory or a file as a *file*. Files contain the data you need. Directories are simply a means of grouping the files.

At the top of the Linux tree is a single directory called root. The root directory is where all other files and directories in the file system stem from. The root directory is created during installation of the operating system and cannot be changed or deleted without losing the operating system and related files. The symbol for the root directory is the forward slash (/). You must use this symbol when accessing the root, or top-level, directory.

Both files and directories are ultimately stored on disk.

Quick Access

Generally, when you create directories, you group and store similar files together. This directly benefits you and also translates to quicker access when you need to find a file. If you know what type of file you are looking for, you can go straight to the directory in which it is located. Consider this example. You work in the payroll department for Townsend Toyota and you are responsible for making sure payroll goes out on a monthly basis. Because the company pays its employees monthly, you have twelve payroll files. The files are named "Jan.dat," "Feb.dat," "Mar.dat," and so on. How would you organize these in the tree? You could put them in separate directories or even scattered in a directory with other unrelated files.

However, when you try to locate them, you may not be able to find them quickly because they are not organized in a central location. A better design is to create a directory named Payroll and place all the monthly payroll files in it. Then, near payday, you simply look in the Payroll directory, find the files you need, and process the payroll data.

As another example, if you had several files dealing with your personal information, you might create a directory called Personal and place your resume, sample cover letters, school documents, and e-mail messages in that directory. Ultimately, it is easier for you to find the files because you have organized them.

The "Garden Store Tree" Analogy

The Linux file system hierarchy is analogous to an actual tree you might purchase at a garden store that has its root system wrapped in canvas. If you turn that garden store tree upside down in your mind, you have the concept of the Linux tree hierarchy. The root system is now at the top, just like the Linux root directory. The branches and leaves stem from the root. A directory in Linux is analogous to a branch on the garden store tree. A leaf is analogous to a file because a leaf cannot contain branches or other leaves just as a file cannot contain directories or other files; however, a file does have contents. Just as a directory can contain other subdirectories and files, a branch can contain other branches and leaves.

Consider this example. Townsend Toyota has a Linux system which contains files and directories. It has created directories to represent its business departments. There are files within the directories that contain business-related data. Figure 2-1 shows the tree structure of Townsend Toyota. The **tree** command displays a hierarchical listing of the directory. Notice that the root, (/), directory is near the upper-left corner. The directories and files are organized into logical groupings beneath the directory named TownsendToyota which is immediately beneath the root, (/). The directories named Accounting, IT, Marketing, and Production are on the same level, falling immediately within the TownsendToyota directory. Look at the Accounting directory and see the four directories beneath it—AccountsPayable, AccountsReceivable, GeneralLedger, and Payroll. Recall that the directory named Payroll contains the payroll files mentioned in the previous example.

 You can use the **tree** command to show a snapshot of a subdirectory too. If you want to see the tree structure just for the directory named Marketing, you enter **tree Marketing**.

```
[toddm@s1 /]$ tree / | more
/
|-- TownsendToyota
|   |-- Accounting
|   |   |-- AccountsPayable
|   |   |-- AccountsReceivable
|   |   |-- GeneralLedger
|   |   `-- Payroll
|   |       |-- Apr.dat
|   |       |-- Feb.dat
|   |       |-- Jan.dat
|   |       |-- Jun.dat
|   |       |-- Mar.dat
|   |       `-- May.dat
|   |-- IT
|   |   |-- Project1
|   |   |   |-- Work1
|   |   |   |-- Work2
|   |   |   `-- Work3
|   |   |-- Project2
|   |   `-- Project3
|   |-- Marketing
|   |   |-- Promotions
|   |   `-- Sales
|   |       |-- East
|   |       |-- North
|   |       |-- South
|   |       `-- West
|   `-- Production
|       |-- Shift1
|       |-- Shift2
|       `-- Shift3
--More--
```

Figure 2-1   Tree hierarchy for Townsend Toyota

The `tree` command is useful for showing the tree structure; however, when writing shell programs, you need to understand how to get to those file or directories within the tree. If you wanted to access the May.dat file from the root directory, you would have to follow the lines in Figure 2-1 down and over to the right until you finally got to the file. You would end up going through the TownsendToyota, Accounting, and Payroll directories, respectively.

 You can think of the output of the `tree` command as a map to get to a file or directory. A map shows you towns you must go through to get to your destination. The `tree` command shows you the directories you must go through to get to your files.

Linux System Directories

Linux stores many of its system files in various subdirectories beneath the root directory. These are created during installation of the operating system and should not be deleted or renamed. You need to understand the purpose of the Linux system directories, shown in Table 2-1, in case your scripts refer to commands or files contained within them.

Table 2-1   Some of the Linux system directories

Directory	Purpose
/bin	Holds many binary executable programs
/boot	Holds the Linux kernel
/dev	Contains device files for all the devices in the Linux file system
/etc	Holds configuration files; many are written using shell script programs. Configuration files are files that various programs read in order to know what they are supposed to do.
/home	Default location which contains user directories; when users log in to a Linux system, their current directory is /home/*username*. For example, a user named Marissa has a home directory of /home/marissa.
/lib	Contains files and executable programs used by the system
/mnt	Contains mounted drives
/root	The Linux superuser, or root user's home directory
/sbin	Contains additional binary executable programs normally used by the root user
/tmp	Used for temporary file and directory storage
/usr	Contains other subdirectories for applications, such as X11 (for X Windows on Linux), HTML files, library files, and games; also included are header files for C programs. Two of the most widely used subdirectories within /usr are usr/bin and /usr/sbin. These contain directories and binary executables.
/var	Contains both files and directories; typically, the type of files in /var vary in size, such as the log files for various processes located in /var/log. The system log file, /var/log/messages, is also held here.

NAVIGATING THE TREE HIERARCHY

Now that you understand how the hierarchy is set up, you need to learn how to navigate the Linux file system. Look at the sample hierarchy tree shown in Figure 2-2, the top-level directory is root, shown by the forward slash symbol, (/). Other directories branch beneath it. Under the user's home directory, represented by the variable $HOME, the directories named dirA and dirB exist. A variable is used for flexibility, so that users and shell scripts can refer to $HOME, and it equates to their individual home directory. Beneath each of these are other directories. Ultimately, files are stored at the bottom of the tree. Directories on the same level and having the same parent directory are considered **sibling directories**. Said another way, dirA and dirB are **child directories** of $HOME, their parent.

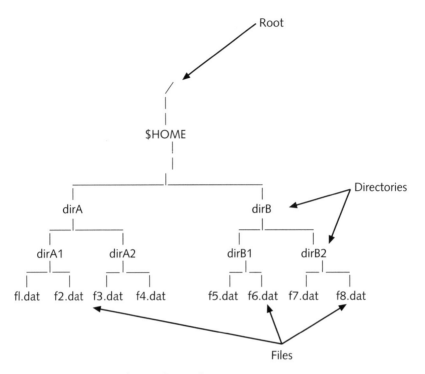

Figure 2-2   A sample tree hierarchy

When a user account is created, a home directory is automatically created for that user. The home directory is usually located in /home as described in Table 2-1. The system uses a variable named $HOME which equates to your home directory.

The contents of the variable named $HOME is different for each user. It is just a method of saying your own home directory. For example, Mary Phan's $HOME may literally be equal to /home/maryphan; while Harold Patel's $HOME directory may literally be equal to /home/haroldpatel.

Your **current directory** denotes where you are within the file system. Think of it as where you are in a building when looking at a building evacuation map. The makers of the map assume you are in a certain room when they created the evacuation plan. They even have a red "You Are Here" dot with a red arrow representing a path showing how to exit the building. The Linux tree operates similarly. The "You Are Here" dot represents your current directory and the long red arrow represents how to get to another location, such as another directory.

When navigating you need to know two things—where you are and where you want to go within the tree hierarchy.

Changing Directory Locations

If you want to change your current position to the root directory, you have to use the cd command. This command allows you to "change directory" locations within the tree to another directory. It takes the general form:

    cd *directory*

Think of the cd command as changing your "You Are Here" location in the tree.

The *directory* is a directory location within the tree that you want to go to.

To help you navigate through the tree, you need to understand the terms full path and partial path. The **full path** specifies the complete path from root. A full path always begins from the root directory. The **partial path** specifies a certain point in the directory path, which is simply the name of the directory that you would like to change to relative to your current location. It never begins at root.

The full or partial path can be used with most any command.

Imagine someone asks you for directions from his house to your house. You would give him directions that would take him from his front door to yours. Essentially, you would be providing him with the full path. If that same person was already on the way to your house and perhaps became lost, you wouldn't give them the full path directions, instead you would provide directions relative to where he currently is located, in other words, the partial path.

Changing Directory Locations to the / Directory

Assume your current directory is dirA in Figure 2-2. In order to change to the root directory using a full path, you would issue this command:

    cd /

Figure 2-3 shows changing directory locations to the root directory. Notice that the before the cd command is performed, the user is in the toddm directory.

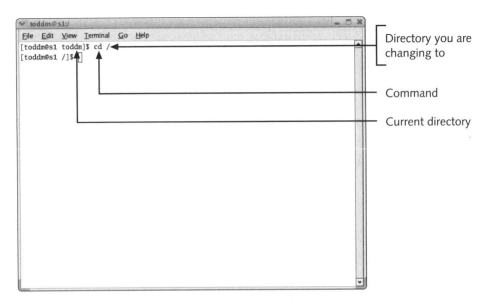

Figure 2-3   Running the cd to change the root directory

Changing Directory Locations to a Parent Directory

In order to change to a parent directory, you use a special notation. In Linux, the parent directory is represented by the use of two dots (. .) notation. Let's say your current directory is dirA1 as shown in Figure 2-2. The command to navigate to the parent directory, dirA is:

    cd ..

The use of the two dots, . ., is an example of a partial path. Every directory, except the root directory, has a parent directory, or . .. The root directory cannot have a parent directory because it is the top directory. A way you can remember this is that you have two parents, one mom and one dad, and in the tree hierarchy, they are collectively referred to as the "parent." Figure 2-4 shows changing directory locations to the parent directory.

Changing Directory Locations to a Child Directory

In order to change directory locations to a child directory, you refer to the child by its name. Here is the general form:

    cd *child-directory*

This is where *child-directory* is the name of the child directory you want to change directory locations to. If you want to change from the current directory of dirA to one of its child directories, such as dirA1, as shown in Figure 2-2, you would issue this command:

    cd dirA1

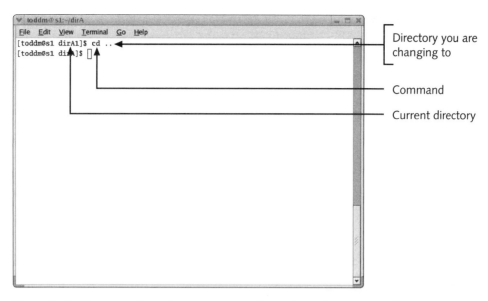

Figure 2-4   Running the cd .. command to navigate to a parent directory

Figure 2-5 shows changing directory locations to a child directory

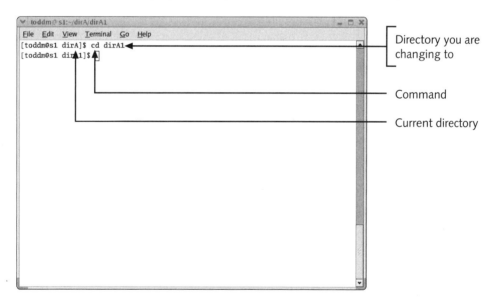

Figure 2-5   Changing to a child directory using the cd command

Changing Directory Locations to a Sibling Directory

A sibling directory is a peer directory of your current directory. In Figure 2-2, the directories dirA and dirB are sibling directories. Also, dirA1 and dirA2 are siblings, as well as dirB1 and dirB2. However, even though dirA1 and dirA2 are on the same level as dirB1 and dirB2 they are not siblings because they have different parents.

To change to any sibling directory, the syntax is:

    cd ../*sibling*

Assume your current directory is dirB, and you want to change directory locations to dirA. You would use the code:

    cd ../dirA

In the command, **cd ../dirA**, the two dots represent the parent directory, in this case **$HOME**, and the forward slash is a separator between the parent and child levels of root and dirA. Figure 2-6 shows changing directory locations to a sibling directory.

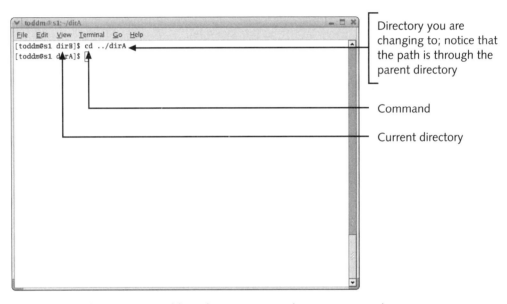

Directory you are changing to; notice that the path is through the parent directory

Command

Current directory

Figure 2-6   Changing to a sibling directory using the cd command

Changing Directory Locations Across Multiple Levels

In order to change directory locations across multiple levels you refer to each parent in the hierarchy tree. Here is the syntax:

    cd ../../*directory*

If your current directory is dirA1 as in Figure 2-2, you navigate to dirB as follows:

    cd ../../dirB

The first pair of dots represents the parent of dirA1 which is dirA. The second pair of dots represents the parent of dirA which is $HOME. This happens to be the grandparent of dirA1. Finally, you include the directory name you want to navigate to that is multiple levels away, which in this case is dirB. Figure 2-7 shows changing directory locations across multiple levels.

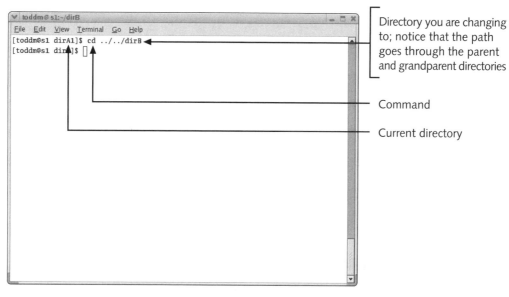

Figure 2-7 Changing directories across multiple levels

UNDERSTANDING DIRECTORY MANAGEMENT COMMANDS

In order to be a proficient Linux System Administrator, you must be aware of many of the commands used to manage the Linux file system. Each command executes and generates one of the following:

- *No output*—The command worked successfully.

- *Output*—The command worked successfully.

- *An error*—The command did not work correctly.

The Linux commands are divided into three main categories:

- *Directory commands*—Commands that work with directories

- *Editor commands*—Commands that allow you to manipulate the file system

- *File commands*—Commands that work with files

The main commands that deal with directories are summarized in Table 2-2. These are the most commonly used commands relating to the file system. It is important that you learn these commands because they allow you to manage the Linux file system, and understanding them gives you greater control over the file system.

Table 2-2   Directory commands

Directory Command	Purpose
pwd	Displays the name of your current directory
ls	Displays both files and directories; by default, it displays the files and directories in the current directory
cd	Changes directory locations
mkdir	Creates or makes a directory
rmdir	Deletes or removes a directory

The pwd Command

The pwd command displays your current working directory and returns output to the screen. Although it does not have very many practical options, it is one of the most important commands because it lets you know where you are in the tree hierarchy. To execute the command, you simply type pwd on the command line, and then press Enter. This displays your current directory location on the screen.

The ls Command

The ls command lists a directory's contents. You use this command to determine what is in a directory. The ls command has a variety of uses and many different options for listing directories. For example, if you wanted to see the size of a file in bytes, you would attach the appropriate option to the ls command. Like the other directory commands, the command is written:

    ls option path-name

The symbol for indicating an option is typically either a single dash (-) or a double-dash (--), and it is followed by the option. So, the -l option when attached to the ls command as in ls -l gives additional information about the files and directories—such as the size of the files and the permissions.

 The command ls -l uses a lowercase letter l (as in lucky), not the numeral one. Don't make the mistake of putting a one after the dash symbol; it results in an error.

The path name is optional. If you leave it off, the ls command default is to show you the contents of the current directory.

The -l Option on the ls Command

One of the most common options for the ls command is -l which is short for long listing. The term "long listing" means that more information—type of file, permissions, links, owner, group, size in bytes, date and time, and name—is displayed on the screen when you use this option than if you don't. Figure 2-8 shows the output of the ls command with the –1 option. Table 2-3 provides an overview of the various fields represented in the figure.

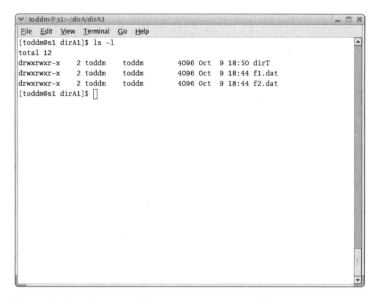

Figure 2-8   Output of the ls –1 command

Table 2-3   Table of the column fields in a long listing

Type	Permissions	Links	Owner	Group	Size in Bytes	Date and Time	Name
d	rwxrwxr-x	2	toddm	toddm	4096	Aug 30 20:52	dirT
-	rw-rw-r--	1	toddm	toddm	37	Aug 31 6:48	f1.dat
-	rw-rw-r--	1	toddm	toddm	102	Aug 31 6:48	f2.dat

The Type Column   The first field of the long listing format is the Type field. Table 2-4 provides a listing of the various types of items that can appear here.

Table 2-4   Possible values of the type field of the long listing

Type Value	Description
d	File is a directory
-	File is a file
c	File is a character device
b	File is a block device

The Permissions Column The next nine characters after the file type represent permissions for the file or directory. These are grouped into three sets of three. The first three characters represent permissions for the owner, the second set of three characters represents permissions for the group, and the last set of three characters represents permissions for other users, commonly known as the world. Table 2-5 provides comprehensive definitions of the permissions.

Table 2-5 Permissions

Letter Abbreviation	Description
r	Indicates that the file or directory can be read
w	Indicates that the file or directory can be written to
x	Indicates that the file can be executed; shell scripts always have the x permission turned on. An x permission for a directory indicates that you can take a directory listing of the directory to see its subdirectories and files.
-	Indicates the permission is not granted

Note that the permissions are positional. They are always in this order: read, write, and execute. If a dash exists in place of the permission, then the permission is turned off or not available. For example, if the permissions are r-x, then the permissions are for read and execute, but no write permission is given.

Additional Columns The remaining six columns are a bit more straightforward in their presentation. The Links column represents the number of links or shortcuts to the file or directory. The Owner column represents the actual user who owns the file. Generally, this is the person who created it. Notice that "toddm" is the owner. The owner of the file or directory receives the owner set of permissions (the first set of read, write, and execute permissions after the Type field). The Group column represents the group membership. If a user is a member of the group, they get the group set of permissions (the middle set of read, write, and execute permissions) in the permissions fields. If you are not the owner or a member of the group, then you get the last set of permissions.

The Date and Time column is the date and time stamp the file or directory was created. The Size in bytes column is the size of the file or directory. And finally, the Name column is the Linux name used when referring to the file. A Linux filename can be no more than 256 characters long.

The −a Option on the ls Command

The −a option is used to display all files and directories. What makes it different from the −l option is that it is used to display hidden files in your own directory. Hidden files begin with a dot or period. Knowing how to list hidden files can be very useful. You may find it necessary to hide files in order to protect them from being deleted or seen

2

by a user. There are several hidden files that are created by default when a user account is created. When you use the `ls -l` command, you'll notice a directory named dot (.) and one named dot dot (..). The single dot represents your current directory—every directory has one of these. The two dots represent the parent. The existence of a directory named dot dot is why you can issue the `cd ..` command to navigate to your parent directory.

Next you will use these two options with the `ls` command.

To execute the `ls` command:

1. Log in to the Linux system as a user, and then open a Terminal emulation window.

2. Type `ls -l`, and then press **Enter**. A long listing of your current directory appears.

3. Record the number of directories and files.

4. Record the permissions for one of the files.

5. Type `ls -a`, and then press **Enter**. A listing of hidden files in your current directory appears.

6. Record the number of hidden files.

7. Now, combine these options on one line. Type `ls -al`, and then press **Enter**. A listing of hidden files in your current directory appears as well as all other files. (The order of the options does not matter. So, `ls -la` would work, too.)

8. Record the permissions of just the hidden files.

9. To exit the Terminal emulation program, type **exit**, and then press **Enter**.

10. Log out.

The `mkdir` and `rmdir` Commands

The `mkdir` command, which creates a new directory, normally returns no output to the screen. The `mkdir` command takes the following form:

```
mkdir directory
```

The path can be either full or partial. For example, to create a directory called paychecks, you would execute the following command:

```
mkdir paychecks
```

Conversely, you use the `rmdir` command to remove an empty directory. The `rmdir` command takes the following form:

```
rmdir directory
```

The path can be either full or partial.

 When removing a directory with the `rmdir` command, the directory must be empty and your current directory cannot be the directory you are trying to remove.

To remove the paychecks directory just shown you would use the `rmdir` command:

```
rmdir paychecks
```

Next you will create a directory named Class, and then remove it.

To create and remove a directory:

1. Log in to the Linux system as a user, and then open a Terminal emulation window.

2. Type **pwd**, and then press **Enter**. Your current working directory is displayed.

3. Type **mkdir Class**, and then press **Enter** to create a new directory named Class.

4. To remove the directory you just created, type **rmdir Class**, and then press **Enter**.

5. Create the Class directory again using the **mkdir** command.

6. Navigate to the Class directory, by typing **cd Class**, and then press **Enter**.

7. Type **pwd**, and then press **Enter**. Notice that Class directory is your present working directory.

8. Type **rmdir Class**, and then press **Enter**. An error message results. Figure 2-9 shows a result of attempting to remove your present directory.

9. To navigate to the parent directory, type **cd ..**, and press **Enter**.

10. Type **pwd**, and then press **Enter**. Your current working directory is displayed. Record it now.

11. Type **rmdir Class**, and then press **Enter**. You are now able to remove the Class directory because it is no longer your current working directory.

12. To exit the Terminal emulation program window, type **exit**, and then press **Enter**.

13. Log out.

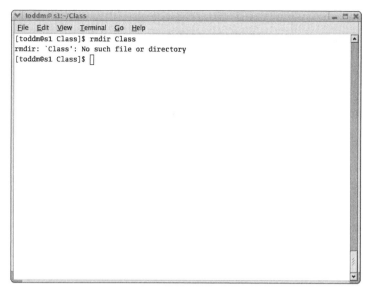

Figure 2-9   Message displays when you attempt to remove your parent directory

Using Editing Commands

In the Linux system you use editors to create shell script programs. **Editors** are programs that allow you to create, copy, and remove text within a file. Editors are similar to word-processing software. There are several different editors, so you need to try out a variety of them in order to determine the one that fits your needs and style best. It is important that you familiarize yourself with these programs because you occasionally need to use them within shell script programs.

Table 2-6 lists the most commonly used editor programs.

Table 2-6   Editor programs

Editor Program	Purpose
vi	Allows you to create a new file; it is somewhat more difficult to navigate than most graphical word-processing programs. The vi editor is the most commonly used editor on Linux systems.
gedit	User-friendly graphical text editor

The vi Program

Visual Interface or **vi**, as it's more commonly called, operates in several modes. While the **vi editor** is not as user-friendly as some of the other editors, particularly the graphical ones, it is the most commonly used editor on most Linux platforms. It operates in two modes. **Command mode** is when you input commands, telling the `vi` editor what you want to do. **Text mode** is when you type in your text or code. Because you use the keyboard to enter commands and text, the Escape key allows you to toggle back and forth between command mode and text mode. It is important to remember that you must issue one of the commands listed in Table 2-7 before you enter any text.

Table 2-7   Common `vi` commands

Command	Description
I	Inserts or moves the cursor to the beginning of the current line and allows you to enter text there
i	Inserts text at the current location of the cursor
O	Opens or adds a new blank line above the current line
o	Opens or adds a new blank line below the current line
A	Appends a new blank line to the end of the current line
a	Appends a new blank line immediately after the current location of the cursor
R	Represents the replace command mode; characters you type replace current characters starting at the location of the cursor
r	Replaces the character at the location of the cursor
k or UP ARROW	Moves up one line
j or DOWN ARROW	Moves down one line
h or LEFT ARROW	Moves one character position to the left
l or RIGHT ARROW	Moves one character position to the right
w	Moves the cursor to the next word
b	Moves the cursor to the previous word (b for back)
Shift+G	Moves the cursor to the end of the file
N followed by Shift+G	Moves the cursor to the Nth line (where N represents a number) in the file. For example, 3 followed by Shift+G, takes you to the third line.
D	Deletes text from the current cursor position to the end of the current line
de or dw	Deletes the current word
db	Deletes the previous word (b for back)
d(	Deletes all the text from the current cursor location to the beginning of the line
d)	Deletes all the text from the current cursor location to the end of the line
dh	Deletes the previous letter
dl or x	Deletes the current letter
dd	Deletes the current line
dw	Deletes the current word

Table 2-7 Common `vi` commands (continued)

Command	Description
u	Undoes the previous command
yy	Yanks, or copies, one line into the vi buffer; the buffer is simply an area of memory for holding data
p	Puts or pastes lines previously yanked and residing in the vi buffer to a new location
Nyy	Yanks, or copies, N lines (where N represents a number) into the vi buffer
:wq!	Writes and then quits vi

You can run the `vi` editor by simply typing the command `vi` in the Terminal emulation window. Then, you can enter your text and save it to a file. However, `vi` is normally executed with the file's path, as in this example:

```
vi payroll
```

Next you will use the `vi` editor to create a file and manage text and code within that file.

To use `vi` to create and manage a file:

1. Log in to the Linux system as a user, and then open a Terminal emulation window.

2. Type `vi file42.txt`, and then press **Enter**. A screen like the one shown in Figure 2-10 appears. The `vi` editor opens the file named file42.txt. (Note that the ~ symbol is called the tilde.)

3. To insert text, press **Esc**, and then type **i**. You are now in the text mode.

4. Enter the following text (be sure to press Enter at the end of each line). Note: If you make a mistake when typing in the text, you'll need to use the Escape key to toggle back and forth between text and command mode. Refer to the commands in Table 2-7.

   ```
   Line 1 of the vi editor.
   Line 2 of the vi editor.
   Line 3 of the vi editor.
   Last line of the vi editor.
   ```

5. To copy the first two lines and place them at the end of the file, move your cursor to the first character on the first line. Press **Esc**, type **2**, and then type **y** twice. This yanks or copies, the first two lines and places them in the `vi` buffer.

6. Move your cursor to the end of the file by pressing **Shift+G**. The cursor moves to the first character on the last line.

7. To put or paste the two previously yanked lines, type **p**. Notice that this places a copy of the two lines at the end of the file.

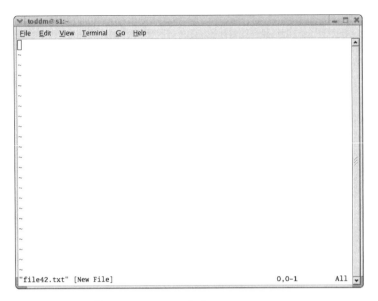

Figure 2-10 The vi command changes

8. To delete the first two lines, move the cursor to the first character on the first line by pressing **1** followed by **Shift+G**. Your cursor moves to the first line.

9. Press **d** twice to delete the first line of text.

10. Repeat Step 9 to delete the second line of text. When complete, the file should look like Figure 2-11.

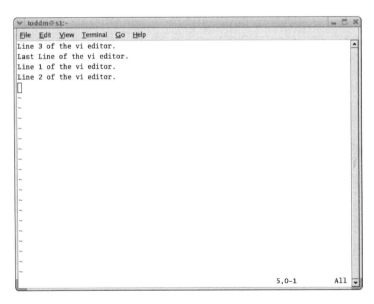

Figure 2-11 The output of the vi command

11. Type **:wq!**, and then press **Enter**. The file is saved and your prompt is returned.

12. Close your window, and then log out.

2

UNDERSTANDING FILE MANAGEMENT COMMANDS

File management commands help you manipulate files. While you use the editor commands to manipulate file content, you use file management commands to manipulate the files themselves such as when you create copies of existing files, move or rename existing files, or even merge text from multiple files. It is important to understand these commands because you will use them on a daily basis. They can also be used in shell scripts. Table 2-8 includes some of the more commonly used file management commands.

Table 2-8   File management commands

cp	Creates a copy of an existing file
mv	Moves or renames an existing file
sort	Sorts a file's fields in either ascending or descending order
cut	Pulls text out of a file; the original text within the file remains intact
paste	Merges the text from multiple files
diff	Displays the differences between two files; this is useful for verifying the integrity of a file against a master file
rm	Removes a file
uniq	Removes duplicate records from a sorted file

The cp Command

The **cp** command allows you to make a copy of a file. It takes the general form:

    cp *option source destination*

This is where ***source*** is the source file—the file you want to copy. The source file must exist or the **cp** command generates an error. The ***destination*** is the file to where you want to copy the source data. The destination file does not have to exist. It is user defined, meaning that the user can change the destination filename. When you use the **cp** command with the **-i** option for interactive mode, if the destination file *does* exist, a message is displayed asking whether or not you would like to overwrite the file.

The cp Command with a Full or Partial Path for Both the Source and Destination Filenames

The **cp** command accepts any combination of full and partial paths for the source and destination files. Let's look at an example. Refer back to Figure 2-1 of the Townsend Toyota tree structure. In order to copy the Apr.dat file from the Payroll directory to the

/TownsendToyota/IT/Project3 directory, you can execute the following command using full paths:

```
cp /TownsendToyota/Accounting/Payroll/Apr.dat/
TownsendToyota/IT/Project3/Apr.dat
```

Once successfully completed, you have a copy of Apr.dat in both the /TownsendToyota/Accounting/Payroll and /TownsendToyota/IT/Project3 directories.

In order to copy the Feb.dat file, located in the /TownsendToyota/Accounting/Payroll to another file called Febbackup.dat within the same directory, you would issue this partial path:

```
cp Feb.dat Febbackup.dat
```

Once successfully completed, you have two files: the original, Feb.dat and the duplicate copy, Febbackup.dat. Both are in the same directory.

Using the `cp` Command to Copy a File to the Parent Directory or a Sibling Directory

In order to copy the May.dat file to the parent directory, you use a partial path for the destination file as shown in this example:

```
cp May.dat ../May.dat
```

Once successfully completed, you have a copy of May.dat in the parent directory.

In order to copy the Jun.dat file, located in the /TownsendToyota/Accounting/Payroll to the sibling directory named /TownsendToyota/Accounting/GeneralLedger, you can use a partial path on the destination as shown in this example:

```
cp Jun.dat ../GeneralLedger/Jun.dat
```

Once successfully completed, you have a copy of Jun.dat in the /TownsendToyota/ Accounting/GeneralLedger sibling directory.

The `mv` Command

The `mv` command allows you to move, or rename, a file or directory. It takes the following form:

```
mv source destination
```

As with the `cp` command, the source file must exist. The destination can be user defined.

 While you use the `mv` command to both move and rename files and directories, the term move is used when the source path and the destination path are in different directories. The term rename is used when the source path and the destination path is in the same directory.

Like the `cp` command, if you use the `-i` option with the `mv` command, it prompts you before it moves a source file to an existing destination file.

The source and destination paths can be either a full or partial path to a file or a directory. However, the source and destination cannot be identical—you cannot move a file to itself.

Using the `mv` Command to Rename a File or Move a File to Another Directory

To rename a file, consider the following example where a file called x.file is changed to the new name y.file. The contents of the newly changed filename remain the same. Because you are renaming and not copying, the original file named x.file no longer exists.

```
mv x.file y.file
```

You can also use the mv command to change the location of the file. As in the previous example, the contents remain the same, but the file is moved and has a new name. Think of the move as if you were physically moving something from one place to another. Its location changes but the contents do not. In the following example, the x2.file is moved to the dirA directory and renamed y2.file.

```
mv x2.file /dirA/y2.file
```

Using the `mv` Command When the Source and Destination Have the Same Name

The only time the source and destination file can have the same name is when you are moving it to another directory. As previously noted, you cannot rename a file to its same name. Yet, in this example, `mv /dirB/x2.file /dirA/x2.file`, the actual filename stays the same—x2.file. This is because the directory name of the source, dirB, and the directory name of the destination, dirA, are different. This results in two completely different paths, hence two completely different filenames as far as Linux is concerned.

Next you will use the `cp` and mv commands to become familiar with how they work.

To copy and move files:

1. Log in to the Linux system as a user, and then open a Terminal emulation window.

2. Type **mkdir dirA1**, and then press **Enter**.

3. First, you need to create a file to duplicate. Use **vi** to create a file named **f1.dat**.

4. Type **cp f1.dat f8.dat**, and then press **Enter** to copy the file you created in the previous step.

5. Type **ls**, and then press **Enter**. Notice that the listing of files includes the file you just created as well as the copy of that file.

6. Type **cp -i f1.dat f8.dat**, and then press **Enter**. The command interactively prompts you asking if you want to overwrite the file.

7. Type **y**, and then press **Enter**.

8. Type **mv f1.dat f9.dat**, and then press **Enter**. The f1.dat file is moved to f9.dat.

9. Type **mv -i f8.dat f9.dat**, and then press **Enter**. The command interactively prompts you, asking if you want to overwrite the file.

10. Type **y**, and then press **Enter**.

11. Type **ls**, and then press **Enter**. Notice that the f9.dat file no longer exists, but the f1.dat file does. Now look at Figure 2-12; it shows the commands as you've used them in this exercise. You can see a listing displaying the files in the directory, in this case dirA1, before they are copied or moved. You can also see the message generated from the **-i** option when it is used with the **cp** and **mv** commands.

12. To exit the Terminal emulation program, type **exit**, and then press **Enter**.

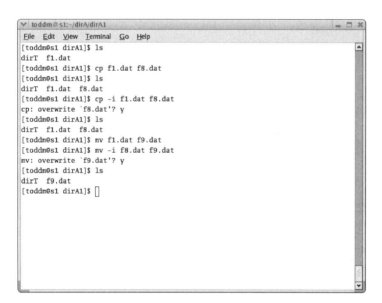

Figure 2-12   The output of the cp and mv commands

The sort Command

The **sort** command is used to sort data either in ascending or descending order. For example, if you want to alphabetically sort a file containing employee names, you use this command. Or, if you want to sort a numeric field in descending order, you also use the **sort** command. The basic syntax of the **sort** command is:

```
sort filename
```

In order to run the **sort** command for a file named unsort.dat, you enter the following command:

```
sort unsort.dat
```

When you use the **sort** command, the default is for the output to be displayed on your screen. However, you can redirect the output to a file by using the greater-than operator, **>**. The following example sorts a file named unsort.dat and places the output to a new file named sort.dat. The original file remains intact. There is no output to the screen because it is being redirected to a file. The name of the file following the greater-than symbol is user defined.

```
sort unsort.dat > sort.dat
```

By default, the **sort** command sorts in ascending order, or lower to higher. You can sort in descending order, called reverse order, using the **-r** option as in this command:

```
sort -r filename
```

The cut Command

The **cut** command allows you to strip text out of files and display the cut text on the screen or redirect the text to another file. This command is most often used to cut fields within a file. The data is not permanently cut from the file. The command does not alter the original file and it automatically opens the file for you. The basic syntax for the **cut** command is:

```
cut options filename
```

You need to be aware of two important options. The **-d** option is used to identify the delimiter in the file. The colon is generally used as a separator or **delimiter** between fields, letting programs know where one field begins and one ends. For example, **-d:** identifies the colon as a delimiter. The **-f** option is used to identify which field you want based on the delimiter. For example, consider the following record for an animal clinic:

```
1001:King Pup:Dog
```

The first field, "1001," represents the ID, the second field, "King Pup," represents the animal's name, and the third field, "Dog," represents the type of animal. Colons are used to delimit the fields in this example. You use a colon, or some other character, instead of a space to separate fields. The space can not be used because it may actually separate words in a field, such as "King Pup."

Assuming the file is named animal.dat, the command to display the first field is: **cut -d: -f1 animal.dat**. The command to display the first and third fields would be: **cut -d: -f1,3 animal.dat**.

Next you will create a file with several employee records in it. Each record will consist of two fields—an employee number followed by a colon and the employee name.

To use the cut command in a file:

1. Log in to the Linux system as a user, and then open a Terminal emulation window.

2. Create a file named **unsort.dat** using the vi editor.

3. Enter the data in two fields. Note in the data below, that the format is *number:name* where *number* represents the first field and *name* represents the second field. The colon (:) is the delimiter. Place the following data in the file noting that there are duplicate 3:Jessie records. (You will use these two records later when you learn about the uniq command.) After you enter the data make sure you press Enter at the end of each line, save the file, and then exit the vi editor.

   ```
   3:Jessie James Garcia
   3:Jessie James Garcia
   2:Zachary Scott Pheng
   4:Lorenzo Todd Von Schloss
   1:Micki McSunday-Washington
   ```

4. To cut the first field, type **cut -d: -f1 unsort.dat**, and then press **Enter**. See Figure 2-13; the first field appears on your screen, but the data has not been removed from the original file.

5. To cut the second field, the names, and then send the output to a file named name.dat, type **cut -d: -f2 unsort.dat > name.dat**, and then press **Enter**. See Figure 2-13.

6. To display the contents of the new file, type **cat name.dat**, and then press **Enter**. See Figure 2-13; notice that the new file only has the names in it.

7. To ensure that the original contents of unsortcut.dat have not been literally cut, type **cat unsort.dat**, and then press **Enter**. The original contents that were created in Step 3 appear unchanged on your screen as shown in Figure 2-13.

8. To exit, type **exit**, and then press **Enter**.

9. Log out.

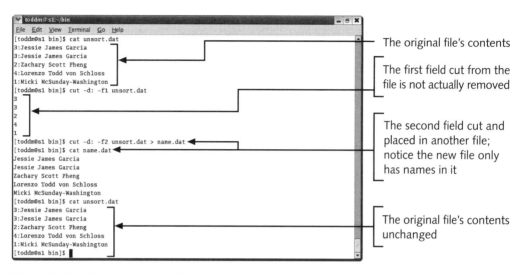

Figure 2-13   Demonstrating the cut command

The paste Command

Whereas the **cut** command cuts file fields, the **paste** command pastes, or merges, data from one file to another. The data can then be merged into a new file. The basic syntax of the **paste** command is:

```
paste filename_one filename_two
```

The above code merges each line from file two with each line of file one. For example, assume you had two files each containing name data. The last.dat file contents are **Smith Jones Adams**, and the first.dat file contents are **Joe Mary Sue**. If you enter the command **paste first.dat last.dat**, then your output to the screen would be:

```
Joe Smith
Mary Jones
Sue Adams
```

If you had entered the command **paste last.dat first.dat**, then your output would be:

```
Smith Joe
Jones Mary
Adams Sue
```

The contents of the original files remain the same. You can also create an altogether new file using the redirect output (>) symbol. If you enter the command **paste first.dat last.dat > first_last.dat**, you would create a new file called first_last.dat with the pasted data from the first.dat and last.dat files.

Suppose that Mama's Hardware Store maintains two separate files. One file is called product and contains the names of top selling sale items, and the other file is called quantity and contains the amount of the sales items that have been ordered. The owners would like the information to appear in one file named orders. To do that, you need to paste these files together. Figure 2-14 shows the contents of the two original files as well as the use of the **paste** command to merge these files and redirect the contents to the new file.

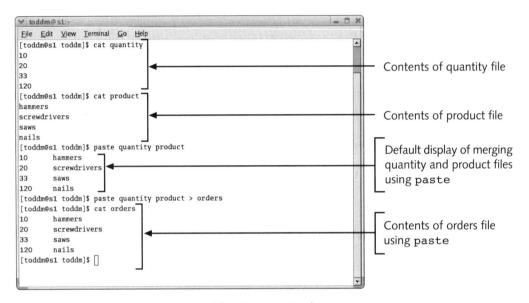

Figure 2-14   The paste command for Mama's Hardware Store

The rm Command

The **rm** command is used to remove a file permanently from the file system tree hierarchy. There is no way to recover a removed file. The basic syntax of the command is:

```
rm filename
```

In the following example, the file named resume.dat is removed.

```
rm resume.dat
```

Some versions of Linux ask you to verify that you really want to remove a file before it is removed. Other versions simply remove the file without asking. Use caution and consider testing this concept by removing a test file before removing any files from your file hierarchy.

The uniq Command

The uniq command is to used to find duplicate lines from a sorted file. This is a particularly helpful programming technique to use if redundant records happen to exist in a file. The uniq command does not remove the duplicate lines; it just displays them on the screen. The uniq command opens the file for you. The basic syntax of this command is:

```
uniq filename
```

The output defaults to the screen, displaying the duplicates. You can also redirect the output to a user-defined filename using the following command:

```
uniq duplicates.dat > uniq.dat
```

In this case, the repeating lines from the duplicates.dat file are redirected to the uniq.dat file. You use redirection when you want to refer to the original data file. In this case, you would process the uniq.dat file because any redundant records have already been removed from the file.

The uniq command has a useful option for counting the number of occurrences of a line in a file. This is helpful when you want to identify the number of duplicates you have in a file. The following uniq command with the attached **-c** option accomplishes this:

```
uniq -c duplicates.dat
```

Next you will use the uniq command to remove duplicate items from a grocery list where several people in the household have added redundant items.

To use the uniq command to remove duplicates from a file:

1. Log in to the Linux system as a user, and then open a Terminal emulation window.

2. Create a file named **grocery.dat** using the vi editor.

3. Enter the following data. As you enter the data, make sure you press Enter at the end of each line. Save the file, and then exit the vi editor.

```
soup
soup
pizza
turkey
lettuce
lettuce
lettuce
apples
bananas
grapes
grapes
```

4. To remove the duplicate grocery items, type **uniq grocery.dat**, and then press **Enter**. See Figure 2-15.

5. To redirect this to a file that you can take to the grocery store, type **uniq grocery.dat > list.dat**, and then press **Enter**.

6. To display the contents of the new list, type **cat list.dat**, and then press **Enter**. See Figure 2-15. Notice that now the items are part of the list.dat file.

7. To exit, type **exit**, and then press **Enter**.

8. Log out.

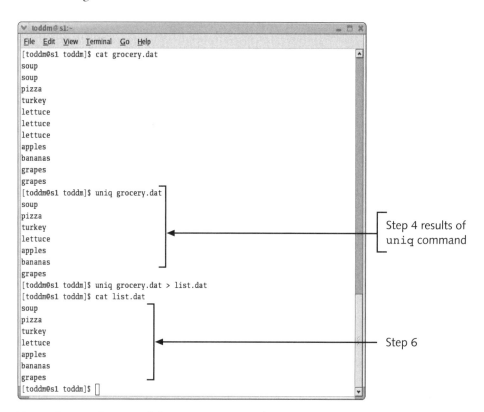

Figure 2-15   Output of the uniq command

CHAPTER SUMMARY

❑ The Linux file system is designed for storage and quick access. Directories contain other directories or files. Files contain only data. The Linux file system is hierarchical, or treelike, in nature. In the Linux file system, the root directory (/) is the top of the tree. All files and folders branch from the root directory. The system directories are created during the installation of the Linux operating system, and they should not be modified or deleted.

❑ When navigating the tree hierarchy, you need to be aware of where you are, or what your current directory is. With the hierarchy structure, there is a parent-child relationship. The parent directory is referred to as dot dot (..). A child directory is referred to by name. Siblings have the same parent. A full path begins at the root directory. A partial path does not include the root directory.

❑ Directory management commands deal with manipulating and displaying the directories in the tree. The most commonly used commands are **cd** for changing the current directory location, **pwd** for displaying the current directory location, and **ls** for displaying the contents of a directory.

❑ Editors and editor commands allow you to manipulate the contents in a file. The most commonly used editor is **vi**. It can be used to add, copy, delete, insert, or modify data within a file.

❑ The file management commands allow you to manipulate the actual files within the tree. The **cp** command is used for copying an existing file to another file, creating two files. The **mv** command is used for moving or renaming an existing file; however, you end up with just one file when you use this command. The **rm** is used to remove a file.

REVIEW QUESTIONS

1. Use the _____ command to change directory locations.

    a. cd

    b. rm

    c. mkdir

    d. cut

2. Which of the following are considered full paths? (Choose all that apply.)

    a. /dirA

    b. ../dir2

    c. payroll

    d. /

3. Use the _____ command to delete a directory.

   a. `delete_dir`

   b. `mkdir`

   c. `rmdir`

   d. `cat`

4. Which of the following are considered partial paths? (Choose all that apply.)

   a. /dirA

   b. ../dir2

   c. payroll

   d. /

5. Which of the following are text editors? (Choose all that apply.)

   a. `vi`

   b. `emacs`

   c. `ls`

   d. `cat`

6. The _____ command sorts data in descending order.

   a. `sort -r`

   b. `sort`

   c. `mkdir`

   d. `reverse`

7. To change the working directory location to a sibling directory named dir2, you enter the _____ command.

   a. `cd /`

   b. `cd \`

   c. `cd ..\dir2`

   d. `cd ../dir2`

8. The _____ directory holds mounted drives.

   a. /root

   b. /boot

   c. /mnt

   d. /var

9. The _____ file system holds files and directories that vary in size.

    a. /root

    b. /boot

    c. /mnt

    d. /var

10. The _____ command creates a directory named winchester in the root directory.

    a. `mkdir /winchester`

    b. `mkdir ../winchester`

    c. `mkdir \winchester`

    d. `md /winchester`

11. The _____ option for the `ls` command displays a long listing.

    a. `-i`

    b. `-a`

    c. `-l`

    d. `-c`

12. Which of the following represents your parent directory?

    a. `..`

    b. `.`

    c. `/`

    d. `\`

13. The _____ command allows you to change directory locations to a child directory named child1.

    a. `mkdir child1`

    b. `cd ../child1`

    c. `cd child1`

    d. `cd /`

14. In `vi`, the command to change to insert mode is:

    a. `o`

    b. `O`

    c. `i`

    d. `d`

15. The _____ command deletes a file.

    a. rmdir

    b. cd

    c. rm

    d. pwd

16. The _____ command displays your present working directory.

    a. cat

    b. cd

    c. touch

    d. pwd

17. The _____ system directory contains the Linux kernel.

    a. /boot

    b. /root

    c. /dev

    d. /var

18. The _____ in the **vi** editor allows you to save and quit the program.

    a. :wq

    b. q!

    c. w!

    d. !

19. The command to rename a file is _____.

    a. mv

    b. cp

    c. del

    d. rename

20. The _____ command makes a duplicate of a file.

    a. mv

    b. cp

    c. del

    d. rename

HANDS-ON PROJECTS

Project 2-1

In this project, you will compare your own family tree to the Linux file system. Research your family tree no further than your grandparents. Draw your family tree on a separate piece of paper, and then explain how your family tree compares to what you've learned about the Linux file system in this chapter.

Project 2-2

In this project, you will compare a building's evacuation plan for one room to the use of paths in the Linux file system. You will first need to get a copy of a building evacuation plan for one room from your local church, school, or work. Then, write a description of how the evacuation plan relates to a path in the Linux file system hierarchy.

Project 2-3

In this project, you will execute various commands in your home directory.

1. Log in to the Linux computer as a user, and then open a Terminal emulation window.
2. Type **touch file1.dat**, and then press **Enter**.
3. Repeat Step 2 three additional times; however, change the number at the end of the filename each time, e.g., file2.dat, file3.dat, file4.dat.
4. Create a hidden file by typing **touch .hiddenfile.txt**, and then press **Enter**.
5. Issue a long listing of all the files in the directory by typing **ls -al**, and then press **Enter**.
6. On a separate sheet of paper, label and identify each column that is displayed.
7. Close your window, and then log off.

Project 2-4

In this project, you will search the Red Hat Web site for information on various Linux commands in order to learn how to use the Web site as a research tool. You will need access to the Internet.

1. Open a Web browser.
2. In the Address or location box on your browser, type ***http://www.redhat.com***, and then press **Enter**. The Red Hat Web site appears.

3. In the Search Red Hat: text box, type **ls**, and then click the **Go** button. The screen displays a listing of the links to documents related to the **ls** command.

4. Click one of the documents and review it. Keep checking documents until you locate one that gives you additional insight into the **ls** command.

5. Based on your findings at this Web site, identify something new you've learned about the **ls** command.

6. Repeat Steps 3 through 5 for the **pwd** command.

7. Repeat Steps 3 through 5 for the **cp** command.

8. Repeat Steps 3 through 5 for the **vi** editor.

9. Close your Web browser.

Project 2-5

In this project, you will execute commands, and then draw the resulting tree structure.

1. Log in to the Linux system as a user, and then open a Terminal emulation window.

2. Type **mkdir Project2-5**, and then press **Enter**.

3. Type **cd Project2-5**, and then press **Enter**.

4. Type **mkdir R**, and then press **Enter**.

5. Type **mkdir S**, and then press **Enter**.

6. Type **mkdir T**, and then press **Enter**.

7. Type **cd T**, and then press **Enter**.

8. Type **touch t1.dat**, and then press **Enter**.

9. Type **touch t2.dat**, and then press **Enter**.

10. Type **touch t3.dat**, and then press **Enter**.

11. Type **cd ../R**, and then press **Enter**.

12. Type **touch r1.dat**, and then press **Enter**.

13. Type **touch r2.dat**, and then press **Enter**.

14. Type **cd ../S**, and then press **Enter**.

15. Type **touch s1.dat**, and then press **Enter**.

16. Type **touch s2.dat**, and then press **Enter**.

17. Type **cd ..**, and then press **Enter**.

18. Draw the resulting tree structure.

19. Close your window, and then log out.

Project 2-6

In this project, you will create a directory tree based on the output of the `tree` command shown in Figure 2-16.

2

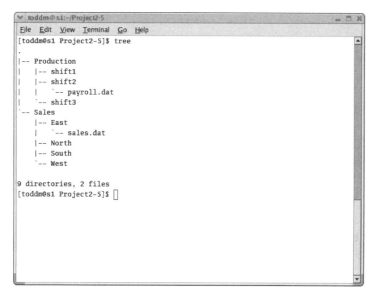

```
  toddm@s1:~/Project2-5                                                 _ □ x
 File   Edit   View   Terminal   Go   Help
[toddm@s1 Project2-5]$ tree
.
|-- Production
|   |-- shift1
|   |-- shift2
|   |   `-- payroll.dat
|   `-- shift3
`-- Sales
    |-- East
    |   `-- sales.dat
    |-- North
    |-- South
    `-- West

9 directories, 2 files
[toddm@s1 Project2-5]$
```

Figure 2-16   Tree you will create for Project 2-6

1. Log in to the Linux system as a user, and then open a Terminal emulation window.
2. Create the directory tree shown in Figure 2-16. You need to use these commands to complete this project: **cd**, **pwd**, **mkdir**, and **rmdir**.
3. Record the order in which you used each command to create the tree.
4. Close your window, and then log out.

Project 2-7

In this project, you will create the directory shown in Figure 2-17 in order to reinforce your understanding of the Linux file system hierarchy. You will need to use these commands to complete this project: **cd**, **pwd**, **mkdir**, and **rmdir**. Finally, record the commands in the order in which you used them to create the tree.

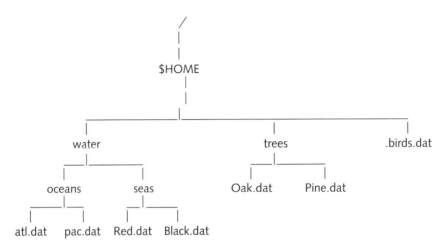

Figure 2-17   Tree you will create for Project 2-7

Project 2-8

In this project, you will use the tree structure from Project 2-5 to manipulate the files and directories created. Project 2-8 requires completion of Project 2-5.

1. Log in to the Linux system as a user, and then open a Terminal emulation window.

2. Type **cd Project2-5**, and then press **Enter**.

3. Type **cd T**, and then press **Enter**.

4. Type **ls**, press **Enter**, and then record the output.

5. Type **cp t1.dat t11.dat**, and then press **Enter**.

6. Type **cp t2.dat t22.dat**, and then press **Enter**.

7. Type **ls**, press **Enter**, and then record the output.

8. Type **mv t3.dat t33.dat**, and then press **Enter**.

9. Type **ls**, press **Enter**, and then record the output.

10. Record the difference between the **cp** and **mv** commands.

11. Type **cd ../S**, and then press **Enter**.

12. Type **ls**, press **Enter**, and then record the output.

13. Type **cp s1.dat ../R/r5.dat**, press **Enter**, and then record what this command does.

14. Type **cd ../R**, and then press **Enter**.

15. Type **ls**, press **Enter**, and then record the output.

16. Close your window, and then log out.

2

Project 2-9

In this project, you will use **vi** to create a data file with records. You will then sort the data.

1. Log in to the Linux system as a user, and then open a Terminal emulation window.

2. Type **mkdir Project2-9**, and then press **Enter**.

3. Type **cd Project2-9**, and then press **Enter**.

4. Type **vi infile.dat**, and then press **Enter**. The **vi** editor opens.

5. To insert text, press **Esc**, and then type **i**.

6. Enter the following text and make sure you press Enter at the end of each line. (Each row is considered an employee record with colons separating the fields. The first field is the employee number. The second field is the employee name, and the third field is the employee salary.)

   ```
   401:Sue Fanglee Tuen:$34000
   104:Sammy Jones:$55402
   207:Tammy Phang:$50040
   214:Zoe Buhari-Jones:$56000
   505:James Brongan:$50500
   ```

7. To save the file, press **Esc**, and then type the colon symbol (**:**). The cursor moves to the bottom of the screen with a colon to its left.

8. To write the file, type **wq!**, and then press **Enter**. The prompt returns.

9. Sort the data in ascending order by typing **sort infile.dat**, press **Enter**, and then record the output.

10. Sort the data in descending order by typing **sort -r infile.dat**, press **Enter**, and then record the output.

11. Sort the data in descending order and redirect the output to another file by typing **sort -r infile.dat > reverse_sort.dat**, and then press **Enter**.

12. Sort the data in ascending order, redirect the output to another file, and then record the command you used.

13. Close your window, and then log out.

Project 2-10

In this project, you will use the files created in Project 2-9. Project 2-10 requires completion of Project 2-9.

1. Log in to the Linux system as a user, and then open a Terminal emulation window.

2. Type **cd Project2-9**, and then press **Enter**.

3. Cut the first field.

4. Cut the second field.

5. Cut the third field.

6. Cut both the first and third field and redirect the output to a new file named **salary.dat**.

7. Make a duplicate of infile.dat by typing `cp infile.dat infile2.dat`, and then press **Enter**.

8. Open the file named **infile2.dat**, and add five additional records. Add a sixth record that has your name. Also, create a fictitious employee number and employee salary to complete your record.

9. Type `diff infile.dat infile2.dat`, and then press **Enter**. Record the output.

10. Close your window, and then log out.

CASE PROJECTS

Case 2-1

You have been hired by TMI to design an application using shell script programs. TMI needs you to design and create a new directory structure.

The company has several departments: accounting, sales, manufacturing, information technology, and headquarters. The accounting department has accounts receivable, accounts payable, and payroll functions within it. The manufacturing department runs three shifts and a weekend shift. The information technology department has five projects in progress. The sales department has offices located in the West, East, North, and South.

First, design the Linux file system hierarchy on paper. Keep in mind that the departments, functions, shifts, regions, and projects need to translate into directories. Next, you need to create this hierarchy on the Linux system. Create at least one empty file in each directory. Use the department, function, shift, region, or project name as the filename and include an extension of .dat.

Case 2-2

Zonka Corp. has sales offices in five countries: the United States, Canada, Spain, Singapore, and France. Design your directory structure on paper and then implement it. Make sure that each country is represented by a directory. Next, create two files in each directory named first.dat and last.dat. These will be used to hold employees' names with an employee's first and last names split between two files. In the file named first.dat, add the first name of five employees. In the file named last.dat, add the corresponding last name of the same five employees. Then, using the **paste** command, merge the first two files together into a new file. For each employee, the new file must have the first name followed by the last name on one line. Then, merge the first two files into another file. For each employee, this file must have the last name followed by the first name on one line. Finally, make backup copies of the newly merged files.

3

SHELL BASICS

In this chapter, you will:

♦ Understand the shell login and logout files
♦ Learn about shell variables
♦ Become familiar with the shell environment
♦ Learn about shell builtin commands
♦ Learn about shell grammar
♦ Understand command types

The Linux shell is the program that acts as the interface between you and the operating system kernel. The shell accepts input in the form of your commands, and then gives the commands over to the processor for execution. You see evidence of the shell when you log in and go to a command prompt. In this chapter, you will learn how the shell is executed and understand the purpose of the shell and shell grammar. Redirection will also be discussed.

UNDERSTANDING THE SHELL LOGIN AND LOGOUT FILES

When you log in, a shell is executed and provides you with a shell prompt. You type your commands to the right of the prompt. From your previous experience, you know that you need a username to log in and interact with the operating system. However, when a user account is created, it is given a default shell, which is what allows you to access the operating system. For Red Hat Linux, the default shell is **bash**.

 As you know from Chapter 1, there are several different shells. This book focuses on the bash shell.

The bash shell is an Institute of Electrical and Electronic Engineers (IEEE) Portable Operating Systems Interface standard (POSIX) developed by the Free Software Foundation. This means it is a standard that comes free with the operating system.

The /etc/profile Script File

There are startup files in the Linux directory hierarchy, which are used to set up default settings for the user's environment. The startup files are read and executed in a specific order as the user logs in. The logout file is read and executed as the user logs out.

The shell reads and executes commands in the /etc/profile file, if it is present. Figure 3-1 shows what's included in this file. This file is actually a script. It is important because it is executed for every user. However, your file content may differ. If you wanted all users to have a script execute when they log in or if you wanted to display a message that all would see as they log in, you would modify this file accordingly. You typically place any statements at the end of this file so you won't interfere with other statements already contained within it. The permissions on this file are read and write for the root user and read for all other users; therefore, you must be logged in as root to modify this file. Users cannot modify it. Although you may not understand all the code at this point, it will become clear as you work your way through this book.

Let's look at a statement in the /etc/profile script to give you an idea of what happens with this script. Recall from Chapter 1 that the `history` command allows you to keep up to 1,000 commands. If you look at Figure 3-1, you notice a `HISTSIZE=1000` statement. This sets the number of commands that the `history` command keeps to 1,000. As root user, you could change it to 10,000 or even just 100. If you increase it, you keep more commands in the history list. This is helpful because you can see previous commands in cases where you want to verify the exact syntax of a command. However, if you increase the size of this file, the file that keeps the history list, called ~/.bash_history, will also increase over time. This means you will use more disk space for the enlarged history list.

```
# /etc/profile
# System wide environment and startup programs
# Functions and aliases go in /etc/bashrc
if ! echo $PATH | /bin/grep -q "/usr/X11R6/bin" ; then
  PATH="$PATH:/usr/X11R6/bin"
fi
ulimit -S -c 1000000 > /dev/null 2>&1
if [ `id -gn` = `id -un` -a `id -u` -gt 14 ]; then
        umask 002
else
        umask 022
fi
USER=`id -un`
LOGNAME=$USER
MAIL="/var/spool/mail/$USER"
HOSTNAME=`/bin/hostname`
HISTSIZE=1000
REPLY="Y"
if [ -z "$INPUTRC" -a ! -f "$HOME/.inputrc" ]; then
        INPUTRC=/etc/inputrc
fi
export PATH USER LOGNAME MAIL HOSTNAME HISTSIZE INPUTRC REPLY
```

Figure 3-1   The /etc/profile script file

You can also see that a variable called $LOGNAME is set in this file. The $LOGNAME equates to the user account of the user that is currently logged in. As a System Administrator you might use this information for auditing purposes.

The ~/.bash_profile Script File

After the shell executes the /etc/profile script file for all users, another script executes; it is called ~/.bash_profile. However, this file, in each user's home directory, is hidden (notice the dot prior to the filename). The file is hidden so you won't accidentally delete it. The permissions for this file are read and write for the owner and read for all other users; that way each user can customize this file. Figure 3-2 shows what's included in this file. Again, your content may vary. This file exists so that users can customize their own login processes. They can modify this script and place their own commands in the file. For example, if a user wants to display a calendar or the date on the screen each time he or she logs in, it can be done by changing this file. This script file also adds the directory $HOME/bin to the PATH so that users can execute their own scripts without entering a full path.

The tilde, ~, is used to represent the user's home directory. The ~ symbol and $HOME are equivalent. Thus ~/.bash_profile is a hidden file in each user's home directory.

```
# .bash_profile
# Get the aliases and functions
if [ -f ~/.bashrc ]; then
. ~/.bashrc
fi
# User specific environment and startup programs
PATH=$PATH:$HOME/bin
BASH_ENV=$HOME/.bashrc
export BASH_ENV PATH
unset USERNAME
```

Figure 3-2   The ~/.bash_profile script file

Next you will modify and test the ~/.bash_profile file to become more familiar with its operation.

To modify and test the ~/.bash_profile file:

1. Log in to the Linux system as a user, and then open a Terminal emulation window.

2. Type **vi .bash_profile**, and then press **Enter**. The shell script is displayed on the screen. You don't need to include the tilde for your home directory because when you log in, your position in the Linux tree already is your own home directory.

3. Press **Shift+G**. Your cursor moves to the bottom of the screen.

4. Type **o** to open a line of text in vi.

5. Type **echo "Hello"**, and then press **Enter**.

6. Save the file, and then close the editor.

7. In order to test .bash_profile, type **bash .bash_profile**, and then press **Enter**. The text "Hello" appears on the screen.

8. To exit the Terminal emulation program, type **exit**, and then press **Enter**.

9. Log out.

The ~/.bash_profile executes another hidden file, called ~/.bashrc, if it exists on the system. The ~/.bashrc script in turn executes another script that sets your prompt; it is called /etc/bashrc and can only be modified by the root user. Remember that the ~/.bashrc is able to be changed by the user, but that the /etc/bashrc file can only be changed by the root user.

The ~/.bash_logout Script File

There is another hidden file located in each user's home directory, which is read and executed each time a user logs out of the Linux system; it is named .bash_logout. A practical use of the ~/.bash_logout file is to check when a user logs off by redirecting the output of the **date** command to a file. Then, you can determine exactly when a user logged off the system.

Next you will perform an exercise where you change the ~/.bash_logout file, and then test it. The goal of this exercise is to have you modify the file to understand what happens when you change it.

To modify and test the ~/.bash_logout file:

1. Log in to the Linux system as a user, and then open a Terminal emulation window.

2. Type **vi .bash_logout**, and then press **Enter**. The shell script is displayed on the screen.

3. Press **Shift+G**. Your cursor moves to the bottom of the screen.

4. Type **o** to open a line of text in vi.

5. To ensure that you are properly logging out, you can add a closing response by typing **echo "Good Bye!"**, and then press **Enter**.

6. Save the file, and then close the editor.

7. In order to test the **.bash_logout** file, type **bash .bash_logout**, and then press **Enter**. The text "Good Bye!" appears on the screen.

8. To exit the Terminal emulation program, type **exit**, and then press **Enter**.

9. Log out.

Another way to invoke the shell is by entering bash at the command prompt. It is located in the /bin directory.

LEARNING ABOUT SHELL VARIABLES

A **shell variable** is a keyword that is set by the shell for a specific use. It is typically entered in all uppercase letters. This is different from most commands, which are entered in lowercase. Each shell variable is used for a different purpose. Notice some of the shell variables, such as PATH and HOSTNAME in Figures 3-1 and 3-2.

You can display the contents of an individual variable by using the echo command and placing a dollar sign ($) prior to the variable's name. For example echo $HOME displays the home directory. Note that echo ~ also displays the home directory.

A few of the shell variables are listed in Table 3-1. You can refer to the man pages on bash for others.

Table 3-1   Some of the important shell variables

Shell Variable	Description
PWD	The most recent current working directory set with the cd command
OLDPWD	The previous working directory set by the cd command
BASH	The full path name used to invoke the bash shell
RANDOM	Generates a random integer between 0 and 32,767
HOSTNAME	The current hostname of the system running Linux
IFS	IFS or Internal Field Separator, used as a separator between words in the shell or shell scripts
PATH	Contains a list of directories that are used to search for commands within the Linux tree hierarchy
HOME	The home directory of the current user. Each user has a home directory when his or her account is created. This is the default location for storing files and directories for a user.
PS1	Represents the prompt
PS3	Represents the prompt for the select statement
TMOUT	Represents the amount of time the shell waits, without user input, before exiting the current shell; TMOUT means to "timeout" the user's session after a specific amount of time passes

Next you will display the contents of a few shell variables so you can understand how to access them in case you need to retrieve them either at the shell prompt or in a shell script.

To display the contents of shell variables:

1. Log in to the Linux system as a user, and then open a Terminal emulation window.

3

2. Type **echo $PWD**, and then press **Enter**. The current working directory is displayed. See Figure 3-3.

3. Type **echo $BASH**, and then press **Enter**. The full path of the default shell, bash, is displayed. See Figure 3-3.

4. Type **echo $RANDOM**, and then press **Enter**. A random number is displayed on the screen. See Figure 3-3; notice that the number is 22,178. You might use the RANDOM shell variable in a program that creates random passwords for users.

5. Type **echo $PATH**, and then press **Enter**. The command search path is displayed on the screen. See Figure 3-3. Here the path is quite long and includes many directories.

6. To exit the Terminal emulation program, type **exit**, and then press **Enter**.

7. Log out.

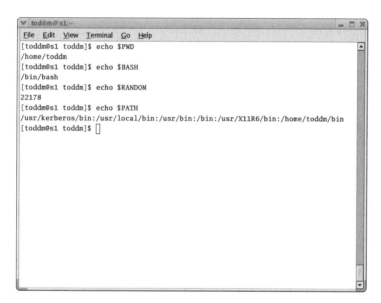

```
[toddm@s1 toddm]$ echo $PWD
/home/toddm
[toddm@s1 toddm]$ echo $BASH
/bin/bash
[toddm@s1 toddm]$ echo $RANDOM
22178
[toddm@s1 toddm]$ echo $PATH
/usr/kerberos/bin:/usr/local/bin:/usr/bin:/bin:/usr/X11R6/bin:/home/toddm/bin
[toddm@s1 toddm]$
```

Figure 3-3   Contents of a few shell variables

The contents of a variable set in the ~/.bash_profile file override the contents of a variable in the /etc/profile script file.

BECOMING FAMILIAR WITH THE SHELL ENVIRONMENT

When you enter a command using a partial path, such as **cp**, how does the shell know how to execute it? When a partial path is used when executing a command, the shell looks at the contents of the **PATH** variable until it finds the directory in which the command is located. Look again at Figure 3-3 and you see the contents of the **PATH** shell variable for the user toddm. Notice that a delimiter, in this case a colon, separates each of the directories in the path listing. When searching for the directory that a command is in, the shell searches each directory, separated by the delimiter in the path list starting from left and moving to the right. If the directory where the command is located is found in the **PATH** variable, the command is executed from that directory. Otherwise, the shell generates an error message indicating the command could not be found.

When executing a command using its full path, such as **/bin/cp**, the shell does not refer to the **PATH** contents. Instead it goes directly to the command using the specified path. For the command **/bin/cp**, the shell moves directly to the **/bin** directory, which is one of the system directories that you learned about in Chapter 2.

The File System Hierarchy Standard

Red Hat supports the **File System Hierarchy Standard**, which has been developed to standardize some of the system directories on computers running the Linux operating system. One important aspect of the standard is to use the /usr/local/bin directory to store all of your shell scripts that need to be available to many users. Note that only the root user can place scripts here, but all others can read and execute scripts within it. If users want to create their own scripts, they can place the script in a **$HOME/bin** directory, but they have to create the **$HOME/bin** directory first. This directory does not exist unless a user creates it. If you look at the **PATH** listing in Figure 3-3, you notice that each of these directories—/usr/local/bin and /home/toddm/bin (**$HOME/bin**)— are listed with the displaying of the shell variable, **$PATH**.

LEARNING ABOUT SHELL BUILTIN COMMANDS

A **builtin command** is a command that is part of the shell program, hence the term "builtin." These commands are actually compiled into the shell, thereby making the shell an executable command containing other commands. You cannot modify or delete builtin commands, and in fact, they are not available in any system directory. The only way you can find out more about these commands is to refer to **man** on **bash**. Table 3-2 shows the common builtin commands. You have seen some of these commands in Chapters 1 and 2. You need to understand these commands because they are used at the command line and in shell scripts.

Table 3-2   Some common shell builtin commands

Builtin Command	Description	Example(s)
`. filename`	Reads and executes commands from specified filename in the current shell environment	`. script1`
`cd`	Changes the current directory (See Chapter 2 for additional coverage)	`cd /`
`declare` or `typeset`	Declares a variable; the -r option makes the variable read-only	`declare var2` `declare —r ReadOnlyVar2`
`echo`	Displays output on the screen	`echo$ y echo "Hello"`
`exec`	Causes a command to replace the current shell; no new process is created	`exec ls`
`exit`	Causes the shell to exit with a status	`exit 1`
`export`	Exports the variable to a spawned shell; this allows a parent shell to set a variable that can be used by a child shell	`export x="Howdy!"`
`history`	Displays history of commands previously entered	`history`
`kill`	Sends a signal to a PID. If you run `kill —l`, you can see all the kill signals. You use this option to kill or stop background processes or daemons.	`kill 1409`
`let`	Evaluates an arithmetic expression	`let x=5`
`local`	Creates a local variable	`local x=5`
`logout`	Exits a login shell	`logout`
`pwd`	Displays current working directory (See Chapter 2 for additional coverage)	`pwd`
`read`	Reads characters from the keyboard	`read x`
`readonly`	Reads characters from the keyboard; once a variable is declared readonly, it cannot be changed	`readonly y`
`return`	Causes a function to exit with a certain value; a return value of 1 indicates failure and a return value of 0 indicates success	`return 1`
`set`	Sets and displays shell variables.	`set —xv`

3

Table 3-2 Some common shell builtin commands (continued)

Builtin Command	Description	Example(s)
`shift`	Shifts positional parameters	`shift 1`
`test`	Evaluates expressions. This works the same as the `[[expression]]` command. Also, you can use the `[[expression]]` command in place of the `test` command.	`test -d fileA.txt`
`trap`	Catches a signal sent to the shell; displays the message "Trapped signal 3" when signal 3 is sent to the shell	`trap "Trappedsignal 3" 3`

LEARNING ABOUT SHELL GRAMMAR

Shell grammar is defined as the rules that must be followed for proper operation of the shell. Basically, for the shell to function correctly, a specific set of syntax rules must be maintained just like in any spoken language. There are several fundamental building blocks in shell grammar. You need to understand these building blocks to best comprehend how the shell interprets the commands given to it. A thorough understanding can help you when you encounter shell errors. The building blocks of shell grammar are as follows:

- Blank
- Word
- Name
- Metacharacter
- Control operator
- Reserved word

A **blank** is defined as a space or a tab and is used to separate items in the shell. A **word** is defined as a sequence of characters that is considered a single unit by the shell. A word is also commonly known as a **token**. A **name** is a word that consists only of letters, numbers and the underscore. A **metacharacter** is a character that is used for a specific purpose by the shell; each purpose is unique to the character. A metacharacter is used to separate words. For example, you have seen the greater-than symbol, >, used as a metacharacter to redirect the output of a command. Table 3-3 contains the metacharacters used by the shell.

3

Table 3-3   Shell metacharacter symbols

Metacharacter Symbol(s)	Metacharacter Name	Purpose
|	The pipe symbol	Allows you to pass command output to another command
&	Ampersand	Allows you to run a job in the background
;	Semicolon	Allows you to sequence commands on the command line
( )	Left and right parentheses	Allows you to run a command in a subshell
<	Less-than symbol	Allows you to redirect input
>	Greater-than symbol	Allows you to redirect output and create a new file
Space	Spacebar	Allows you to separate words

Let's look at an example to help you understand how shell grammar works. In the following statement, echo "This is the production file">production.txt, the command echo is a word. The space immediately following this command is a blank that is used to separate this word from the next. The next word is literally "This is the production file". Next, the redirection operator, >, appears and is a metacharacter. Although most of the time you surround the redirection operator with a space, it is not mandatory because a metacharacter separates words. The redirection operator separates the text being echoed and the filename which is a name.

A **control operator** is a token that performs a specific control function. It modifies how the shell processes commands. Table 3-4 contains the control operator symbols.

Table 3-4   Shell control operators

Symbol(s)	Name	Function
||	Two pipe symbols	Causes one command to execute depending upon the failure of another
&&	Two ampersand symbols	Causes one command to execute depending upon the successful completion of another
&	Single ampersand	Allows you to run a job in the background
;	Semicolon	Allows you to run commands in a sequence
( )	Left and right parentheses	Allows you to run a command in a subshell
|	Pipe symbol	Allows you to pass command output to another command

In the next example, each command is executed from left to right in sequence:

```
echo "howdy" ; who ; pwd ; date
```

If you enter the commands in sequence without the semicolon, you would receive an error. Next you will perform an exercise to help you understand the importance of shell operators.

To use a shell control operator:

1. Log in to the Linux system as a user, and then open a Terminal emulation window.

2. Run the following commands, and then record the output.

   ```
   ls ; pwd ; who ; date ; cal 12 2005
   ```

3. Run the following commands, and then record the output.

   ```
   ls pwd who date cal 12 2005
   ```

4. Run the following commands, and then record the output.

   ```
   (ls; pwd; who; date; cal 12 2005;)
   ```

5. Run the following commands, and then record the output.

   ```
   pwd && date
   ```

6. Run the following commands, and then record the output.

   ```
   date & who
   ```

7. To exit the Terminal emulation program, type **exit**, and then press **Enter**.

8. Log out.

A **reserved word** is defined as a word that has special meaning to the shell. Such words cannot be used for any other purpose unless it is in quotes or not the first word in a command. Reserved words have specific syntax that must be followed; each is different. For example, the `if`, `then`, `else`, and `fi` statements are reserved to test conditions in a decision and you could not use them to accomplish something else. As another example, the `while`, `do`, and `done` statements are reserved for processing loops. You will learn the purpose of most of the remaining reserved words as you work your way through the remaining chapters.

UNDERSTANDING COMMAND TYPES

Now, that you have learned about the building blocks of shell grammar, you need to understand the major components, specifically, command types. Having a solid working knowledge of command types gives you the ability to properly structure commands in your shell scripts. The major components of shell grammar are listed in descending order of complexity of the command type.

- Compound commands
- Lists

- Pipelines
- Simple commands

Think of the command types as being structured in a pyramid in terms of complexity, with simple commands at the bottom and compound commands at the top of the pyramid. Refer to Figure 3-4 for the pyramid view of the command types.

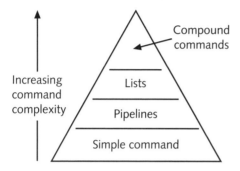

Figure 3-4   Command types pyramid

Simple Commands

A **simple command** is a set of words separated by blanks. It is also the most basic type of operation you can do within the shell. A shell control operator terminates a simple command. A simple command takes the general form:

> *command —options arguments*

As you already know, the *command* is the name of the command; the hyphen (–) signifies that one or more options are to follow. An *option* adds extra features or characteristics to the command. An *argument* is usually one or more filenames that the command is going to use.

 A synonym for argument is parameter.

Not all commands have options, nor do they all take filenames as arguments. Because each command has its own purpose and particular syntax, you should refer to the man pages for a given command to see specific information about the command's syntax.

Below are a few examples of simple commands. You have been executing simple commands since Chapter 1, so these types of commands should be familiar to you.

```
ls -l /etc
touch file1.txt
pwd
echo "Hi"
cd /usr/sbin
clear
```

Each command returns an exit status to the shell once the command completes. An exit status of zero indicates that the command succeeded. A nonzero exit status indicates that the command failed. The concept of an exit status will become important in later chapters when you want to test whether or not a command completed successfully or not.

Pipelines

The next level up in the command-type pyramid is the pipeline command. A **pipeline** is a sequence of simple commands separated by the pipe symbol character (|).

 Although the pipe symbol (|) prints as a solid vertical bar, it is shown as a broken vertical bar on most keyboards. You will usually find it above Enter on the same key as the backslash. The term pipe and pipeline are synonymous.

The pipeline allows data to be passed between processes. A pipeline takes the following general form:

command1 | *command2* | *command3* …

This is where *command1*, *command2*, and *command3* are Linux commands separated by the pipe (|) symbol. The presence of the three dots implies you can add several pipelines. Below are examples of commands using the pipe symbol:

```
ls | more
ls | sort
who | sort | more
history | sort | more
```

To understand the pipeline process you need to realize that the output of the command on the left side of the pipe symbol is used as input for the command on the right side of the pipe symbol. The command on the right modifies the output in some way prior to displaying the output on the screen. For example, the command `ls | more` directs the output of the `ls` command as input to the `more` command. The `more` command then displays one page at a time on the screen. By combining these two commands together, the `ls | more` pipeline causes a directory listing to be displayed one page at a time. If you entered just `ls`, and the output was more than a page, the output would scroll off the screen and you would be unable to see the portion that scrolled. Here is another example: `ls | sort | more`. This pipeline sorts a directory listing before displaying it one page at a time.

A good analogy for pipelines is a water-filtering system. Some people have filters beneath their kitchen sinks to purify drinking water. Water, representing data, flows from the outside pipes as input to the filtering system, representing a command. The physical pipe represents the Linux pipeline. The filter purifies the water, or in the case of a pipeline, modifies its input. The output of the filter is input into your glass—the output you see on your screen.

Next you will perform an exercise to help you better understand the use of the pipe symbol.

To use the pipe symbol:

1. Log in to the Linux system as a user, and then open a Terminal emulation window.

2. Type **ls | more**, and then press **Enter**. The listing is displayed on the screen. Depending upon the number of files and directories to list, the listing may appear one page at a time.

3. Type **cat .bash_history | more**, and then press **Enter**. The file .bash_history appears on the screen one page at a time.

4. Type **who | sort | more**, and then press **Enter**. The output of the who command is sorted and displayed on the screen. Depending upon the number of users logged in, the output may appear one page at a time.

5. To exit the Terminal emulation program, type **exit**, and then press **Enter**.

6. Log out.

List

Up one level from a pipeline is a list. A **list** is a sequence of one pipeline or multiple pipelines which are separated by one of these operators: **;**, **&**, **&&**, or **| |**. A list is terminated by either a **;**, **&**, or a newline character. Each of these operators will be discussed next.

The ; Operator

Like pipelines, commands separated by a **semicolon (;)** are executed sequentially by the shell. Use of the **;** operator takes the following general form on the command line:

    command1; command2

This is where *command1* and *command2* are Linux commands, executed in sequence, separated by the semicolon symbol. After the first command completes its execution, the shell executes the next command in sequence. Unlike pipes where the commands execute as parts of one process, each command separated by the semicolon is a separate process, and is given its own PID. Let's look at an example of a list using the **;** operator. The command list **ls ; pwd** executes the **ls** command first. When it completes, the shell executes the **pwd** command. The subsequent command executes whether or not the previous command executed successfully.

The & Operator

If a command is followed by the **& operator**, it is executed in the background in a subshell. A **subshell** is a shell that is spawned, or generated, from the current shell. A **background process** is a process that can neither read from nor write to the terminal. Because of this, the shell does not wait for the background process to complete before returning the prompt. The shell normally executes a command as a **foreground process**—process that can read from or be written to the terminal. The shell must wait for a foreground process to complete before returning the prompt.

Normally, if a command executes in the foreground, you can stop it by pressing Ctrl+C. However, you cannot stop a background process by pressing Ctrl+C. Instead, you need to issue the `kill` command to stop a background process. Use of the & operator takes the following general form on the command line:

    command1 & command2

This is where *command1* and *command2* are Linux commands, executed concurrently and separated by the ampersand symbol. *command1* is executed in a subshell at the same time that *command2* is executed in the current shell. Using the & symbol allows both commands to be executed at the same time. Note *command2* is optional. If you leave it off, then the shell simply executes *command1* in the background as in: *command1* &.

Here is an example using the & operator. In the command list `ls & pwd`, the `ls` command executes in the background, while the `pwd` command executes in the foreground. Because they are not executed sequentially, the `ls` command may actually complete after the `pwd`, even though it is listed first. In this list command example, the command completion sequence would be determined by the number of directories and files in the current directory.

The && Operator

The **&& operator** causes the shell to execute a command only if the immediately preceding command completes successfully (exit status of zero). This is different from the & operator. With the && operator, the commands are executed sequentially in the same shell—not concurrently in a subshell. Use of the && operator takes the following general form on the command line:

    command1 && command2

This is where *command1* and *command2* are Linux commands separated by two ampersand symbols. The command specified as *command2* only executes if *command1* executes successfully (with an exit status of zero).

 With the & operator, even if the first one fails, the second command executes. With the && operator, if the first command fails, the second command will *never* execute.

For example, in the list `rm file1.txt && pwd`, the `rm file1.txt` command executes first. If it completes successfully, the `pwd` executes after it. If `rm file1.txt` fails (exit status is nonzero), because the file to be removed does not exist, the `pwd` never executes.

Let's look at another example. In the list `lsxxx && pwd`, the `pwd` command never executes because the `lsxxx` command does not exist and returns a nonzero exit status.

The || Operator

The **|| operator** causes the shell to execute a secondary command in the event that the first command fails. Use of the || operator takes the following general form on the command line:

```
command1 || command2
```

This is where *command1* and *command2* are Linux commands separated by two pipe symbols. Even though the || operator uses two pipe symbols, its use here is unrelated to the functionality of a single pipe symbol in pipelines. The command specified as *command2* only executes if *command1* executes unsuccessfully (with an exit status not equal to zero).

For example, in the list `rm file1.txt || pwd`, if the `rm file1.txt` command fails to execute successfully (nonzero exit status), the second command, `pwd`, executes. If the first command in the list, `rm file1.txt || pwd`, completes successfully, the `pwd` command never executes. In the following list, `lsxxx || pwd`, the `lsxxx` command does not exist and returns a nonzero exit status for being unsuccessful, so the `pwd` command executes.

Combining Commands and Operators

The shell allows you to combine operators on the command line. When using the `&&` and || operators, the commands in the list are executed sequentially. In a list that includes both the `&&` and || operators, equal precedence exists between the two operators. The operator that appears first, from left to the right, is executed first. In a list that only includes both the `;` and `&` operators, equal precedence exists between these two as well. The operator appearing first, in left to right order, is executed first. However, in a list that includes all four operators, the `&&` and || operators are evaluated before the `;` and `&` operators.

Let's combine a few of these operators to see how they work together. In the list example, `date; pwd && who | more`, there are two simple commands, `date` and `pwd`, separated by the control operator, `;`. Then the `&&` operator is used with the `who | more` pipeline. This list executes the `who | more` pipeline only if the preceding commands, `date; pwd` complete successfully. Thus, the `date` command runs first. Then, the `pwd` command executes. Next, the shell must determine if the preceding command failed. If so, it stops and processes no other statements. If the commands have succeeded, then the `who | more` command executes. Refer to the first command list in Figure 3-5. You can see that both commands on the left and right side of the `&&` operator executed.

In the preceding example, all commands should execute. However, in the command, `date; pwdx && who | more` where `pwdx` is misspelled, only the `date` command executes. The `pwdx` fails because it is invalid. Because the sequence of commands on the left side of the `&&` operator failed, the pipeline on the right side does not execute.

Consider this list example, `date; pwd || who | more` which uses the `||` operator. Here the `who | more` pipeline only executes if the preceding commands, `date; pwd`, do *not* complete successfully. Figure 3-5 shows a sample screen shot of this list.

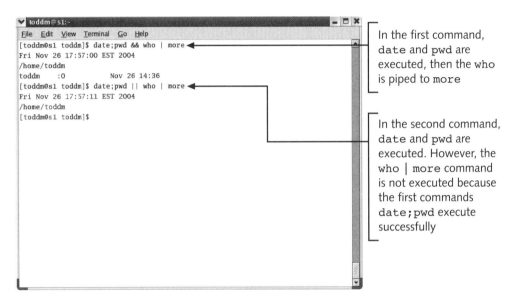

In the first command, `date` and `pwd` are executed, then the `who` is piped to `more`

In the second command, `date` and `pwd` are executed. However, the `who | more` command is not executed because the first commands `date;pwd` execute successfully

Figure 3-5   Output of two list commands

Compound Commands

At the top of the command-type pyramid, is the compound command; thus, it is the most powerful of the command types. **Compound commands** allow you to perform calculations, assign variables, perform decision tests, and create loops. A compound command can include any of the previous command types plus the following types:

- Group commands
- Expressions
- Decision constructs
- Looping constructs

Group commands and expressions will be discussed here. Decision and looping constructs will be discussed in Chapters 6 and 7, respectively.

Group Commands

A **group command** is a list of commands either executing in a subshell or the current shell. A group command is made up of one of the following formats:

- `(list)`
- `{ list; }`

The `(list)` Group Command

With a `(list)` group command, the list of commands is executed in a subshell. Because the commands in the list are executed in a subshell, any variables assigned within the list do not remain intact once the list completes. Let's look at an example. In Figure 3-6, the variable assignment **y=5** sets y to the value of 5. Next the **echo $y** command displays the contents of the variable "y," which is 5. In the next statement, which is a list group command, **(y=50)**, "y" is set to the value of 50 in a subshell. However, the result of the last **echo $y** command shows that "y" is still set to 5. This is because the commands in the `(list)` group command are executed in a shell spawned from the current shell. The current shell is not affected by commands executed in the shell spawned from it. You would use this group command when you wanted a variable to remain unaffected by a command in the current shell.

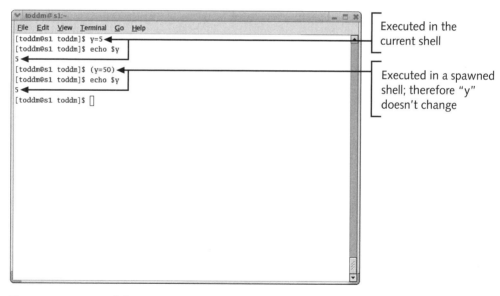

Figure 3-6   Use of the `(list)` group command

A variable is assigned by inputting a name, the equal sign, and then the value. For example, y=5 assigns the value 5 to the variable "y." You must precede a variable name with a dollar sign in order to use the contents. For example, in the command echo $y the dollar sign immediately prior to the variable name, "y," is required. If you left off the dollar sign, as in, echo y, the shell would literally display the letter "y."

You could also use the (list) group command structure if you wanted to execute multiple commands in the background. Using the & operator causes a command to be executed in the background as in who &. However, you can only place one command before the & operator. With the group command, you can execute multiple commands in the background. For example, the group command (pwd; who; ls) & causes each command within the parentheses to be executed collectively in the background. They will take only one PID.

When a subshell is spawned, it takes on a unique PID. Its PPID is the PID of the parent shell that spawned it.

The { list; } Group Command

With a {list; } group command, the list of commands is executed in the current shell. The list must be terminated with a semicolon ; or newline. Because the commands in the list are executed in the same shell, any variables assigned within the list remain once the list completes.

This type of group command is useful when you want to apply other operators to the commands in the list as a whole. For example, if you execute the who and ls -l commands, their output may scroll off the screen. You could use the pipe operator and the more command to scroll the output one screenful at a time. You could enter the commands as a group command, { who; ls -l;} | more. Then, the collective output of the commands between the { } symbols would be piped to the more command. Figure 3-7 shows a screenshot of the previous group command. Notice that the collective output is piped to the more command.

Let's look at another example dealing with variables. In Figure 3-8, the variable assignment y=5 sets "y" to the value of 5. Next the echo $y command displays the contents of the variable "y," which is 5. In the next statement, { y=50; }, "y" is set to the value of 50 in the current shell. The result of the last echo $y command shows that "y" now possesses the new value—50. Again, this is because the commands in the list execute in the current shell.

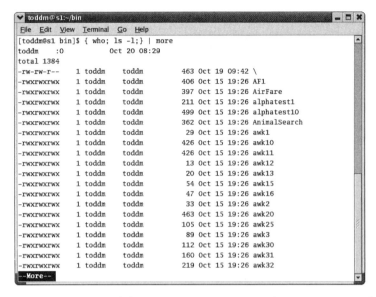

Figure 3-7   Use of the {list;1;} command grouping several commands

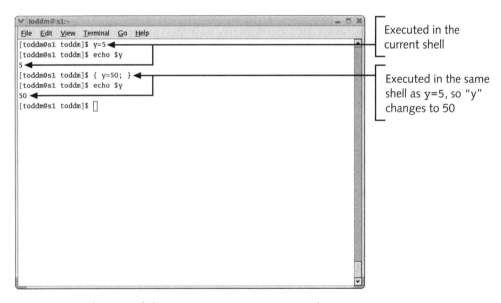

Figure 3-8   The use of the {list;} group command

If you look again at Figure 3-6 and compare it with Figure 3-8, you see that in the (y=5) group command, the value of "y" does not change because the statement is executed in a subshell and does not affect the current value of "y." In Figure 3-8, the { y=50; } group command does change it because it is performed in the same shell.

Expressions

An **expression** is used when you want to assign a value to a variable, perform an arithmetic calculation using variables, or test for values meeting certain conditions. An expression is made up of one of these formats:

- `((expression))`
- `[[ expression ]]`

The `((expression))` command

You use the `((expression))` compound command to evaluate an arithmetic operation. The expression generally takes one of the following forms:

```
((variable-name = value1 operator value2))
((value1 operator value2))
```

This is where *value1* and *value2* are variable assignments or integers. The term *operator* represents an arithmetic operation that is performed on the values. A partial list of operators is shown in Table 3-5. The first statement of the expression is used for variable assignment, as in: `((y=5 + 6))`. Note that *variable-name* is a variable assigned by you.

Table 3-5   Various operators used with the `((expression))` compound command

Operator	Name	Example
Variable-name++	The increment operation	`((t = x++))`
Variable-name--	The decrement operation	`((t = x--))`
**	Exponentiation	`((x = 2**3))`
*	Multiply	`((x = 4*5))`
/	Division	`((x = 10 / 2))`
+	Addition	`((x = 10+2))`
-	Subtraction	`((x = 10 - 2))`
%	Remainder	`((r = 100 % 4))`
= =	Equal to	`(($x = = 2))`
! =	Not equal to	`(($x ! = 2))`
>=	Greater than or equal to	`(($x >= $y))`
<=	Less than or equal to	`(($t <= 10))`
>	Greater than	`(($x > 5))`
<	Less than	`(($t < $x))`
&&	AND operation	`(($y = = 5 && $t = = 5))`
||	OR operation	`(($y = =$r || $t = = 5))`

You can use `let "expression"` instead of `((expression))` for arithmetic operations. The `"expression"` in the `let "expression"` statement uses the same syntax as `((expression))`. For example, `((y=500))` is equivalent to `let "y=500"`.

3

Next you will become familiar with the syntax of expressions because you will use expressions in future chapters.

To understand expressions:

1. Log in to the Linux operating system as a user, and then open a Terminal emulation window.

2. To multiply two numbers, type **((x=5 * 6))**, and then press **Enter**. The variable "x" now contains the number 30. However, nothing is displayed yet.

3. To add a variable and a number, type **((y=$x+4))**, and then press **Enter**. The variable "y" now contains the number 34. Again, nothing is displayed yet.

4. To display the contents of the two variables, type **echo $x $y**, and then press **Enter**. The numbers 30 and 34 are displayed on your screen.

5. To exit the Terminal emulation program, type **exit**, and then press **Enter**.

6. Log out.

The Increment and Decrement Operators

Now, look at the increment and decrement operators listed in Table 3-5. These are extremely useful operators because they allow you to add one to a value or subtract one from a value efficiently in a script. Two addition symbols, + +, are used as the increment operator. Two subtraction symbols, − −, are used as the decrement operator. Let's say you wanted to increment the value of a variable named **value1**, by 1; you could use the increment operator as follows:

```
((value1++))
```

The increment operator can be used in a script as a counter when you want to count items you have processed. Other ways to increment a value are: `((value1=value1+1))`, `let "value1++"`, or `let "value1= value1+1"`

Figure 3-9 illustrates the use of the increment operator to increment a value. In the figure, value1 is set to 100 and then incremented using the **value1++** statement. Notice the **echo** statements result in 100 before and 101 after the value is incremented.

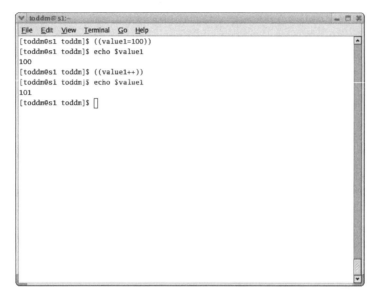

```
[toddm@s1 toddm]$ ((value1=100))
[toddm@s1 toddm]$ echo $value1
100
[toddm@s1 toddm]$ ((value1++))
[toddm@s1 toddm]$ echo $value1
101
[toddm@s1 toddm]$ []
```

Figure 3-9   Using the increment operator to increment a value

Now, suppose you wanted to decrement the value of the variable named **value1** by 1. You could use the decrement operator as follows:

```
((value1--))
```

Figure 3-10 illustrates the use of the decrement operator to decrement a value. You can see the variable with a value of 100 is displayed before it is decremented and then the value changes to 99 after the variable contents are decremented.

The Exponentiation, Multiplication, Division, Addition, Subtraction, and Remainder Operators   You are probably familiar with the mathematical concepts of exponentiation, multiplication, division, addition, and subtraction. The idea of placing the remainder into a variable may be new to you; it will be covered at the end of this section. First, look at how these operators are set up in examples so you can understand how to implement them in shell scripts. These operators are important because they allow the shell to perform calculations and can be used in scripts.

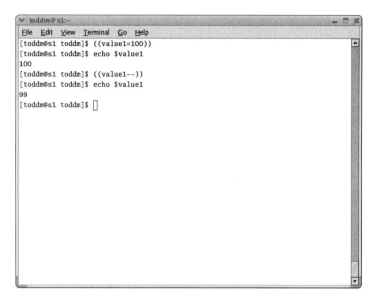

Figure 3-10   Using the decrement operator to decrement a value

First consider exponentiation—raising a number to a power. To do this, you use two asterisks, **. Look at an example:

```
((x = 4))
((y = 2**x))
```

In this example, the variable "x" is set to 4. In the expression, ((y=2**x)), the variable "y" is equal to 2 raised to the power of "x" which is 4. Thus, the answer is "y" equals 16.

Here are some multiplication, division, addition, subtraction, and remainder examples to consider. Figure 3-11 shows the results of these expressions.

```
((x = 4))
((y = 2))
((m=x*y))
((d=x/y))
((a=x+y))
((s=x-y))
((r= x%y))
```

```
toddm@s1:~                                                    _ □ X
File  Edit  View  Terminal  Go  Help
[toddm@s1 toddm]$ ((x=4))
[toddm@s1 toddm]$ ((y=2))
[toddm@s1 toddm]$ ((m=x*y))
[toddm@s1 toddm]$ ((d=x/y))
[toddm@s1 toddm]$ ((a=x+y))
[toddm@s1 toddm]$ ((s=x-y))
[toddm@s1 toddm]$ ((r=x%y))
[toddm@s1 toddm]$ echo $x
4
[toddm@s1 toddm]$ echo $y
2
[toddm@s1 toddm]$ echo $m
8
[toddm@s1 toddm]$ echo $d
2
[toddm@s1 toddm]$ echo $a
6
[toddm@s1 toddm]$ echo $s
2
[toddm@s1 toddm]$ echo $r
0
[toddm@s1 toddm]$ []
```

Figure 3-11   The results of various arithmetic expressions

 Tip When using the % operator, the variable to the left of the % operator is divided by the variable to the right of the % operator. Then, the remainder of this division is placed into the variable name. So, in ((x=10%2)), "x" equals zero, and in ((x=11%2)), "x" has a remainder value of 1.

Arithmetic expressions follow precedence. The order of what takes precedence is listed in Table 3-6. Operators listed within the same cell of the table have equal precedence, so if two operators with equal precedence are given in an expression, they are evaluated from left to right. For example, the increment and decrement operators have equal precedence and are evaluated before anything else.

Table 3-6   Precedence of arithmetic operations listed in descending order

Operators
`Variable-name++, Variable-name--`
`**, *, /, %`
`+, -`
`<=, >=, <, >`
`= =, ! =`
`&&`
`||`

You can alter the order by placing parentheses around lower-precedence operations so that they are evaluated before higher ones. If you have multiple parentheses, the operations within the innermost parentheses are performed first. For example, in the statement ((y=5+3*2)), the multiplication operation is evaluated first. So, the number 3 is multiplied by the number 2, resulting in 6. Then, the number 5 is added to the number 6, and "y" is set to 11. However, if you placed parentheses around the addition operation, as in ((y=(5+3)*2)), it would evaluate first. So, 5 is added to 3 resulting in 8. Then, the number 8 is multiplied by the number 2, and "y" is set to 16.

Next you will complete an exercise to help you understand the use of parentheses in expressions.

To understand the use of parentheses in expressions:

1. Log in to the Linux system as a user, and then open a Terminal emulation window.

2. Type **((x=100-3**2))**, and then press **Enter** to change the value of "x" by first raising 3 to the power of 2 and then subtracting the result from 100.

3. Type **((y=(100-3)**2))**, and then press **Enter** to change the value of "y" by first subtracting 3 from 100 and then raising that result to the power of 2.

4. Type **echo $x $y**, and then press **Enter**. The numbers 91 and 9409, are displayed on the screen respectively.

5. To exit the Terminal emulation program, type **exit**, and then press **Enter**.

6. Log out.

Expressions operate only on integers. Division by zero results in an error.

The [[expression]] command   You can use the [[expression]] command, or the **test** command, to test attributes of a file or directory, perform character string comparisons, and perform numeric comparisons. A **string** is a set of one or more alphanumeric characters—either a number or a character. The [[expression]] commands have several formats. You would use the **if** command to make decisions with the [[expression]] command. The **if** command is covered in Chapter 6.

CHAPTER SUMMARY

❏ The shell can be invoked by either logging in or by entering the name of the shell at the shell prompt. The shell uses startup files to customize the user's environment. The login files are /etc/profile, ~/.bash_profile, and ~/.bashrc. The /etc/profile script file is read and executed for all users as they log in. The root user account can only change this script file. The other two, ~/.bash_profile and ~/.bashrc, located in each user's home directory, are executed if they exist. Each user can change these files. The ~/.bash_logout is executed when a user logs out and can be modified by the user.

❏ The shell has its own variables that are reserved specifically for its use. They must be entered in uppercase. The **PATH** shell variable contains a list of directories the shell searches when attempting to locate a script or command. To display the contents of a shell variable, precede it with a dollar sign, as in this example: **$PATH**.

❏ The File System Hierarchy Standard supports placing scripts used by all users in the /usr/local/bin directory and having users place their own scripts in ~/bin. The ~/bin directory must be created before any scripts can be placed in it.

❏ Shell builtin commands are commands that are compiled as part of the shell. You can't find them in any directory, and you have to refer to the man pages for the shell instead of for an individual command.

❏ It is important to understand the grammar of the shell because the shell is a language and a strong understanding of the fundamentals can help you troubleshoot problems when you are entering commands. The basic building blocks of shell grammar are: blanks, words, names, metacharacters, control operators, and reserved words. A blank is a space or tab and is used to separate items entered at the shell prompt. A word is a sequence of characters the shell uses as a unit. A name is a word consisting only of letters, numbers, and the underscore. A metacharacter is a character that has a special purpose to the shell. A control operator modifies how the shell processes commands. A reserved word is a word that is used by the shell and is generally a command.

❏ The shell provides for several command types. These include simple commands, pipelines, lists, and compound commands. You need to understand these different types in order to properly construct commands to accomplish a certain task without the threat of generating an error. A simple command is a set of words separated by blanks. A pipeline is used to process data between commands. A list is a series of pipelines separated by a control operator. A compound command allows you to assign variables, perform computations, and execute decisions and loop structures.

REVIEW QUESTIONS

1. _____ is the login startup file that is read first.

   a. /etc/profile

   b. ~/.bash_logout

   c. ~/.bash_profile

   d. ~/.bashrc

3

2. Which term is used to define a space or tab in shell grammar?

   a. metacharacter

   b. word

   c. name

   d. blank

3. A _____ process always executes in a subshell.

   a. foreground

   b. background

   c. simple command

   d. control operator

4. The _____ script file is read and executed when the user terminates his session.

   a. /etc/profile

   b. ~/.bash_logout

   c. ~/.bash_profile

   d. ~/.bashrc

5. Which term is used to describe a character that has special meaning to the shell?

   a. token

   b. word

   c. blank

   d. metacharacter

6. A _____ process can read data from the terminal.

   a. foreground

   b. background

   c. control operator

   d. token

7. Which is the name of the symbol that allows the output of one command to be filtered as input to another?

   a. greater-than

   b. pipe

   c. double greater-than

   d. less-than

8. _____ is the symbol used for executing a job in the background of the shell.

   a. &

   b. <

   c. ;

   d. ?

9. _____ is the symbol used to separate commands in a list, which are executed sequentially.

   a. ;

   b. <

   c. >>

   d. ?

10. _____ is the operator that is used when you want one command to execute only if another command executes successfully.

    a. *

    b. ||

    c. &&

    d. <

11. Which group command executes commands in a subshell?

    a. `((n++))`

    b. `((expression))`

    c. `{ list };`

    d. `(list)`

12. You use the _____ group command to execute commands in the current shell.

    a. `((n++))`

    b. `((expression))`

    c. `{ list };`

    d. `(list)`

13. Which group command is used to evaluate arithmetic operations?

    a. `[ list ]`

    b. `((expression))`

    c. `{ list };`

    d. `(list)`

14. Which of the following is an example of the increment operator?

    a. {{n++}}

    b. ((n--))

    c. ((n++))

    d. ((+n+))

15. The remainder symbol is _____.

    a. *

    b. /

    c. &

    d. %

16. Which command is synonymous with the [[**expression**]] command?

    a. **pwd**

    b. **test**

    c. **((expression))**

    d. **{list}**

17. Which term describes a set of one or more alphanumeric characters?

    a. token

    b. string

    c. list

    d. blank

18. A command that is part of the shell is called a _____ command.

    a. export

    b. import

    c. builtin

    d. inherent

19. Which command is used to send a signal to a PID?

    a. **pwd**

    b. **kill**

    c. **ls**

    d. **signal**

20. The _____ shell variable is used to locate the directory a command is stored in.

    a. `$path`

    b. `$PATH`

    c. /etc/profile

    d. `$TMOUT`

HANDS-ON PROJECTS

Project 3-1

In this project, you will change the ~/.bash_profile file so you can see it execute as part of the login process. This will help reinforce your understanding of its role in the login process.

1. Log in to the Linux system as a user, and then open a Terminal emulation window.

2. Type **vi .bash_profile**, and then press **Enter**. The shell script is displayed on the screen. Note there will be other commands currently there.

3. Press **Shift+G** to move the cursor to the bottom of the file.

4. Type **o** to open a line of text in **vi**, and then input the following lines of code to change the ~/.bash_profile file:

```
echo "Executing the .bash_profile login file."
echo "A list of current users:"
who
echo "The current directory is:"
pwd
echo "The end of the .bash_profile login file."
```

5. Save the file, and then close the editor.

6. Execute the script.

7. Record the output.

8. Delete the lines of code in the ~/.bash_profile file that you added.

9. Close your window, and then log out.

Project 3-2

In this project, you will change the ~/.bashrc file so you can see it execute as part of the login process.

1. Log in to the Linux system as a user, and then open a Terminal emulation window.

2. Type **vi .bashrc**, and then press **Enter**. The shell script is displayed on the screen.

3

3. Go to the end of the file and append the following lines of code:

```
echo "Executing the .bashrc login file."
date
echo "The end of the .bashrc login file."
```

4. Telnet to your system.

5. As you are logging in, notice the screen, and record what occurs.

6. Compare the execution of Project 3-1 and this project. Which script executes first?

7. Delete the lines in the ~/.bashrc file that you added.

8. Save the file, and then close the editor.

9. Close your window, and then log out.

Project 3-3

In this project, you will create a shell script and change the .bash_logout file to execute that shell script. You will display the user's login name set in the /etc/profile, as well as display the host name followed by the date. Finally, you will test the script. The goal of this project is to reinforce your knowledge of the login and logout shell script files.

1. Log in to the Linux system as a user, and then open a Terminal emulation window.

2. Type **vi LogOut**, and then press **Enter**.

3. Insert the following lines to display the user's login name, hostname, date, and time the user logged out:

```
echo -n $LOGNAME "logged out" $HOSTNAME "at"
date
```

4. Save the file, and then close the editor.

5. Open the **.bash_logout** file, and then insert the LogOut script you just created at the bottom of the screen.

6. Press **Shift+G** to move the cursor to the bottom of the file.

7. Type **o** to open a line of text in vi.

8. Type **bash LogOut**, and then press **Enter**.

9. Save the file, and then close the editor.

10. Telnet to your system.

11. Log out, notice the screen, and then record the results.

12. Close all windows.

Project 3-4

In this project, you will reinforce your understanding of shell variables.

1. Log in to the Linux system as a user, and then open a Terminal emulation window.

2. Create a shell script named **Project3–4** located in a directory supported by the File System Hierarchy Standard.

3. You need to perform the steps shown in pseudocode in the order shown:

```
Change to the /tmp directory
Change to your home directory
Display the previous working directory using a shell
variable
Display your home directory using a shell variable
Display your home directory using an alternate method to
using a shell variable
Display the amount of time the shell will wait for user
input before the current shell is terminated using a shell
variable
Set the previous variable to 120
Display the amount of time the shell will wait for user
input before the current shell is terminated using a
shell variable
Set the previous variable to 0
```

4. Save the file, and then close the editor.

5. Execute the script.

6. Record the commands used, and then record or print your script.

7. Close your window, and then log out.

Project 3-5

In this project, you will reinforce your understanding of what happens to variables when using group commands. You will also see how a formula changes when parentheses are added or removed from an arithmetic expression.

1. Log in to the Linux system as a user, and then open a Terminal emulation window.

2. Create a shell script named **Project3–5** located in a directory supported by the File System Hierarchy Standard that contains the following lines of code:

```
a=100
b=10
y=0
echo $a $b $y
( ((y=($a+4)*$b)); echo $y )
echo $y
( ((y=$a+4*$b)); echo $y)
echo $y
{ ((y=($a+4)*$b)); echo $y; }
echo $y
{ ((y=$a+4*$b)); echo $y; }
echo $y
```

3. Print the script.

3

4. Save the file, and then close the editor.

5. Execute the script.

6. Write down the output to the right of each command that executes. Why does the value of "y" either change or remain the same after each of the echo $y statements that are on a line by themselves?

7. Close your window, and then log out.

Project 3-6

In this project, you will use the increment operator as a counter. You will also use the decrement operator to reinforce your understanding of the use of expressions.

1. Log in to the Linux system as a user, and then open a Terminal emulation window.

2. Create a shell script named **Project3-6** located in a directory supported by the File System Hierarchy Standard.

3. The script needs to perform the following pseudocode in the order shown:

```
Set a variable named "n" to 10
Display the contents of "n"
Use the correct expression to increase "n" by 1
Display the contents of "n"
Use the correct expression to decrease "n" by 1
Display the contents of "n"
Increase the variable "n" again using a different
expression
Display the contents of "n"
Decrease the variable "n" again using a different
expression
Display the contents of "n"
```

4. Save the file, and then close the editor.

5. Execute the script, and then record the command used.

6. Record or print your script.

7. Close your window, and then log out.

Project 3-7

In this project, you use additional arithmetic operators in the ((expression)) commands. The goal of this project is to reinforce your understanding of arithmetic operations.

1. Log in to the Linux system as a user, and then open a Terminal emulation window.

2. Create a shell script named **Project3-7** located in a directory supported by the File System Hierarchy Standard.

3. The script needs to perform the following pseudocode in the order shown:

```
Set a variable named "x" to 10
Set a variable named "y" to 100
Display the result of dividing "y" by "x" and place the
result into variable "t"
Display the result of dividing "y" by 0
Display the result of multiplying "y" by "x" and place the
result into variable "t"
Display the result of adding "y" and "x" and place the
result into variable "t"
Display the result of subtracting "x" from "y" and place the
result into variable "t"
Display the result of raising "y" to the power of 2 and
place the result into variable "t"
Display the result of taking the remainder of "y" divided
by "x" and place the result into variable "t"
```

4. Save the file, and then close the editor.

5. Execute the script, and then record the commands used.

6. Record or print your script.

7. Close your window, and then log out.

Project 3-8

In this project, you will gain an understanding of how to use various command types at the command line.

1. Log in to the Linux system as a user, and then open a Terminal emulation window.

2. Create a shell script named **Project3-8** located in a directory supported by the File System Hierarchy Standard.

3. The script needs to perform the following pseudocode in the order shown:

```
Display the list of current users sequentially followed by
the current directory
Display the list of current users as a background process
Update the modification time of a file named cactus.dat
Issue the command to display a message indicating a file
named cactus.dat was removed only if the command to remove
it succeeds
Issue the command to display a message indicating a file
named cactus.dat was not removed only if the command to
remove it fails
Display a long listing of the /tmp directory one screen at
a time
```

4. Save the file, and then close the editor.

5. Execute the script, and then record or print your script.

6. Close your window, and then log out.

CASE PROJECTS

Case 3-1

TMI has hired your consulting firm to assist their Linux users. You get a call from Marge who is just learning the Linux system. She has saved up several questions and needs you to respond to these issues:

1. She needs to locate additional documentation on the `cd`, `pwd`, and the `history` commands, but she is having difficulty finding anything.

2. She has a script that one of the programmers wrote. It takes a long time to execute. She wants to be able to execute it and have the prompt immediately return.

3. She would like to add a message to all users as they log in. She would like a different message added for her own account.

Case 3-2

The Santiago Law Firm has recently purchased a Linux computer system. You interview the users and determine a shell script is needed to exit a user's process when he or she has not pressed a key after 60 seconds. When each user logs in, a list should be displayed of current users so everyonse can see who is logged in and presumably, working. Additionally, the Santiago Law Firm wants each user to see what system he or she is logged on to. Also, the firm would like a calendar for the current month to be displayed. (*Hint*: This requires modification to the ~/.bash_profile file. The **TMOUT** shell variable must be set and exported to 60 seconds.) Finally, the ~/.bash_logout file needs to display the message "Exiting the Santiago system" when a user exits a Terminal emulation window.

4

THE SHELL ENVIRONMENT

In this chapter, you will:

- ◆ Understand redirection
- ◆ Understand pattern matching
- ◆ Understand the use of quoting
- ◆ Understand expansion
- ◆ Learn additional commands

In this chapter, you will understand how to redirect the flow of a command's input or output. You will also learn how to match specific patterns to access a subset of the files in a given directory and how to use quoting to protect certain metacharacters. You will see how various commands and operators expand into additional items. Finally, you will learn some additional commands that will help you perform your job better in a Linux operating system environment.

UNDERSTANDING REDIRECTION

Redirection means to direct the flow from one place to another. In Linux, you can redirect the flow of input or output from their normal default location. Why would you want to do this? Redirection gives you flexibility in terms of where your data is either coming from (input) or going to (output). For example, you might redirect output if you wanted to save the result of a command. Because output redirection typically results in a file being generated, you are able to review the file that contains the output of the command, either presently or at a later date. Input redirection is used less often than output redirection. With input redirection, the default location for a command's input is changed. However, most of the commands that accept filenames as part of their syntax usually don't require the input redirection operator.

Linux refers to **standard input (stdin)** as the default location for inputting commands. The default location for standard input is the keyboard. Linux refers to **standard output (stdout)** as the default location for outputting commands. Standard output defaults to the display screen. The term **standard error (stderr)** is the default location of errors generated from commands. Standard errors also default to the display screen. Redirection allows you to change the default locations of standard input, standard output, and standard error.

Linux uses the term **file descriptor** to describe a number that refers to a file. Each time a command runs, it has three file descriptors—one for stdin, stdout, and stderr. It uses these to handle input and output operations as well as error handling. Table 4-1 shows the file descriptors for standard input, output, and error.

Table 4-1   File descriptors for standard input, output, and error

File	File Descriptor	Location
Standard input	0	/dev/stdin
Standard output	1	/dev/stdout
Standard error	2	/dev/stderr

Linux treats the keyboard and the display screen as files. Linux also treats other hardware devices such as tape backup devices, floppy devices, and CD-ROM devices similarly. If you execute the `ls` command in the /dev directory, you will see the device files.

Redirecting Standard Input

Redirecting input causes a program to read from a file instead of the keyboard. The symbol to redirect input is the less-than symbol (<). The arrow points toward the command for redirecting input. The general form is:

```
command < filename
```

This is where *command* is a command, and *filename* is a Linux file. For example, the `sort` command typed in without any options sorts the data from standard input, or the keyboard. However, you can sort a file if you use a redirection symbol, for example, `sort < personnel.txt`. This command takes the input for the `sort` command directly from the personnel.txt file instead of the keyboard. The original file remains intact and the output is sent to standard output, or the screen.

Next you will learn how to redirect input. In this exercise, you will enter employee names in a payroll file. You will use the `sort` command to sort the payroll file, which will be redirected as input to it.

To redirect input:

1. Log in to the Linux system as a user, and then open a Terminal emulation window.

2. Create a file named **pay.dat** in your **$HOME/bin** directory that includes the following records:

   ```
   Smith, Jay
   Patel, Arnie
   Trang, Vingh
   Adams, Claude
   DeRue, Jacques
   ```

3. Save the file, and then close the editor.

4. To redirect input, type **sort < pay.dat**, and then press **Enter**. See Figure 4-1. The data is sorted on the screen. The original pay.dat file is intact.

5. To verify the original file has not changed, type **cat pay.dat**. See Figure 4-1. Notice the order of employee names is the same as you originally input it in Step 2.

6. Close the window, and then log out.

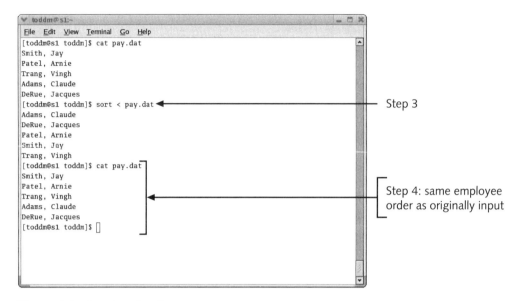

Figure 4-1 Input redirection

Redirecting Standard Output

Redirecting output causes the command to redirect its output from the display screen to a file. Redirecting output is useful when you want to keep the output of a command for later review. There are two forms of redirecting standard output. They are redirecting output to create a new file and redirecting output to append to an existing file.

Redirecting Output to Create a New File

Using the single greater-than (>) symbol to redirect output allows you to send the output of a command to a file. If the file exists, its current contents are overwritten. If the file does not exist, it is created. Notice that the arrow points away from the command for redirecting output. You might redirect output to a new file if you wanted to keep the listing of a command for later review. The general form is:

        command > filename

For example, the `ls` command displays a directory listing to standard output, or the display screen. You can redirect standard output to a file named lslist.txt by typing `ls > lslist.txt`. This results in standard output being redirected to the specified file. When you use a single greater-than symbol, it causes a new file to be created as long as a file by that name doesn't already exist. If the file exists, then that file is overwritten.

Let's look at an example.

```
ls > file2.txt
cat file2.txt
who > file2.txt
cat file2.txt
```

The `ls > file2.txt` command causes the output of the `ls` command to be redirected to a file named file2.txt. The output is placed at the beginning of the file. If file2.txt already exists, any previous data in that file is lost. The second command, `cat file2.txt`, proves the output has been redirected. The third command, `who > file2.txt`, causes the output of the `who > file2.txt` command to be redirected to the same file, overwriting any previous data. Again, the output is placed at the beginning of the file. Ultimately, you only end up with the output from the `who > file2.txt` command as is proven by the last command, `cat file2.txt`. Figure 4-2 shows the results of the previous commands.

Figure 4-2 Output redirection to create a new file

 You can redirect input and output in a single command. For example, the command `sort -r < input.txt > output.txt` sorts the file input.txt in reverse sort order, and then redirects that output to a file named output.txt.

Redirecting Output to Append to a File

You use two greater than symbols to append output to a file. If the file exists, the output of the command adds its output just below the last line of the existing file. If the file does not exist, it is created. You perform the redirect append (>>) operation if you want to preserve the current contents of a file. You perform the redirect create (>) operation if you want to remove the previous contents of the output file. The general form is:

```
command > filename
```

Consider what happens if you issue the following sequence of commands:

```
ls > file2.txt
cat file2.txt
who >> file2.txt
cat file2.txt
```

The first command's output is redirected to the file; the second command's output is placed after the first. In this case, you would have the output of both commands in one file. Figure 4-3 shows a screenshot of these commands.

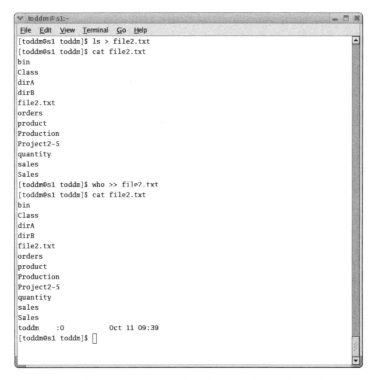

Figure 4-3 Redirecting output and appending it to a file

Compare Figures 4-2 and 4-3 and notice how they differ. In Figure 4-2, file2.txt contains just the output of the very last command. In Figure 4-3, file2.txt contains the output of both commands.

Next you will redirect output.

To redirect output:

1. Log in to the Linux system as a user, and then open a Terminal emulation window.

2. To redirect output and create a new file, type **ls -l > file3.txt**, and then press **Enter**. The output of the **ls -l** command does not appear on the screen because it was sent to the file named file3.txt.

3. To redirect output and append to a file, type **pwd >> file3.txt**, and then press **Enter**. The output of the **pwd** command does not appear on the screen because it was sent to the file named file3.txt.

4. To redirect output and append to a file, type **date >> file3.txt**, and then press **Enter**. The output of the **date** command does not appear on the screen because it was sent to the file named file3.txt.

5. To redirect output and append to a file, type **echo "The End" >> file3.txt**, and then press **Enter**. Again, the output of the **echo** command does not appear on the screen.

6. To display the contents of the file, type **cat file3.txt**, and then press **Enter**. See Figure 4-4; notice that the output that was redirected in Steps 2 through 5 now appears on the screen.

7. To exit the Terminal emulation program, type **exit**, and then press **Enter**.

8. Log out.

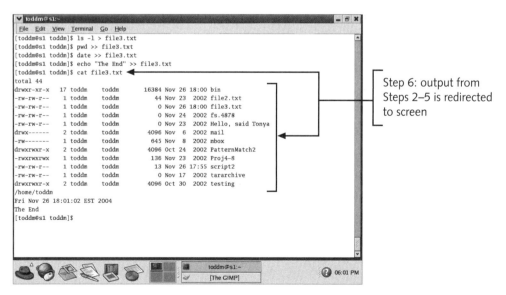

Figure 4-4   Redirecting output to both create and append to a file

Redirecting Standard Error

Most commands also send their error messages to the screen. If you want to capture that output to a file for later review, you can redirect standard error. Let's say you are working on the Linux help desk for a company, and a customer calls saying she is getting an error message. One solution is to have the customer redirect standard error to a file, and then send the file to you for inspection. Redirecting standard error is similar to redirecting standard output except you must refer to the file descriptor, 2, for standard error to redirect it. The general form is:

```
2>filename
```

For example, if you want an error message from the **rm** command to be redirected, you enter **rm 2>rmlist.err**. Then, you can issue the **cat rmlist.err** command to display the contents of the rmlist.err file.

Typically, standard error is combined with standard output. However, to redirect standard output and standard error to different files, you enter **rm >rmlist.txt 2>rmlist.err**. You implement this form of redirection if you want to send standard output and standard error to different files.

You typically redirect both standard output and standard error if a command runs automatically, for example, at night when you are not there to see the output on the screen. In this case, you would want to have the output sent to a file for review the next day.

 Setting up scripts to run automatically will be discussed in Chapter 12.

If you want standard output and standard error to go to the same file, the general form is:

```
&>filename
```

The use of the ampersand (**&**) tells the shell to redirect standard error and standard output to a file other than the default; you use the ampersand method with the redirection symbol. If you want to redirect both standard output and standard error in one file, you also use the method using the ampersand. For example, the following command tells the shell to redirect both standard output and standard error to the same filename.

```
rm &>rmlisting.txt
```

Next you will learn how to redirect standard output and standard error.

To redirect standard output and standard error:

1. Log in to the Linux system as a user, and then open a Terminal emulation window.

2. To redirect standard output and standard error to different files, type **(ls -l; who; rm t5) >listing.txt 2> errlisting.txt**, and then press **Enter**. There is no output displayed to the screen. (*Note:* The file t5, if it exists, should be removed prior to performing this step so an error will be generated.)

3. To display the contents of the listing.txt file, type **cat listing.txt**, and then press **Enter**. See Figure 4-5. The output is displayed on the screen.

4. To display the contents of the errlisting.txt file, type **cat errlisting.txt**, and then press **Enter**. See Figure 4-5. The output is displayed on the screen.

5. To combine standard output and error to a single file, type **(ls -l; who; rm t5) &>combolist.txt**, and then press **Enter**.

6. To display the contents of the combolist.txt file, type **cat combolist.txt**, and then press **Enter**. See Figure 4-6. The output is displayed on the screen.

7. Close the window, and then log out.

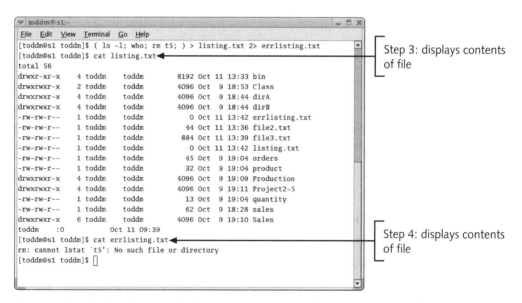

Figure 4-5   Redirecting standard output and standard error to separate files

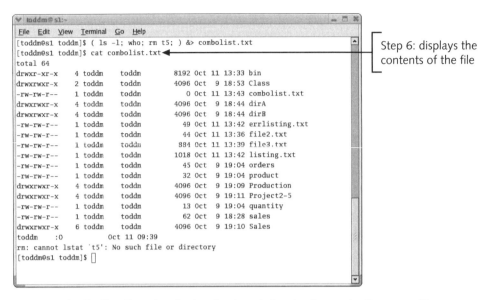

Figure 4-6   Redirecting standard output and standard error to the same file

UNDERSTANDING PATTERN MATCHING

Pattern matching is a technique that uses metacharacters to match characters based upon a certain pattern. For example, you use pattern-matching techniques to list all files that started with a "j." Or, if you want to match all characters with a .dat extension, you can use pattern-matching techniques. Pattern matching usually results in a subset of the total number of items available. For example, if you want to display all files beginning with a "j," then this would most likely be a subset of the total number of files in the given directory.

 You can think of pattern matching as "searching" for specific files or directories in a given directory.

There are several methods for matching various patterns of characters. The pattern-matching techniques are as follows:

- To match any character use the (*) symbol
- To match a single character use the (?) symbol
- To match any one of several characters use the ([...]) symbol

Matching Any Character

You use the asterisk symbol to match any character. This type of pattern matching usually concludes in the largest number of results returned because it matches any character. You use this pattern-matching technique if you want to match patterns that match a lot of characters. The asterisk symbol matches any character position. For example, the command `cp *.dat /dirA` tells the shell to copy all files with a "dat" extension in the filename to the directory named dirA. The command `ls -l t*` tells the shell to list all of the files that begin with a lowercase "t." The command `rm G*.txt` tells the shell to remove all files that begin with an uppercase "G" and that have a "txt" extension.

Next you will learn how to match any character.

To match any character:

1. Log in to the Linux system as a user, and then open a Terminal emulation window.

2. Create a directory named **PatternMatch1** in the `$HOME` directory.

3. Change directory locations to **PatternMatch1**.

4. Use the `touch` command to create these files in the PatternMatch1 directory: **file1.dat**, **GreatBig.txt**, **file2.dat**, **file3.dat**, **file5.txt**, and **file6.txt**, and then list all the files with the `ls` command.

5. To list all files that begin with the letter "f," type `ls f*`, and then press **Enter**. See Figure 4-7. Only files beginning with an "f" are displayed.

6. To list all files that begin with the letter "G," type `ls G*`, and then press **Enter**. See Figure 4-7. Only files beginning with a "G" are displayed.

7. To list all files with an extension of "txt," type `ls *.txt`, and then press **Enter**. See Figure 4-7. Only files with an extension of "txt" are displayed.

8. To list all files that begin with the letter "f" and have an extension of "txt," type `ls f*.txt`, and then press **Enter**. See Figure 4-7. Only files beginning with an "f" *and* having an extension of "txt" are displayed.

9. Close your window, and then log out.

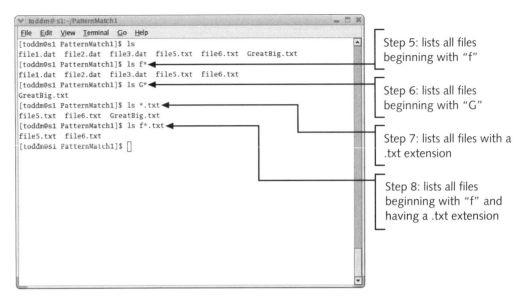

Figure 4-7   Pattern matching of any character

Another term that is used to describe the concept of matching any character is "wildcard." Sometimes an asterisk is called the wildcard symbol. The term comes from playing with a deck of cards where a card can be any card the player chooses. Thus, pattern matching is synonymous with wildcarding.

Match a Single Character

To match a single character position, you use the question mark symbol. This type of pattern matching is usually more restrictive than matching any character because you can actually control which character position to match. For example, if you wanted to display only files that had a "2" in their fourth character position regardless of what follows the fourth character position, you would enter `ls ???2*`. If you had entered `ls *2*`, the result would be any file with a "2" anywhere in the filename, so the use of ? is required to establish proper placement of the character for which you are searching.

Next you will perform a search to match a single character.

To match a single character:

1. Log in to the Linux system as a user, and then open a Terminal emulation window.

2. Create a directory named **PatternMatch2** in the **$HOME** directory.

3. Change directory locations to **PatternMatch2**.

4. Use the **touch** command to create these files in the **PatternMatch2** directory: **filemonkey.txt**, **filesilly.dat**, **file123.dat**, **t1.dat**, **t2.dat**, **t3.dat**, **tell.dat**, **telecommute.dat**, and **tv.txt**.

5. List all the files with the **ls** command.

6. To list all files that begin with a "t," are followed by a single character, and have a "dat" extension, type **ls t?.dat**, and then press **Enter**. See Figure 4-8. Notice that only the matching files are listed.

7. To list all files that begin with a "t," followed by a single character and have three characters in the extension, type **ls t?.???**, and then press **Enter**. See Figure 4-8. Notice that only matching files are listed.

8. To match files containing four characters with a three-character extension, type **ls ????.???**, and then press **Enter**. See Figure 4-8; notice that only the matching file is listed.

9. To remove all files that begin with a "t," have only one remaining character in the second character position, and have a three-character extension, type **rm t?.???**, and then press **Enter**. See Figure 4-8; notice that only the matching files, in this case, t1.dat, t2.dat, t3.dat, and tv.txt are removed.

 In some versions of Linux you may receive an interactive prompt from the rm command asking if you want to delete each file. To remove the files in question, you must answer in the affirmative.

10. List all the files using the **ls** command.

11. To list the files previously removed, type **ls t?.???**, and then press **Enter**. See Figure 4-8. A message appears indicating there are no such files.

12. Close your window, and then log out.

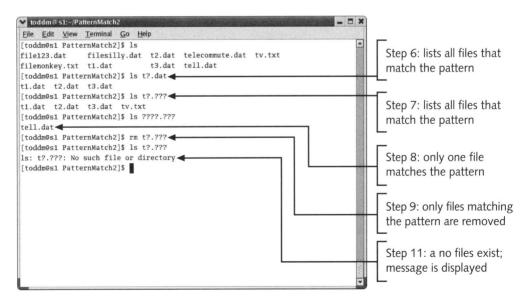

Figure 4-8   Pattern matching a single character

Match Any One of Several Characters

The use of square brackets allows you to match any one of the characters contained within the square brackets. You use this type of pattern matching for matching files containing uppercase and lowercase filenames. Linux filenames are case sensitive, meaning that the following files are considered different: FUN.DAT, Fun.Dat, fun.dat, FuN.DaT and fuN.dAt. Consequently, if you want to match any files beginning with either an uppercase "T" or a lowercase "t," you would enter ls [Tt]*. Like the question mark symbol, use of square brackets is positional.

This pattern-matching technique also allows you to match a range of characters. For example, if you want to list all files that begin with any of the uppercase letters "L" through "P," you enter ls [L-P]*. To match these same lowercase characters, you enter ls [l-p]*.

Next you will use pattern matching to match one of several characters.

To match one of several characters:

1. Log in to the Linux system as a user, and then open a Terminal emulation window.

2. Change to the **PatternMatch2** directory.

3. Use the **touch** command to create these additional files in the **PatternMatch2** directory: **zorro.txt**, **pecan.dat**, **apples.dat**, **water.dat**, and **bread.txt**.

4. List all the files.

5. To list all files beginning with either an "f" or "t," type ls [ft]*, and then press **Enter**. See Figure 4-9. Only matching files are listed.

6. To list all files beginning with "tel" and having either an "l" or an "e" in the fourth character position, type ls tel[le]*, and then press **Enter**. See Figure 4-9; notice that only the telecommute.dat and tell.dat files are displayed.

7. To list all files that begin with a letter in the range of "f" through "z," type ls [f-z]*, and then press **Enter**. See Figure 4-9. Notice that only matching files beginning with any letter starting with "f" through the letter "z" are listed.

8. To list all files that begin with "file" with the letters "m" through "s" as the fifth character position, type ls file[m-s]*, and then press **Enter**. See Figure 4-9. Only matching files are displayed.

9. Close your window, and then log out.

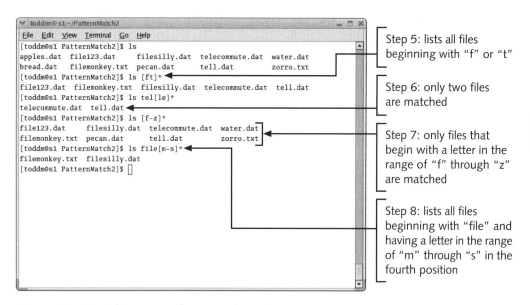

Step 5: lists all files beginning with "f" or "t"

Step 6: only two files are matched

Step 7: only files that begin with a letter in the range of "f" through "z" are matched

Step 8: lists all files beginning with "file" and having a letter in the range of "m" through "s" in the fourth position

Figure 4-9   Matching more than one character

Understanding the Use of Quoting

If you have to use one of the metacharacters discussed in Chapter 3, or one of the pattern-matching characters, you need a way to distinguish between the literal symbol and the symbol's use as a metacharacter or pattern-matching character. This is called **quoting** and it allows you to distinguish between the literal value of the symbol and the symbols used as code. To do this, you must use one of these three symbols:

- Backslash (\)
- Single quote (')
- Double quote (")

A Backslash (\)

A backslash is also called the **escape character**. When you use the backslash symbol when you are quoting, it allows you to preserve only the character immediately following it, with the exception of a newline character. For example, consider the greater-than symbol. You know that the greater-than symbol is a shell metacharacter that redirects output to create a new file. To stop the shell from interpreting the greater-than symbol as the redirection symbol, you need to protect it. If you want to create a file named "tools>," you do so by entering the following command: `touch tools\>`. In this example, it is the backslash symbol that preserves the literal meaning of the greater-than symbol. If you enter `touch tools>`, the shell generates an error because the shell uses the greater-than symbol as a redirection operator, and it is expecting a filename to follow this operator.

 In general, it is not advisable to use metacharacters as symbols when naming a file.

Next you will use the backslash symbol to preserve the meaning of a metacharacter.

To use the backslash to preserve the literal meaning of a metacharacter:

1. Log in to the Linux system as a user, and then open a Terminal emulation window.

2. Type **touch TimeKeeper>**, and then press **Enter**. An error message is displayed on the screen. This is because the backslash was not included in the filename, so the shell tried to interpret the greater-than symbol as a redirection operator and failed because a filename was not following the greater-than symbol.

3. To create a file with the greater-than metacharacter in the filename, type **touch TimeKeeper\>**, and then press **Enter**. The prompt returns.

4. Type **ls TimeKeeper>**, and then press **Enter**. Again, you receive an error because the **ls** command could not handle the greater-than metacharacter correctly.

5. To list the file with the greater-than metacharacter in the filename, type **ls TimeKeeper\>**, and then press **Enter**. Notice that this time, the file is displayed.

6. To exit the Terminal emulation program, type **exit**, and then press **Enter**.

7. Log out.

A Single Quote (')

Like the backslash, a single quote is used to protect the literal meaning of metacharacters. However, it differs from the backslash in that it can protect all characters within the single quotes. The only character it cannot protect is itself. Usually, you use single quotes if you want to display a quote from someone. For example, the command echo 'Joe said "Have fun!"' results in the shell placing double quotes around the text "Have fun!".

A single quote cannot occur with other single quotes even if preceded by a backslash. For example, the command echo 'Joe said 'Have fun'' would not result in the shell placing single quotes around the text 'Have fun'. Instead, the shell simply displays Joe said Have fun. To display the quotes, you enter echo 'Joe said "Have fun" '.

Next you will protect text and metacharacters using single quotes.

To use the single quotes to preserve the literal meaning of characters within the quotes:

1. Log in to the Linux system as a user, and then open a Terminal emulation window.

2. Type `touch ' "Hello", said Tonya'`, and then press **Enter** to create a file with this unusual name.

3. List this file with the `ls ' "Hello", said Tonya'` command. The file is listed on the screen.

4. Insert the following lines of code to create and display the file:

   ```
   touch ''Hello', said Tonya'
   ls ''Hello', said Tonya'
   ```

   The text Hello does not have quotes around it when the filename is displayed. Remember, you cannot embed single quotes within single quotes.

5. Close your window, and then log out.

A Double Quote (")

You use double quotes to protect all symbols and characters within the double quotes. However, double quotes will not protect these literal symbols: $, ', and \, even though they are metacharacters. Recall that single quotes will protect these symbols. If you want to display these characters or have them as part of a filename, you need to use single quotes. For example, the command `echo '$5.00'` displays the text $5.00 correctly.

If you want to display a single quote, as an apostrophe, then you need to use double quotes. For example, to display the text, Ross' Farms, Inc., you use double quotes because single quotes cannot contain single quotes. To create a file named "Micki's file", you enter `touch "Micki's file"`.

Next you will preserve the literal meaning of a metacharacter using double quotes.

To use double quotes:

1. Log in to the Linux system as a user, and then open a Terminal emulation window.

2. To correctly display the text **I've gone fishin'**, enter `echo "I've gone fishin'"`, and then press **Enter**. Notice that the text is correctly displayed on the screen.

3. To correctly display the text **Jake won $500.00**, enter `echo 'Jake won $500.00'`, and then press **Enter**. Again, the text is correctly displayed on the screen. You could have entered it this way too: `echo Jake won '$'500.00` because you only need to protect the dollar sign.

4. To correctly display the text **You've earned $5.00**, enter `echo "You've" earned '$5.00'`, and then press **Enter**. You are required to form the statement this way because the apostrophe (a single quote) in the contraction

must be protected with double quotes. The dollar sign must be protected with the single quotes.

5. Close your window, and then log out.

UNDERSTANDING EXPANSION

Expansion is the process of changing metacharacters and special symbols into something else. The shell uses special symbols to expand or substitute words that are entered on the command line. You have already seen expansion as it applies to the shell variables in previous chapters. For example, $HOME expands, or turns, into your home directory. The $PATH variable expands into the list of directories the shell uses to search for locating commands. Expansion occurs when you use these variables. There are several types of expansion but only a few will be discussed in this chapter. They are listed below:

- Tilde

- Parameter and variable

- Command substitution

Tilde Expansion

A **tilde-prefix** is the part of a command that begins with the tilde symbol (~) and is followed by additional characters. The tilde (~) expands to the user's login name home directory. For example, if you execute the **cd** ~ command, your current directory changes to your home directory. If you enter the command cp ~/victory.dat /tmp, the file named "victory.dat" from your home directory would be copied to the /tmp directory.

If the tilde-prefix is part of the ~+ command, then the value of the shell variable PWD is substituted for the tilde-prefix. For example, if you enter the command echo ~+, your current working directory is displayed. In this case, the tilde-prefix with the plus sign achieve the same results as the **pwd** command.

If the tilde-prefix is part of the ~- command, then the value of the shell variable OLDPWD is substituted for the tilde-prefix and hyphen. If you enter the command echo ~-, your previous working directory is displayed.

Parameter (or Variable) Expansion

Parameter expansion, in general, substitutes values for parameter or variable names. Parameters and variables are discussed further in Chapter 5. For now, think of them as names that can contain values. The dollar sign ($) is used for parameter expansion. For example, you can set the variable Text1 to be "Please enter menu selection: " with the command **Text1="Please enter menu selection: "**. However, in order to access the contents, you must precede the variable with the dollar sign. So, **echo $Text1** displays the contents of Text1 on the screen. In this example, the variable $Text1 is substituted with its contents, "Please enter menu selection:". There are a variety of ways you can achieve parameter substitution depending upon the expansion command you choose to use.

Use of the ${name} method

The use of braces is designed to allow you to mix variables and numbers in the shell. For the most part their use is not needed, but there are some circumstances where braces are required. This type of expansion takes the following general form:

```
${name}
```

For example, suppose you work for an international bank and you want to display a currency value symbol that you have stored in a variable named currency. You also want to display a credit transaction by a customer to show "Credit $500.00." To do so, you enter the following statements:

```
currency='$'
echo "Credit" ${currency}500.00
```

These commands display what you intended on the screen-"Credit $500." If you don't include the braces around the variable, you get unexpected results. Here the variable currency is equal to the number 500. Figure 4-10 demonstrates this use of braces for parameter substitution from the previous example. Notice the second example in Figure 4-10 does not contain braces. Without them, the dollar sign and the number are not displayed.

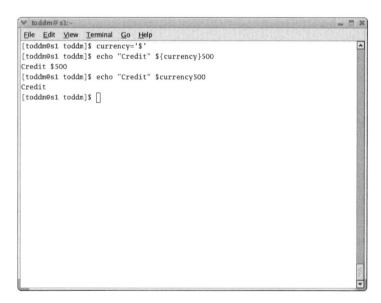

Figure 4-10 Use of braces in parameter substitution

Specifying Part of a Value Using ${name:offset:length}

You can use parameter expansion to specify a portion of a parameter's value by using the following form:

${name:offset:length}

The *name* value is the name of the variable. The *offset* position is the beginning position within the value you want, and the length number is the number of positions of the value you want. The *offset* position begins at zero. The use of braces is required. If you leave them off, you get unexpected results. Consider an example where you have a parameter named "p" that contained the value "abcde." Letter "a" is in position, or offset, zero; letter "b" is in position, or offset, one; and so on. If you want to specify the third and fourth character positions for "c" and "d," then you use the statement echo ${p:2:2}. The first "2" is the offset and the second "2" is the length. If you want to display the first four positions, you use the statement echo ${p:0:4}. A practical use of this type of parameter expansion might be using a portion of your Social Security Number (SSN) as a password. Many systems set your initial password to the last four digits of your SSN. So, the statement, password=${SSN:5:4} initially sets the password to the last four digits of your SSN.

Specifying a Variable's Length

There may be times when you want to determine the length of a variable. For instance, if you want to determine if a user has entered the appropriate number of characters in a field on the screen. To determine the length of a variable you use the following general form:

${#variable}

To display the length for a variable named "T," you type echo ${#T}.

Next you will complete an exercise to increase your understanding of parameter expansion.

To understand parameter expansion:

1. Log in to the Linux system as a user, and then open a Terminal emulation window.

2. To set a variable for use, type **p="56789"**, and then press **Enter**.

3. To display the first two character positions of "p," type **echo ${p:0:2}**, and then press **Enter**. See Figure 4-11. The characters, "5" and "6," are displayed.

4. To display two character positions of "p" starting with the third position, type **echo ${p:2:2}**, and then press **Enter**. See Figure 4-11. The characters, "7" and "8" are displayed.

5. To display the last character position of "p," type **echo ${p:4:1}**, and then press **Enter**. See Figure 4-11. The last character is displayed.

6. To verify the need for braces, type **echo $p:4:1**, and then press **Enter**. See Figure 4-11. Notice that the text "56789:4:1" is displayed, which is not what you intended.

7. To display the length of "p," type **echo ${#p}**, and then press **Enter**. See Figure 4-11. The numeral five is displayed indicating that the length of the variable is five positions.

8. Close your window, and then log out.

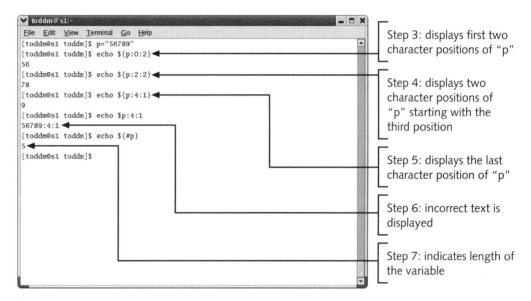

Figure 4-11   Use of parameter expansion

Command Substitution

Command substitution allows you to substitute the output of a command in place of the command itself. This is typically used in combination with parameter or variable substitution. For example, you know that the **pwd** command displays your current working directory. What if you want to keep this information? You can use command substitution to set a variable to equal the output of the **pwd** command. Then, you can display the contents of the variable using parameter substitution. There are two forms of command substitution. They are:

- $(*command*)
- `*command*`

In both cases, ***command*** is a Linux command. The $(*command*) is the newer of the two forms of command substitution and treats everything within the parentheses as part of the command.

The single back quote (`) is used in `command`. It is on the same key as the tilde symbol.

Let's look at an example. If you enter the **t=`ls`** command, followed by the **echo $t** command, the contents of the variable named "t" are the output of the **ls** command. If you choose to use the other syntax, you enter **t=$(ls)**.

You can also nest command substitutions. Nesting means placing a command substitution with another command substitution. The innermost nested command executes first. For example, in the **t=$(ls $(pwd))** command, the content of the variable "t" first contains a listing of the current working directory, which is the output of the **$(pwd)** command that is substituted first. Next, the output of the **ls** command is substituted. Ultimately, the contents of "t" are the directory listing of the current directory in this example.

You cannot use the single back quotes when nesting. You will get unexpected results.

Next you will complete an exercise to help you understand command substitution.

To understand command substitution:

1. Log in to the Linux system as a user, and then open a Terminal emulation window.

2. Type **echo "User" $(whoami) "is on system" $(hostname)**, and then press **Enter**. The text "User *username* is on system *system-name*" is displayed on the screen. See Figure 4-12. Note that toddm is the username shown and the system name is s1. Your *username* and *system-name* will be different.

3. Type **echo "Your current directory is: " $(pwd)**, and then press **Enter**. The text "Your current directory is: *directory-name*" is displayed on the screen. In Figure 4-12 the current directory shown is /home/toddm/Ch4. Your *directory-name* will be different.

4. To implement an alternate form of command substitution, type **echo "Your current directory is: " `pwd`**, and then press **Enter**. See Figure 4-12. Notice that the results are the same for this step and the previous one.

5. To display the date, type **echo "Today is" `date`**, and then press **Enter**. The text "Today is *current-date*" is displayed on the screen. Your *current-date* will be different than what is shown in Figure 4-12.

6. To display the current year, type **echo "The year is" `date +%Y`**, and then press **Enter**. The text "The year is *current-year*" is displayed on the screen. Your *current-year* will be different than what is shown in Figure 4-12.

7. Close your window, and then log out.

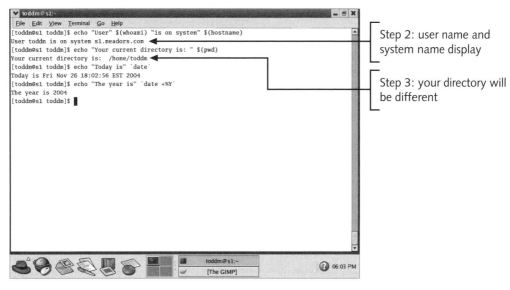

4

Step 2: user name and system name display

Step 3: your directory will be different

Figure 4-12   Use of command substitution

LEARNING ADDITIONAL COMMANDS

In this section, you will learn several additional Linux commands. These commands will help enhance your Linux skills; they are highly useful commands when implemented in shell scripts. The following is a list of additional commands:

- find
- tr
- tee
- mail

The find Command

The **find** command allows you to search for files in the directory tree. You use this command when you do not know where a file is located. This command locates the directory the file is in. You can also use this command with options to find files that are a certain size, owned by a specific user, or older than a specified number of days. The **find** command locates the files in the directory tree based upon the criteria specified in the options. While the **find** command has numerous options, only a few will be covered in this section. If you want to find out about additional options, refer to the **man** pages for the **find** command. The **find** command takes this general form:

    find *path expression*

This is where *path* is either a full or partial path. Note that only the current directory is searched if you do not specify a path. An *expression* can be comprised of options, tests, and actions. Only tests will be discussed in this section. There are several available actions, but the default action is to display text to the screen. Table 4-2 shows a list of some of the more important *find* tests.

Table 4-2   A few **find** tests

Test	Description	Example
-mtime *number-of-days*	Finds files modified a specified *number-of-days* ago	find -mtime 5
-name *pattern*	Searches for a directory based upon a specified *pattern*	find -name ltm1
-size *number*	Finds files that are a minimum size. The *number* specifies the size used to compare. After the number, you can use a term. Some valid terms are: "k" for kilobytes "c" for bytes	find -size 1k
-type	Finds files of a certain type. Some valid types: "d"=directory "f"= file	find -type d
-user *username*	Find files owned by *username*	find -user toddm

Consider the example shown in the table used for finding a specific file named ltm1, **find -name ltm1**. The output returned for this example is the full path to the file in the tree. You don't have to be in the directory the file is located in to use the **find** command. The **find** command looks in all directories starting in the current directory. This is a particularly useful command when you don't know where a file is located.

You can use pattern matching techniques with the **find** command, too. For example, to find all files with a first character in the range of "a–c", you enter **find [a-c]***.

If you want to locate all files that have not been modified in the last seven days, you enter **find -mtime 7**. A list of files not modified in the last seven days appears. The **find** command searches all subdirectories. Use of the modification option is very helpful when you want to clean up your system by deleting "older" files.

Another application of the **find** command is listing all files as opposed to directories. To do so you enter **find -type f**, and a listing of all files along with their full paths is displayed. To locate only directories, you enter **find -type d**, and a listing of all directories is displayed. The **find** command is also useful for finding files created by a particular user. To display all files owned by a user named "Sally," you enter **find -user Sally**, and all of her files are displayed.

You can even locate files that are a specific size. To find all files that are at least 10 kilobytes (10,000 characters), you enter **find -size 10k**. This application is useful for locating large files in the directory tree that might be occupying a lot of disk space.

Next you will complete an exercise to help you understand the **find** command.

To understand the find command:

1. Log in to the Linux system as a user, and then open a Terminal emulation window.

2. To locate all files and directories in the current directory, type **find**, and then press **Enter**. All files and directories appear on the screen.

3. To locate directories, type **find -type d**, and then press **Enter**. This time, only directories appear on the screen.

4. To locate files, type **find -type f**, and then press **Enter**. Now, only files appear on the screen.

5. To find files over 1 kilobyte, type **find -size 1k**, and then press **Enter**. Only files at least 1 kilobyte in size appear.

6. To find files owned by a user, type **find -user *username***. Replace *username* with your own name. All files that you own are displayed.

7. Close your window, and then log out.

The tr Command

The **tr** command translates or deletes characters. It is very useful for translating lowercase characters to uppercase when testing for user input in a shell script. It takes the following general form:

```
tr option set1 set2
```

This is where *set1* are either characters or classes of characters that are to be translated into characters or classes of characters specified in *set2*. The original characters in *set1* are translated into the characters in *set2*. If you wanted to translate all lowercase letters to uppercase using a class of characters, you enter **tr [:lower:] [:upper:]**. Or, you could reverse the two and convert uppercase to lowercase as in **tr [:upper:] [:lower:]**.

From a programming standpoint, translating characters gives you greater control over the characters because fewer possible variations exist. As a shell programmer, there may be times when you request a user to input data at a prompt. You can use the **tr** command to translate all the characters to uppercase, and continue your script based on uppercase input data. For example, suppose you wrote a shell script that checked whether a user entered a "Y," for "Yes," in order to perform a certain task. What if the user entered a lowercase "y"? Remember that uppercase and lowercase letters are different. One option is to write a script that accounts for all the possibilities, or you could just translate the lowercase "y" to an uppercase "Y," and then check for this.

 You can use the "-d" option to delete characters.

Next you will use the `tr` command to translate uppercase and lowercase letters.

To understand the `tr` command:

1. Log in to the Linux system as a user, and then open a Terminal emulation window.

2. To translate lowercase characters to uppercase, type **tr [:lower:] [:upper:]**, and then press **Enter**. The cursor moves to the beginning of the next line. The `tr` command is awaiting your input.

3. At the beginning of the next line, type **linux is fun!**, and then press **Enter**. See Figure 4-13. The characters are translated to uppercase.

4. Press **Ctrl+D** to terminate the command.

5. To translate uppercase characters to lowercase, type **tr [:upper:] [:lower:]**, and then press **Enter**. The cursor moves to the beginning of the next line. The `tr` command is awaiting your input.

6. At the beginning of the next line, type **THIS is cool.**, and then press **Enter**. See Figure 4-13. The uppercase characters are translated to lowercase. The already existing lowercase characters do not change.

7. Press **Ctrl+D** to terminate the command.

8. To translate just one character, type **tr y Y**, and then press **Enter**.

9. At the beginning of the next line, type **The answer is "y".**, and then press **Enter**. See Figure 4-13. The only character translated is "y." It is translated from lowercase to uppercase.

10. Press **Ctrl+D** to terminate the command.

11. Close your window, and then log out.

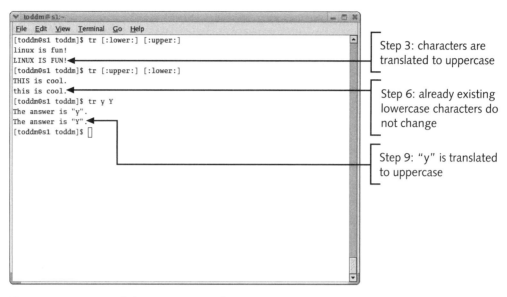

Figure 4-13 Use of the `tr` command

The `tee` Command

The **tee** command is a useful command because it reads from standard input and writes both to standard output and to files. You use this command if you want to see the output of a command as well as keep the output of the command in a file for later review. The following is the general form:

        tee *option file*

The **tee** command only has a few options; the most important one is the **-a** option used for appending. Consider a possible use for this command. One example might be displaying the output of the **who** command on the screen and then capturing that same output to a file for later review. You can use the **tee** command to accomplish this. Suppose you enter the **who | tee wholist.txt** command. Recall that the vertical bar is the pipe symbol discussed in Chapter 2. The output goes to the screen, and then the **tee** command sends the output to the wholist.txt file. This differs from redirection because with the **tee** command you get output in two places—the screen and a file. With (or without) redirection, you only get output in one place—either the screen or a file.

Next you will use the **tee** command to send output to two places.

To understand the `tee` command:

1. Log in to the Linux system as a user, and then open a Terminal emulation window.

2. To display the list of current users and send the output to a file named "output.txt," type **who | tee output.txt**, and then press Enter. Figure 4-14 shows possible results of this command. Your results will differ.

3. Display the content of the output file.

4. To display the list of current users and append the output to the output.txt file, type **who | tee -a output.txt**, and then press **Enter**. The listing of users should be similar to what was displayed in Step 2.

5. Display the contents of the output file. See Figure 4-14. Notice that the **cat** command is used to display the output.txt file. The original output that was sent to this file in Step 2 as well as the output appended in Step 4 is shown. Your results will differ.

6. To display the current directory, and then append the output to the output.txt file, type **pwd | tee -a output.txt**, and then press **Enter**. Your present working directory is displayed.

7. Display the contents of the output.txt file. See Figure 4-14. Notice that the information from Steps 2 and 4 is included as well as the result of the **pwd** command from Step 6. Your results will differ.

8. Close the window, and then log out.

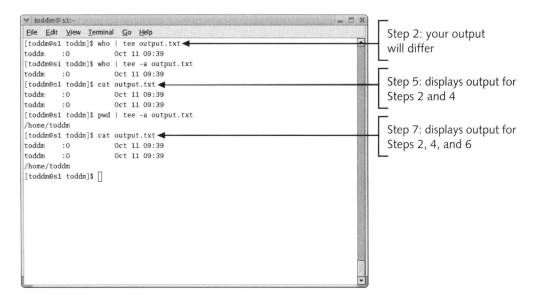

Figure 4-14   Use of the `tee` command

The `mail` Command

The `mail` command is used to send and receive electronic messages. To run the `mail` command, simply type `mail` at the command prompt. Because most people are already familiar with the concepts of sending and receiving e-mail, you will next perform an exercise to show you how it works on the Linux operating system.

To use the `mail` command:

1. Log in to the Linux system as a user, and then open a Terminal emulation window.

2. To send an e-mail to a user, type **mail *username***, and then press **Enter**. Be sure to replace *username* with your own username. The `mail` command displays a Subject: line.

3. On the Subject: line, type **Price Quote**, and then press **Enter**. The cursor moves to the beginning of the next line. This is one of the message lines where you will enter the text you want to send.

4. On the first message line, type **The price quote for customer 1001A for Purchase Order 1122-EG is $199.99.**, and then press **Enter**. On the next message line, type **Thanks,**, and then press **Enter**. The cursor moves to the beginning of the next message line. See Figure 4-15.

5. Press **Ctrl+D**. The Cc: line appears. This is for "Courtesy copy" in case you want to send this message to another user.

6. Press **Enter**. The Linux prompt returns.

7. Wait a few minutes for the mail daemon to send the message. To receive your mail, type **mail**, and then press **Enter**. An ampersand appears. This is the `mail` prompt. See Figure 4-15. One or more lines are displayed indicating you have a message. You should see the letter "N" for "New" message and a number to the right of the "N." This is the message number used for referencing the message.

8. Type in the message number of your new message, and then press **Enter**. The message appears. In Figure 4-15, the message number is "1."

9. Review the message, press **q**, and then press **Enter** to quit `mail`.

10. Close your window, and then log out.

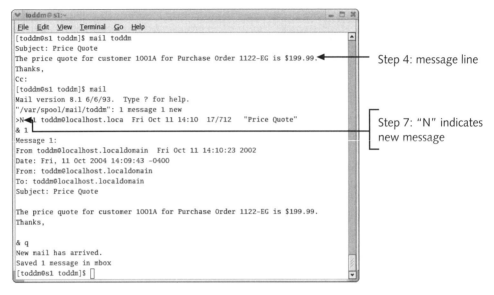

Figure 4-15   Use of the `mail` command

Chapter Summary

❐ Redirection changes the default locations of standard input, standard output, and standard error. The symbol for redirecting standard input is the less-than symbol (<). The symbol for redirecting standard output and creating a new file is the single greater-than symbol (>). The symbol for redirecting standard output and appending it to a file is made up of two greater-than symbols (>).

❐ Pattern matching can be used to find characters. The symbol to match zero or more characters is the asterisk (*). The symbol to match a single character position is the question mark (?). To match several characters, you enclose a list or range of characters to be matched within brackets, ([...]).

❐ The use of quotes preserves the literal meaning of metacharacters. The backslash, \, preserves the meaning of the character immediately following it. Using two single quotes, ' ... ', protects characters within the quotes. Single quotes preserve the meaning of all characters within them with the exception of another single quote. The use of two double quotes, " ... ", preserves the meaning of all characters within double quotes with the exception of $, ', and \.

❐ Expansion is the process of changing the metacharacters into something else. The shell uses special symbols known as metacharacters to expand words or substitute values. The types of expansion discussed in this chapter include tilde, parameter, or variable, and command. Tilde expansion converts the metacharacter ~ into your home directory. Parameter, or variable, expansion allows you to use metacharacters to combine numbers and characters. To work with portions of a parameter, you use the (`${name:offset:length}`) form. To determine the length of a parameter, you use the (`${#name}`) form.

❑ The `find` command allows you to locate files and directories within the Linux tree based upon size, owner, age, and other criteria. The `tr` command translates and deletes characters. The `tee` command sends output both to the screen and to a file. The `mail` command allows you to send and receive e-mail messages.

4

REVIEW QUESTIONS

1. Which command is used to locate files?

   a. `who`

   b. `find`

   c. `tr`

   d. `mail`

2. Which command is used to send and receive messages?

   a. `who`

   b. `find`

   c. `tr`

   d. `mail`

3. You use _____ to redirect input.

   a. `>>`

   b. `<`

   c. `>`

   d. `$(...)`

4. The file descriptor for standard error is _____.

   a. 1

   b. 0

   c. 9

   d. 2

5. You use _____ to redirect output and create a new file.

   a. `>>`

   b. `<`

   c. `>`

   d. `$(...)`

6. You use _____ to redirect output and add data to the end of a file.

   a. >>

   b. <

   c. >

   d. $(...)

7. The _____ option on the `tee` command allows you to append to a file.

   a. -o

   b. -a

   c. >

   d. >>

8. The default location for standard input is the _____.

   a. printer

   b. hard disk

   c. screen

   d. keyboard

9. Which is used to perform command substitution?

   a. '...'

   b. <

   c. >

   d. `...`

10. The _____ command translates uppercase letters to lowercase letters.

    a. `tr`

    b. `tee`

    c. `mail`

    d. `find`

11. The _____ metacharacter preserves all characters except a single quote.

    a. \

    b. "

    c. `

    d. '

12. The _____ metacharacter preserves all characters except the dollar sign, the single back quote, and the backslash.

    a. \
    b. "
    c. `
    d. '

13. The _____ metacharacter preserves the character following it.

    a. \
    b. "
    c. `
    d. '

14. To nest using command substitution, you use the _____ form.

    a. '...'
    b. "..."
    c. `...`
    d. $(...)

15. To locate files that are 2 kilobytes, you use the _____ command.

    a. `ls -l 2k`
    b. `find -size 2k`
    c. `find -length 2k`
    d. `find -size 2c`

16. To locate files owned by Marge, you use the _____ command.

    a. `ls -owner=Marge`
    b. `find -who Marge`
    c. `find -owner Marge`
    d. `find -user Marge`

17. To convert the letter "v" to uppercase, you use the _____ command.

    a. `tr v V`
    b. `tr V v`
    c. `ls v | tee -a out.txt`
    d. `tr [:upper:] [:lower:]`

4

18. To redirect standard error of the **pwd** command to a file named Error.txt, use the _____ command.

    a. pwd &>2

    b. pwd 2>error.lst

    c. pwd 2>Error.txt

    d. pwd > Error.txt

19. To redirect standard output and standard error of the **who** command to a file named wholist.txt, use the _____ command.

    a. who &>1 & 2

    b. who>>wholist.txt

    c. who 2>wholist.txt

    d. who &> wholist.txt

20. To display the output of the **ls** command to the screen and to a file named lslisting.txt you use the _____ command.

    a. ls | tr lslisting.txt

    b. find -name lslisting.txt

    c. ls | tee -a lslisting.dat

    d. ls | tee lslisting.txt

HANDS-ON PROJECTS

Project 4-1

In this project, you will reinforce your knowledge of redirecting input and output. The goal of this project is to use redirection to alter where the input of a command is coming from or where the output of a command is going to.

1. Log in to the Linux system as a user, and then open a Terminal emulation window.

2. To redirect output, type **who > x.dat**, and then press **Enter**.

3. To redirect and append output, type **ls >> x.dat**, and then press **Enter**.

4. To redirect and append output, type **pwd >> x.dat**, and then press **Enter**.

5. To redirect and append output, type **date >> x.dat**, and then press **Enter**.

6. To redirect and append output, type **echo "The end" >> x.dat**, and then press **Enter**.

7. To display the contents of the output file, type **cat x.dat | more**, and then press **Enter**.

8. Record the output.

9. To overwrite the output file previously used by redirecting the output and creating a new file, type **echo "Oops" > x.dat**, and then press **Enter**.

10. To display the contents of the output file, type **cat x.dat**, and then press **Enter**.

11. Record the reason for difference in this output compared with the output you recorded in Step 8.

12. To redirect standard input, you first need to create a file to work with. Create a file named **unsort.dat** with the following data:

    3

    1

    2

13. To redirect input, type **sort < unsort.dat**, and then press **Enter**.

14. Record the output.

15. To redirect input and output, type **sort < unsort.dat > sort.dat**, and then press **Enter**.

16. Type **cat unsort.dat**, and then press **Enter**.

17. Record the output.

18. Type **cat sort.dat**, and then press **Enter**.

19. Record the output.

20. Record the reason the two previous files differ.

21. Close your window, and then log out.

Project 4-2

In this project, you will reinforce your knowledge of redirecting standard output and standard error. The goal of this project is to use redirection to alter where the output of a command and any resulting error messages are sent.

1. Log in to the Linux system as a user, and then open a Terminal emulation window.

2. Create a file named **P4-2.dat**.

3. To redirect standard output and standard error to different files, type
   ls P4-2.dat > List.txt 2> ListError.txt, and then press **Enter**.

4. Display the contents of both files.

5. Remove the file named **P4-2.dat**, so you can generate an error in the next command.

6. To see what happens when an error is generated, repeat Step 3.

7. Display the contents of both files.

8. Record the output and the reason for the output.

9. To redirect standard output and error to the same file named both.txt, type
   ls P4-2.dat &>both.txt, and then press **Enter**.

10. Display the contents of the file named **both.txt**.

11. Record the output and the reason for the output.

12. Close your window, and then log out.

Project 4-3

In this project, you will reinforce your knowledge of the concept of pattern matching. The goal of this project is to create several files, and then write a script to perform pattern matching techniques for the listing of files.

1. Log in to the Linux system as a user, and then open a Terminal emulation window.

2. Create the following files in the same directory: **pay042004.dat, pay022004.dat, pay122004.dat, pay042003.dat, pay062004.dat, pay102004.dat, sales012004.dat, sales052004.dat, sales102004.dat,** and **sales042004.dat**. The files have a three character name followed by a two digit month and a four digit year. The file extension is "dat."

3. Create a script named **Project4-3** in the **$HOME/bin** directory.

4. List all files beginning with any letter in the range "a"–"r."

5. List all files beginning with an "s."

6. List all sales files that include the year 2004.

7. List all pay files for April.

8. List all files with a "txt" extension.

9. Save the script, and then close the editor.

10. Run the script, record the commands used in Steps 9-12, and then record or print the script.

11. Close your window, and then log out.

Project 4-4

In this project, you will reinforce your knowledge of the concepts of redirection and pattern matching. The goal of this project is to use the files created in Project 4-3, then write a script to perform both redirection and use pattern-matching techniques.

1. Log in to the Linux system as a user, and then open a Terminal emulation window.

2. Create a script named **Project4-4** in the **$HOME/bin** directory.

3. List all files beginning with "pay," and then redirect output to a file named PayList.txt.

4. List all sales files for August, redirect output to a file named AugList.txt, and then redirect standard error to ErrorList.txt.

5. List all pay files with a .txt extension, and then redirect both standard output and error to PayTxtList.txt.

6. List all files beginning in the range of "a-z," and then redirect both standard output and error to azList.txt.

7. Save the script, and then close the editor.

8. Run the script, record the commands used in Steps 3-6, record the command used, and then record or print the script.

9. Close your window, and then log out.

Project 4-5

In this project, you will reinforce your knowledge of the concept of quoting. The goal of this project is to have you write a script that quotes metacharacters, and then redirect that output to a file. By combining the quoting and redirection in one project, you will see the importance of quoting. (*Hint*: If you don't put the correct quoting characters in the correct place, you could end up with errors.)

1. Log in to the Linux system as a user, and then open a Terminal emulation window.

2. Create a script named **Project4-5** in the **$HOME/bin** directory.

3. Insert the following lines of code:

```
echo "This file has single quotes 'see'." > echolist.txt
echo "I've earned '$'500.00 "in sales this week." >> echolist.txt
echo "James' " '$'Money'$' "list" >> echolist.txt
echo The prompt on some systems has this symbol \>.  >> echolist.txt
```

4. Save the script, and then close the editor.

5. Run the script, record the commands used in Step 3, and then record or print the script.

6. Close your window, and then log out.

Project 4-6

In this project, you will reinforce your knowledge of expansion. The goal of this project is to help you understand the concepts of tilde expansion, parameter or variable expansion, and command substitution.

1. Log in to the Linux system as a user, and then open a Terminal emulation window.

2. To display your current working directory using tilde expansion, type **echo ~+**, and then press **Enter**.

3. To display your previous working directory using tilde expansion, type **echo ~-**, and then press **Enter**.

4. To use tilde expansion to change to your home directory, type **cd ~**, and then press **Enter**.

5. To set a value to be used with parameter expansion, type **Value="ABC123"**, and then press **Enter**.

6. To display the last three character positions, type **echo ${Value:3:3}**, and then press **Enter**.

7. To display the last (sixth) character position, type **echo ${Value:5:1}**, and then press **Enter**.

8. To display the length of the variable Value, type **echo ${#Value}**, and then press **Enter**.

9. To use command substitution to set a variable equal to the output of the previous command, type **len=$(echo ${#Value})**, and then press **Enter**.

10. Display the contents of the variable named len.

11. To use command substitution to set a variable named password equal to the last three characters in the value, type **password=$(echo ${Value:3:3})**, and then press **Enter**.

12. Display the contents of the variable named password.

13. Close your window, and then log out.

Project 4-7

The goal of this project is to help reinforce your understanding of the **find** command.

1. Log in to the Linux system as a user, and then open a Terminal emulation window.

2. To locate directories and redirect the output to a file, type **find -type d > dirlist.txt**, and then press **Enter**.

3. To locate files that are 3k (kilobyte) in size or larger and redirect the output, type **find -size 3k > ThreeK.txt**, and then press **Enter**.

4. To locate files that haven't been modified in seven days and redirect the output to a file, type **find -mtime 7 > SevenDays.txt**, and then press **Enter**.

5. To locate files that haven't been modified in three days and that are 1k in size, type **find -type f -size 1k -mtime 3**, and then press **Enter**.

6. To locate files that haven't been modified in 30 days, that are 10k in size, that are owned by your username, and then to redirect standard output and error to a file, type **find -type f -size 10k -mtime 30 -user *username* &> findlist.txt**, and then press **Enter**. Replace *username* with your own user name.

7. Close your window, and then log out.

Project 4-8

The goal of this project is to help reinforce your understanding of the **tee** command.

1. Log in to the Linux system as a user, and then open a Terminal emulation window.

2. Create a script named **Project4-8** in the **$HOME/bin** directory.

3. Run the correct command to display a long listing to the screen, and then place the results of the long listing in a file named **Project4-8list.txt**.

4. Run the correct command to display the currently logged in users to the screen, and then append the results to a file named **Project4-8list.txt**.

5. Run the correct command to find only files in the current directory and display them on the screen, and then append the results to a file named **Project4-8list.txt**.

6. Run the correct command to find only files in the current directory that begin with letters in the range "a–z" and display them on the screen, and then append the results to a file named **Project4-8list.txt**.

7. Save the script and then close the editor.

8. Run the script, record the command used, and then record or print the script.

9. Close your window, and then log out.

CASE PROJECTS

Case 4-1

You have been hired by TMI to create a shell script using pattern-matching techniques. The payroll department needs the following files created and then placed in the Payroll directory that you created in Case 2-1:

jan07.dat	dec04.dat	jul04.dat	feb06.dat	apr06.dat	dec06.dat
jan02.dat	feb14.txt	jun06.dat	feb16.dat	aug06.txt	jun04.dat
jan03.dat	jul04.txt	jul13.txt	feb26.dat	may06.txt	jun06.txt
oct27.txt	feb07.dat	dec07.dat	apr28.dat	mar06.dat	apr09.txt

Because the IT staff has a limited knowledge of the Linux operating system, they want you to help them perform the following tasks. Run the commands at the command line to make sure you get them to work properly. Once they are correct, place these commands in a shell script. Then, test and run the script.

The script must include a Linux statement for each step below:

1. Display all files with an extension of "dat."

2. Display only files for "January."

3. Display all files that begin with a "j" and have an extension of "dat."

4. Display all files only for the seventh of every month.

5. Display all files that begin with the letter "j" or the letter "d."

Case 4-2

Jenny's Motorcycle and Sidecar Shop has a Linux system used to run their main sales shop and two satellite sales offices. Recently, their Linux System Administrator left, and they need you to write a script for them. The script must perform the following and redirect output and errors to one or more files in your home directory:

- Find all files that are at least 10 kilobytes.

- Find all files owned by root that are 100 kilobytes in length.

- Use the **man** pages to construct the correct command to locate only files with the permissions of read, write, and execute for all files owned by root.

- Display the contents of the output file(s), and then translate all lowercase letters to uppercase.

- Print the output file(s) within the script.

5

SHELL SCRIPT PROGRAMMING CONCEPTS

In this chapter, you will:

♦ Understand the sequential flow of shell scripting
♦ Manage shell scripts
♦ Understand the basic components of a shell script
♦ Understand parameters
♦ Create interactive scripts
♦ Understand debugging

This chapter gives you an overview of shell script programming. You need to understand the flow of shell scripting in order to effectively write shell scripts. You will learn how to manage shell scripts, which entails changing the permissions on a script to allow you to execute it by simply entering the script name. You will also learn how the shell executes a script. By placing the script in a directory which is on the search path, you will be able to run the script from any directory location. You will learn the basic components of a script which include adding comments to a script and adding a usage clause which indicates to the user how to run the script. Allowing your script to accept values from the command line or interact with the user will also be discussed. Finally, you will learn how to debug and troubleshoot your script to handle any execution errors you may run into.

UNDERSTANDING THE SEQUENTIAL FLOW OF SHELL SCRIPTING

Shell scripts allow you to combine programming logic with operating system commands to automate parts of your job. The term **sequential**, as it applies to shell scripting, means one command executes at a time. All programming languages execute their statements in sequential order. You can alter this order with decision statements, looping structures, and functions. These concepts are discussed in later chapters.

Let's look at an example taken from most everyone's day—getting ready for school or work. This overall task can be set up in a series of sequential steps in pseudocode. As an example, here is the list of steps that one could use to get ready for school or work:

1. *Turn alarm clock off.*

2. *Get out of bed.*

3. *Shower and clean up.*

4. *Dress.*

5. *Eat breakfast.*

6. *Brush teeth.*

7. *Drive to school or work.*

Granted, some steps in this list can be done in a different order. You might say that you eat breakfast before you shower and dress. Or, you may be late so you skip eating breakfast and brushing your teeth. However, you must do some of these steps prior to others. You must get out of bed before you dress or even drive to school or work. And, if you complete the list of steps in the order shown, then you have a routine, or program, for getting ready for school or work everyday.

The getting-ready-for-school-or-work routine parallels the concept of a sequential flow of a shell script. In the above example, each of the individual steps is equal to a command. The collective steps are considered the program. In shell scripts like the getting-ready-for-school-or-work program, some commands may be executed before other commands, and there are some commands that must be executed before others.

 A shell script is a program.

In order to help understand the sequential flow of shell scripting, you will create a simple three-line shell script. The following steps are the pseudocode for the shell script. As you may already know, pseudocode allows you to concentrate on the logic of your program instead of being concerned about the specific syntax. Review the following pseudocode:

1. Change directory locations to root.

2. Run a listing on the directory.

3. Display the current working directory.

Next you will turn this pseudocode into a shell script.

To create a shell script from pseudocode:

1. Log in to the Linux system as a user, and then open a Terminal emulation window.

2. To change to the bin directory, type **cd bin**, and then press **Enter**.

3. To create the shell script with the name ListRoot, type **vi ListRoot**, and then press **Enter**.

4. Type **i** to insert a line of text. The text "—INSERT—"appears at the bottom of the window.

5. To mirror the pseudocode statements, insert the following lines of code to the ListRoot script:

```
cd /
ls
pwd
```

6. In order to save the script, press **Esc**, type **:wq!**, and then press **Enter**.

7. In order to execute the ListRoot script, type **bash ListRoot**, and then press **Enter**. The shell script executes and performs the statements you added in Step 4—specifically, changes to the root directory, performs a directory listing, and then displays the present, or current, working directory. Figure 5-1 shows the ListRoot script and its execution.

8. Close your window, and then log out.

When you create a shell script, you must arrange the commands in a logical order. The logical order depends upon the task you are trying to accomplish. In the ListRoot script, if you placed the **pwd** command before the **ls** command, the order of processing would change. In this case, the **ls** would execute last. Although this is a minor change in this shell script, in some cases, if you place the commands out of order, it can create unexpected results. Take for example, a shell script that redirects output to a file.

You learned in Chapter 4 the difference between using a single greater-than symbol and two greater-than symbols to redirect output. The single greater-than symbol overwrites the current contents of the file. Using two greater-than symbols appends to a file.

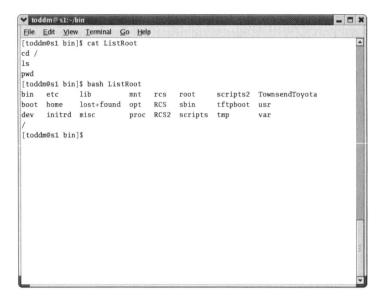

Figure 5-1   The ListRoot script

In the following sequence of commands, the first **echo** command is redirecting the text "output" to a file named **output.txt**. Any previous data is overwritten. The next two **echo** statements are appending to the same filename.

```
echo "output" > output.txt
echo "more output" >> output.txt
echo "even more output" >> output.txt
```

What would happen if you placed the first line at the end of the list of commands? In other words, if you used the following code instead of the previous code:

```
echo "more output" >> output.txt
echo "even more output" >> output.txt
echo "output" > output.txt
```

The answer to this question is that any previous data in the file would be lost. Although the first two commands are appending output, thus preserving any previous data in the file; the last statement is using a single greater-than symbol to overwrite the file, thus resulting in any prior data being lost. What you will have in the file, after the last statement is executed, is simply the text "output" in the file—nothing else. This is a problem if you want to keep any existing data.

The best way to ensure the correctness of your shell script is to write the logic on paper as pseudocode. Then, if possible, have your instructor review it. Next, convert the pseudocode statements into commands using an appropriate Linux editor. Finally, run the shell script.

MANAGING SHELL SCRIPTS

In this section, you will learn how to manage shell scripts. When you manage a shell script, you are making the script executable in a location where the users will be able to run it. Managing shell scripts involves the following:

- Modification of a shell script's file access permission
- Placement of shell scripts

Modification of the File Access Permission of a Shell Script

As you have learned, you can execute a shell script by entering the shell's name, such as bash, followed by the script's name. For example, to execute a shell script named paychecks, you enter **bash paychecks** at the command line. However, if you use a script frequently, there is a method that is more streamlined and that is widely used among programmers. Instead of entering the name of the shell (in this case bash) you can modify the permissions of your script so you can execute it by simply entering the script's name. The **chmod** command allows you to modify the file access permission on a file or directory. Recall that you learned about permissions in Chapter 2. The permissions are read, write, and execute for the user who owns the file, the group ownership of the file, and others. When a file is first created, it has certain default permissions. For nonroot users, the default file permissions are read and write for the user who owns the file as well as the group membership on the file, and just read for others. For the root user, the permissions are read and write for the owner and read for the group and others. The **chmod** command takes the following general form:

```
chmod ugo +-= rwx filename
```

In this syntax, u represents the user or owner of the file, g represents the group permissions on the file, and the o represents the other users. The + sign means to add a permission to the current permission set, the − sign means to remove a permission from the current permission set, and the = sign creates a new permission set. Recall that r, w, and x stand for read, write, and execute. The command syntax places the *filename* after the permissions. You can use any or all of these symbols to achieve the necessary level of permission you seek for your file. Next you will change the execute permission using the letter notation of the **chmod** command so you can simply enter the shell script name at the command line.

To modify the execute permissions of a file using letter notation so you can simply enter the script's name:

1. Log in to the Linux system as a user, and then open a Terminal emulation window.

2. Move **ListRoot** to the **~/bin** directory.

3. Change directory locations to the **~/bin** directory.

4. Type **chmod ugo+x ListRoot**, and then press **Enter**. The prompt returns.

5. To verify that the execute permission has been set, type **ls —l ListRoot**, and then press **Enter**. Notice that the execute permission has been added.

6. Run the script by simply entering **ListRoot**. Notice that the command executes just by entering the script's name.

7. Close your window, and then log out.

Now that you know how to modify the permissions of a script in order to make it executable, you will utilize this concept in subsequent exercises and labs as well as on the job.

Another method of changing permissions with the **chmod** command is to use numbers to represent the permissions for the user, group, and other users. This method takes the general form:

```
chmod nnn filename
```

Here, *n* represents a number from 0 to 7. Each *n* represents the permission number for the user owner, group, and other users. Table 5-1 shows the permissions and numbers to which they refer.

Table 5-1   Permission numbers for the **chmod** command

Permissions	Number
---	0
--x	1
-w-	2
-wx	3
r--	4
r-x	5
rw-	6
rwx	7

The best way to use this table is to look for the permission you want and then look to the right to find the appropriate number you need. The three permission columns represent a 4, 2, and 1 for read (**r**), write (**w**), and execute (**x**), respectively for the user owner, group, and other users. You add up the numbers for the permissions you want. For example, if you want read-only, you simply need 4 for the permission. If you want read and write, you would add 4 and 2 to get the number 6. If you want read, write and execute, you add up 4, 2, and 1 to get the number 7.

So, if a file named program1 needed to have read, write and execute for the user owner, read and execute permissions for the group, and no permissions for all others, you would enter chmod 750 program1.

Next you will perform an activity using the chmod command with the number notation. The end result is the same as the letter notation of the chmod command—to be able to execute a script by entering just the name on the command line. However, you can use the chmod command to modify other permissions.

To modify the execute permissions of a file using number notation:

1. Log in to the Linux system as a user, and then open a Terminal emulation window.

2. Change to the **bin** directory.

3. Create a shell script that displays the current date and a list of users logged on the system. (*Hint*: use the **date** command followed by the **who** command.) Be sure to save the script with the name **LoggedOn** in the **bin** subdirectory of your home directory, and then close **vi**.

4. The current permissions are **rw-** for user owner and group and **r- -** for all others. To add execute permission for all three permission sets, type **chmod 775 LoggedOn**, and then press **Enter**. By using "775," you are setting the permissions to **rwx** for the user owner and group and **r-x** for all others. You are only adding execute.

5. To verify the permissions type **ls -l LoggedOn**, and then press **Enter**.

6. Execute the script named **LoggedOn**.

7. Close your window, and then log out.

Some users find the number method easier to enter from the keyboard once they understand its methodology. As a user writing shell scripts, you need to understand both methods. One reason is that there are process startup scripts located in the /etc/rc.d/init.d directory that use both methods. You will need to understand the startup scripts in order to troubleshoot the Linux system. For example, if you execute the command grep chmod * in the /etc/rc.d/init.d directory you will see scripts that use either method. The grep command allows you to search for text in files and will be covered in Chapter 10. The command given above searches for the text "chmod" in all files.

Exercise caution when using the chmod command. You don't want to inadvertently give group owners or other users excess permissions. For example, if a file named fileA.txt is created, it would have default permissions of rw-rw- - r- -. If you executed chmod 777 fileA.txt, then everyone on the system would have all permissions, including write. This would give anyone access to modify or even delete fileA.txt whether you intended this or not.

Placement of Shell Scripts

When you create a script or want to find an existing script, it's a good idea to understand how the shell locates scripts that are to be executed. Here's how it works. If you enter a command or script name using its full path, the shell attempts to locate the command in the specified directory. Say you entered the following command at the shell prompt:

```
/scripts/script1
```

Assuming the script is executable, how does the shell know how to locate the script named script1 in order to execute it? Simply put, the shell attempts to locate the shell script named script1 in the /scripts directory because you told it to look there when you entered the full path on the command line. If the shell script is not present, the shell generates an error message indicating the shell script file cannot be found.

Now, if you enter the command or script name using the partial path instead of the full path, the shell attempts to locate the directory the script is in a little differently. Say you executed the same script as above but left off the root symbol and directory location as follows:

```
script1
```

How does the shell know in which directory the script is located? The shell searches each element of the **PATH** shell variable for a directory containing the script file. If the directory is located that houses script1, the file is executed. Otherwise, an error is displayed. Figure 5-2 displays the contents of the **PATH** variable. The command used to display the contents of the **PATH** variable is **echo $PATH**. This variable is often called the search path.

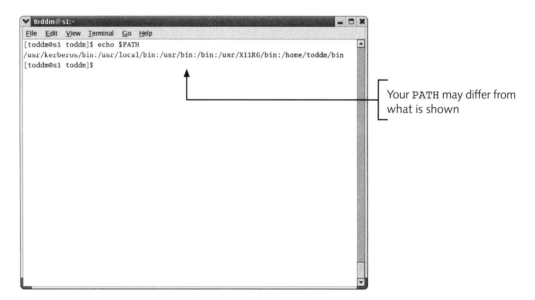

Figure 5-2 Contents of the PATH shell variable

In this example, you can see that there are six directories on the search path. Your actual search path may be different if a System Administrator changed the setting of the **PATH** variable. Changing the **PATH** is typically done in one of the startup files for the user account. In Figure 5-3 you can see the first directory listed is searched first. The next directory in the list is searched only if the script file is not found in the first directory. This process continues until the directory containing the file is found or the last directory is reached. If the shell cannot locate the script in any of the directories listed, then an error appears indicating the shell cannot find the script.

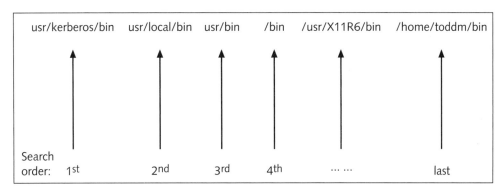

Figure 5-3   Search order of the search path

 You can also display the contents of the **PATH** shell variable using the env command. This command displays all variables for a given user account. The important thing to note here is that this command shows a colon separating each directory for the **PATH** variable.

The main reason for the search path is to make your job easier. It is much easier on you, the Linux user, if you can just enter the script name without having to enter the directory in which it is located. There is less to enter at the keyboard, resulting in fewer typos and errors. In order to run a shell script without using the full path name, you follow one of two methods. First, you can create a directory, place the shell scripts in the directory, and then add the directory to the search path. This method is useful when you have a shell script that needs to be used by many users or when you have a set of scripts you want to test. Next, you will see how this method works by creating a directory named testing where you will later place shell scripts that you are testing and don't want other users to access.

To create a directory and place it on the search path:

1. Log in to the Linux system as a user, and then open a Terminal emulation window.

2. Create a directory in your home directory named **testing**.

3. Type **PATH=$PATH:$HOME/testing**, and then press **Enter**. This command appends the current path, $PATH, with the directory, $HOME/testing. The text PATH= sets the path.

4. Change your current directory to the **$HOME/testing** directory.

5. Use the **vi** editor to create a shell script, named **display_hi** that displays the text "Hi."

6. Save the script, and then close **vi**.

7. Change to the **$HOME** directory to demonstrate the search path is used.

8. Type **bash display_hi**. The text "Hi" should appear on the screen.

9. Close your window, and then log out.

Another method for running the script without using the full path name is to place your shell script in one of the directories listed in the current search path. When you install the Linux operating system, there are a few directories that are used for the purpose of customization. For example, you can place your scripts in the /usr/local/bin directory or the $HOME/bin directory because both of these directories are on the search path. You can also place your scripts in the $HOME/bin directory as you have already done in previous exercises in this chapter. Either method works fine, but if you want to separate your scripts for testing, you should create a separate directory and place the directory name in the search path.

> The naming of scripts should be meaningful and unique. The script name must not duplicate the name of some other executable in the user's current path unless it will always be run using the full path name or an appropriate partial path name.

UNDERSTANDING THE BASIC COMPONENTS OF A SHELL SCRIPT

In this section, you will learn about the basic components of a shell script. All shell scripts can be broken down into the following list of components:

- Command interpreters
- Comments
- Variables

Specifying the Command Interpreter

You should place a statement that refers to the command interpreter that is being used in the very first line of your script. Remember from Chapter 1 that several shells, or command interpreters, exist in the Linux environment. Each shell has its own syntax rules, so commands that work in one script may not work in another. If you have multiple scripts that use different shells, you should place statements referencing the command interpreters at the beginning of each script. The advantage of specifying the command, or shell, interpreter in your program is that you ensure that later statements execute in the shell you want.

To specify the shell that is used to process subsequent commands in your script, place the statement `#!`, followed by the full path to the shell, as the very first line of your script. Consider the following example:

```
#!/bin/bash
# Comments
pwd
```

The first line references the command interpreter, the second includes any additional comments, and finally the third line contains the command statements.

> There are no spaces in the statement `#!/bin/bash` and no spaces or characters follow the `#!` symbols.

Table 5-2 provides a list of the common Linux shells and their full paths.

Table 5-2   Full paths of common Linux shells

Shell	Path
Bash	/bin/bash
Ksh	/usr/bin/ksh
Sh	/bin/sh
Csh	/bin/csh

> You can use the `which` command to determine the full path of the shells, or any commands. For example, `which bash` displays the full path of the bash shell.

Consider the script named MAIN shown in Figure 5-4. MAIN is written in the bash shell. However, it references other scripts written in different shells. Each of these scripts references the appropriate shell to be used for processing the commands within it. As each script completes, it returns to the MAIN script. Then, the next command or script in sequence executes.

Comments

Comments are placed in shell scripts so you and others understand what the programmer was thinking when he created the script. Anyone who has write permission to the script can place comments in it. This way, when the time comes for modification, you have a complete understanding of the programming that has already taken place. Accurate comments are essential to the programming process. Inaccurate comments are worse than no comments at all because they lead you to think one way when the program is doing something completely different. You implement or place comments by using the # symbol anywhere on a line. Commands or text following the # symbol will *not* be executed.

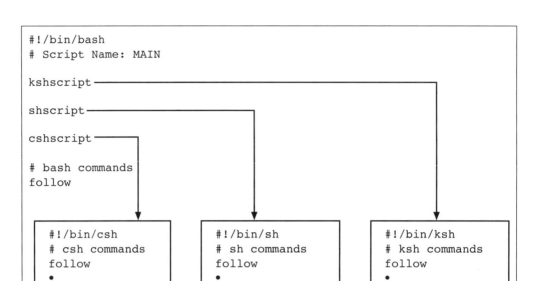

Figure 5-4   Specifying command interpreters in scripts

The use of # for comments causes the shell to ignore the line. You can place comments prior to a command to cause the shell to ignore the command. This can be useful if you are testing new statements in a script but are not sure if these statements will work as you've planned. For example, # pwd causes the shell to treat the **pwd** command as part of the comment text following the # symbol. If the # symbol were removed, the **pwd** command would execute normally.

In general, there should be a comment section at the beginning of every script so it is the first thing someone opening your script sees. Comments should contain the author of the script, a description of the script, the name and version number of the script, required parameters, the date modified, and a description of the modification. Figure 5-5 shows a script that uses comments. Note this is only a partial script.

At times, you may want to place comments close to actual code statements. In the following example, a comment is placed prior to each statement indicating what the next statement will do.

```
# Computes the new salary for the sales representatives
((Salary=$Salary+$Bonus))
# Displays the output to the screen
echo "Salary for $SalesPerson is $Salary and bonus amount is $Bonus"
```

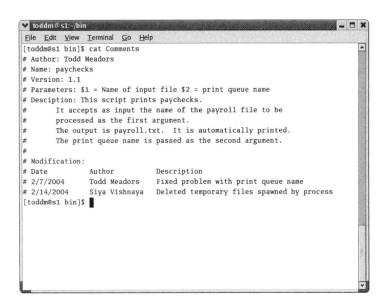

```
[toddm@s1 bin]$ cat Comments
# Author: Todd Meadors
# Name: paychecks
# Version: 1.1
# Parameters: $1 = Name of input file $2 = print queue name
# Description: This script prints paychecks.
#       It accepts as input the name of the payroll file to be
#       processed as the first argument.
#       The output is payroll.txt.  It is automatically printed.
#       The print queue name is passed as the second argument.
#
# Modification:
# Date          Author          Description
# 2/7/2004      Todd Meadors    Fixed problem with print queue name
# 2/14/2004     Siya Vishnaya   Deleted temporary files spawned by process
[toddm@s1 bin]$
```

Figure 5-5   Use of comments in a script

In this next example, comments are placed to the right of commands. Each command executes normally because the # symbol follows, rather than *precedes* the command. You see this approach used often in shell scripts because it saves space in the script file and places the comment closer to the actual command it references.

```
pwd     # Prints current directory
ls −l   # Displays a long listing
```

Although time consuming, the use of comments can reduce the time it takes to make modifications to the script. Even if you are the only one modifying the script, you should use comments. It's not unheard of for experienced System Administrators or programmers to sometimes forget why they wrote something a certain way when they created the script. Although placing comments in your script may take some time now, it will save a lot of time later when you need to remember why you did something.

Variables

A **variable** is used to represent data. It is composed of the variable name and the data, or contents. For example, the variable name "x" may have the number 5 as its data. The variable can be assigned by setting x to 5 as in the statement **x=5**. The contents of a variable are held in memory while in use. You can think of a variable as a cell in a spreadsheet.

A variable is sometimes called a field or a data name. To refer to the contents of a variable in the bash shell script, you precede the variable name with a dollar sign, $, as in $NetPay. For example, the command echo $NetPay displays the contents of the variable named NetPay.

Programmers try to assign variable names that describe the data they contain. For example, if the data contains a net pay amount, then a descriptive name assignment would be NetPay or NET_PAY. Programmers also make the variable names readable. For example, the variable named inventoryquantityonhand is not very easy to read. Unfortunately, most programming languages, including shell scripts, do not allow you to place a space or a hyphen between the words in the variable name. The variable names Net Pay and Net-Pay are not allowed. So, a programmer places underscores between the words of the name, uses common abbreviations, or capitalizes the first letter of each word to make the variable easier to read when reviewing a script. Thus, the following variable names would be acceptable: InventoryQuantityOnHand, InvQtyOnHand, QuantityOnHand, or Qty_On_Hand.

You can also indicate the type of data that a variable can contain as well as the size of the data. For example, if you have a variable such as NetPay and you know it should contain only numbers, you can indicate that NetPay is a numeric or an integer data type. For variables that only contain characters, you define them as a character string. When you define the size of the variable, you need to make the size large enough to hold all of the data. For example, if you define a character field to be five characters, and you try to store data with more than five characters, the data would be truncated on the right.

Variable declaration is the act of specifically defining the variable name and type. When you declare a variable, memory space is allocated for the variable's name and type. It is a good idea to define your variables near the beginning of your script or just prior to using them in a script. There are two commands that allow you to declare a variable in a script. They are the **declare** command and the **typeset** command. Their functions are identical. For example, to declare a variable as an integer for arithmetic evaluation and another variable as integer and read-only, you enter the following:

```
declare —i TotalSales
declare —i —r InterestRate
```

 The shell dynamically creates variables for you if you don't declare them. However, you have much greater control over the type of data they can contain, when you declare them manually.

Initialization is the act of setting a variable to a beginning value. Although not required, it is advisable to set your variables to initial values so you know what they contain prior to using them. In the case of setting integer variables, you will most likely set your initial values to zero, for example, **NetPay=0**. You can either initialize your variable in an initialization section at the beginning of your script or in the script prior to using the variable.

A variable that has been initialized, or set, can be unset with the shell `unset` command. For example, to unset the variable named MonthlySales that has previously been set to a value, you enter `unset MonthlySales`.

Next you will create a script that contains comments, variable declarations, and initialization statements to further your understanding of these topics.

To understand how to implement comments, variable declarations, and initialization statements in a script:

1. Log in to the Linux system as a user, and then open a Terminal emulation window.

2. Create a script named **BasicComponents** in the **$HOME/bin** directory.

3. Insert the following lines of code to initialize the shell interpreter, add comments, declare and set a variable, and display a variable's contents. (*Note*: put your name in place of *your_name* and today's date in place of *today's_date*):

```
#!/bin/bash
# Author: your_name
# Date: today's_date
declare SalesRegion
SalesRegion="Eastern"
echo "The sales region is:" $SalesRegion
```

4. Make sure you save the script, close **vi**, and change permissions so you can execute the script by name.

5. Execute the script. The script displays "The sales region is: Eastern" on the screen.

6. Close your window and then log out.

UNDERSTANDING PARAMETERS

It is important to understand parameters because they allow you to provide a script with data. This allows you to make your scripts much more flexible because you can vary the data that goes into the script. Also, parameters give you information such as the status of a statement or the number of parameters entered. A **parameter** is a name, number, or special character that stores a value. A parameter is considered to be set if it has a value and can be set to a number, letters, or the null value. Null means the variable is set to no value.

There are two types of parameters used by the shell:

- Positional parameters
- Special parameters

Positional Parameters

You can make a shell script more flexible using positional parameters to apply values within your script. The parameters are called "positional" because they refer to the numeric position of the value in the list that follows the script's name. Once the values are given to the script, you can use these values within the script itself. You use positional parameters by entering the shell script name followed by multiple values on the command line. The general form for using positional parameters is:

```
script-name value1 value2 value3…value9
```

This is where *value1*, *value2*, *value3*, and so forth are positional values given, or passed, to the shell script. The positional parameters are called by number—1, 2, 3 and so on, and respectively represent *value1*, *value2*, *value3*, through *value9*.

You will learn how to pass more than nine parameters using additional commands later in this chapter.

If you want to refer to the contents of a parameter, you precede the parameter with a dollar sign ($) followed by its positional number. So, the positional parameter $1 receives the value specified as *value1*. The positional parameter $2 receives the value specified as *value2*. The name of successive parameters is incremented by one until you reach $9. The $0 parameter takes the value of the actual script name itself.

You cannot use $0 for passing values to the script.

Look at the following single line shell script named display_it below:

```
echo $1 $2
```

The display_it shell script displays two positional parameters in this example. The programmer does not know what the data is at the time the script is written. That is what makes positional parameters so flexible. The programmer does need to know how many parameters to account for. To enter the values for this shell script, you enter the following:

```
display_it a b
```

The first value, "a," is passed to the script as $1. The second value, "b," is passed to the script as $2. When executed, this shell script displays the values "a" and "b" on the screen. Figure 5-6 offers further explanation of this example.

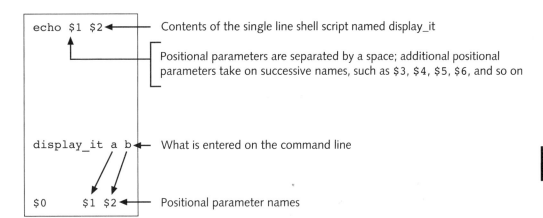

Figure 5-6   Understanding positional parameters

The benefit of using positional parameters is that you are able to write scripts that refer to parameters regardless of the value. This is a powerful feature of shell scripting. You can give a script many values and refer to the positional parameter name to get the actual value. You could rerun the previous script as **display_it The End** to display the text "The" and "End" on the screen. This is just an example. You could execute the script to display any two values as long as you separated them on the command line by a space.

You can also use positional parameters in conjunction with commands. For example, you can create a script to display the contents of a directory and pass the directory name as a positional parameter on the command line. The following code demonstrates how you can modify the ListRoot script to accept any directory as the first positional parameter.

```
cd $1
ls
pwd
```

For example, to execute this script and pass the /tmp directory to it, you enter **ListRoot /tmp**. The first positional parameter is /tmp. Thus, the script changes directory locations to /tmp, displays a listing of that directory, and then displays the present working directory.

 The shell knows when one value ends and the other begins by using the builtin variable named IFS, which stands for Internal Field Separator. It is set to space, tab, and newline and uses these as default separators. So, by entering display_it The End on the command line, the shell looks for either a space, tab, or newline to delimit each value. That's why "The" sets to $1 and "End" sets to $2.

Next, you will use your knowledge of expression from Chapter 3 to create a script that adds any two numbers passed to it.

To create a script that accepts and sums two positional parameters:

1. Log in to the Linux system as a user, and then open a Terminal emulation window.

2. Change to the **$HOME/bin** directory.

3. Open the **vi** editor.

4. Type the following lines of code to create a variable named Sum1 that is the sum of two positional parameters, and then display the Sum1 on the screen:

   ```
   ((Sum1 = $1 + $2))
   echo $Sum1
   ```

5. Save the script as **AddThem**, and then exit **vi**.

6. To make it executable, type **chmod ugo+x AddThem**, and then press **Enter**.

7. To execute the script, type **AddThem 10 5**, and then press **Enter**. The sum of 15 is displayed.

8. Rerun the script and pass the values 500 and 200 respectively. The sum of 700 is displayed.

9. Close your window, and then log out.

Now, you have created a shell script that is flexible in terms of data that can be passed to it.

Next, you need to understand what happens when you have more than nine positional parameters that you want to pass to a shell script. To accomplish this you use the **shift** command. The **shift** command allows you to use more values in the shell by shifting them around. The general form is:

```
shift n
```

This is where *n* is a number that indicates how many positional parameters to shift. Take a look at the following shell script named ShiftThem:

```
echo $1 $2 $3 $4 $5 $6 $7 $8 $9
shift 1
echo $1 $2 $3 $4 $5 $6 $7 $8 $9
```

If you executed the script as follows:

```
ShiftThem 1 2 3 4 5 6 7 8 9 10
```

The output would be:

```
1 2 3 4 5 6 7 8 9
2 3 4 5 6 7 8 9 10
```

Figure 5-7 shows the flow of the **shift** command in action.

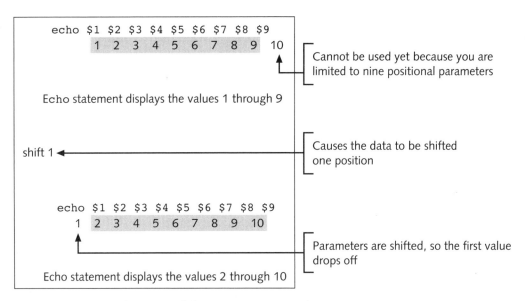

Figure 5-7 An explanation of the shift command

Figure 5-8 displays the script called ShiftThem along with the output of its execution.

```
toddm@s1:~/bin                                        - □ ✕
File  Edit  View  Terminal  Go  Help
[toddm@s1 bin]$ cat ShiftThem
echo $1 $2 $3 $4 $5 $6 $7 $8 $9
shift 1
echo $1 $2 $3 $4 $5 $6 $7 $8 $9
[toddm@s1 bin]$ ShiftThem 1 2 3 4 5 6 7 8 9 10
1 2 3 4 5 6 7 8 9
2 3 4 5 6 7 8 9 10
[toddm@s1 bin]$ ▌
```

Figure 5-8 The ShiftThem script and the output of its execution

What would happen if you shifted the positional parameters more than one number, for instance, three positions? The answer is that the positional parameters shift the number you specify, or three in this case. Figure 5-9 shows a breakdown of shifting three parameters.

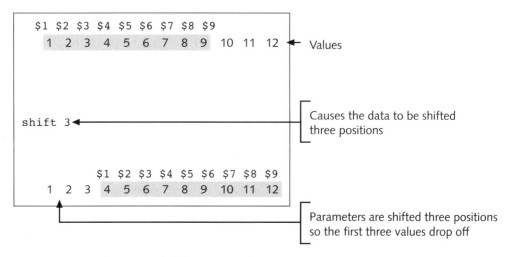

Figure 5-9   Explanation of shifting more than one parameter

Let's take a look at a practical implementation using the **shift** command. Imagine you need to add together 10 donations raised at a charity auction. Because you can only pass nine arguments to a script at one time, you have to shift the values to different positional parameters. The script, named DonatedSum, follows:

```
((DonatedSum=$1 + $2 + $3 + $4 + $5 + $6 + $7 + $8 + $9 ))
shift 9
((DonatedSum=$DonatedSum + $1))
echo $DonatedSum
```

In this sample code, the variable named DonatedSum is equal to the summation of the first nine positional parameters. Next, the **shift 9** command shifts the parameters to the right nine positions so the new value of **$1** becomes the 10th parameter. The parameter **$1** no longer contains the first value. Figure 5-10 shows the DonatedSum script with output. The variable sum contains the summation of the values of all of the positional parameters.

Next you will create a script that uses shifting positional parameters.

To create a script that shifts positional parameters:

1. Log in to the Linux system as a user, and then open a Terminal emulation window.

2. Change to the **$HOME/bin** directory.

3. Open the **vi** editor.

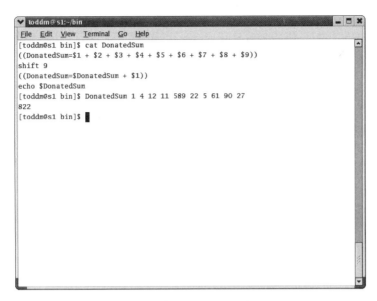

Figure 5-10   The DonatedSum script with output

4. Type the following lines of code to create a script that shifts the parameters two times:

```
echo $1 $2 $3 $4 $5 $6 $7 $8 $9
shift 5
echo $1 $2 $3 $4 $5 $6 $7 $8 $9
shift 2
echo $1 $2 $3 $4 $5 $6 $7 $8 $9
```

5. Save the file as **ShiftThemAgain**, and then close `vi`.

6. Type **chmod ugo+x ShiftThemAgain**, and then press **Enter**.

7. To execute the script, type **ShiftThemAgain 1 2 3 4 5 6 7 8 9 10 11 12 13 14 15 16**, and then press **Enter**.

8. Rerun the script and pass 16 different values to it on the command line.

9. Close your window, and then log out.

Now you have created a script for passing and shifting values. You can modify it as you see fit. Consider the potential tasks for which you could use this script. How might you modify it to make it best serve your needs?

As you can see, it is an advantage to be able to pass parameters to a script. However, the names of the positional parameters do not describe the data they contain, and this can seem like a complication whether you are using two parameters or several. Fortunately, you can have positional parameters take on more descriptive names. For example, if $1 represented someone's name and $2 represented his salary, you could write a shell script that set the variables to the positional parameters. Review the shell script, named NameSalary:

```
Name=$1
Salary=$2
echo $Name
echo $Salary
```

You could execute the script as `NameSalary "Jose Cruz" 50000`. In the above script, the first statement, the variable named "Name" contains the contents of the first parameter, which is "Jose Cruz." Quotes are required so the shell knows that both the first and last name represents the first positional parameter. If you leave the quotes off, the shell interprets "Jose" as `$1` and "Cruz" as `$2`, or Salary.

In the second statement, the variable named Salary contains the contents of the second parameter. Finally, the two `echo` statements display the contents of the Name and Salary variables, respectively.

The benefit of setting a descriptive name to equal the contents of a positional parameter is you can reference the data by using a variable that actually describes the data. In other words, `$Name`, brings to mind someone's name, whereas `$1` does not. You can later refer to Name and feel confident this variable contains someone's name, and this makes modifications to your script easier. Figure 5-11 shows the NameSalary script as well as two executions of that script and their output. The first command, `cat NameSalary`, displays the contents of the script. The second command, `NameSalary "Jose Dutch" 50000`, executes it correctly because quotes are included around the name. However, the third command, `NameSalary Jose Dutch 50000`, executes the script incorrectly; notice there are no quotes around the name Jose Dutch.

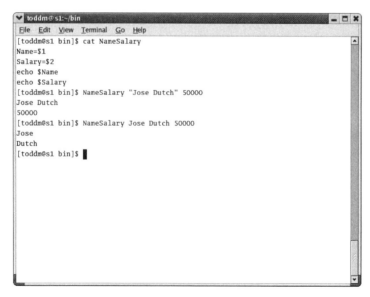

Figure 5-11   NameSalary script along with two executions and their respective output

Special Parameters

The shell uses special parameters to perform specific tasks such as referring to such items as the number of positional parameters given to a script, the name of the script, the PID of the shell, or the status of a command. Special parameters cannot be assigned values by you. You can only reference the contents of special parameters using the special parameter symbols. The actual symbols expand into other values. Some of the special parameters used by the shell are described in Table 5-3.

Table 5-3   Description of some of the special parameters used by the shell

Special Parameter	Description
@	Expands into all of the positional parameters starting at 1
#	Expands to the number of positional parameters
?	Expands to the exit status of the command previously executed as a foreground process
$	Expands to the PID of the shell
!	Expands to the PID of the previously executed background process

As with positional parameters, in order to reference a special parameter, you must precede it with the dollar sign ($). For example, if you wanted to display the current PID of your shell, you would enter `echo  $$` at the command line. By combining text with special parameters you can create more user-friendly scripts. For example, if you place the command `echo "The number of parameters is:"  $#` in a script, the command displays the text "The number of parameters is:" followed by the actual number of parameters passed to the script.

Take a look at the code for the sample script named ExitStatus shown in Figure 5-12, which utilizes the special parameter `$?` to determine the exit status of a previously executed command. Notice also that Figure 5-12 includes a breakdown of how each line of code functions.

Recall that an exit status of zero indicates success, and a nonzero exit status indicates failure. Thus, the second `rm payroll.dat` will fail because the file was previously removed. Figure 5-13 shows the output of this script, showing both the successful and failed exit statuses.

Of course, this is merely an example, you would not place two `rm` statements in tandem that remove the same file. However, what you can learn from this is that you can use the exit status to determine if a command failed or not. If the script did fail, you could send a message to the user, append the message to a file, or both.

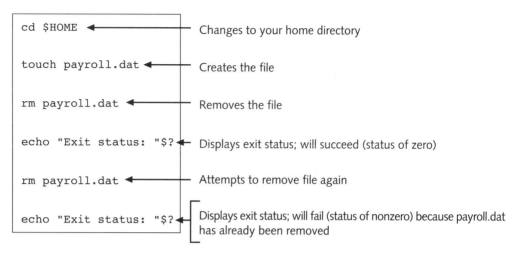

Figure 5-12   Code and its explanation for the ExitStatus script

Figure 5-13   The ExitStatus script and its output

Next you will further your understanding of special parameters.

To understand special parameters:

1. Log in to the Linux system as a user, and then open a Terminal emulation window.

2. Create a script named **SpecialParams** in the **$HOME/bin** directory.

3. Insert the following lines of code, noting that the command named `pwdx` intentionally fails and the resulting exit status reflects this:

```
pwd
echo "Exit status of last command is:" $?
pwdx
echo "Exit status of last command is:" $?
echo "Script name is:" $0
echo "The number of parameters passed is:" $#
```

4. Save the script, close **vi**, and then change the file permissions so you can execute the script by name.

5. Execute the script. The script executes and displays an exit status of zero for the command that runs correctly and displays a nonzero exit status for the invalid or incorrect command. Figure 5-14 shows the contents of the SpecialParams script followed by its output.

6. Close your window, and then log out.

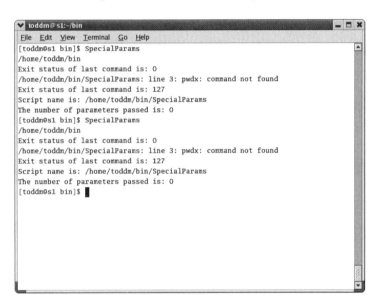

Figure 5-14   The contents of the SpecialParams script and its output

Using a Usage Clause

You can use the special parameter `$#` to determine if the appropriate number of parameters are entered by the user. This implementation is called a usage clause. A **usage clause** is a statement that displays a message indicating how to execute the script if it is executed incorrectly. Usage clauses are typically used with positional parameters that are entered on the command line following the script name. For example, if a script requires three positional parameters, and you only enter two of them, the script can detect that only two were entered, and then display a usage clause indicating how to execute the script successfully. The special parameter $#, used to reference the total number of positional parameters, is used in an if statement. (The details of if statements are covered in Chapter 6.) The following example checks to see if three positional parameters have been entered on the command line. The special parameter contains the actual number of positional parameters entered, in this case three. If a programmer enters less than three parameters, then a usage clause message is displayed. Finally, any subsequent statements execute.

```
if [ $# -lt 3 ]
then
        echo "Usage $0 value1 value2 value3"
fi
```

Figure 5-15 shows a sample script that contains the components used in this section.

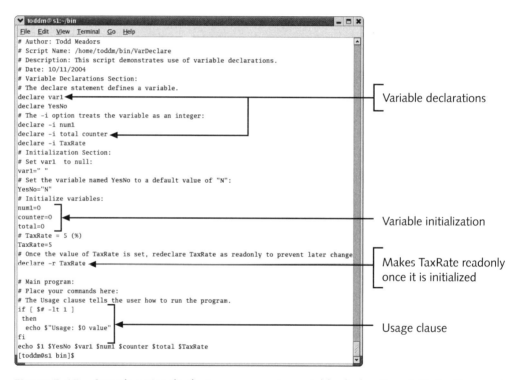

Figure 5-15   Sample script displaying comments, variable declaration, initialization, and a usage clause

CREATING INTERACTIVE SCRIPTS

Although you can use positional parameters to input data into a script, there is another approach that allows you to prompt the user for data called the **interactive method**. The interactive method uses the **read** command to prompt for user input.

The benefit of using the **read** command is that you can prompt users for input at the time you need the input. With positional parameters, all of the input must be known prior to command execution. With the **read** command, you can create a descriptive variable name to contain the data without having to rename it as you saw in an earlier section of this chapter. Later, in the script, you can refer to the data by using the variable name. There are no positional parameter names to worry about.

A common use of the **read** command in scripts is when you want a user to respond with either "Yes" or "No" to a prompt such as "Do you want to continue?". The **read** command follows the general format:

```
read variable-name
```

This is where **variable-name** is the name of a variable, not a positional parameter. Once you read data in the variable name, you can display the data by referencing the variable by name. Look at this simple example.

```
read value1
echo $value1
```

In this script there are two statements. The first statement reads data from the keyboard and places it into a variable named value1. The shell waits for the user input data followed by Enter. The second statement displays the variable's content on the screen.

You can make the script a bit more user-friendly by indicating the type of data you are requesting from the user. If you precede the **read** statement with the **echo -n** statement, you can display a message, thereby letting the user know what he or she needs to enter. The **-n** option of the **echo** statement suppresses a newline, so the cursor does not move to the next line. Next, you will use the **read** command to accept data.

To understand the read command:

1. Log in to the Linux system as a user, and then open a Terminal emulation window.

2. Create a script named **ReadHobby** in the **$HOME/bin** directory

3. Type the following lines of code to display a message statement, read the value entered, and then display the value:

```
echo -n "Enter your favorite hobby:"
read hobby
echo "You entered:" $hobby
```

4. Save the script, close **vi**, change the file permissions so you can execute the script by name, and then execute the script. Refer to Figure 5-16 and you see the contents of the script and execution with the text "Weight Lifting" entered into the script. Once entered, the text is displayed.

5. Modify the script to remove the **−n** option of the **echo** statement.

6. Execute the script again noticing the difference when using the **−n** option and not using it.

7. Close your window, and then log out.

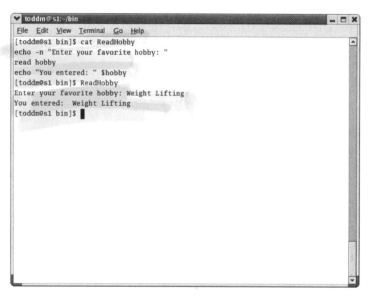

Figure 5-16 ReadHobby script and its output

Like many of the other commands that you've learned about, the **read** command has some important options. They are listed in Table 5-4.

Table 5-4 Some options used by the **read** command

Option	Description
−p *prompt*	Use to display *prompt* as a text message to prompt the user for input; this is an alternative to using the **echo** −n statement
−s	Use to suppress echoing characters on the screen; useful for suppressing passwords
−t *timeout*	Use to time out, or expire, the command once *timeout* seconds have been exceeded
−a *array-name*	Use to read data into an array (arrays are discussed in Chapter 8)

Let's use a few of these options in the following script:

```
read -t 3 -s -p "Enter password:" password
echo $password
```

In the first statement of this script, the **read** command displays the text "Enter password:" on the screen which is the text for the prompt that follows the **-p** option. The **-s** option suppresses the characters displayed on the screen when the user enters characters in response to the prompt. The data is placed in the variable named password. The **-t 3** option specifies that if a key is not pressed within three seconds, the command times out, or stops. Processing then continues with the next statement.

 You don't have to use all of the options on the **read** command at the same time. You can use each option individually.

Protecting a Variable

Once you have set a variable, there may be times when you don't want it to change. What can you do to protect the contents of your variable against accidental change once its value has been set? You can use the **readonly** command to ensure that another user cannot change the variable.

The advantage of using the **readonly** command is that you are able to protect the contents of a variable. This can prove useful for constant values you don't want to change once set. An example might be the tax rate. You may want the user to enter a tax rate for different states. If the tax rate is entered as 5, for 5%, you don't want this to be changed to a different value later in the script. Use of the **readonly** command in this case serves to protect the value of the variable. Look at the following sample code for a script named ZipCode:

```
read -p "Enter Zip Code: " Zip
echo "Zip Code is: " $Zip
readonly Zip
read -p "Attempting to change Zip Code: " Zip
echo "Zip Code is: " $Zip
```

Figure 5-17 displays the ZipCode script output. Notice the value is initially set to "30044." Next, the variable is set to read-only. Then, there is an attempt to set it to "60505," resulting in an error because the variable is read-only. The last statement displays the original value, "30044."

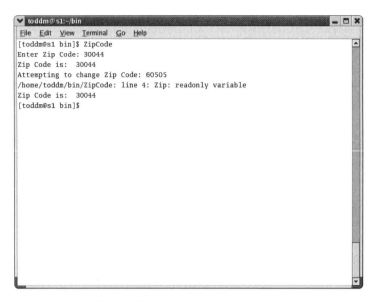

Figure 5-17   The ZipCode script output

UNDERSTANDING DEBUGGING

One important aspect of learning any programming language is understanding how to debug a program. **Debugging** is troubleshooting errors that may occur during the execution of a script. You need to understand debugging techniques so you can quickly and effectively locate an error and correct it. The following two commands can help you debug a shell script:

- echo
- set

Using echo

The simplest method you can utilize for debugging is to use the **echo** statement to display the contents of a variable at different points in the script. Recall the ZipCode script; the **echo** statement is used there to display the contents of a variable. First, the data is entered, and then it is displayed on the screen. If you are only using the **echo** statement for debugging purposes, you should consider removing it once the user works with the script to keep your script clean and to the point. While displaying additional values may help you, especially when you are debugging, these values may just confuse other users.

Although the **echo** statement can show you the value in a variable or parameter, it cannot very easily show you the flow in a script. To accomplish this, you use the **set** command.

Using set

Another approach to debugging is to use the **set** command. The **set** command is a shell builtin command that has numerous options. Two of its options used in combination allow you to see line by line what is going on in the script. You want to use this approach if you need to understand the logical flow of a script. The **-v** option prints each line as it is read. The **-x** option displays the command and its arguments. You can arrange the options in any order with the **set** command.

 You should not keep the **set** options on for users. The **set** command gives them too much detail and may result in unnecessary phone calls asking for help.

The minus sign allows you to use the options. You turn the options off using the plus sign. For example, **set -xv**, turns the options on while **set +xv** turns them off. Although this may seem contradictory, it is how they work.

Generally, you place the statement **set -xv** at the beginning of the script or immediately prior to the statement you want to begin debugging. You place the statement **set +xv** at the end of the script or someplace in the script where you are certain you no longer need it. Next you will use the **set** command to debug the ZipCode script.

To understand the set statements in order to debug:

1. Log in to the Linux system as a user, and then open a Terminal emulation window.

2. Create a script named **ZipCode** in the **$HOME/bin** directory. This is the same code that is used to create the results shown in Figure 5-17.

3. To set debugging on, enter the following statement as the first line of the script:

```
set -xv
```

4. Now, enter the code for the script:

```
read -p "Enter Zip Code: " Zip
echo "Zip Code is: " $Zip
readonly Zip
read -p "Attempting to change Zip Code: " Zip
echo "Zip Code is: " $Zip
```

5. To set debugging off, enter the following statement as the last line of the script:

```
set +xv
```

6. Save the script, and then close **vi**.

7. Change the file permissions so you can execute the script by name, and then execute the script. Type **30044** at the first prompt for setting the value of Zip. Type **44440** at the second prompt where you attempt to change the Zip Code.

The result is you cannot change the value at the second prompt. Also, extra text is displayed due to debugging. Figure 5-18 shows the ZipCode script with debugging options. The first statement simply displays the contents of the ZipCode script. The second statement is the script's execution. Notice as the script runs, the two plus symbols, ++, are located to the left of the statement as it is executing.

8. Close your window, and then log out.

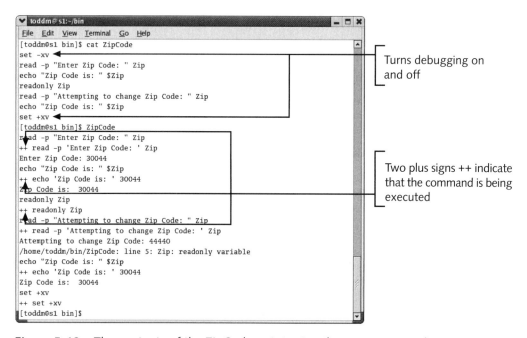

Figure 5-18   The contents of the ZipCode script using the set command

 You can also use a command named `script` for debugging purposes. You run the command prior to executing the script. When the script is finished, press Ctrl+D to terminate the `script` command. The output is contained in a file named "typescript." This is very similar to using the `set` command.

CHAPTER SUMMARY

- Programs execute statements sequentially, or one after the other. Because a shell script is a program, it follows the same rule. You can break down the logic of a problem's solution into pseudocode using statements that are not specific to the programming language. A pseudocode statement describes what is needed to accomplish a task without being concerned with the actual syntax of the language.

- In managing shell scripts, you must be aware of two factors: modifying the permissions of a script and placement of the script. You use the chmod command to modify a script's permissions. In order to execute the script by simply specifying the script's name on the command line, you need to give the script execute permission and place the script in a directory that is on the search path. The $PATH variable contains a list of directories that are searched when the shell attempts to locate a command.

- To have a complete understanding of the basic components of a script you need to be familiar with how to use comments, specify the command interpreter, manage variables, and use a usage clause. You should place comments in your script to describe the goal of the script. The comments should include your name, the date, the name of the script, required positional parameters, and any modifications you make to your script. Comments tell others what your script is doing. You should also specify the command interpreter to ensure that all commands are running in the correct shell. Variable names need to describe their contents. You should declare and initialize all variables used in your program. Also, you should use a usage clause when using positional parameters in a script.

- The shell uses two types of parameters—positional parameters and special parameters. Positional parameters allow you to place values on the command line following the script's name. This data can be used inside the script. The positional parameters range from 0 to 9. The $0 positional parameter represents the script's name. If you have more than nine, you must shift the parameters using the shift command. The shell uses special parameters to accomplish tasks such as displaying the exit status of a command or displaying the number of parameters passed to a script. You cannot change special parameters. The most useful special parameter is ? which is used for checking exit status.

- You can create scripts that allow for user interaction by using the read command. This allows you more control over the variable names because you can define their names at the time you ask for input. You can use the readonly command to prevent a variable's contents from changing.

- You can debug your script with the set -xv command. This command displays each line and variable as it is executed. The set +xv command turns off debugging. You can also use the echo command to display the contents of variables. However, make sure you delete or comment out the echo statement when you no longer need them for debugging purposes.

5

REVIEW QUESTIONS

1. _____ describes a set of statements that establish the logic of actual program code.

   a. Script

   b. Machine code

   c. Pseudocode

   d. Binary executable

2. Which of the following uses the bash shell for the command interpreter in a script?

   a. `/bin/bash`

   b. `# /bin/bash`

   c. `!/bin/bash`

   d. `#!/bin/bash`

3. What is the name of the directory located in your home directory that is usually on the search path? (If a script is in this directory, it can be executed without entering the full path name of the script.)

   a. `$HOME/bin`

   b. /bin

   c. /usr/local/bin

   d. `$PATH`

4. What is the name of the shell builtin variable that is used for searching directories when you enter a command or script name?

   a. `$HOME`

   b. `$ENV`

   c. `$$`

   d. `$PATH`

5. What does the positional parameter `$0` reference?

   a. the first parameter following the script name

   b. the exit status of the previous command

   c. the name of the script

   d. the very last positional parameter

6. _____ is the concept of setting a variable to a beginning value.

   a. Declaration

   b. Initialization

   c. Usage clause

   d. A signal

7. The _____ command is used to set and unset permissions.

   a. `trap`

   b. `kill`

   c. `echo`

   d. `chmod`

8. The _____ command allows you to use more than nine positional parameters.

   a. `trap`

   b. `kill`

   c. `shift`

   d. `chmod`

9. What special parameter is used to determine the exit status of a previously executed command?

   a. `*`

   b. `?`

   c. `#`

   d. `0`

10. What command sets the permissions of a file named payroll.dat to be read, write, and execute for the owner; read and execute for the group; and no access for others?

    a. `chmod 750 payroll.dat`

    b. `chmod 742 payroll.dat`

    c. `chmod 057 payroll.dat`

    d. `chmod 776 payroll.dat`

11. You can implement _____ to indicate to a user how many positional parameters to pass to a script.

    a. a declaration of an integer

    b. an initialization of a variable

    c. a usage clause

    d. pseudocode

12. You use the _____ symbol to mark the beginning of a comment in a script.

    a. !

    b. #

    c. $

    d. <

13. What command sets the permissions of a directory named HumanResources to be read, write, and execute for the owner; read and write for the group; and read for others?

    a. `chmod 764 HumanResources`

    b. `chmod 744 HumanResources`

    c. `chmod 742 HumanResources`

    d. `chmod 706 HumanResources`

14. You can use the _____ command to retrieve data interactively in a script.

    a. `readonly`

    b. `read`

    c. `echo $1`

    d. `shift`

15. What command is used to define a variable as an integer?

    a. `declare -i`

    b. `define -i`

    c. `shift`

    d. `readonly`

16. The _____ command is used to prevent a variable from changing.

    a. `read`

    b. `declare`

    c. `shift`

    d. `readonly`

17. What is the result of the following script?

```
#!/bin/bash
# echo $1 $2
echo $3
echo $?
```

    a. The positional parameters, $1, $2, and $3, and the total number of positional parameters are displayed.

    b. The positional parameters, $1, $2, and $3, and the exit status are displayed.

c. The positional parameter $3 and the exit status are displayed.

d. The positional parameter $3 and the number of positional parameters are displayed.

18. You use the _____ command to determine the PID of a process.

a. ps

b. declare

c. grep

d. readonly

19. You use the _____ command to debug a script.

a. set -xv

b. set +xv

c. grep

d. read

20. What special parameter is used to determine the number of positional parameters passed to a script?

a. *

b. ?

c. #

d. 0

HANDS-ON PROJECTS

Project 5-1

In this project, you will turn pseudocode into an actual shell script.

1. Log in to the Linux system as a user, and then open a Terminal emulation window.

2. Create a shell script named **Project5-1** in your **$HOME/bin** directory for the following pseudocode:

> *Turn debugging on.*
> *Place a reference to the bash shell interpreter in the script.*
> *Place some appropriate comments at the beginning of your script.*
> *Redirect the date to a new file named /tmp/list.txt.*
> *Append a listing of the current users tothe same file.*
> *Append the contents of the search path variable to this same file.*
> *Copy /tmp/list.txt to your home directory and name it $HOME/Project5-1.txt.*
> *Remove the file named /tmp/list.txt.*
> *Turn debugging off.*

3. Save the script, close the editor, make the script executable, and then execute your script.

4. Close your window, and then log out.

Project 5-2

In this project, you will write a script that calculates an average of five values passed as positional parameters.

1. Log in to the Linux system as a user, and then open a Terminal emulation window.
2. Create a script named **Project5-2** in the **$HOME/bin** directory.
3. Insert a reference to the bash shell, appropriate comments, and your name as author.
4. Accept five positional parameters from the command line.
5. Display all five values on the screen.
6. Display a usage clause if the incorrect number of values is entered.
7. Display an average of the five values.
8. Save the script, close the editor, make the script executable, and then execute the script.
9. Record the output.
10. Close your window, and then log out.

Project 5-3

In this project, you will shift positional parameters. You will pass 13 numbers to a script, and then display their sum. You will also modify one of the scripts, named sum1, used as an exercise in this chapter. You will use sum1 as a guide to complete this project.

1. Log in to the Linux system as a user, and then open a Terminal emulation window.
2. Copy **sum1** to **Project5-3** in the **$HOME/bin** directory.
3. Insert a reference to the bash shell with the appropriate comments, including your name as the author. Indicate that this is a modification of the original script, the date of modification, and a description of the modification (see Steps 4 through 8).
4. Clear the screen with the **clear** command.
5. Display the script name. (*Hint*: Use **$0**.)
6. Display today's date.
7. Allow the script to accept 13 values.
8. Display the sum of the 13 values.
9. Save the script, close the editor, make the script executable, and then execute the script.
10. Close your window, and then log out.

Project 5-4

In this project, you will perform calculations in interactive scripts using the **read** command to accept variables from the keyboard and display their average. You will modify the script created in Project 5-2 to read three numbers from the keyboard.

1. Log in to the Linux system as a user, and then open a Terminal emulation window.
2. Create a script named **Project5-4** in the **$HOME/bin** directory.
3. Read three values from the keyboard.
4. Declare the variables as integers, initialize the variables to zero, and then once the variables are read, make them read-only.
5. Set a timeout value of five seconds for each variable.
6. Display the contents of the variables.
7. Attempt to change them again.
8. Save the script, close the editor, make the script executable, and then execute the script.
9. Close your window, and then log out.

Project 5-5

In this project, you will perform exponentiation in interactive scripts using the **read** command to accept two variables and then raise one to the power of the other. Once the answer is displayed, you will unset all variables using the **unset** command.

1. Log in to the Linux system as a user, and then open a Terminal emulation window.
2. Create a script named **Project5-5** in the **$HOME/bin** directory.
3. Declare three variables as integer, x, y, and A. Read x and y in from the keyboard. Compute the answer, A, as x raised to the yth power, and then display the answer.
4. Unset the variable with the **unset** command.
5. Save the script, close the editor, make the script executable, and then execute the script.
6. Close your window, and then log out.

Project 5-6

In this project, you will create a script that accepts a variable. The variable will be suppressed, thereby emulating password entry. You will use the **read** command to accept a variable from the keyboard. When the variable is read, the characters must not be displayed back to the user on the screen.

1. Log in to the Linux system as a user, and then open a Terminal emulation window.
2. Create a script named **Project5-6** in the **$HOME/bin** directory.
3. Clear the screen, and then display the message "Enter password:" on the screen.

4. Read the variable for the password, but suppress characters from displaying on the screen as the user types them. Use a timeout value of your choosing to limit the amount of time the user has to enter the value.

5. Save the script, close the editor, make the script executable, and then execute the script.

6. Close the window, and then log out.

Project 5-7

In this project, you will perform computations on positional parameters as well as implement a usage clause by creating a script that calculates a net amount based on sales (less costs).

1. Log in to the Linux system as a user, and then open a Terminal emulation window.

2. Create a script named **Project5-7** in the **$HOME/bin** directory, and be sure to include the appropriate comments.

3. Set up the script to accept two positional parameters from the command line and display a usage clause if the incorrect number of values is entered.

4. Store the positional parameters as declared integers as follows:

```
Sales=$1
Costs=$2
```

5. Declare a variable named **Net** as an integer. It will contain the difference between Sales and Costs.

6. Calculate the difference between Sales and Costs using the variable named Net to display an appropriate message indicating the difference.

7. Save the script, close the editor, make the script executable, and then execute the script.

8. Close your window, and then log out.

Project 5-8

In this project, you will properly protect data on the command line when it is passed to a script by creating a script where you will pass positional parameters.

1. Log in to the Linux system as a user, and then open a Terminal emulation window.

2. Create a script named **Project5-8** in the **$HOME/bin** directory, and be sure to include the appropriate comments.

3. Clear the screen.

4. To accept name, address, city, state, phone number, fax number, and e-mail account from the command line, use the following positional parameters:

```
$1=name, $2=address, $3=city, $4=state, $5=phone number,
$6=fax number, and $7=email account.
```

Remember you are required to use double quotes in order to assign the value to the correct positional parameters.

5. Display a usage clause if the incorrect number of values is entered.

6. Display all parameters.

7. Save the script, close the editor, make the script executable, and then execute the script.

8. Run the script using the following data:

   Name: Rachael Sing

   Address: 100 East Windam Street

   City: Atlanta

   State: Georgia

   Phone: 555-555-5550

   Fax: 555-555-5551

   Email: rsing@domainname.com

9. Rerun the script with different data of your own choosing.

10. Record the output.

11. Close your window, and then log out.

CASE PROJECTS

Case 5-1

TMI needs help writing a script that calculates net pay. The script needs to support the 11 items of data that are listed below. (*Note*: you must use whole-number amounts.)

- Employee ID
- Gross Pay
- Federal Tax Amount
- Social Security Amount
- 401K Deduction Amount
- Medical Insurance
- Dental Insurance
- Vision Insurance
- Disability Insurance
- Legal Insurance
- Stock Purchase

To complete this case you need to write the pseudocode logic for this script, write the script using positional parameters where all parameters must have an amount even if it is 0, use integers only when inputting the data, use comments, reference the shell, include variable declaration and initialization, and add a usage clause where appropriate. Display the Employee's ID, the Gross Pay, all of the deductions and the Net Pay in an appropriate manner. (*Hint*: the Net Pay is the Gross Pay after all the deductions have been accounted for.)

Case 5-2

The Antonio Czechos Drywall Firm has hired you to help implement a directory structure for them based on Figure 5-19. Because you were called out of town to aid another customer, you cannot go to the site. In the meantime, you decide to write a script that will create the structure for them. To create the directory structure, complete the following tasks:

1. Write the pseudocode.
2. Write a script to create the directory structure shown in Figure 5-19.
3. The directory structure should start from the AC_Drywall directory from within your home directory.
4. Other issues:
   a. If the item has an extension, treat it as a file. Otherwise, consider it a directory.
   b. Note the hidden file.
   c. The Manager1.txt file must only have these permissions: read and write for the user owner and the group owners. Others should have no access.
   d. The Emp1.txt file must have all permissions turned on.

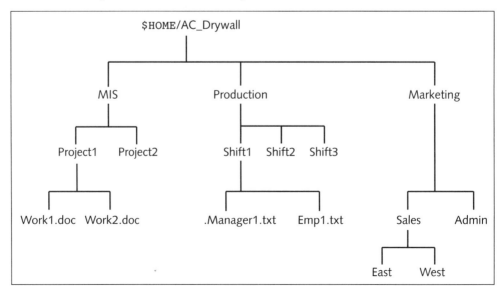

Figure 5-19   AC Drywall directory structure

6

DECISION STRUCTURES

> **In this chapter, you will:**
> - Understand decision-structure theory
> - Understand `if` statements
> - Use logical operators
> - Use the `elif` clause in an `if` statement
> - Nest `if` statements
> - Understand the `case` statement

You learned in Chapter 5 that each statement in a shell script is executed sequentially. There are programming structures, which allow you to change the sequential flow. Decision structures test for a condition and, based upon the result of that test, execute one set of statements or another, but not both. Shell scripts use the `if` statement and the `case` statement for decision making.

UNDERSTANDING DECISION-STRUCTURE THEORY

Before you learn about the decision statements, you need to understand how decision theory works in scripts. A **decision** is a choice made from possible alternatives based on some condition. You make decisions on a daily basis—deciding what to wear, choosing which movie to see, and scheduling time to study for a test. Once you've made your decisions, there is usually no turning back. For example, if you have just enough money for one movie, and you purchase a ticket for a specific one, you cannot go back and purchase another ticket for a different movie. You made your decision.

Here's another example. You probably have more than one route you can take from your home to your school. Let's say you are driving to school, but you are running a little late for the final exam for your programming class. You notice that the road ahead is blocked due to an accident. At this point, you must make a decision. Do you wait for the accident to clear, or do you take an alternate route? Let's say that the logic is that if the road is blocked, you will take the alternate route. Once your decision is made, you need to follow through on the chosen path.

A decision has one entry point and one exit point. In other words only one set of instructions can be followed based on the decision.

This type of decision making can be implemented in shell scripts as well. In writing your shell scripts, you may need to have the script make a decision about a condition before it takes a course of action. Once a decision is made, the script executes only one set of statements. In Linux you use the `if` statement as a form of decision making. It takes the following general form:

If condition then

  Do activity if condition is true

End-if

This is where *condition* is evaluated as either true or false. If the *condition* evaluates as true, then the activity immediately following it is performed. If the *condition* evaluates as false, then no *activity* is performed. The clause *End-if* is used to terminate the *if* logic in this pseudocode sample. Also, the term **clause** refers to words that are used in conjunction with a statement, such as *then* or *End-if*. The clause *then* is required in shell scripts as well as many other programming languages.

When referring to decision structures, the term "statement," or "command," is used to refer to an actual decision statement, such as `if`.

The `if` structure applies to all programming languages. As you are aware, you cannot implement the above logic in a shell script without converting it into the specific syntax for the shell's implementation of the `if` statement.

Here's how you can turn a decision into pseudocode logic. In the previous example, if the road is indeed blocked, you plan to take the alternate route. Otherwise, you continue on your normal path. Here is the pseudocode that demonstrates this decision:

Get ready for school

Drive to school

If road is blocked then

> *Take alternate route*

End-if

Take final exam

Statements that come before or after the `if` are unaffected by the condition it tests. Here is what happens. All statements are executed sequentially prior to the `if` statement. The `if` statement is then executed. Once the condition is evaluated, statements that follow `if` are executed sequentially as normal. For example, you *Get ready for school* and *Drive to school* in that order, before you deal with the `if` statement. Once the decision has been made regarding an alternate route, you still *Take final exam* once you arrive at school, regardless of the route taken. What would happen in the previous statement if the road were not blocked? The answer is that the condition of *If road is blocked then* would evaluate false. You would not take the alternate route but you would still take the final exam.

Flowcharts and Decision Making

In programming, one of the tools used to help you understand the logic of decisions is the flowchart. The **flowchart** uses symbols to help you understand the overall flow of a program. The flowchart symbols and their use are listed in Table 6-1.

Table 6-1 Description of the flowchart symbols

Name	Symbol	Usage
Oval		Used to indicate where the flowchart begins and ends
Parallelogram		Used to represent the input and output of data
Square		Used to represent a processing activity
Diamond		Used to represent a decision

Figure 6-1 shows a flowchart for the decision made while driving to school.

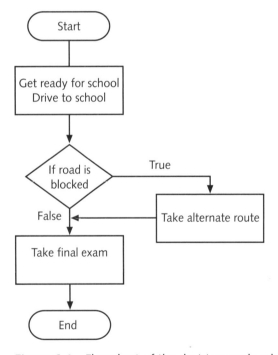

Figure 6-1 Flowchart of the decision made while driving to school

Understanding the *else* Decision Structure

What would you do if you wanted to perform an activity for the false condition of an *if* statement? Because the *if* statement tests for a true condition, you need to add logic to your *if* statement that handles the false condition. To do this, you use the *else* clause.

Here's how the *else* works. The condition is tested. If the condition tests true, then the code statements immediately following the `if` statement, stopping prior to the `else` clause, are executed. If the condition tests false, then the code statements immediately following the *else* clause, stopping prior to the *End-if* clause, are executed. Only one set of statements is executed, either the true condition statements or the false condition statements. Refer to the following pseudocode for logic using *else* in an *if* statement:

If condition then

> *Do activity if condition is true*

Else

> *Do activity if condition is false*

End-if

Here's an example to help understand this concept. The Blue Skydiving Company sells sky diving gear and rides. The management wants to determine if they earned a profit or incurred a loss this quarter.

Figure 6-2 shows the pseudocode that has been developed to evaluate the company's profitability. First the pseudocode determines the Sales and Costs amounts. Next, the Net difference is calculated. Then, a decision must be made. If the difference between Sales and Costs is greater than zero, then the company earned a profit and the profit amount is displayed. If the difference between Sales and Costs is not greater than zero, then the company incurred a loss and the amount of the loss is displayed. A third possibility is that the Sales and Costs could be the same, resulting in a zero difference.

Get Sales

Get Costs

Net=Sales-Costs

If Net>0 then

       Display "Profit of:"Net

Else

       Display "Loss of:"Net

End-if

Figure 6-2   Profitability pseudocode for the Blue Skydiving Company

UNDERSTANDING `if` STATEMENTS

You can implement decision theory in the shell similarly to how you do it using pseudocode. One of the statements the shell uses to make decisions is `if`. Understanding the syntax of `if` will help you to write it correctly in a script. If you misspell any word in the syntax, the script generates a syntax error and your script does not successfully execute. The syntax of the `if` statement is as follows:

```
if list
then
        statement1
        statement2
        ...
        statementN
fi
```

The `if`, `then`, and `fi` clauses are required. First, the commands in the *list* execute. (Refer to Chapter Three for a review of lists.) Then the *list* terminates with an exit status. The exit status is what is tested, not the commands in the *list*. If the exit status is zero, the command statements, *statement1* through *statementN*, following the `then` clause, but prior to the `fi` clause, are executed. If the exit status is nonzero, then the command statements are not executed. Processing continues with subsequent statements in the script. The clause `fi`, which is "if" spelled backwards, terminates the `if` statement.

An alternate way for writing the shell's `if` statement is using `else` to execute statements if the exit status of *list* is nonzero. The `else` clause is optional but is needed when you want to process commands when a false condition is reached. Using the `else` clause in an `if` statement takes the following form:

```
if list
then
        statements
else
        statements
fi
```

Notice the indention of statements within the `if` statement. Although indenting statements is not required, it makes the code more readable in case the script needs to be modified later. Generally, you indent the statements following `then` as shown in the various examples in the section.

To help you understand what this means, let's look at Figure 6-3 as an example. Sven's Fruit Stand is asking each customer what his or her favorite fruit is. If the customer's favorite fruit is the same as Sven's, then the customer receives free groceries for the day. Figure 6-3, shows a detailed explanation of the script.

Remember that in shell programming, an exit status of zero is true and an exit status of one is false.

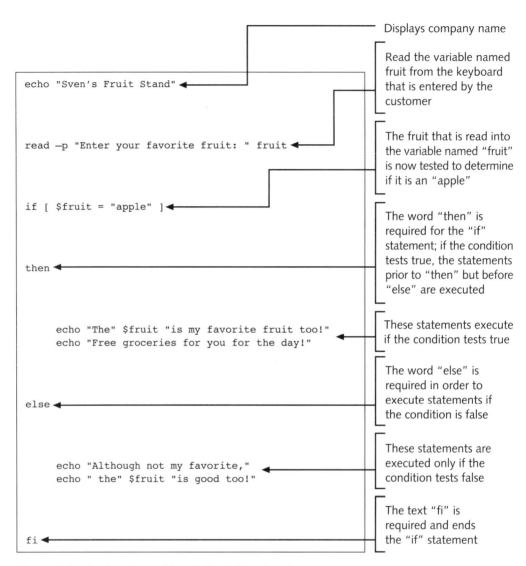

Figure 6-3   Explanation of Sven's Fruit Stand code

Next you will create a script that tests whether the **mv** command successfully moved a file by using the **if** statement to test the exit condition of the list command.

To create a script that tests the exist status of a command:

    1. Log in to the Linux system as a user, and then open a Terminal emulation window.

    2. Create a script named **MoveTest** in the **$HOME/bin** directory.

3. Insert the following lines of code to create an `if` statement that checks to see if the `mv` command moved the specified file:

```
#!/bin/bash
if mv bike1.txt bike2.txt
then
        echo "Move completed successfully — file moved.
           Status " $?
else
        echo "Move completed unsuccessfully — file not
           moved. Status " $?
fi
```

4. Save the script, quit the editor, and then make the script executable.

5. Create a file named **bike1.txt**. Make sure you save the file, and then quit the editor.

6. Execute the script. The bike1.txt file is moved. You know this because of the message echoed to the screen. See Figure 6-4.

7. Execute the script again. See Figure 6-4. A message indicating the file has not been moved is displayed. This is because the file, bike1.txt no longer exists. It was moved in the previous step.

8. Close your window, and then log out.

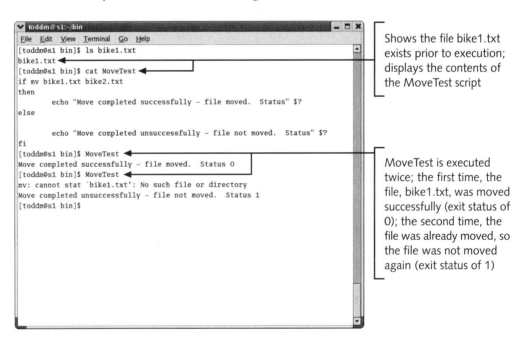

Shows the file bike1.txt exists prior to execution; displays the contents of the MoveTest script

MoveTest is executed twice; the first time, the file, bike1.txt, was moved successfully (exit status of 0); the second time, the file was already moved, so the file was not moved again (exit status of 1)

Figure 6-4   The MoveTest script and resulting output

Using Conditional Expressions in an `if` Statement

You can use conditional expressions as well as commands in an `if` statement. Using conditional expressions allows you to compare numbers, make string comparisons, and perform command substitutions. The conditional expression takes the following general form:

```
[[ conditional expression ]]
```

This is where the *conditional expression* tests for values being equal, greater than, less than, or not equal. (Refer to Chapter 3 and the `man` pages for additional conditional expressions.)

 There is a space before and after each pair of square brackets, `[[` and `]]`. If you do not put a space before and after each pair, you receive an error when executing a script that uses these.

Next you will create a few scripts that utilize the `if` statement and that perform various tests. The scripts will be explained prior to creating and running them. You can then use these samples as guides to help you create additional scripts later.

The first script tests two positional parameters and displays a message only if the first number is larger than the second. The goal of this activity is to help you understand how to implement the `if` statement to perform comparisons of numbers.

To create a script that uses the `if` statement to compare positional parameters used as numbers:

1. Log in to the Linux system as a user, and then open a Terminal emulation window.

2. Create a script named **NumberGreater** in the **$HOME/bin** directory.

3. Insert the following lines of code to create an `if` statement that utilizes a conditional expression to compare two positional parameters:

```
#!/bin/bash
if [[  $1 -gt  $2  ]]
then
      echo $1 " is greater than " $2
else
      echo $1 " is less than " $2
fi
```

4. Save the script, and then quit the editor.

5. Make the script executable, and then execute the script using **4** as the first parameter and **3** as the second parameter. See Figure 6-5. A message displays indicating that the first parameter, 4, is greater then the second parameter, 3.

6. Execute the script again. This time use **6** as the first parameter and **9** as the second parameter. See Figure 6-5. Compare the differences in output of this step with Step 4. A message indicates the first parameter, 6, is less than the second parameter, 9. This is different from the previous run because there are different values being compared.

7. Do not log out.

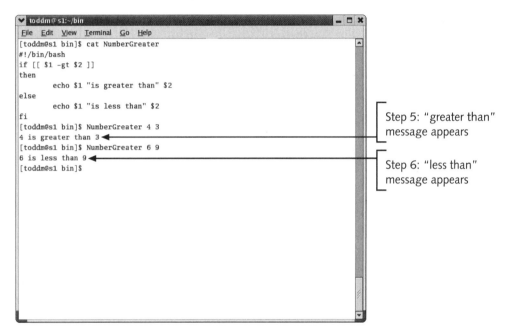

```
[toddm@s1 bin]$ cat NumberGreater
#!/bin/bash
if [[ $1 -gt $2 ]]
then
        echo $1 "is greater than" $2
else
        echo $1 "is less than" $2
fi
[toddm@s1 bin]$ NumberGreater 4 3
4 is greater than 3
[toddm@s1 bin]$ NumberGreater 6 9
6 is less than 9
[toddm@s1 bin]$
```

Step 5: "greater than" message appears

Step 6: "less than" message appears

Figure 6-5   The NumberGreater script and resulting output

Next you will create a script that tests a declared variable named "Color" that is read into the script using the **read** statement. The script will display a message if the value is equal to the literal string "red." The goal of this exercise is to help you understand how to implement the **if** statement to perform string comparisons. The practical use of this script is to test whether or not a value entered is equal to a string of letters.

To create a script that uses the if statement to determine if a value read from the keyboard is equal to a literal string:

1. Create a script named **ColorRed** in the **$HOME/bin** directory.

2. Insert the following lines of code. Notice that you are using the **read** statement instead of positional parameters.

```
#!/bin/bash
declare Color
read -p "Enter color: " Color
```

```
if [[  $Color = "red"  ]]
then
      echo "The color is red"
else
      echo "The color is not red - it is " $Color
fi
```

3. Save the script, and then quit the editor.

4. Make the script executable, and then execute it. Type **red** when prompted to enter a color. See Figure 6-6. A message indicating that the color is red appears.

5. Execute the script again. Type **blue** when prompted to enter color. See Figure 6-6. The message "The color is not red — it is blue" is displayed.

6. Do not log out.

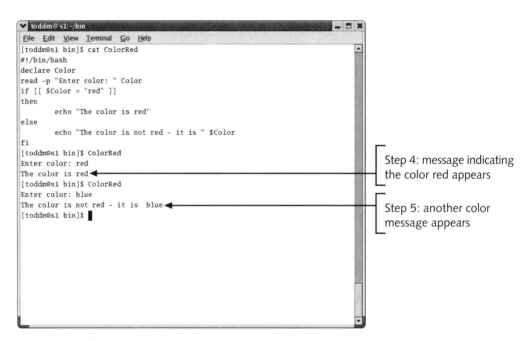

Figure 6-6   The ColorRed script and resulting output

In this third script you will use command substitution to determine if the current directory is equal to a specific directory. The goal of this exercise is to help you understand how to implement the `if` statement using command substitution. One practical application for this script might be to determine if a user's current directory is a directory they should not be in.

To create a script that uses the `if` statement to determine if the current directory is a specific one:

1. Create a script named **IsDirTmp** in the $HOME/bin directory.

2. Insert the following lines of code to display a message based upon your current directory. If your current directory is /tmp, you are instructed to change to your home directory. Otherwise, your current directory is displayed. Note the command `dir1=`pwd`` uses command substitution. This is discussed in Chapter 4. Also, the variable dir1 contains the output of the `pwd` command. So, if the present working directory is /tmp, then dir1 literally equals /tmp.

```
#!/bin/bash
dir1=`pwd` # The variable dir1 contains the output of the
 pwd command.
if [[   $dir1 = "/tmp"   ]]
then
      echo "Your current directory is /tmp"
      echo "Change to $HOME immediately"
else
      echo "Your current directory is " $dir1
fi
```

3. Save the script, quit the editor, and then make the script executable.

4. If you are not in the $HOME/bin directory change to it, and then execute the script. See Figure 6-7. A message displaying your current directory appears.

5. Change to the **/tmp** directory, and then execute the script. See Figure 6-7. A message appears indicating your current directory is /tmp and that you need to change out of the /tmp directory. If you compare this step to the previous step, you see a difference in the messages displayed. In the previous step, because you are in your home directory, you are not told to change directory locations.

6. Close the window, and then log out.

You should now be able to adapt the concepts presented in these scripts to other scripts you may write in the future.

 You can place the entire `if` statement on a single line. However, you must use a semicolon to separate each element of the statement. The syntax is `if` *list*; then *statements*; `fi`. One line is considered to be `if` *list*, the next is `then` *statements*, and the last one is `fi`. To execute the ColorGreen script on a single command line, you enter `if [[ $Color = "green"]]; then echo "The color is green"; fi`.

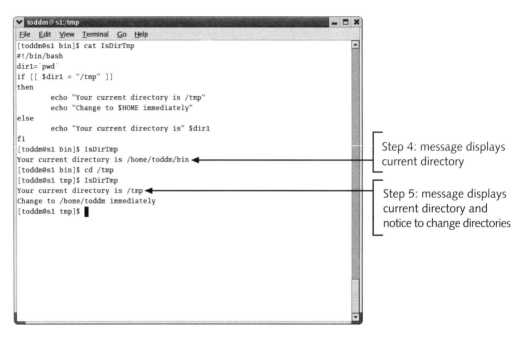

Step 4: message displays current directory

Step 5: message displays current directory and notice to change directories

Figure 6-7   The IsDirTmp script and resulting output

Conditional Processing Using Single Square Brackets

Instead of using double square brackets for conditional processing, you can use single square brackets, [and], or the **test** command. Because there is no set standard in the Linux operating system and often several ways to accomplish the same thing, script programmers and System Administrators write in a style with which they are most comfortable. However, you need to beware of these alternatives because the system scripts in the etc/rc.d/init.d directory use them.

Figure 6-8 demonstrates the use of double and single square brackets and the **test** command. The script contains the same logic implemented three different ways to give you an idea how to use [ ] and **test** as alternatives. The results are the same provided you input the same data. Another alternative is to write three different scripts to do the same as this one script. You can see from the script that you could adapt this code to a script that inquires of a user whether he or she wants to continue or not. This type of prompting logic is useful in menu structures, which will be covered in Chapter 9.

```
toddm@s1:~/bin
File  Edit  View  Terminal  Go  Help
[toddm@s1 bin]$ cat YesNo
read -p "Do you want to continue? (Using double square brackets) " YesNo
if [[ $YesNo = "Y" ]]
then
        echo "You entered" $YesNo
fi
read -p "Do you want to continue? (Using single square brackets) " YesNo
if [ $YesNo = "Y" ]
then
        echo "You entered" $YesNo
fi
read -p "Do you want to continue? (Using test command) " YesNo
if test $YesNo = "Y"
then
        echo "You entered" $YesNo
fi
[toddm@s1 bin]$ YesNo
Do you want to continue? (Using double square brackets) Y
You entered Y
Do you want to continue? (Using single square brackets) Y
You entered Y
Do you want to continue? (Using test command) Y
You entered Y
[toddm@s1 bin]$ YesNo
Do you want to continue? (Using double square brackets) n
Do you want to continue? (Using single square brackets) n
Do you want to continue? (Using test command) n
[toddm@s1 bin]$
```

Figure 6-8   The YesNo script and its resulting output

The single square brackets are actually a link to the `test` command. So, using the single square brackets and the `test` command are the same. They exist for compatibility with other shells and versions of the operating system. Because single square brackets are built into the shell and remain in memory, their use is more efficient because the shell does not have to locate them on disk. However, what to use is the preference of the script programmer.

USING LOGICAL OPERATORS

You can implement the *AND*, *OR*, and *NOT* pseudocode logical operators in the shell. These logical operators allow you to test multiple commands and conditional expressions, as well as allow you to make decisions based upon multiple criteria. The result of using these operators is a more powerful and flexible logic in your scripts.

Let's look at the *AND* operator first. The shell uses **&&**, two ampersand symbols, for the *AND* operator. It takes the following form in the shell, given two conditions:

```
if [[ condition1 && condition2 ]]
then
      statements
else
      statements
fi
```

6

This is where each condition, *condition1* and *condition2*, is an exit status from executed commands. The results of each condition must return an exit status of zero, for true, in order for the statements following **then** to execute. If either condition results in an exit status of one, for false, then the *statements* following **else** execute.

Next, let's look at the *OR* operator. The shell uses ||, two vertical bars, for the *OR* operator. It takes the following form in the shell with two conditions:

```
if [[ condition1 || condition2 ]]
then
      statements
else
      statements
fi
```

In the case of ||, only one of the conditions must have an exit status of zero in order for the statements following **then** to execute. The statements following **else** only execute if *both* conditions return an exit status of one.

Lastly, consider the *NOT* operator. The shell uses !, a single exclamation point, as the *NOT* operator. It takes the following form in the shell:

```
if [[ ! condition ]]
then
          statements
else
          statements
fi
```

Here is how this logical operator works. An exit status is returned from the command, as a *condition*. This *condition* is then negated. That is, an exit status of zero becomes a one and an exit status of one becomes zero. Thus, the ! operator negates the *condition*. It is the negated *condition* that gets evaluated; other than that, it works the same as the previous operators. If the negated *condition* has an exit status of zero, the statements following **then** execute. If the negated *condition* has an exit status of one, the statements following **else** execute.

> The logical && operator is more restrictive than the logical || operator because both conditions must return an exit status of zero.

Look at the following sample business scenario that creates scripts that use these conditions. The Have Fun Hotel and Resort Software Company writes application software for beach and mountain lodges. The company management would like to give the technical support personnel who are hourly employees (**Status = "H"**) and who work the third shift (`Shift=3`) an annual bonus of $500. Before you can write this script, you need to turn this problem into pseudocode. Here is the logic:

Bonus=500

Read Status

Read Shift

If Status="H" AND Shift=3

Then

   Display "Your bonus is "

Else

   Display "You are only eligible for a bonus if you are hourly working shift 3"

End-if

Next you will create the resulting script.

To create a script that uses the && operator:

1. Log in to the Linux system as a user, and then open a Terminal emulation window.

2. Create a script named **ShiftBonus** in the `$HOME/bin` directory.

3. Insert the following lines of code to initialize the bonus variable, read data from the keyboard, and then display results of the data based on an `if` statement that makes use of the `&&` operator. Figure 6-9 displays the contents of the ShiftBonus script.

```
Bonus=500
read -p "Enter Status: " Status
read -p "Enter Shift: " Shift
if [ $Status = "H" ] && [ $Shift = 3 ]
then
    echo "Your bonus for working shift $Shift is"
       '$'$Bonus"."
else
    echo "You are only entitled to a bonus if you are
       hourly and work shift 3."
fi
```

4. Save the script, quit the editor, and then make the script executable.

5. Execute the script, and then type **H** when prompted for Status and type **2** when prompted for Shift. See Figure 6-10. A message indicating you do not receive a bonus appears.

6. Execute the script again, and then type **H** when prompted for Status and **3** when prompted for Shift. See Figure 6-10. A message indicating you do receive a bonus appears.

7. Execute the script a third time, and then type **S** (for Salaried) when prompted for Status and **3** when prompted for Shift. See Figure 6-10. A message indicating you do not receive a bonus appears.

8. Do not log out.

Figure 6-9   Contents of the ShiftBonus script

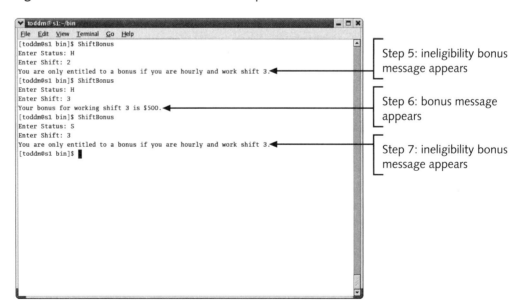

Figure 6-10   Output of the ShiftBonus script

If you use the || operator in the ShiftBonus script instead of the &&, the logic would provide for a bonus if either the Status equaled "H" or the Shift equaled 3. Only one of the conditions needs to be true in order for the true condition statements to execute. Using the correct logical operator is important. Otherwise, you can experience logic problems. Even when the script is syntactically correct, the logic you use to set up your script can be incorrect.

In this next example, the management at the Have Fun Hotel and Resort Software Company has decided to reward the technical support personnel in the call center based upon the amount of calls they take and the amount of calls they close. Calls Handled is the amount of calls a support person takes. Calls Closed is the amount of calls that are completed to customer satisfaction. Here is the partial logic:

If Calls Handled > 150 OR Calls Closed > 50

Then

   Display "You are entitled to a bonus"

Else

   Display "You are only entitled to a bonus if the calls handled exceeds 150 or calls closed exceeds 50"

End-if

Next you will create the script for the Have Fun Hotel and Resort Software Company using the logical *OR* operator.

To create a script that uses the || operator:

1. Create a script named **Calls** in the **$HOME/bin** directory.

2. Insert the following lines of code to read data from the keyboard and create an `if` statement that makes use of the || operator:

```
read -p "Enter the calls handled: " CallsHandled
read -p "Enter the calls closed: " CallsClosed
if [[ $CallsHandled -gt 150 || $CallsClosed -gt 50 ]]
then
        echo "You are entitled to a bonus."
else
        echo "You are only entitled to a bonus if the calls
            handled exceeds 150 or calls closed exceeds 50."
fi
```

3. Save the script, quit the editor, and then make the script executable.

4. Execute the script, and then type **159** when prompted for calls handled and **40** when prompted for calls closed. See Figure 6-11. A message indicating you are entitled to a bonus appears.

6

5. Execute the script again, and then type **120** when prompted for calls handled and **76** when prompted for calls closed. See Figure 6-11. A message indicating you are entitled to a bonus appears.

6. Run the script a third time, and then type **76** when prompted for calls handled and **44** when prompted for calls closed. See Figure 6-11. A message indicating you are only entitled to a bonus when you exceed 150 calls handled or 50 calls closed appears.

7. Do not log out.

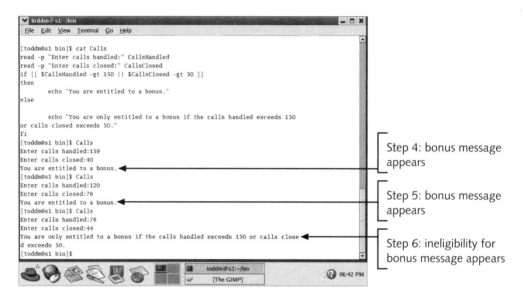

Figure 6-11   The Calls script and resulting output

In the Calls script, consider what the result would be if one of the conditions were left off or the **&&** operator were used instead of the **||** operator. The script would be syntactically correct. However, it would logically be incorrect because it would not follow the desires of the management. In the case of the input for Steps 4 through 6, only one employee would be eligible for the bonus, not two.

In this final example for the Have Fun Hotel and Resort Software Company, the management wants a script created that indicates whether personnel with 25 years of service can retire. Here is the partial logic using the *NOT* logical operator.

If Years of Service is NOT less than 25

Then

    Display "You can retire now."

Else

    Display "You will need 25 years to retire."

End-if

Next you will create the script using the logical *NOT* operator.

To create a script that uses the ! operator:

1. Create a script named **Retire** in the **$HOME/bin** directory.

2. Insert the following lines of code to read data from the keyboard and create an `if` statement that makes use of the ! operator:

```
read -p "Years of Service: " Years
if [[ ! $Years -lt 25 ]]
then
        echo "You can retire now."
else
        echo "You will need 25 years to retire."
fi
```

3. Save the script, quit the editor, and then make the script executable.

4. Execute the script, and then type **32** when prompted for Years of Service. See Figure 6-12. A message indicating you can retire now appears.

5. Execute the script again, and then type **21** when prompted for Years of Service. See Figure 6-12. A message indicating you need 25 years to retire appears.

6. Close your window, and then log out.

Note that if you left off the ! operator, the code would indicate that that you could retire *only* if you had been there less than 25 years. Of course, this would be incorrect based upon the requirements of the scenario.

Although you created the Retire script using the ! operator, you could have written it without using this operator. You could modify the script as follows:

```
read -p "Years of Service: " Years
if [[ $Years -ge 25 ]]
then
        echo "You can retire now."
else
        echo "You will need 25 years to retire."
fi
```

6

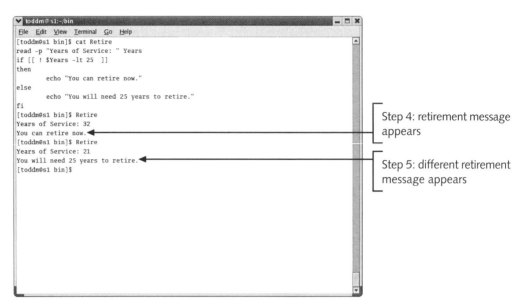

Step 4: retirement message appears

Step 5: different retirement message appears

Figure 6-12   The Retire script and resulting output

Notice the main difference between the two versions is that they are opposite in terms of logic.

Now that you've looked at some sample scripts using the `if` statement and logical operators, review Table 6-2 for a summary of the conditions used in this section. You read this table by looking at the evaluation of the conditions in the Condition 1 and Condition 2 columns. Next, look to the right under the heading for the operation you are using. For example, if Condition 1 is true and Condition 2 is false, then the *AND* operator result would be false, and the *OR* operator result would be true. In the last column, only one condition is tested, which is Condition 1. So, in this case if Condition 1 is true, false is the result of the *NOT* condition operator.

Table 6-2   Logical operators

Condition 1	Condition 2	Condition 1 AND Condition 2 Result (Script uses &&)	Condition 1 OR Condition 2 Result (Script uses ||)	NOT Condition 1 (Script uses !)
True	True	True	True	False
True	False	False	True	False
False	True	False	True	True
False	False	False	False	True

You can have multiple conditions with these logical operators. For example, `if true && true && true; then echo "True"; else echo "False"; fi` displays "True" on the screen. Also, `if true && false && true; then echo "True"; else echo "False"; fi` displays "False" on the screen. However using the `||` operator, `if true || false || true; then echo "True"; else echo "False"; fi` displays "True" on the screen. But, `if false || false || false; then echo "True"; else echo "False"; fi` displays "False" on the screen.

USING THE `elif` CLAUSE IN AN `if` STATEMENT

The `if` statement allows you to use the optional `elif` clause to further test a false condition of an `if` statement. Figure 6-13 shows the placement of the `elif` clause within the `if` statement.

The phrase `elif` stands for "else if." It is part of the `if` statement and cannot be used by itself. In other words, you could not have just the `elif` clause followed by a condition.

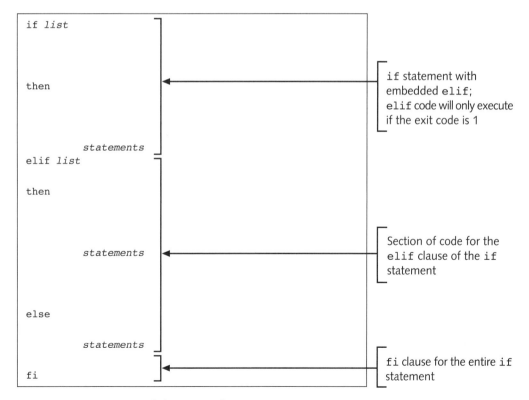

Figure 6-13   Position of the `elif` clause in an `if` statement

Using this form of the if statement, then if *list* must return an exit status of one in order for the elif clause to process. Once control passes to the elif clause, processing occurs as if this were an if statement. The commands that are executed for the elif clause begin with the then clause and end with the last statement prior to fi. Note that there is only one fi clause for the entire if statement.

If the condition for the elif *list* clause returns an exit status of zero, then the then statements within the elif statements are executed. If the condition for the elif *list* clause returns an exit status of one, then the else statements are executed.

If if *list* returns an exit status of zero, the statements immediately following the first then clause are executed up to the elif clause. Then, processing skips the elif clause altogether and resumes after the fi clause.

To help you understand this, take a look at another business scenario. Rose's Bubblegum and Popcorn Factory is interested in knowing whether they have made a profit, experienced a loss, or broken even with respect to their cash flow. They want a script that reads in sales and costs and calculates their difference. If the difference is zero, they have a breakeven. If the difference is greater than zero, they have a profit; otherwise, they have a loss.

Next you will write the shell script to determine profitability for Rose's Bubblegum and Popcorn Factory, using the elif clause.

To create a script that uses the elif clause in the if statement:

1. Log in to the Linux system as a user, and then open a Terminal emulation window.

2. Create a script named **ProfitLossBreakeven** in the $HOME/bin directory.

3. Insert the following lines of code. The code is structured this way because you have three possible scenarios—profit, a loss, or a breakeven. In this exercise, the breakeven possibility is tested first. This is simply programmer preference. You could test any of the three conditions first. However, you would have to change the existing code.

```
#!/bin/bash
read -p "Enter Sales Amount: " Sales
read -p "Enter Costs: " Costs
((Net=$Sales - $Costs))
if [[ $Net -eq "0" ]]
then
        echo "Profit and Costs are equal — breakeven."
elif [[ $Net -gt "0" ]]
   then
        echo "Profit of: " $Net
   else
         echo "Loss of: " $Net
fi
```

4. Save the script, and then quit the editor.

5. Make the script executable, and then execute the script inputting **5000** when prompted for Sales Amount and **6500** when prompted for Costs. See Figure 6-14. Because Sales is less than Costs, a loss of -1500 is reflected in a message.

6. Execute the script again. This time input **6500** when prompted for Sales Amount and **6500** when prompted for Costs. See Figure 6-14. Here is the breakeven. Both Sales and Costs are the same resulting in neither a profit nor a loss. Thus, a message indicating a breakeven has occurred is displayed.

7. Execute the script one final time and input **6500** when prompted for Sales Amount and **5000** when prompted for Costs. See Figure 6-14. In this execution, a profit of 1500 is displayed because Sales exceeds Costs by that amount.

8. Close your window, and then log out.

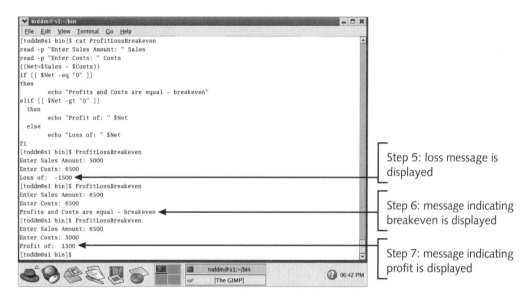

Figure 6-14   The ProfitLossBreakeven script and its resulting output

There are a variety of ways to write a script that yields identical results. Let's look at an alternative to this script, named ProfitLossBreakeven2. In this alternate version, there are two `elif` clauses used—one nested within the other. The way this works is that if the net amount is not equal to zero, for a breakeven, then the first `elif` is tested. If the net amount is zero, the fact that a breakeven exists is displayed and the script terminates.

With the first `elif` clause, if the net amount is greater then zero, you have a profit. The amount of profit is displayed and the script terminates. Only if the net amount is less than zero will the second `elif` be tested. In this case, the amount of the loss is displayed. Because the second `elif` is nested, testing of the second `elif` is conditional; it is only tested if the first `elif` results in false. Look back to Figure 6-14 and you see only one elif clause. Look at Figure 6-15 and you see two elif clauses. If you compare the figures, you see the end result is the same.

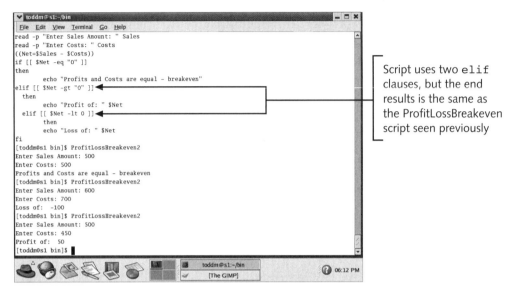

Script uses two elif clauses, but the end results is the same as the ProfitLossBreakeven script seen previously

Figure 6-15   The ProfitLossBreakeven2 script with two elif clauses

NESTING if STATEMENTS

As you are creating more and more complex scripts, you may find that one condition depends on the result of another. Similar to nested elif statements, the shell allows you to nest your if statements, meaning that you can create a complete if...then...fi statement within another if...then...fi statement. With nesting, you can have whole sections of code embedded within other whole sections of code.

Consider the following example. An organization named Lucy's Books and Tapes, Inc. has specific retirement requirements. An employee must have 25 years of service regardless of age, or an employee must have 10 years of service and be at least 60 years of age in order to retire. Figure 6-16 demonstrates this example. The first if is a data validation test. Although not a stated requirement, it makes sense for the employee's age to be less than the number of years. If this were not in the script, then the script would technically allow someone to be 15 years old with 30 years of service. Because it is not possible for the age to be less than the years of service, it needs to be considered as part of the script. Many times, you must go beyond the stated requirements of a program to prevent inaccurate data from getting into the scripts.

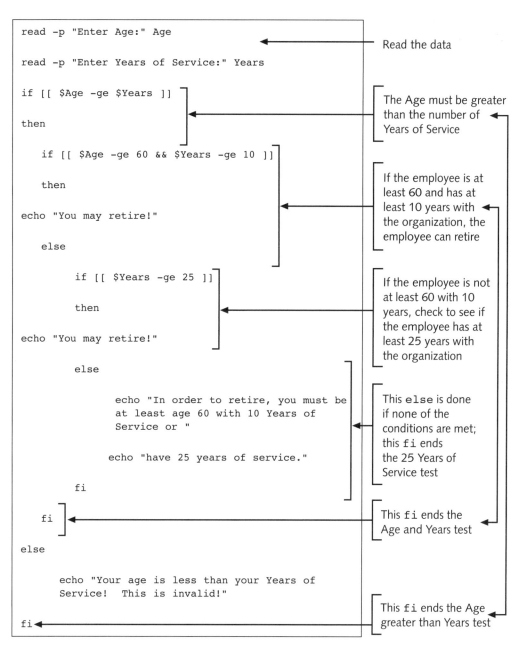

```
read -p "Enter Age:" Age                                              Read the data

read -p "Enter Years of Service:" Years

if [[ $Age -ge $Years ]]
                                                                      The Age must be greater
then                                                                  than the number of
                                                                      Years of Service
    if [[ $Age -ge 60 && $Years -ge 10 ]]
                                                                      If the employee is at
    then                                                              least 60 and has at
                                                                      least 10 years with
echo "You may retire!"                                                the organization, the
                                                                      employee can retire
    else

        if [[ $Years -ge 25 ]]
                                                                      If the employee is not
        then                                                          at least 60 with 10
                                                                      years, check to see if
echo "You may retire!"                                                the employee has at
                                                                      least 25 years with
        else                                                          the organization

            echo "In order to retire, you must be                     This else is done
            at least age 60 with 10 Years of                          if none of the
            Service or "                                              conditions are met;
                                                                      this fi ends
            echo "have 25 years of service."                          the 25 Years of
                                                                      Service test
        fi

    fi                                                                This fi ends the
                                                                      Age and Years test
else

    echo "Your age is less than your Years of
    Service!  This is invalid!"
                                                                      This fi ends the Age
fi                                                                    greater than Years test
```

Figure 6-16 Lucy's Books and Tapes, Inc. retirement requirements script

Data integrity is discussed in greater detail in Chapter 9.

Next you will create the script shown in Figure 6-16.

To create a script that uses the nested `if` statements:

1. Log in to the Linux system as a user, and then open a Terminal emulation window.

2. Create a script named **RetirementStatus** in the `$HOME/bin` directory.

3. Insert the lines of code shown in Figure 6-16 to create a script that uses nested `if` statements.

4. Save the script, and then quit the editor.

5. Make the script executable, execute the script, and then input **50** when prompted for Age and **10** when prompted for Years of Service. See Figure 6-17. A message indicating you have not met the requirements appears.

6. Execute the script again. This time input **62** when prompted for Age and **26** when prompted for Years of Service. See Figure 6-17. A message indicting you have met the requirements appears.

7. Execute the script one last time. Input **15** when prompted for Age and **20** when prompted for Years of Service. See Figure 6-17. A message indicating that your input is invalid appears.

8. Close your window, and then log out.

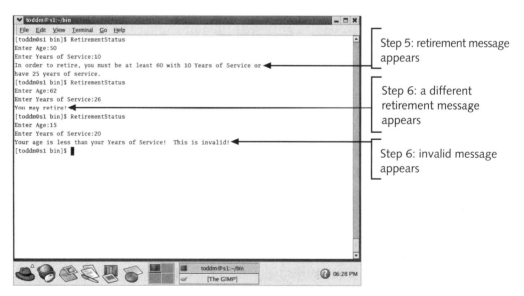

Step 5: retirement message appears

Step 6: a different retirement message appears

Step 6: invalid message appears

Figure 6-17   Execution of the RetirementStatus script

Let's take a look at a more complex example of a script using nested `if` statements. In this example, Hugh Nguyen Airways needs a script to help with the passenger-booking system. This script will serve as a prototype for the company's main booking system that will be written in another programming language. The company needs a program that determines the price of a fare for a booking. Figure 6-18 demonstrates the logic that the script needs to follow to meet the demands of the passenger-booking system.

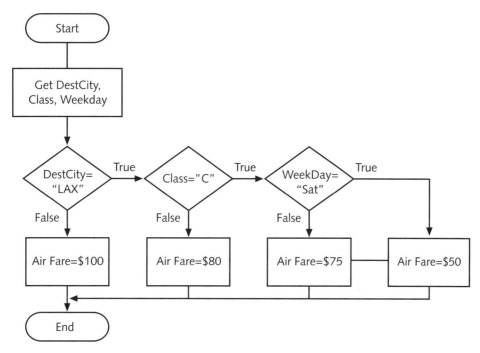

Figure 6-18   Flowchart of the logic for calculating airfare prices

Figure 6-19 shows the actual script that applies the logic shown in the flowchart in Figure 6-18. Notice that the AirFare script shown in Figure 6-19 accepts three variables—DestCity, Class, and WeekDay, and determines the price based upon these inputs. The logic established in Figure 6-18 maintains that if the passenger travels to Los Angeles (city code of "LAX") and is in Coach class (Class "C"), he or she will pay an airfare of $50 for travel on a Saturday and $75 for travel any other day. If the passenger travels to Los Angeles in any other class, he or she pays an airfare of $80. Airfare to any other city is $100.

```
toddm@s1:~/bin                                           _ □ ✕
File  Edit  View  Terminal  Go  Help
[toddm@s1 bin]$ cat AirFare
read -p "Enter Destination City" DestCity
read -p "Enter Class" Class
read -p "Enter Day of Week" WeekDay
if [[ $DestCity -eq "LAX" ]]
then
# Class C is Coach
   if [[ $Class = "C" ]]
        then
            if [[ $WeekDay = "Sat" ]]
            then
                ((AirFare = 50))
            else
                ((AirFare = 75))
            fi

   else
        ((AirFare=80))
   fi
else
  ((AirFare = 100))
fi
echo "Air Fare: "'$'$AirFare
[toddm@s1 bin]$
```

Figure 6-19   Airfare calculation script for Hugh Nguyen Airways

UNDERSTANDING THE case STATEMENT

The case statement is another implementation of the decision structure. You should use the case statement when you have a decision that is based upon multiple inputs such as the feedback received from a user based on several menu options.

 Although there are no set rules, you should consider using the case statement when you have three or more decisions. Again, it is up to the programmer to decide which approach to use.

Generally, using the case statement instead of an if statement is more readable for a programmer when there are several inputs. Logically speaking, the case statement functions similarly as one large if statement.

Pseudologic of the case Statement

Let's first look at the general logic of the case statement:

Case variable-name

   Case1: Perform activity if contents of Case1 are equal to the contents of variable-name

   Case2: Perform activity if contents of Case2 are equal to the contents of variable-name

   Case3: Perform activity if contents of Case3 are equal to the contents of variable-name

Case Else: Perform activity if none of the previous Cases are equal to the contents of the variable-name

End-Case

Here's how the **case** statement works. The *variable-name* is tested to see if the contents match one of the cases, specified as *Case1*, *Case2*, or *Case3*, then the activity to the right of the match is performed. Once the match occurs, none of the other cases is tested. Processing continues to statements that come after the **case** statement. You can use a **case else** clause in the event there are no matches. This clause is useful if a user has not entered a value from a list of choices that have been given.

Syntax for the case Statement

Let's look at the shell's implementation of the **case** statement:

```
case word   in
        pattern1) statements
                statements
                  ;;
        pattern2) statements
            statements
              ;;
        patternN) statements
            statements
                  ;;
    esac
```

The **case** statement, and the **in** and **esac** clauses are required. The phrase **case** *word* **in** is required. This code phrase is analogous to the verbal phrase "What case is the pattern to match?". The *word* is a variable that matches one of the patterns. For a pattern, you can use characters and numbers. You can also use the pattern-matching symbols, *, for matching all characters; ?, for matching a single character; or [...], for matching a range of characters.

 Most scripts use * as a form of the *case else* pseudocode. It matches anything, and it is generally placed at the end of a **case** statement for catching cases that do not match any previous pattern.

The right parenthesis symbol,) is required for each *patternN* and separates each individual case from the statements that are to be performed if a match occurs for that case. The ;; symbols are required and are used to terminate each case. The **esac** clause terminates the entire **case** statement. Similar to **if** and **fi**, **esac** is "case" spelled backwards.

Next you will create a simple shell script using the `case` statement.

To create a simple script that uses the case statement:

1. Log in to the Linux system as a user, and then open a Terminal emulation window.

2. Copy the script named `$HOME/bin/ColorRed` used in an earlier exercise to a new script named `$HOME/bin/ColorRed1`.

3. Modify the script so it contains the following lines of code:

```
read -p "Enter color: " Color
case $Color in
   red) echo "The color is red"
       ;;
   *) echo "The color is not red — it is " $Color
esac
```

4. Save the script, and then quit the editor.

5. Execute the script. Input **red** when prompted for color.

6. Execute the script again. This time input **blue** when prompted for a color.

7. Close your window, and then log out.

Pattern matching and the `case` Statement

Suppose you want to write a script that asks users to respond to a yes or no question in order for a specific activity to occur. They might input a "Y," "y," or "Yes" for a positive response. You can set up your code to allow several patterns to be matched for one case. To do this, you need to use the vertical bar, |, to separate the patterns that are possible. So, in the ColorRed1 script, you could modify the first pattern statement, `red) echo "The color is red"` with `red|Red|RED) echo "The color is red"` to accept either "red," "Red," or "RED" as valid input. Any one of these three causes "The color is red" to display on the screen. You can think of the | operator as a logical *OR* in this case.

Next you will learn how to use the | operator to match one of several possible values in a variable. You will use the `tr` command to translate the answer into uppercase and test the translated result. Another alternative to attempting to guess the patterns a user may input using the | operator, is to combine the | operator with the `tr` command to translate the user's input into all uppercase letters, and thus limit the number of possible inputs your script needs to anticipate. For example, when translating characters, you won't have to worry about testing multiple combinations of "Yes," "yes," "Y," or "y" for a positive response on the part of the user. Command substitution is used to hold the translated result, and that is what is tested in the `case` statement.

To create a script that uses the | operator for pattern matching in a case statement:

1. Log in to the Linux system as a user, and then open a Terminal emulation window.

2. Create a script named **YesNoCase** in the `$HOME/bin` directory.

3. Insert the following lines of code to accept input from a user, translate the user's input into all uppercase, and create a case statement to display the desired files:

```
read -p "Do you want to see all files? (Y or N)" YesNo
YN=`echo $YesNo | tr [:lower:] [:upper:]`# Turn the
response into uppercase.
case $YN in
     Y|YES)
          echo "Displaying all files..."
          ls -a
          ;;
     N|NO)
          echo "Displaying all files except hidden..."
          ls
          ;;
     *) echo "Invalid response!" ;;
esac
```

4. Save the script, and then quit the editor.

5. Make the script executable, and then execute the script. Input **Y** when prompted. Because "Y" is entered, the `ls -a` command is executed and displays all files, including hidden files.

6. Execute the script again. Input **y** when prompted. Because "y" is entered, it is translated to an uppercase "Y." Again, the `ls -a` command is executed and displays all files, including hidden files.

7. Execute the script again. Input **N** when prompted. Because "N" is entered, the `ls` command is executed and displays all files, except hidden files.

8. Execute the script another time. Input **No** when prompted. Because an "n" is entered, it is translated to an uppercase "N." The `ls` command again executes and displays all files, excluding hidden files.

9. Execute the script one last time. Input **Ok** when prompted. A message indicating an invalid response was entered is displayed.

10. Close your window, and then log out.

Note in the next to the last statement that the `;;` symbols for ending a case are on the same line as the statement. This is acceptable and saves some space in your script.

6

Command Substitution and Pattern Matching

You can also use the `case` statement to perform pattern matching on a command's output. You learned about command substitution in Chapter 4. When combining command substitution with pattern matching, you use the `` `...` `` or `$(...)` characters to substitute the command's output in place of the command. Then, you use the `case` statement to test the result. For example, say the `pwd` command displays "/tmp" as your current directory. Then the command `case` `` `pwd` `` `in` literally translates to "case /tmp in." You must then create the cases for the patterns you want to match.

Next you will use the `case` statement, along with command substitution, to determine if the current directory is /. If it is (/), then the current directory is changed to the user's home directory using the `cd $HOME` command.

To create a script that incorporates command substitution in a case statement:

1. Log in to the Linux system as a user, and then open a Terminal emulation window.

2. Create a script named **DirRootCase** in the `$HOME/bin` directory.

3. Insert the following lines of code to create a `case` statement that changes the directory to the user's home directory when the current directory is (/):

```
case `pwd` in
      /) echo "Changing to $HOME"
         cd $HOME # Note: cd or cd ~ would also work.
      ;;
esac
```

4. Save the script, quit the editor, and then make the script executable.

5. Change to root.

6. Execute the script. A message is displayed indicating the current directory is being changed to your home directory.

7. Close your window, and then log out.

Matching Individual Positions

You can create a script that uses pattern-matching techniques to match individual character positions. Figure 6-20 shows a script written for Samuel's Movie Theater that helps determine the price of an admission ticket based upon the age of the movie goer. The owners of the theater want the price of admission to be as follows: if the patron is 12 years of age and younger, the price is $3.00. If the patron is between 13 and 59, the price is $6.00. If the patron is a senior citizen, above age 60, the price is $4.00. The first pattern-matching code, `[1-9]|[1][0-2]`, accounts for the ages 1 through 9 or 10, 11, or 12. The next pattern matching code, `[1][3-9]|[2-5][0-9]`, matches the ages 13 through 19, or 20 through 59. The next pattern matching code, `[6-9][0-9]`, matches the ages 60 through 99.

```
ChildPrice=3

AdultPrice=6

SeniorPrice=4

read -p "Enter your age: " age

case $age in

    [1-9]|[1][0-2]) echo "Price is Child's price of " $ChildPrice ;;

    [1][3-9]|[2-5][0-9]) echo "Price is Adult price of " $AdultPrice ;;

    [6-9][0-9]) echo "Price is Senior price of " $SeniorPrice ;;

    *) echo "Enter a valid selection" ;;

esac
```

Figure 6-20   Samuel's Movie Theater admission pricing script using case statements to create menus

The **case** statement is an ideal tool to use when you want to create a menu system where a user can enter one of several choices.

 In Chapter 7, you will learn how to build a loop around the case statement so the menu processes a selection and then refreshes the screen choices for further selection. This is known as a true menu system.

Next you will combine some of the concepts you've learned so far into a partial menu script. This script is partial in that each selection is processed and then the script terminates. This helps you get familiar with the fundamentals for building a menu system.

To use the case statement to build a partial menu system:

1. Log in to the Linux system as a user, and then open a Terminal emulation window.

2. Create a script named **Choices** in the **$HOME/bin** directory.

3. Insert the following lines of code. These statements create the menu selection numbers for the script. A user will be able to select a number to run a command.

```
echo "1.  The ps command"
echo "2.  The who command"
echo "3.  The ls command"
```

```
echo "4.  View a file using the cat command"
read -p "Enter Selection: " Answer
```

4. Now, insert these lines of code. This creates the first two possible statements to be executed. For example, if the user selects "1," then the **ps** command executes. If the user selects "2," then the **who** command executes.

```
case $Answer in
1)  ps  ;;
2)  who ;;
```

5. Now, insert these lines of code. This creates the third possible set of statements to be executed. For example, if the user selects "3," then the user is prompted to enter "Y" for a long listing. If the user enters a "Y," a long listing is executed. If "N" is entered, then a regular listing is executed.

```
3) read -p "Do you want a long listing? (Y or N) " YesNo
        YN=`echo $YesNo | tr [:lower:] [:upper:]`
        case $YN in
              Y)  ls  -l  ;;
              *)  ls  ;;
        esac ;;
```

6. Now, insert these lines of code. This creates the fourth possible set of statements to be executed. For example, if the user selects "4," then the user is prompted for a filename to enter. If the file exists, then it is displayed. If it does not exist, a message appears indicating that the file does not exist.

```
4)    read -p "Enter file name to view: " FileName
      if [ -a $FileName ]
      then
              cat $FileName | more   # Or more $FileName
      else
              echo "File does not exist!"
      fi  ;;
*) echo "Enter a valid selection"  ;;
esac
```

7. Save the script, quit the editor, and then make the script executable.

8. Execute the script for choice **1**. A process listing is displayed because the **ps** command executes.

9. Execute the script for choice **3**. Input **Y** when prompted to answer the question about the long listing. A long listing appears.

10. Execute the script for choice **2**. A listing of users currently logged on is displayed because the **who** command executes.

11. Execute the script for choice **4** to view an existing file. Type **ColorRed** to display the contents of this file. The ColorRed file is displayed.

12. Close your window, and then, log out.

CHAPTER SUMMARY

❑ A decision is a choice of possible alternatives. Once a choice has been made, the path of the program is set. You can use decision structures to change the flow of a program, thereby creating powerful programming constructs. Flowcharts utilize symbols and arrows to represent program flow. The flowcharting symbol for a decision is the diamond.

❑ One of the shell's decision statements is the `if` statement. It allows you to test a condition, and then perform statements based upon the condition.

❑ The shell uses the `&&` operator for a logical *AND*, a `||` operator for a logical *OR*, and a `!` operator for a logical *NOT*.

❑ The optional `elif` clause allows you to test another condition in the event the `if` condition tests false. When using the `elif` clause, there is only one `if` for each `if...elif` pair.

❑ You can nest `if` statements by placing whole `if` statements within other `if` statements. You should consider nesting `if` statements when you have a condition that depends upon the result of a previous condition.

❑ The shell allows you to use the `case` statement as a substitute for the `if` statement. The best use of the `case` statement is when one variable has several potential values.

REVIEW QUESTIONS

1. The _____ is the flowcharting symbol used for a decision.

   a. diamond

   b. oval

   c. parallelogram

   d. square

2. Which of the following uses symbols to assist you in understanding the flow of a program?

   a. Pseudocode

   b. Flowchart

   c. The `case` statement

   d. The `if` statement

3. Given the following script, which of the subsequent answers is true?

```
#!/bin/bash
((x=1)); ((y=2))
if [ $x -gt $y ]
then
        echo $x $y
```

```
        else
                echo $y $x
        fi
```

a. The use of semicolons is incorrect.

b. The output is 2 1.

c. The output is 1 2.

d. The use of square brackets is incorrect.

4. Given the following script, which of the subsequent answers is true?

```
#!/bin/bash
((x=2)); ((y=(3*$x)/2))
if [ $x -le $y ]
then
        echo $x $y
else
        echo $y $x
fi
```

a. The use of semicolons is incorrect.

b. The output is 3 2.

c. The output is 2 3.

d. The terminating word is misspelled.

5. A _____ is used as a delimiter when an `if` statement is on a single line.

a. colon

b. comma

c. semicolon

d. question mark

6. When using an `if` statement, you use the _____ symbol to test that a variable is either "cat," "Cat," or "CAT".

a. &&

b. !

c. -

d. ||

7. You use the _____ symbol to negate a condition in a shell script.

a. &&

b. !

c. -

d. ||

8. You use the _____ symbol as a logical AND condition in a shell script.

   a. &&

   b. !

   c. -

   d. ||

9. Which clause would you use if you wanted to further test a false condition in an if statement?

   a. case

   b. !=

   c. else

   d. elif

10. _____ is the terminating clause for the if statement.

    a. end-if

    b. fi

    c. elif

    d. esac

11. _____ is the terminating clause for the case statement.

    a. end-if

    b. fi

    c. elif

    d. esac

12. Placing a complete if statement within another complete if statement is called _____.

    a. flowcharting

    b. nesting

    c. conditional processing

    d. using a usage clause

13. Given the following script, which of the following is true?

```
#!/bin/bash
((x=5)); ((y=10))
if [[ $x -eq 5 || $y -gt 12 ]
then
        echo "Hello"
else
        echo "Bye"
fi
```

a. The output displays "Hello."

b. The output displays "Bye."

c. There is a square bracket missing.

d. The ((x=5)) statement contains incorrect syntax.

14. Given the following script, which of the following is true?

```
#!/bin/bash
((x=5)); ((y=10))
if [[ $x -eq 5 || $y -gt 12 ]]
then
        echo "Hello"
else
        echo "Bye"
fi
```

a. The output displays "Hello."

b. The output displays "Bye."

c. There is a square bracket missing.

d. The ((x=10)) statement contains incorrect syntax.

15. Given the following script, which of the following is true?

```
#!/bin/bash
((x=5)); ((y=10))
if [[ $x -eq 5 && $y -gt 12 ]]
 then
        echo "Hello"
else
        echo "Bye"
fi
```

a. The output displays "Hello."

b. The output displays "Bye."

c. There is a square bracket missing.

d. The ((x=5)) statement contains incorrect syntax.

16. Given the following script, which of the following is true?

```
#!/bin/bash
((x=5)); ((y=10))
if [[ $x -lt 5 || $y -gt 84 ]
then
        echo "Hello"
else
        echo "Bye"
if
```

a. The output displays "Hello."

b. The output displays "Bye."

c. There is a square bracket missing.

d. There is no terminating clause.

17. Given three *AND* conditions, what is the end result if one of the conditions is false?

a. The end result is true.

b. The end result is false.

c. You cannot have three *AND* conditions.

d. Statements following the `then` in an `if` execute.

6

18. Given the following script, which of the following is true?

```
#!/bin/bash
((x=5)); ((y=10))
case $x in
        [1-5]) echo $x
        ;;
        echo $y
        ;;
esac
```

a. The output displays 5.

b. The output displays 10.

c. There is a square bracket missing.

d. There is no terminating clause.

19. Given the following script, which of the following is true?

```
#!/bin/bash
((x=5)); ((y=10))
if [[ $x -eq 4 ]]
then
        if [[ $y -ge 10 ]]
        then echo $x $y
        else echo $y $x
else echo "Hi"
fi
```

a. The output displays 5 10.

b. The output displays 10 5.

c. The output displays "Hi."

d. There is no terminating clause.

20. Given the following script, which of the following is true?

```
#!/bin/bash
((x=4)); ((y=10))
if [[ $x -eq 4 ]]
then
        if [[ $y -ge 10 ]]
        then echo $x $y
        else echo $y $x
else echo "Hi"
fi
```

   a. The output displays 4 10.

   b. The output displays 10 4.

   c. The output displays "Howdy."

   d. There is no terminating clause.

HANDS-ON PROJECTS

Project 6-1

In this project, you will create a shell script that tests whether a file has been removed with the rm command. You will test for the exit status of a command's execution and use a decision structure to determine if the command successfully executed or not. If the exit status of the rm command equals zero, then the file has been removed. If the exit status of the rm command equals one, then the file has either been removed or never existed. Remember to turn on debugging with set -xv if you need to troubleshoot the script. Turn it off with set +xv when through debugging the script.

  1. Log in to the Linux system as a user, and then open a Terminal emulation window.

  2. Create a shell script named **Project6-1** in your **$HOME/bin** directory.

  3. Insert the following lines of code:

```
touch FileIsHere.txt
rm FileIsHere.txt
FileHereStatus=$?
if [[ $FileHereStatus -eq 0 ]]
then
        echo "File successfully removed"
else
        echo "File not present"
fi
rm FileNotHere.txt
FileNotHereStatus=$?
if [[ $FileNotHereStatus -eq 0 ]]
```

```
then
        echo "File successfully removed"
else
        echo "File not present"
fi
```

4. Save the script, and then quit the editor.

5. Make the script executable, and then execute the script.

6. Record the results.

7. Close your window, and then log out.

Project 6-2

6

In this project, you will create a shell script that uses the **case** statement to implement a usage clause (refer to Chapter 5 for more on usage clauses). The script requires only three positional parameters. An appropriate message is displayed if an incorrect number of parameters are entered.

1. Log in to the Linux system as a user, and then open a Terminal emulation window.

2. Create a shell script named **Project6-2** in your **$HOME/bin** directory, translate the following pseudocode into actual lines of code, and then enter the appropriate code into the Project6-2 script:

Case number-of-positional-parameters

> *0: Display a message indicating how to run the script and indicate to the user that no positional parameters were entered.*

> *1 or 2: Display a message indicating how to run the script and display the number of positional parameters entered.*

> *3: Display the three positional parameters.*

> *Case Else: Display an error indicating that too many positional parameters were entered.*

End-Case

3. Save the script, and then quit the editor.

4. Make the script executable, and then execute the script with no parameters.

5. Record the result.

6. Execute the script again with one parameter, execute it again with three parameters, and then execute it once more with five parameters.

7. Record the results.

8. Close your window, and then log out.

Project 6-3

In this project, you will implement the `elif` clause. A nonprofit organization, named Helping Hands for All, has hired several contract programmers to work with their permanent programming staff. They want to give the employees, who are hourly (status of "H") or salaried (status of "S"), a $500 bonus. The programmers with contractor status (status of "C") will not receive a bonus. Any other status is invalid.

1. Log in to the Linux system as a user, and then open a Terminal emulation window.

2. Create a shell script named **Project6-3** in your `$HOME/bin` directory.

3. Insert the following lines of code:

```
read -p "Enter Status: " Status
if [[ $Status = "S" || $Status = "H" ]]
then
        ((Bonus=500))
        echo "You get a bonus of" '$'$Bonus
elif [[ $Status = "C" ]]
then
        echo "You are a contractor. You need to become
          permanent to receive a bonus."
else
        echo "Invalid status"
fi
```

4. Save the script, and then quit the editor.

5. Make the script executable, and then execute the script four times. Input "S," "H," "C," and "T" respectively, when prompted to enter status.

6. Record the output.

7. Close your window, and then log out.

Project 6-4

In this project, you will convert pseudocode that uses a decision structure into a shell script. The script then will accept three grades, calculate an average, and then display a letter grade based upon the average. You will need to use either the `if` statement or the `case` statement to implement this script.

1. Log in to the Linux system as a user, and then open a Terminal emulation window.

2. Create a shell script named **Project6-4** in your `$HOME/bin` directory.

3. Convert the following pseudocode into code for the script:

Read in three grades from the keyboard

Average the grades

Display the appropriate letter grade for the number grade using this scale:

90 to 100: Display a letter grade of "A"

80 to 89: Display a letter grade of "B"

70 to 79: Display a letter grade of "C"

65 to 69: Display a letter grade of "D"

0 to 64: Display a letter grade of "F"

Insert appropriate comments

4. Save the script, quit the editor, and then make the script executable.
5. Execute the script and then input **100**, **90**, and **100** when prompted for each grade.
6. Record the output.
7. Execute the script again. This time input **99**, **68**, and **70** when prompted for each grade.
8. Record the output.
9. Execute the script one last time. Input **80**, **96**, and **72** when prompted for each grade.
10. Record the output.
11. Close your window, and then log out.

Project 6-5

In this project, you will convert pseudocode into a shell script and implement either an `if` or `case` decision structure that determines the bonus level for a salesperson.

1. Log in to the Linux system as a user, and then open a Terminal emulation window.
2. Create a shell script named **Project6-5** in the **$HOME/bin** directory.
3. Convert the following pseudocode into code for the script:

Read SalesPerson and QuarterlySales from the keyboard

Display an appropriate message regarding the bonus when the QuarterlySales for a SalesPerson falls within these ranges:

Over $1,000,000	*$1,500 Bonus*
$100,000 to $999,999	*$750 Bonus*
Under $99,999	*No Bonus*

4. Save the script, and then quit the editor.
5. Make the script executable, and then execute the script inputting **Mike** when prompted for the salesperson and **67000** when prompted for sales.
6. Execute the script again. Input **Mary** when prompted for the salesperson and **1000000** when prompted for sales.

6

7. Execute the script one last time. Input **Lisa** when prompted for the salesperson and **250000** when prompted for sales.

8. Record the output.

9. Close your window, and then log out.

Project 6-6

In this project, you will apply conditional processing logic by writing a shell script that uses the `if` statement to accept one positional parameter from the keyboard. If the parameter does not equal a value specified in the script, display an "invalid data" error message.

1. Log in to the Linux system as a user, and then open a Terminal emulation window.

2. Create a shell script named **Project6-6** in your **$HOME/bin** directory, and then translate the program requirements into the appropriate code:

   The script accepts one positional parameter

   The script verifies a positional parameter was entered; if not, a message is displayed

   The positional parameter is saved as StateCode

   If the positional parameter is equal to "GA" or "KY," display a message indicating a valid StateCode was entered

   If the StateCode does not equal one of the previous codes, display an error indicating an invalid StateCode was entered

   Insert appropriate comments

3. Save the script, and then quit the editor.

4. Make the scripts executable, and then execute the scripts using "GA" as the first positional parameter.

5. Record the result.

6. Execute the scripts using "OK" as the first positional parameter.

7. Record the result.

8. Execute the scripts using "KY" as the first positional parameter.

9. Record the result.

10. Close your window, and then log out.

Project 6-7

The goal of this project is to turn a flowchart into a shell script.

1. Log in to the Linux system as a user, and then open a Terminal emulation window.

2. Create a script named **Project6-7** in your **$HOME/bin** directory.

3. Using the flowchart shown in Figure 6-21 as a guide, create the code that fulfills the program logic shown there.

4. Record or print the script.

5. Execute the script inputting **5** as A and **10** as B.

6. Record the result.

7. Execute the script again. Input **5** as A and **4** as B.

8. Record the result.

9. Execute the script one last time. Input **3** as A and **10** as B.

10. Record the result.

11. Close your window, and then log out.

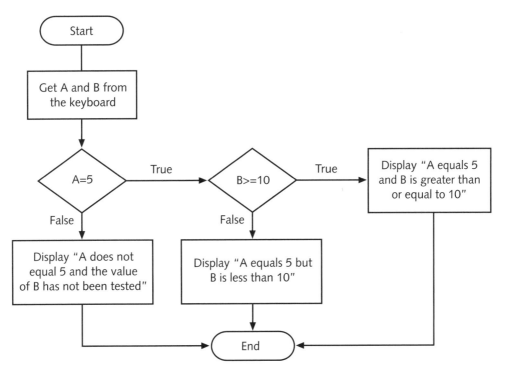

Figure 6-21   Flowchart for Project 6-7

Project 6-8

In this project, you will implement conditional processing and nest **if** statements. The firm named TJ Liu & Associates needs a shell script written. The script needs to accept two values, Status and Years. The status must be either "S," "H," or "C" (for "salary," "hour," and "contract" respectively); otherwise, an error message is displayed. An employee with a status of "H" or "S" and who has been employed for at least two years will receive 50 shares of company stock. A contractor who has been working with TJ Liu & Associates for more than three years will receive a $100 bonus. An appropriate message must be displayed for employees or contractors not meeting the requirements.

1. Log in to the Linux system as a user, and then open a Terminal emulation window.

2. Create a shell script named **Project6-8** in your `$HOME/bin` directory.

3. Insert the following lines of code:

```
read -p "Enter Status " Status
if [[ $Status = "S" || $Status = "H" || $Status = "C" ]]
then
read -p "Enter Years " Years
if [[ $Status = "S" || $Status = "H" ]]
then
        if [[ $Years -ge 2 ]]
        then
            ((NumOfShares=50))
            echo "You get a bonus of" $NumOfShares "shares
              of company stock"
        else
            echo "You must be here at least 2 years for
            receiving company stock."
        fi
   elif [ $Status = "C" ]
   then
        if [[ $Years -gt 3 ]]
        then
            ((Bonus=100))
            echo "You get a bonus of" '$'$Bonus
        else
            echo "You must be here at least 3 years for
              receiving company stock."
        fi
   fi
else
        echo "Invalid status"
   fi
```

4. Save the script, and then close the editor.

5. Make the script executable, and then execute the script. Input **H** when prompted for status and **5** when prompted for years.

6. Record the output.

7. Execute the script again. Input **C** when prompted for status and **2** when prompted for years.

8. Record the output.

9. Execute the script again. Input **S** when prompted for status and **15** when prompted for years.

10. Record the output.

11. Execute the script one last time. Input **T** when prompted for status.

12. Record the output.

13. Close your window, and then log out.

CASE PROJECTS

Case 6-1

TMI has asked you to create a script that will allow the user to enter one of several choices from the command line. The only allowed choices are as follows:

1. Copy one file to another. Allow the user to enter a source filename to copy. If the source file exists, read the name of the destination file and copy the file. Display a message indicating success or failure based on the return status.

2. Remove a file if it exists. Display a message indicating success or failure based on the return status.

3. Display only the current day of the week.

4. Display a calendar.

Case 6-2

Wendy Tran-Patel owns Working Out For Fun, Inc., and wants to create a rewards contest for her customers. She hires you to help develop the rewards program as well as implement it. She would like to give three rewards each month. There will be a $25 movie pass, a $50 restaurant gift certificate, and a $100 cash prize. You are required to propose the method of determining the reward, and write a script to meet your proposal. The methods used to determine the reward can be based upon total number of minutes on a treadmill machine, total pounds lifted, or total number of aerobic workout classes attended. You need to determine appropriate levels for each prize. You must create a flowchart or prepare pseudocode for your proposal, and then implement your proposal in a script that displays the reward given.

7

LOOPING STRUCTURES

In this chapter, you will:

♦ Understand loop theory
♦ Understand the `while` statement
♦ Understand the `until` statement
♦ Understand the `for` statement

Although shell scripts statements are executed sequentially, you can change the flow within the script by implementing looping structures. Looping structures allow your scripts to repeatedly execute the same set of statements for different data as long as some specified condition exists. Once the condition no longer exists, processing continues to the statements following the looping structure. In this chapter, you will learn about the shell's implementation of looping structures using the `while`, `until` and `for` commands.

UNDERSTANDING LOOP THEORY

In programming theory, a **loop** is when a condition causes a specific set of programming statements to be repeated. The statements within the loop repeat until another condition occurs which then terminates the loop. The term **iteration**, or **pass**, refers to each completion of the statements within a loop; therefore, if a loop repeats its statements three times, it has completed three iterations, or passes.

The flowchart in Figure 7-1 shows the general form of the basic looping structure. You can see that a set of statements is executed prior to the condition being tested. If the condition tests true, then the program repeats the statements prior to the decision. If the condition tests false, the program does not repeat the steps, and subsequent statements continue to execute as normal.

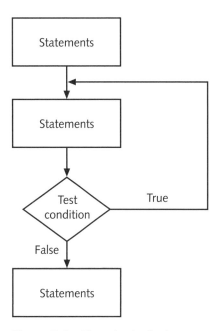

Figure 7-1   Flowchart of a loop

The biggest advantage of using looping structures is that they allow you to enter data without knowing how much data needs to be entered. For example, a bank may need to process thousands of transactions in customer accounts. A program can be created to read all of the records and process them. When there are no more records to read in the file, the loop terminates. Similarly, a teacher may need a program that calculates grades. Because the number of grades the teacher needs to enter may vary, a program can be created using loops to prompt the teacher for each grade. Once all grades are entered, the loop terminates and calculates the grade.

Figure 7-2 shows a more complex example that contains more than one loop. A loop allows code to repeatedly execute until a condition exists. Sally Mingledorf's Ice Cream & Cones, Inc. Main Menu page allows users to access a variety of other sub-menus. A menu uses looping structures to allow the menu selections to continually appear on the screen. Once users choose other menu items, another loop for the sub-menu executes allowing users the ability to choose selections on the submenu. When users are finished with the submenu, they can return to the menu on which they started. Here they can go back into the submenu or go into other submenus which are also made of looping structures. It is the loop that facilitates the ability to go back and forth between menus.

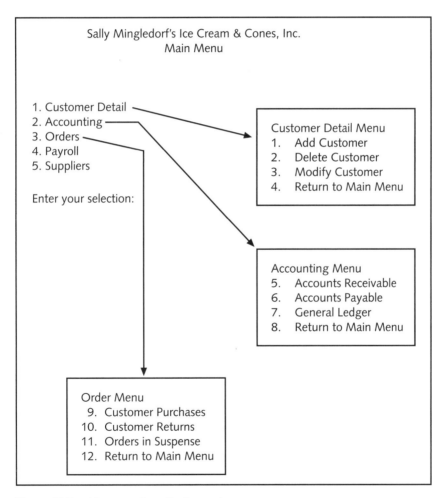

Figure 7-2   Menu system that uses loops

An Infinite Loop

Sometimes the logic of your program can cause the program to go into what is called an infinite loop. An **infinite loop** is a loop that theoretically repeats without end. It does not stop unless you terminate the script's process. You can terminate a script with a `kill` signal.

One disadvantage of a script going into an infinite loop is that it consumes an excessive amount of processing time. You can test this yourself by opening up two windows. In one window, run the `yes` command and in the other run the `top` command. Figure 7-3 and Figure 7-4 show the before and after System Monitor screens for the `yes` command running and consuming all of the CPU time, and then being terminated. Notice the line zigzagging in the "% CPU Usage History" section of the System Monitor window shown in Figure 7-3. Each of the horizontal lines running across the background represents a 20% increment. You can see that utilization started off low because the `yes` command had not been started yet. However, once the command is started, you can see the utilization rise and plateau at the 100% mark. At the time the screenshot was taken, the utilization rose to 101.00%. The act of taking the screenshot is CPU intensive, too. The reason that the utilization exceeds 100% is that this is an average time.

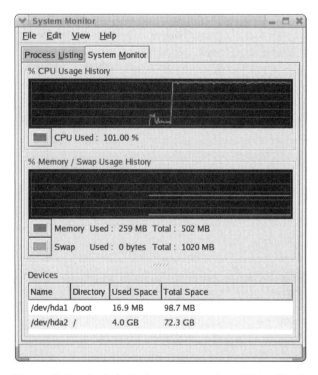

Figure 7-3   An infinite loop consuming CPU utilization

Notice, in Figure 7-4, that the CPU utilization dropped to 11% after the **yes** command is terminated by pressing Ctrl+C.

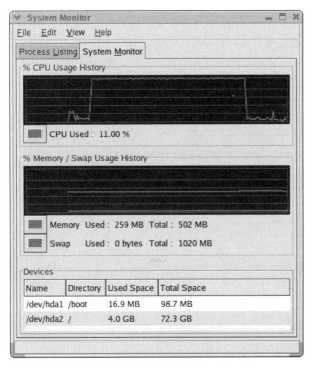

Figure 7-4   Terminating an infinite loop causes CPU utilization to drop

UNDERSTANDING THE while STATEMENT

The theoretical *While* statement tests whether a condition is true or false. If the condition is true, the *While* statement repeats the instructions, following the *Do* clause up to the *End-While* clause. If the condition is false, the loop terminates and program flow continues subsequent statements. The logic of the *While* statement is:

While true-condition

Do

> *Perform activity for true-condition*

End-While

Figure 7-5 shows a flowchart depicting the *While* statement. The shaded area represents the *While* loop.

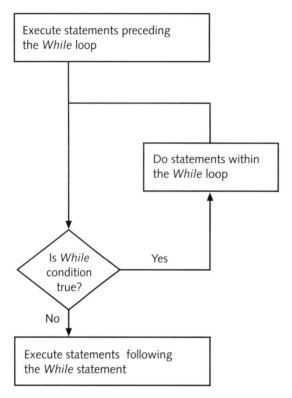

Figure 7-5 Flowchart of the *While* statement

Consider the following business application structured using the pseudocode for the *While* statement. In this example, the *While* loop is used to process multiple records in a file.

Open file

While you have records

Do

        Read record

        Process record

        Write record

End-While

Close file

Notice that first the file containing the records is opened. Then, as long as you have records in the file, they are read and then processed. A record must be read prior to processing it. Processing a record might include performing computations or logic operations on the fields within the record. As long as there are records in the file, they are read and then processed. Once the loop terminates, the file is closed.

The while Statement Syntax

Like the theoretical *While* statement, the shell's while statement also tests for a condition being true or false, and if the condition is true, performs the loop's statements; if false, it bypasses the loop's statements. The while loop in the shell takes the following form:

```
while listA
do
        listB
done
```

The *listA* statements are a set of commands that is executed and that results in an exit status. If the commands in *listA* exit with an exit status of zero, then the commands in *listB* are executed. If the commands in *listA* exit with a nonzero exit status, the commands in *listB* are not executed. The statements following done are executed whether or not commands in *listB* execute.

To prove that the while command performs the do statements as long as the exit status is zero, run this command:

```
while true
do
        echo $?
done
```

The statement true always returns an exit status of zero. It displays the value zero an infinite number of times. You can terminate this statement or any other infinite loop by pressing Ctrl+C.

 You can accomplish the same proof by entering this command: while ! false; do echo $?; done. The statement false always returns an exit status of one. However, by placing the negation operator (!) prior to it, the condition is zero. This loop displays the value zero an infinite number of times.

Using the while Statement

You can use the while statement to test for characters. Consider the script shown in Figure 7-6. In this script, a listing of the users who are logged on as well as a listing of current files are displayed. The script user is then prompted as to whether he would like to stop the script once the network information is displayed. If the user enters a "Y," then the script terminates; otherwise, the loop continues. Let's look at this in closer detail.

In the WhileLoopStop script a variable named Stop is initialized to "N." Next, the while statement uses the logical negation operator to determine if the variable is not equal to "Y." The first time through, the variable named Stop is equal to "N", so the while condition tests true. Because it tests true, the do statements are executed—these are the who, ls, and read statements. The user is then prompted by the read statement for an answer. If the user enters anything but a "Y," the while loop continues.

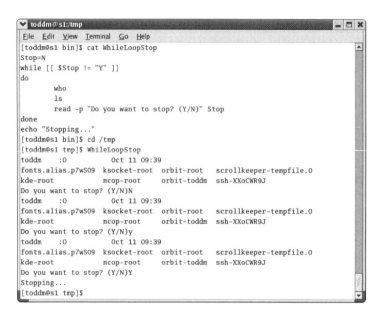

Figure 7-6 WhileLoopStop script that tests for characters

It is important to understand how to use the `while` loop to test for character values because there may be times when you need to do just that. For instance, you may need to loop through code to prompt users to enter certain values, and then test their input. Or, you might need to create a script that repeatedly asks the user to enter a valid password. Next you will create a script that tests a condition. If the condition is true, then the `while` loop will display a listing of processes using the `ps —e | more` command, and then prompt the user to continue.

To create a script using `while` to test character values:

1. Log in to the Linux system as a user, and then open a Terminal emulation window.

2. Create a script named **WhileLoopB** in the `$HOME/bin` directory.

3. Insert the following lines of code to create a loop which shows the processes that are running:

```
Continue=Y
while [[ $Continue = "Y" ]]
do
        ps —e | more    # The "-e" option shows all
        processes.
        read —p "Do you want to continue? (Y)" Con
        Continue=`echo $Con | tr [:lower:] [:upper:]`
            # Convert answer to uppercase and test that.
done
```

4. Save the script, and then quit the editor.

5. Make the script executable, and then execute the script. A listing of all processes is displayed.

6. When prompted, enter "**Y**," and then press **Enter**. Because you answered "Y," a listing of all processes is displayed again. You are prompted again.

7. This time when prompted, enter "**N**," and then press **Enter**. Because you answered "N," the script terminates.

8. Close your window, and then log out.

The while **Statement and Command Exit Status**

You can use the while statement to test the exit status of a command. Why would you want to do this? Testing the exit status of a command in a while statement is useful for determining whether or not a command succeeded or failed. Once you determine the exit status, you can perform iterations based on that knowledge. See the following script:

```
while ! cp fileX.txt fileY.txt
do
        echo "Attempting to copy…"
        sleep 10     # Pause the script for 10 seconds.
done
```

In this example, the while statement attempts to copy a file. If the file is present, it is copied. If the file does not exist, the while statement loops continually until the file gets created. Notice that the negation operator (!) is used. The while statement negates the exit status of the cp fileX.txt fileY.txt command; thus the **copy** command fails if fileX.txt is nonexistent. This results in a nonzero exit status. The negation operator turns that status to a zero, for true. As long as the while ! cp fileX.txt fileY.txt is true the file is never copied. As part of the while loop, a message is displayed indicating that the script will attempt to copy the file again. The script pauses for 10 seconds so you have time to read the message. The script continues to try to copy the file as long as fileX.txt is not present. Once the file is created, it is copied to fileY.txt and the script terminates. It is possible for the file to be created by a background program or by you using another Terminal emulation window. Figure 7-7 shows the WhileCopy script running.

Notice that there are two windows in Figure 7-7. In the window on the left, you can see the contents of WhileCopy and its execution. You can see that it is attempting to copy the file but cannot do so because it did not exist at the time the script was executed. However, in the terminal window on the right in Figure 7-7, you can see that the file, fileX.txt, is created using the **touch** command. It is important to understand that the script in the left window was started before fileX.txt was created. Once fileX.txt is created, the script copies fileX.txt to fileY.txt.

Figure 7-7   The WhileCopy script, its output, and another Terminal emulation window used to create a file

Terminating a Loop

There may be times when you need to terminate a loop before a condition terminates the loop; for instance, if you wanted your loop to terminate prematurely because the script encountered an error within the loop or a user decided to exit a menu that uses a loop. In these cases, you can use the **break** command to end the loop. This command is used within the shell's looping structures and is often accompanied by a variable count. Consider the following code:

```
((count=1))
while true
do
    echo $count
    ((count++))
    if [[ $count —gt 3 ]]
    then
            break
    fi
done
```

In this example, the **while** statement tests for a zero exit status. As you know, the **true** command always returns a zero exit status. You then set a variable count to increment and test if the variable's value is greater than three. Once the variable is greater than three, the **break** command is activated, causing the loop to terminate. Then, control of the script is passed to any statement following the **break** clause.

There may be times when you want to exit just one iteration of the loop instead of terminating the whole loop. In this case, you would use the continue statement.

Nesting while Loops

The shell also allows you to nest **while** statements to create a loop within a loop. One reason you might consider using a nested **while** loop is to create a menu that uses the **while** statement to repeatedly display available options. You could then embed the **case** statement within the **while** statement to handle those options. Also, you could set it up so that one of the options has a loop that requires a specific value to be entered and that displays the same prompt if the correct value is not entered. Thus, you end up with the menu loop, and within it, a nested loop that prompts for a certain value.

Figure 7-8 depicts how nested loops fit together, as well as how you structure the syntax for those loops.

7

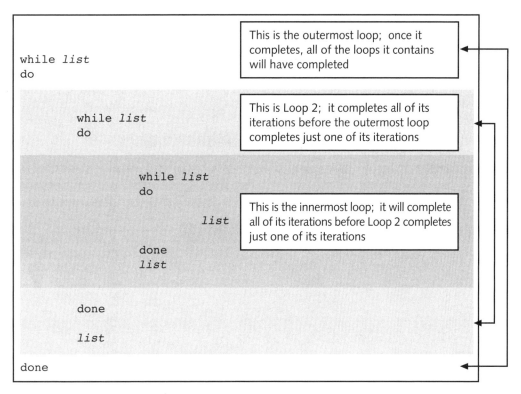

Figure 7-8   Understanding nested loops

In Figure 7-8 there are three loops. The innermost loop's condition is reached before Loop 2's condition is reached. Loop 2's condition is reached before the outermost loop's condition is reached. In other words, each loop completes all of its iterations before the loop surrounding it goes through only one of its iterations.

 When nesting loops, if you have just two loops, the one embedded inside the other is called the inner loop. The other is called the outer loop. When you have more than one nested loop, the additional loops are referred to as "Loop *Number*," where *Number* is the number of the loop beginning from the outer loop. For example, if you have three loops, you would have the outer loop, Loop 2 and then the inner loop.

Figure 7-9 shows an example of nesting `while` loops. The WhileNest script contains two loops. On the first pass of the first while loop, called the outer loop, the condition `$x –le 3` is tested. If "x" is less than three, then the second `while` loop, the inner loop, is tested. This is where the condition `$y –le 3` is tested. As long as "y" is less than three, then the variables are displayed using the statement `echo $x $y`. Then, "y" is incremented with the statement `((y++))`. Once "y" reaches three, then "x" is incremented using `((x++))`. At this point, the inner `while` statement has made three complete iterations. Meanwhile, the outer loop has only made one. So, the outer loop makes one iteration, and the inner loop makes iterations until "x" finally reaches three, and the script terminates. The inner `while` loop then displays the values 1, 2, 3 for every one occurrence of "x."

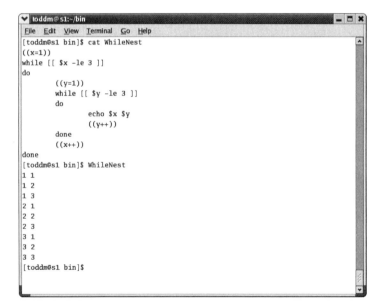

Figure 7-9   A script using nested *while* statements

The result of the WhileNest script's execution displays the "x" variable in the first, or left, column and the "y" variable in the second, or right, column. Notice that the "y" variable changes three times for every one change of the "x" variable. In total, the variables are displayed nine times. In this example, you can multiply the two numbers in each condition, (in this case, three multiplied by three) to determine how many times the inner loop passes through its do statements.

Next you will implement the code in Figure 7-10 to help you understand how to nest while statements. The variables used in this example, "outer" and "inner," are used for incrementing and testing the iterations of the nested loops.

To create a script using nested while statements:

1. Log in to the Linux system as a user, and then open a Terminal emulation window.

2. Create a script named **WhileLoopNest** in the $HOME/bin directory.

3. Insert the following lines of code to use two while statements to implement nested loops:

```
((outer=1))
while [[ $outer -le 3 ]]
do
        ((inner=1))
        while [[ $inner -le 3 ]]
        do
                echo $outer $inner
                ((inner++))
        done
        ((outer++))
done
```

4. Save the script, and then quit the editor.

5. Make the script executable, and then execute the script. Two columns of numbers appear; they are the contents of the variables outer and inner. See Figure 7-10. The first column represents the change of the variable outer within the outside loop. The second column represents the change of the variable inner within the inside loop. Notice that inner changes three times as often as outer because it is incremented in the inner loop.

6. Close your window, and then log out.

7

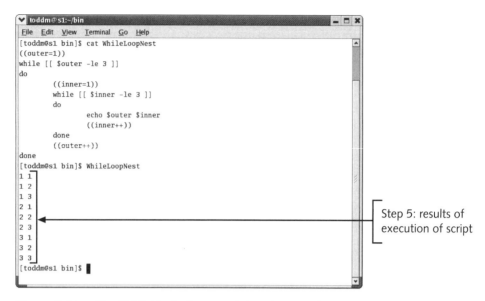

Figure 7-10   The WhileNestedLoop script and a sample run

UNDERSTANDING THE until STATEMENT

Like the theoretical *While* statement, the *Until* statement also tests whether a condition is true or false. The *Until* statement repeats statements until a condition becomes true. Think of the *Until* statement as the opposite logic of the *While* statement. The logic of the *Until* statement is shown below:

Until false-condition

Do

      Perform activity for false-condition

End-Until

Figure 7-11 shows a flowchart displaying the *Until* statement.

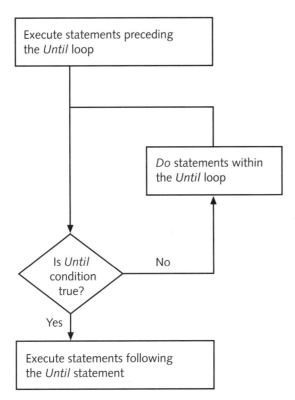

Figure 7-11   Flowchart of the *Until* statement

Recall the pseudocode for the *While* statement used to process records. Now, you will see how to turn the *While* statement into the equivalent *Until* pseudocode. When using the *Until* statement, you need to rephrase the condition. In this case, the condition being tested is, "Are there any more records?" If there are more records, process them. Once there are no more records, terminate the loop, and close the file.

Open file

Until there are no more records

Do

  Read record

  Process record

  Write record

End-While

Close file

Because the logic of *Until* can be a bit tricky, consider one more section of pseudocode for the *Until* statement to help you get a better idea how it works. Take a look at an example that has happened to you—what to do on a rainy day.

In this example, as long as it is raining, you will stay indoors. Once it stops raining the condition turns false, and the loop terminates. Then, you can do an outside activity, such as washing the car or planting vegetables, in this case. Here is the pseudocode:

Until it stops raining

> *Stay inside*

End-Until

Wash car or plant vegetable garden

Now, here's the rainy day pseudocode for the *Until* statement converted into the *While* statement, so you can compare the two. Notice that the logic of the two statements is just the opposite.

While it is raining

> *Stay inside*

End-While

Wash car or plant vegetable garden

The `until` Statement Syntax

Whereas the `while` statement performs its `do` statements if the exit status of the condition or list is a zero or true, the `until` statement performs its `do` statements if the exit status of the condition or list is nonzero, or false. The `until` statement syntax is:

```
until listA
do
          listB
done
```

 Like the `while` statement, you can also write the `until` statement as a single statement, as in: `until listA; do listB; done`.

The *listA* statements are a set of commands that is executed with an exit status. If the commands in *listA* result in a nonzero exit status, then the commands in *listB* are executed. If the commands in *listA* result in an exit status of zero, the commands in *listB* are not executed. In either case, the program flow continues normally after the done clause.

As you saw with the while statement, you can prove this by running the following command:

```
until ! true
        do echo $?
done
```

This command displays the value one an infinite number of times. You can terminate this statement by pressing Ctrl+C.

> You can accomplish the same proof by entering this command: until false; do echo $?; done, which also displays the value one an infinite number of times.

Using the until Statement with Logical Operations

Recall the script named WhileLoopStop that continually displays the logged-in network users and then prompts to see if the script user would like to continue. Consider how this script might function if you modify it to use the until statement. As long as the user does not enter a "Y," the script loops, displaying the currently logged-in users. Notice that the original code for WhileLoopStop has been slightly modified to show you how this script works using the until statement and that it has been renamed the UntilLoopStop script:

```
Stop=N
until [[ $Stop = "Y" ]]
do
        who ls
        read —p "Do you want to stop? (Y)" Stop
done
echo "Stopping…"
```

Figure 7-12 displays the UntilLoopStop script. You can see that the script continues to display the contents of a directory until the user presses "Y" to stop it.

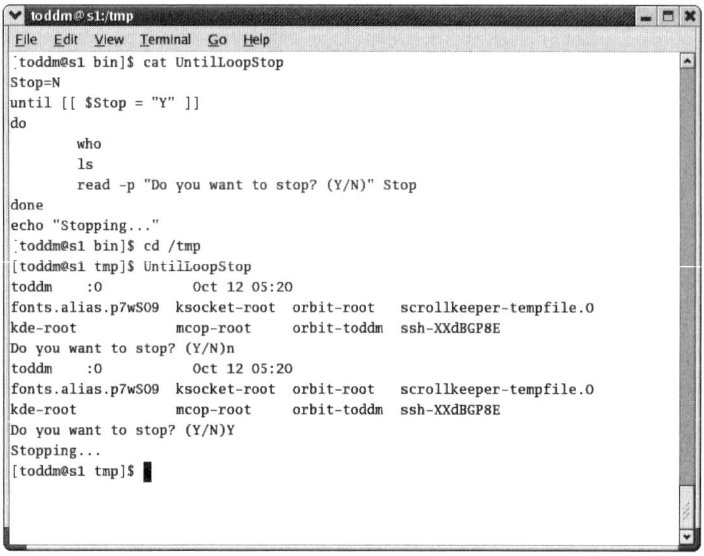

Figure 7-12   The UntilLoopStop script and its output

Consider the following example. Say you work as a shell programmer in the Information Technology Department for Plane Parts, Inc., a manufacturer that produces a generic line of tools used for airplane maintenance. The production manager requires employees to fill out a daily timesheet for the previous day's activities. However, most of the time, employees are days late in filling out the timesheet. She requests your help eliminating the timesheet delay. Next you will write a script to remind employees to complete their timesheets each day. The script runs for the first five minutes of each hour, unless it is terminated. In the script, the variable minute contains the minute derived from the **date** command using the **cut** command. As long as the current system's minute is less than five, then the **until** loop performs an iteration. With each iteration, a message is displayed indicating the user should complete the daily timesheet; a pause of 15 seconds occurs, and then the current minute is derived again. Until the newly determined minute becomes greater than or equal to five, an iteration occurs.

To create a script using the `until` statement:

1. Log in to the Linux system as a user, and then open a Terminal emulation window.

2. Create a script named **TimeSheet** in the **$HOME/bin** directory.

3. Insert the following lines of code to create a message that asks the employee to complete a daily timesheet and displays the message until five minutes after the hour in which the script is run.

```
declare -i minute
minute=`date +%M`
until [[ $minute -ge 5 ]]
        do
                echo "Complete daily timesheet!"
                sleep 15
                minute=`date +%M`
done
```

4. Save the script, and then quit the editor.

5. Make the script executable, and then execute the script to check that it runs correctly. To implement this script, you would add this to one of the login files discussed in Chapter 3. (*Note*: For this to work properly, your system time must be between 0 and 5 minutes past any given hour.) You can either wait for the time to meet this requirement or, within the script, change "5" to "10" for minutes from your current time so the script will work with the current time on your system. See Figure 7-13. Notice that three messages appear on the screen. As long as the minute is less than or equal to five, the message "Complete daily timesheet!" is displayed. Once the minute exceeds five, the message is no longer displayed.

6. Close your window, and then log out.

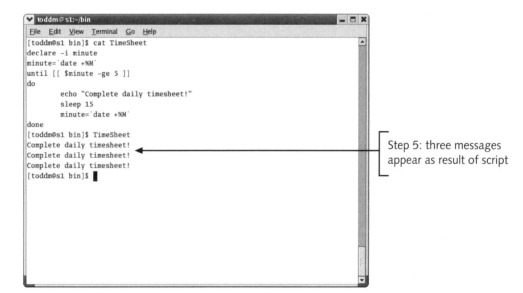

Figure 7-13 The TimeSheet script

Consider one more example. Plane Parts, Inc. wants you to create a script that checks to see if the nightly run for the Accounting program failed. If it did, an error file is automatically created by the program. Also it's important to note that if the nightly run did fail, the application that generated the error will not restart because of the error, and this results in other users being unable to do their work. Next, you will create a script that continually displays a message indicating that an error file exists resulting from an error in the Accounting program. The error file should not be removed before an investigation determines the reason for failure. If the file exists, then an error must have occurred. You can use the `until` loop to determine if the error file does exist, and if it does, then generate messages indicating just that. Have the loop continue until the file no longer exists. In the `until` statement, the –e option returns true if the file exists. This condition is negated with the `!` operator.

In general, it is not uncommon for files to get processed overnight, and if the program processing the files fails, a System Administrator is usually contacted and an error file is left.

To create a script using the `until` loop to test the existence of a file:

1. Log in to the Linux system as a user, and then open a Terminal emulation window.

2. Create the **NightlyRunError.txt** file in your **$HOME/bin** directory.

3. Create a script named **UntilFile** in the **$HOME/bin** directory.

4. Insert the following lines of code to display a message indicating that an error file exists and needs to be deleted before the Accounting program can run. Note the code does not remove the script because the programmer or System Administrator needs to investigate the reason for the failure. When the file is ultimately removed, then the loop terminates, and the Accounting program can be restarted.

```
until [ ! -e NightlyRunError.txt ]
do
    echo "The NightlyRunError.txt file exists and
      it needs to be deleted in order to run the
      Accounting program."
    sleep 3
done
echo "Starting Accounting program..."
# The full path to accounting program would go here.
```

5. Save the script, quit the editor, and then make the **UntilFile** script executable.

6. Execute the script. See Figure 7-14. A message appears indicating the file exists and must be removed in order for the Accounting program to run.

7. Open another Terminal emulation window, and then remove the **NightlyRunError.txt** file so you can see what happens when the file is not present.

8. Execute the script again. See Figure 7-14. The message "Starting Accounting program…" appears on the screen because the NightlyRunError.txt file is not present.

9. Close your windows, and then log out.

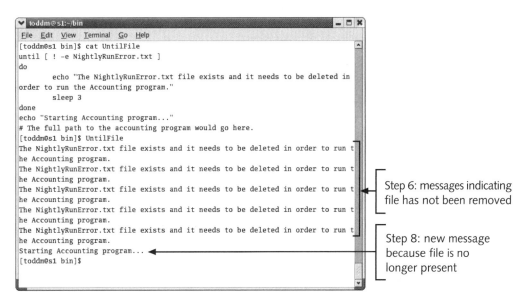

Figure 7-14 The UntilFile script

UNDERSTANDING THE for STATEMENT

The *While* and the *Until* statements are useful when you do not know how much data you have to process. There is another logical looping structure, the *For* statement, that allows you to process a set number of iterations.

Look at the general form of the theoretical *For* statement:

For variable goes from initial-value to ending-value

Do

      Perform activity as long as variable is not equal to the ending-value

      Increment or Decrement value of variable

End-For

The *For* loop begins with a starting value for a *variable*. The starting value is set with *initial-value*. Then, the statements in the loop body are executed. After that, the *variable* is changed; it is either incremented or decremented. The *Do* statements are repeatedly executed until the *variable* reaches the *ending-value*. Figure 7-15 shows a flowchart displaying the *For* statement.

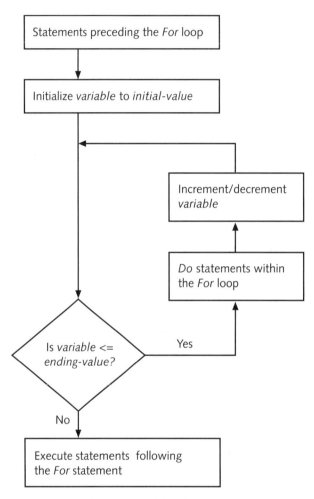

Figure 7-15 Flowchart of the *For* statement

Let's look at an example. In the following pseudocode, the variable "x" starts at one, the contents of "x" are displayed, and then "x" is incremented by one. The loop repeatedly displays the contents of "x" and increments "x" until "x" equals the number five. Here is the pseudocode:

For x in 1 to 5

Do

> *Display x*

End-For

You can also decrement by following the same logic. In this case, the variable "x" starts at five, displays "x," and then automatically decrements "x" by one until it reaches one. The pseudocode for decrementing a variable is:

For x in 5 to 1

Do

> *Display x*

End-For

The `for` Statement Syntax

The advantage of the `for` statement is that it allows you to control the number of iterations a loop performs. Let's say you work for a small radio station, and the on-air meteorologist wants you to take the average of last week's outside temperature. You could use the `for` statement to loop through seven iterations—one for each day of the week. Or, in another scenario, if you want to find the average of five grades for your Advanced Programming class, then you can use a `for` statement to complete this task.

There are two variations of the `for` statement.

- Using `for` with a word list
- Using `for` with an arithmetic expression

You can place both forms on a single line, using semicolons, or on separate lines. The syntax of the two variations is covered in the following sections.

Using `for` with a Word List

You use the word list version of the `for` statement to loop through items in a word list. It is not used for controlling a numeric variable in the word list and incrementing or decrementing it. The arithmetic expression form of the `for` statement does that. Let's look at an example where the `for` statement is performed five times:

```
for number in 1 2 3 4 5
do
        echo $number
done
```

With the statement `for number in 1 2 3 4 5`, the variable named number is assigned to the first item in the list, which is 1. The statement between the do and done clauses is performed for each assignment of the variable. Next, the value of the variable named "number" changes to each item in the list until the last item is reached. Essentially, number is set to 1, then the do statements are executed, then number is set to 2, and the do statements are executed again, and so on until the variable number equals the last item in the list, in this case 5. The do statements are performed for the last item. The numbers are displayed one at a time on one line each.

The variable name is a user-defined name. The items in the word list do not have to be numeric. Next you will create a script that uses characters instead of numbers in the word list.

To create a script using `for` with a word list:

1. Log in to the Linux system as a user, and then open a Terminal emulation window.

2. Create a script named **WordList** in the **$HOME/bin** directory.

3. Insert the following lines of code to create a script that makes use of a `for` loop to insert items, in this case various fruits, in a word list:

```
for fruit in pear banana peach
do
        echo "I need a $fruit from the store."
done
```

4. Save the script, and then quit the editor.

5. Make the script executable, and then execute the script. Three statements appear indicating that a pear, banana, and peach are needed from the store.

6. Close your window, and then log out.

Using Arithmetic Operations

You can also perform arithmetic operations on the words in the word list as long as they are numbers. For example, consider the following lines of code:

```
for var in 2 4 6 8
do
        ((power = $var ** 2))
        echo $var "to the second power is" $power
done
```

In this example, the variable named var is assigned to a number—2, 4, 6, 8, in the word list. In the first iteration, var is set to 2. Then, inside the loop, the variable named power is equal to the value of var, which is 2, to the second power, using `**2`, in the third line. Then, a message is displayed indicating that 2 to the second power is 4.

This repeats for the values in the word list. The output is four lines and indicates that 2 to the second power is 4, 4 to the second power is 16, 6 to the second power is 36, and finally, 8 to the second power is 64.

Next you will create a loop that will allow you to enter seven daily temperatures and display their average.

To create a script using `for` to enter a specific number of temperature values:

1. Log in to the Linux system as a user, and then open a Terminal emulation window.

2. Create a script named **ForAvg** in the **$HOME/bin** directory.

3. Insert the following lines of code to create the loop that iterates seven times:

```
for num in 1 2 3 4 5 6 7
do
```

4. Insert the following lines of code to read the temperature values, accumulate the value in a variable named TempTotal, and then terminate the loop. The accumulation is done because on the next pass of the loop, the current value of Temp changes to the next temperature reading.

```
    read -p "Enter Daily Temperature for day $num:" Temp
    ((TempTotal = $TempTotal + $Temp))
done
```

5. Insert the following lines of code to calculate and display the average:

```
# After $num reaches 7, average the temperatures and
  display the average.
((AvgTemp = $TempTotal / $num))
echo "Average weekly temperature was:" $AvgTemp
```

6. Save the script, and then quit the editor.

7. Make the script executable, execute the script, and then enter the following seven temperatures when prompted: **100**, **90**, **88**, **102**, **91**, **97**, and **95**. See Figure 7-16. A message is displayed indicating that the average weekly temperature was 94.

8. Close your window, and then log out.

7

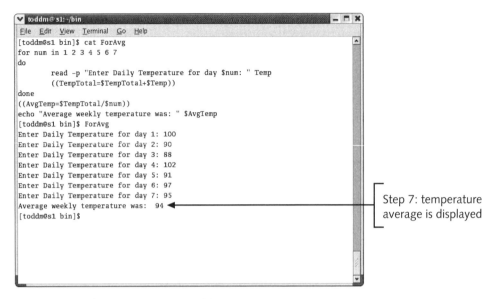

Figure 7-16 The ForAvg script and its output

Using `for` with an Arithmetic Expression

Using a **for** loop with an arithmetic expression allows you greater control over the loop by initializing, testing, and changing a numeric value. The **for** loop uses a control variable to determine the number of loop iterations. There are three parts to this type of looping structure. They are:

- Initialize the loop's control variable with ***expression1***

- Test a conditional operation with ***expression2***

- Change the loop's control variable with ***expression3***

Consider the following example:

```
for ((num=1; num<=5; num++))
do
        echo $num
done
```

In this example, ***expression1*** is num=1, ***expression2*** is num<=5, and ***expression3*** is num++. Here is how it works. The variable num is initialized to a starting value in the first expression. Then, the value of num is compared to five. If num is less than or equal to five, as shown in ***expression2***, then the command(s) in the do *list* are executed. Finally, the variable is incremented in ***expression3***. Then the test starts all over. In this example, the loop continues until the value of the variable num exceeds five. The execution of this script causes the numbers 1 through 5 to appear one after the other on separate lines in one column.

Consider what happens if you modify the ForAvg script by combining the **read** command with the arithmetic expression form of the of **for** statement—you create a very flexible script. Here you have the number of days of temperatures to be entered determined by the user. Here is the code for the ForNum script which is based on the ForAvg script:

```
read -p "Enter the number of days: " Days
for ((num=1; num <=$Days; num++))
do
    read -p "Enter Daily Temperature for day $num: " Temp
    ((TempTotal=$TempTotal+$Temp))
done
((AvgTemp=$TempTotal/($Days)))
echo "Average weekly temperature was: " $AvgTemp
```

This script allows the user to enter any number of days for which temperature averages are taken. See Figure 7-17. Here the user enters the numeral 4 for the number of days, and then inputs the temperatures to obtain the average for those days. There is also another run where the user enters temperatures for two days that are also averaged. You could not do this using the logic in the ForAvg script created in the last exercise.

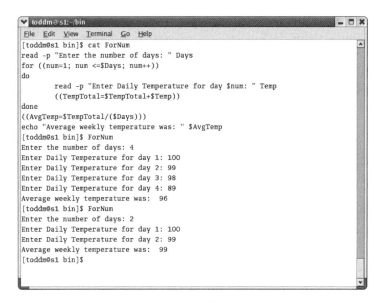

```
[toddm@s1 bin]$ cat ForNum
read -p "Enter the number of days: " Days
for ((num=1; num <=$Days; num++))
do
        read -p "Enter Daily Temperature for day $num: " Temp
        ((TempTotal=$TempTotal+$Temp))
done
((AvgTemp=$TempTotal/($Days)))
echo "Average weekly temperature was: " $AvgTemp
[toddm@s1 bin]$ ForNum
Enter the number of days: 4
Enter Daily Temperature for day 1: 100
Enter Daily Temperature for day 2: 99
Enter Daily Temperature for day 3: 98
Enter Daily Temperature for day 4: 89
Average weekly temperature was:  96
[toddm@s1 bin]$ ForNum
Enter the number of days: 2
Enter Daily Temperature for day 1: 100
Enter Daily Temperature for day 2: 99
Average weekly temperature was:  99
[toddm@s1 bin]$
```

Figure 7-17 The ForNum script and its output

Next you will create a **for** loop, increment the variable num, and use the mathematical operation for squaring the number.

To create a for loop script using expressions:

1. Log in to the Linux system as a user, and then open a Terminal emulation window.

2. Create a script named **SquareLoop** in the **$HOME/bin** directory.

3. Insert the following lines of code:

```
for ((num=1; num <= 10; num++))
do
        ((squared = $num ** 2))
        echo $squared
done
```

4. Save the script, and then quit the editor.

5. Make the script executable, execute the script, and then record the output. The numbers 1 through 10 are squared and the result is displayed.

6. Close your window, and then log out.

Nesting for Statements

You can also nest **for** statements. Like previous looping structures, you must embed a complete **for** statement within another one. With nested loops, the outer loop starts one iteration, and the inner loop must complete all of its iterations before the outer loop begins another iteration. Let's look at the ForNestA script in Figure 7-18. The variable "i" is the control variable for the outer loop and the variable "j" is the control variable for the inner loop.

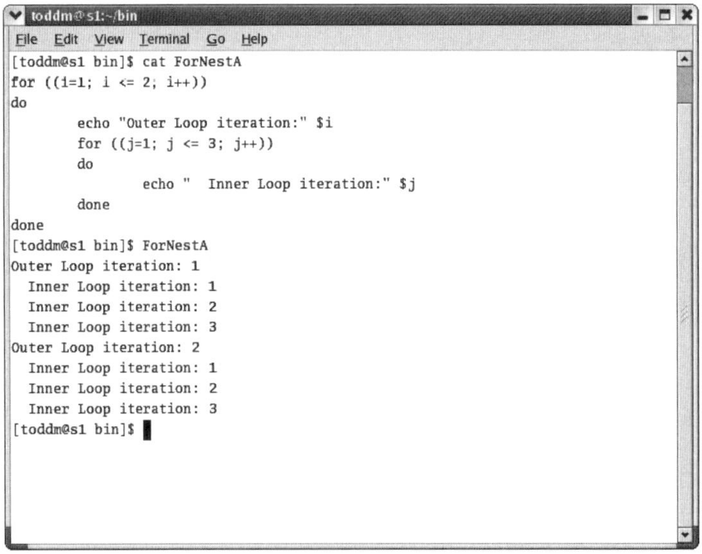

```
[toddm@s1 bin]$ cat ForNestA
for ((i=1; i <= 2; i++))
do
        echo "Outer Loop iteration:" $i
        for ((j=1; j <= 3; j++))
        do
                echo "  Inner Loop iteration:" $j
        done
done
[toddm@s1 bin]$ ForNestA
Outer Loop iteration: 1
  Inner Loop iteration: 1
  Inner Loop iteration: 2
  Inner Loop iteration: 3
Outer Loop iteration: 2
  Inner Loop iteration: 1
  Inner Loop iteration: 2
  Inner Loop iteration: 3
[toddm@s1 bin]$
```

Figure 7-18 The ForNestA script with nested **for** loops and its output

Notice that even though the outer loop begins first, the inner loop must complete its cycle, in this case three iterations, before the outer loop can begin its second iteration, at which point the inner loop must again complete its cycle of three iterations before the outer loop can begin its final iteration.

Next you will nest three `for` loops. The outermost loop uses variable "i," Loop 2 uses variable "j," and the innermost loop uses variable "k." These are displayed in the innermost loop. Notice that for each iteration of "i," "j" changes from 1 to 2 and "k" changes from 1 to 3 twice.

To create a script that uses nested `for` loops:

1. Log in to the Linux system as a user, and then open a Terminal emulation window.

2. Create a script named **ForNested** in the **$HOME/bin** directory.

3. Insert the following lines of code to create a three-level nested loop. The first two lines are heading lines.

```
echo "i j k"
echo "----"
for ((i=1; i <= 3; i++))
do
        for ((j=1; j <= 2; j++))
        do
                for ((k=1; k <=3; k++))
                do
                        echo $i $j $k
                done
        done
done
```

4. Save the script, and then quit the editor.

5. Make the script executable, and then execute the script. See Figure 7-19. After the two heading lines, the output is 18 rows of numbers three columns deep.

6. Close the window, and then log out.

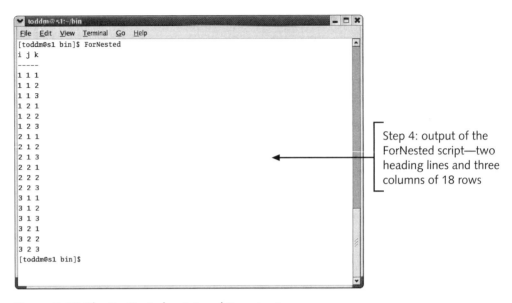

Step 4: output of the ForNested script—two heading lines and three columns of 18 rows

Figure 7-19 The ForNested script and its output

CHAPTER SUMMARY

- A loop is a set of statements that are repeated for some purpose until some condition changes. Once the condition is reached, the loop terminates. An iteration occurs each time the statements within the loop are processed. An infinite loop occurs if no condition exists to terminate the loop; this consumes an excessive amount of processing time and should be avoided. The major looping structures in programming theory are *While*, *Until*, and *For*.

- The while loop is useful when you don't know the number of iterations. You can use it to test the condition of numeric amounts, characters, and commands. The syntax of the shell's while statement tests the exit status of the commands in the *listA* statements. If *listA* returns a zero exit status, then *listB* statements execute. If *listA* returns a nonzero exit status, then *listB* statements are skipped. Statements following the loop structure are executed regardless of the loop's condition. The while statement supports nested loops. Nested loops allow you to implement loops within loops.

- Like the while loop, you use the until statement when the number of iterations is unknown. You can test the condition of numeric amounts, characters, and commands. The shell's until statement tests the exit status of the commands in *listA*. If *listA* returns an exit status of one, then the *listB* statements execute. If *listA* returns an exit status of zero, then the *listB* statements are skipped. Statements following the loop structure are executed regardless of the loop's condition. The until statement supports nested loops.

❏ The shell's **for** statement is used when the number of iterations you want to perform is known. There are two forms of the **for** statement. The word list form is used to loop through any type of item in a word list. These items can be numbers, characters, or commands. The arithmetic expression form is used for incrementing and decrementing numeric values.

REVIEW QUESTIONS

1. Using the _____ statement, the **do** statements are executed for a true condition.

   a. until

   b. break

   c. continue

   d. while

2. A(n) _____ occurs when a set of programming statements are repeatedly executed.

   a. iteration

   b. pass

   c. true condition

   d. loop

3. Using the _____ statement, the **do** statements are executed for a false condition.

   a. until

   b. break

   c. continue

   d. while

4. A(n) _____ is the action of a loop performing its statements one time.

   a. iteration

   b. pass

   c. false condition

   d. loop

5. The _____ statement is used to terminate a loop.

   a. until

   b. break

   c. continue

   d. while

6. The _____ statement is used to terminate the loop for one iteration.

    a. `until`

    b. `break`

    c. `continue`

    d. `while`

7. The following statement will execute _____ time(s).

```
for ((num=1 ; num<=5; num++))
do
        echo $num
done
```

    a. 0

    b. 4

    c. 5

    d. 6

8. The following statement will execute _____ time(s).

```
for ((num=1 ; num<=5; num++))
done
        echo $num
do
```

    a. 0

    b. 1

    c. 5

    d. 6

9. A(n) _____ loop loops forever until terminated.

    a. iteration

    b. pass

    c. infinite

    d. `continue`

10. The following statement will execute _____ time(s).

```
for ((num=1 ; num<5; num++))
do
        echo $num
done
```

    a. 0

    b. 4

    c. 5

    d. an infinite number of

11. What is the result of the following statements?

```
for animal in cat dog bear
do
        echo $animal
done
```

a. The words "cat," "dog," "animal," and "bear" are displayed on the screen.

b. The word "animal" is displayed on the screen.

c. The words "cat," "dog," and "bear" are displayed on the screen.

d. Nothing occurs because the statement has a syntax error.

12. The following statement will execute _____ time(s).

```
((t=0))
while [[ $t=1 ]]
do
        echo "Blue Ocean!"
done
((t++))
```

a. 0

b. 1

c. an infinite number of

d. 2

13. What is the result of the following statements?

```
((t=0))
while [[ $t -lt 3 ]]
        echo "Taco"
done
```

a. The text "Taco" is displayed only once.

b. The text "Taco" is displayed an infinite number of times.

c. The text "Taco" is displayed three times.

d. Nothing occurs because the statement has a syntax error.

14. What is the result of the following statements?

```
((g=5))
until [[ $g -lt 1 ]
do
        echo $g; ((g--))
done
```

a. The numbers 5, 4, 3, 2, 1 are displayed on the screen on separate lines.

b. The numbers 5, 4, 3, 2 are displayed on the screen on separate lines.

c. The numbers 4, 3, 2, 1, 0 are displayed on the screen on separate lines.

d. Nothing occurs because the statement has a syntax error.

15. The following statement displays "Popcorn" _____ times.

```
for ((num1=1 ; num1<=3; num1++))
do
        for ((num2=1; num2<=2; num2++))
        do
                echo "Popcorn"
        done
done
```

a. 0

b. 4

c. 5

d. 6

16. What is the result of the following statements?

```
((g=6))
until [[ $g -lt1 ]]
do
        echo $g; ((g--))
done
```

a. The numbers 6, 5, 4, 3, 2, 1 are displayed on the screen on separate lines.

b. The numbers 5, 4, 3, 2, 1, 0 are displayed on the screen on separate lines.

c. The numbers 5, 4, 3, 2, 1, 0 are displayed on the screen on separate lines.

d. Nothing occurs because the statement has a syntax error.

17. What is the result of the following statements?

```
((i=10)); ((j=2))
while [[ $j -lt $i ]]
do
        echo $j; ((j++))
        if [[ $j -gt 5 ]]
        then break
        fi
done
```

a. The numbers 2, 3, 4, 5, 6 are displayed on the screen on separate lines.

b. The numbers 2, 3, 4, 5 are displayed on the screen on separate lines.

c. The numbers 5, 4, 3, 2 are displayed on the screen on separate lines.

d. The numbers 10, 9, 8, 7, 6, 5, 4, 3, 2, 1 are displayed on the screen on separate lines.

18. Given the following code, what value of the variable named total will be displayed?

```
((total=0))
for ((num1=1 ; num1<=3; num1++))
do
        for ((num2=1; num2<=2; num2++))
        do
                for ((num3=10; num3>=1; num3—))
                do
                        ((total++))
                done
        done
done
echo $total
```

a. 20

b. 30

c. 60

d. 120

19. What is displayed if the following code is executed?

```
for name in 'pwd'; do echo $name; done
```

a. name

b. the present working directory

c. a syntax error message

d. nothing

20. What is displayed if the following code is executed?

```
for name in 'echo hi'; do echo $name; done
```

a. hi

b. echo hi

c. a syntax error message

d. nothing

HANDS-ON PROJECTS

Project 7-1

In this project, you will create a file that contains a list of directories. You will use the for loop structure to control the process. Command substitution is needed to read the contents of the file containing the list of directories. A directory needs to be created for each line in the file.

1. Log in to the Linux system as a user, and then open a Terminal emulation window.

2. Create a file named **inlist** in the **$HOME/bin** directory. This file will contain the list of directories, on separate lines, that are to be created.

3. Insert the following lines of code:

```
Dir1
Dir2
Dir2/Dir2a1
Dir2/Dir2a2
Dir2/Dir2a2/Dir2b1
Dir2/Dir2a2/Dir2b2
```

4. Create a shell script named **Project7-1** in your **$HOME/bin** directory.

5. Insert the following lines of code:

```
for dirname in `cat inlist`
do
        mkdir $dirname
done
```

6. Save the script, and then quit the editor.

7. Make the script executable, and then execute the script.

8. Record the output.

9. Close your window, and then log out.

Project 7-2

In this project, you will use a looping structure that allows you to determine if a host computer is available. You will use the `ping` command to accomplish this. If it is available, you will `telnet` to the host computer.

1. Log in to the Linux system as a user, and then open a Terminal emulation window.

2. Create a shell script named **Project7-2** in the **$HOME/bin** directory.

3. Insert the following lines of code:

```
read -p "Enter IP address or host name to ping " PingName
ping -c 2 $PingName
until [[ $? -eq 0 ]]
do
        sleep 2
        echo "Host not available.  Pinging again..."
        ping -c 3 $PingName
done
echo "The host is available."
echo "Telnetting to the host."
telnet $PingName
```

4. Save the script, and then quit the editor.

5. Make the script executable, and then execute the script, and input an existing host address.

6. Execute the script again. This time use a host that does not exist.

7. Close your window, and then log out.

Project 7-3

In this project, you will create a script that generates a random number using the shell's builtin RANDOM variable. The user will be asked to enter a number between 1 and 10, inclusive. The loop will continue until the user guesses the correct answer. The $RANDOM statement will generate a random number between 0 and 32,767; therefore, a $RANDOM statement within the loop will ensure a random number between 1 and 10, inclusive, is generated by the system.

1. Log in to the Linux system as a user, and then open a Terminal emulation window.

2. Create a shell script named **Project7-3** in the $HOME/bin directory.

3. Insert the following lines of code:

```
read -p "Guess a number between 1 and 10: " guess
rand=$RANDOM
while true
do
if [[ $rand -ge 1 && $rand -le 10 ]]
   then
        if [[ $guess -eq $rand ]]
        then
             echo "Right"
             break
        else
             echo "Try again"
             read -p "Guess a number between 1 and: 10 "
               guess
             rand=$RANDOM
        fi
   else
        rand=$RANDOM
   fi
done
```

4. Save the script, and then quit the editor.

5. Make the script executable, execute the script, and then enter the same number until you guess the number.

6. Record the number of times it takes you to guess correctly.

7. Close your window, and then log out.

Project 7-4

In this project, you will use the `while` and `until` statements as well as nested loops.

1. Log in to the Linux system as a user, and then open a Terminal emulation window.

2. Create a shell script named **Project7-4** in the `$HOME/bin` directory.

3. Insert the following lines of code:

```
let "x=1"                          # Same as ((x=1))
while [[ $x -le 5 ]]               # Outer loop begins
do
        let "y=4"
        until [[ $y -le 1 ]]       # Inner loop begins
        do
                let y--            # Same as ((y--))
                echo $x $y
                let c++            # Same as ((c++))
        done                       # Inner loop ends
        let x++                    # Same as ((x++))
done                               # Outer loop ends
echo "The number of times looped is: " $c
```

4. Save the script, and then quit the editor.

5. Make the script executable, and then execute the script.

6. Close your window, and then log out.

Project 7-5

In this project, you will create a script that displays "Happy Birthday!" if the current month and day happen to match the system date.

1. Log in to the Linux system as a user, and then open a Terminal emulation window.

2. Create a shell script named **Project7-5** in the `$HOME/bin` directory.

3. Insert the following lines of code:

```
read -p "Enter your three-letter birth month
  (e.g., Feb) ?" BirthMonth
read -p "Enter your two-digit birth day
  (e.g., 07) ?" BirthDay
month=`date | cut +%b`
day=`date | cut +%d`
if [[ $BirthMonth -eq $month && $BirthDay -eq $day ]]
then
        HappyBirthday="Y"
else
        HappyBirthday="N"
fi
```

```
while [[ $HappyBirthday = "Y" ]]
do
        echo "Happy Birthday!"
        sleep 10
done
```

4. Save the script, and then quit the editor.

5. Make the script executable, execute the script, and then input your birth month and birthday.

6. Record the result.

7. Execute the script again. This time input the current day and month.

8. Record the result.

9. How would you terminate the script?

10. Close the window, and then log out.

Project 7-6

In this project, you will rewrite the "Happy Birthday!" script using the `case` statement for the decision and the `until` statement for the looping structure.

1. Log in to the Linux system as a user, and then open a Terminal emulation window.

2. Copy **Project7-5** to **Project7-6** in your **$HOME/bin** directory. (If you did not complete Project 7-5, the code for this script is included in Step 3 of that project.)

3. Write the pseudocode or draw a flowchart for using the `case` statement for the decision and the `until` statement for the loop.

4. Modify **Project7-6** to use the `case` statement and the `until` statement.

5. Record the script.

6. Save the script, quit the editor, make the script executable, execute the script, and input your birth month and birthday when prompted.

7. Record the result.

8. Execute the script again. This time input the current day and month.

9. Record the result.

10. Close your window, and then log out.

Project 7-7

In this project, you will create a script that allows the user to enter a password. The password the user enters will be suppressed with the **-s** option of the **read** statement. If the user fails to input the correct password after three tries, then a message will be displayed indicating that the number of attempts has been exceeded, and the script will terminate.

1. Log in to the Linux system as a user, and then open a Terminal emulation window.

2. Create a shell script named **Project7-7** in the **$HOME/bin** directory.

3. Insert the following lines of code:

```
pw=""
password="cactus207"# This is the password to compare.
((count=1))
while [[ $pw != $password ]]
do
    ((count++))
    read  -s -p "Enter password: " pw
    echo ""
    if [[ $pw = $password ]]    # Is there a match?
    then
        echo "Correct!"
        break

    fi
    if [[ $count -gt 3 ]] # Limit the number of times to 3.
    then
        echo "Too many attempts!"
        break
    fi
done
```

4. Save the script, quit the editor, and then make the script executable.

5. Execute the script several times using the correct password (cactus207) and incorrect passwords.

6. Close your windows, and then log out.

Project 7-8

In this project, you will create a menu script allowing a user to enter options to run Linux commands.

1. Log in to the Linux system as a user, and then open a Terminal emulation window.

2. Create a shell script, named **Project7-8** in the **$HOME/bin** directory.

3. Insert the following lines of code:

```
YN="Y"
while [[ $YN = "Y" ]]
do
        clear
        echo "  MAIN MENU"
        echo " 1.  Long Listing"
        echo " 2.  Current Users"
        echo " 3.  Process Listing"
        read -p "Enter a valid selection [1-3]" selection
        case $selection in
```

```
        1) ls -l | more ;;
        2) who | more;;
        3) ps | more;;
        *) echo "Enter a valid selection [1-3]" ;;
   esac
   read -p "Continue (Y/N) ?" YesNo
   YN=`echo $YesNo | tr [:lower:] [:upper:]`
done
```

4. Save the script, quit the editor, and then make the script executable.

5. Execute the script, inputting the numbers **1**, **2**, and **3** for the menu options.

6. Record your observations.

7. Close your windows, and then log out.

7

CASE PROJECTS

Case 7-1

TMI is requesting your services again. You are to create a menu script that allows the user to enter all of the options given in Case 1 in Chapter 6. Be sure to create a flowchart or pseudocode before implementing your script. Make sure you run and test your script.

Case 7-2

You are to create a menu of Linux commands that a user can run. You will need to copy the Project7-8 script and modify it. There will be a fourth menu option that brings up another menu, called the Remote System Menu. Users must enter a password to gain access to this menu. The password should not be displayed on the screen. If an incorrect password is entered, an appropriate message is displayed indicating an invalid password and the user is returned to the MAIN MENU. If the user enters a correct password, then two options are displayed. The first option allows the user to ping to another system. You need to allow for the user to input either an IP address or hostname to ping. For the second option, allow the user to telnet to another system. Provide for the user to input either an IP address or hostname for use with telnet. You will use a looping structure within the Remote System Menu to allow the user to ping or telnet until he or she decides not to continue.

8

FUNCTIONS AND ARRAYS

In this chapter, you will:

♦ Understand functions

♦ Understand function parts

♦ Implement functions

♦ Implement a function library

♦ Understand arrays

♦ Declare arrays and assign array values

♦ Access and clear values in an array

♦ Create records using arrays

In this chapter, you will learn how to implement functions and arrays. Functions are small miniscripts that aid in the development of programs because their code can be used numerous times and achieve consistent results. Functions also facilitate the use of a function library—a collection of functions that multiple users can utilize. Arrays allow you to assign multiple values to a single variable name. This is useful because it allows you to reference all the elements of the array using a single variable name. You can also use looping structures to easily manipulate the data within an array.

UNDERSTANDING FUNCTIONS

A **function** is a set of statements that can be used to perform a specific task. Functions are self-contained blocks, or "chunks," of code that can be used multiple times simply by referencing the function name.

 Functions can accept values and return a result. Functions are called subprograms, subroutines, or modules in other programming languages.

Functions are similar to scripts in that both contain shell statements. However, functions execute within the current shell and scripts are spawned as subshells in a child process. Because a script creates a new process, the operating system has more to manage in the process tree, which translates to the additional use of processor time and memory. Functions, on the other hand, do not require additional processor time or memory. A few other benefits of using functions include reusability, reduction of redundancy, and modularization.

Function Reusability

Functions are reusable. Because of this, you do not need to recreate them to complete the same tasks over and over. Using the same functions multiple times saves you time and helps to errorproof future programs that use the original, proven functions. For example, say you are a shell programmer for a large international bank, The Big Bank. They want you to write a program, which converts currency from U.S. dollars to Eurodollars and vice versa, and that can be used by several different users and scripts throughout the day. One way to complete this task is to create a function. A user could give the function a value of either U.S. dollars or Eurodollars to convert, and the function would return the converted value. At a large international bank, many users could implement this function over the course of the business day. The same conversion program could be written using a script; however, you would have the added overhead with the associated child processes. Functions are executed by simply entering their names, or they can be accessed within a shell script. You reuse the code in a function by referring to it as many times as you need it in a script.

Functions Reduce Redundancy

The use of functions also reduces the redundancy in a programming environment. In many large programming shops there may be multiple programmers working on the same problem separately and without knowledge of the other people's work. At best, although the programmers may solve the problem correctly, they duplicated effort. At worst, the programmers may end up with different solutions to the same problem, where one or both are incorrect. One or more programmers working on a single problem and implementing common functions can reduce this redundancy.

Take a typical programming task that could be worked on by several programmers that is conducive to the use of a function. For example, the programming staff at The Big Bank needs to convert dates to and from different formats. Some date formats are MM/DD/YYYY, while others use the numeric Julian date of YYYYDDD, and still others employ one of the European formats, typically DD-MMM-YYYY. One or more functions could be created to convert one date format to another. Once the data conversion function is complete, all programmers and users can implement the function when needed without having to recreate the conversion code.

Let's look at an overview of how functions can be created and used within a script. Figure 8-1 shows a portion of a script that contains two functions and calls the functions several times. Note this script does not work as is, but is intended to help you understand the placement and usage of functions within a script. In Figure 8-1, a programmer with The Big Bank has created two functions, DateConversion and CurrencyConversion, defined and called within the Accounting script. Although not coded in the figure, these functions have their own commands that accomplish their intended goals. For example, the DateConversion function converts one date format to another. The CurrencyConversion function converts one currency rate to another. As with actual scripts, the main portion of the script, which falls under the comment "The Accounting Script" in the figure, is located below the definition of the functions. Once a function is created, it can be used any number of times in the script simply by referencing its name followed by any necessary parameters. Notice that `CurrencyConversion $Amount` is listed twice in Figure 8-1; this means that this function is called two times in the script.

Keep in mind that the programmers writing the scripts are responsible for writing the functions. They must understand what each function does so they know when to reference it by name and what, if any, parameters are needed for processing. If the programmers wanted the DateConversion function to process data again, they would have to place another reference to it in the script. For the CurrencyConversion function, the parameter, `$Amount`, is the data that the function processes. For the DateConversion function, the parameter `$DateToConvert` is processed. For now, just understand that this is an overview of the placement and usage of functions within scripts. The actual creation and implementation will be discussed later in this chapter.

Modularization

Modularization is the process of breaking a program into manageable parts, called **modules**. Functions are often called modules. In Figure 8-1, you see two defined modules—the two functions and one main program calling them. Because functions allow you to break your program into smaller components, you can isolate a problem to a specific area in the program. In Figure 8-1, if there were a problem with the currency amount not converting correctly, you could isolate the problem related to that function instead of having to reexamine the code in the date conversion function or somewhere else in the script.

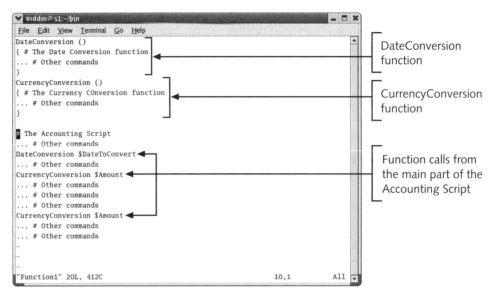

Figure 8-1   Use of functions in shell scripts

Understanding Function Parts

Functions are implemented within a shell script and are usually placed at the beginning of the script. Here is the general format of a function:

```
function function-name ( )
{
list
}
```

The name of the function is required, and you as the programmer need to decide what to name it. You need to include either the keyword `function` at the beginning of the function or use a pair of ending parentheses `( )` after the function name. However, if you choose to, you can use both. The use of the keyword `function` or the parentheses are what define the function in the script. The left `{` and right `}` braces are required and indicate the function's beginning and end and act as the function's boundaries. The left brace can be placed on the same line as the function declaration as in `function function-name ( ) {`. The right brace can be placed on the last line as long as it is preceded by a semicolon. You can also place the right brace on its own separate line. It is important to understand the concept of boundaries because if you place a command *inside* the function that should have been placed *outside* the function, you most likely will encounter logic errors or syntax errors. The commands in the `list` are any valid Linux commands.

You can also place the function on a single line using either of the following methods: function *function-name* { *list;* } or *function-name* (){ *list;* }. Note that the semicolon is required after *list* when you create a function on a single line.

Consider the following example. The function named DisplayHello has only one statement, echo "hello". When the function is referenced or called, it simply displays the text "hello" on the screen.

```
function DisplayHello ( ) {
echo "hello"
}
```

In a script, you make use of the commands in a function by mentioning, or referencing, the function by name, in this case **DisplayHello**. This is known as a **function call**. Think of it as calling upon the function to do its work.

When you put the function and the function call together, you get the following completed script that displays "hello" on the screen and can be added to an existing script or program:

```
function DisplayHello ( ) {
echo "hello"
}
DisplayHello
```

IMPLEMENTING FUNCTIONS

As you know, functions are generally located at the beginning of the script, and their statements are only executed if the function is called. This is because the shell needs to be aware of the function before the shell calls it. In other words, you need to define and create your function before you utilize it. You can place commands before the function as long as they don't reference the function. When the shell interprets a script, it reads past the function and executes statements after it. Once the function is called, the shell executes the statements within the function. After the function has completed, the shell returns control to the statements following the function call.

You need to understand placement of the function in shell scripts because improper placement can cause your script to result in an error. Figure 8-2 shows the shell's response to the DisplayIt script that contains a function that is defined after the function call. When the DisplayIt script executes, the shell cannot find the function and results in a "command not found" error.

In Figure 8-3, the DisplayIt script has been modified to place the function call after the function. When the script executes, the shell can locate the function. You can see that the script displays the text "it" on the screen.

8

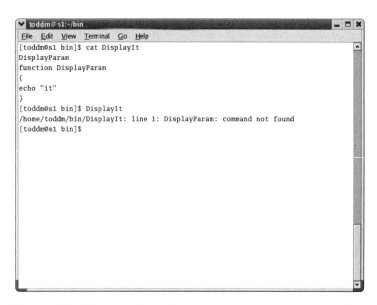

Figure 8-2   Error resulting from an improperly placed function

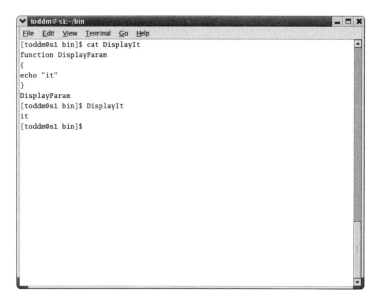

Figure 8-3   Results of correctly placed function

Functions Calling Functions

You can use the code of an existing function within another function. This allows you to use an existing function that is already present—there is no need to rewrite the code. Look at an example dealing with pay for regular time versus pay for overtime. As you know, if a worker's hours are less than or equal to 40, then the pay for regular time is cal-culated as hours multiplied by rate of pay. If the hours worked exceed 40, then the over-time pay is comprised of two parts, the amount of overtime pay plus the amount of pay for regular time. For the overtime pay, the calculation is the number of hours over 40 multi-plied by one and a half (1.5) and then multiplied by the rate of pay. To this, you add the regular time calculation. You must code for the possibility of both regular and overtime cal-culation. So, for the regular time calculation, you can create a function called RegularTime. For the overtime calculation, you can create a function called OverTime. It needs to include a calculation for the first component, which is the actual overtime pay calculation. For the second component of the overtime calculation, you can simply call the RegularTime func-tion. Figure 8-4 shows a partial script that implements this example. Note the script can-not run as is. It is simply used to show you how functions within functions can be used.

8

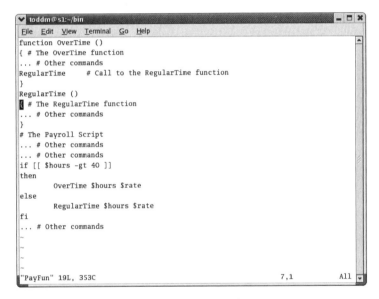

Figure 8-4 A function calling another function

In terms of how to set up a function call within another function, the general format is:

```
functionA ()
{
commands
functionB          # Call to other function
}
functionB ()       # Called from functionA
{
commands
}
# Main section
functionA
```

Look at a simple example. Figure 8-5 shows the contents of a script named FunctionLink. The main section of the script calls the function named Apple and passes program control to it. The first statement within the Apple function displays the text "Apple," and then calls the function named Grapes and control passes to the Grapes function. The Grapes function displays the text "Grapes" on the screen. When the Grapes function completes, control returns to the Apple function. Because there are no other statements within the Apple function, control returns to the statement following the original function call to Apple in the main section of the script.

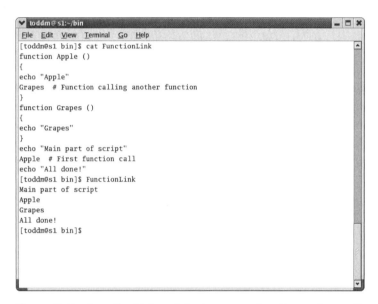

```
[toddm@s1 bin]$ cat FunctionLink
function Apple ()
{
echo "Apple"
Grapes  # Function calling another function
}
function Grapes ()
{
echo "Grapes"
}
echo "Main part of script"
Apple  # First function call
echo "All done!"
[toddm@s1 bin]$ FunctionLink
Main part of script
Apple
Grapes
All done!
[toddm@s1 bin]$
```

Figure 8-5   FunctionLink script where one function calls another

Avoiding Syntax Errors

There are lots of syntax errors you can avoid just by paying careful attention when you type your scripts. However, here are a couple of the more common syntax errors that can occur when you are creating functions. As you know, when creating a function, you must use either the keyword `function` prior to the name of the function or use the parentheses, ( ) after the name of the function. However, if both are left off, the shell generates an error message. This is a common mistake that is easily avoided by making sure you are using the correct format when creating functions. So, *function-name* ( ), `function` *function-name*, or `function` *function-name* ( ) are acceptable.

Another potential problem common among programmers who are familiar with Java and other languages that make greater use of parentheses, is adding the parentheses ( ), after the function name when calling the function. For example, if you create a function

named WhoList, then you call it in a script by simply using `WhoList`, *not* `WhoList ( )`.
If you add parenthesis, the shell generates an error.

Next you will create a simple function to get started.

To create a script that uses a function to display the text "howdy" on the screen:

1. Log in to the Linux system as a user, and then open a Terminal emulation window.

2. Create a script named **FunHowdy** in your **$HOME/bin** directory.

3. Insert the following lines of code to create and call the function:

```
function howdy ( )
{
echo "howdy"
}
howdy
```

4. Save the script, and then close the editor.

5. Make the script executable, and then run the script. Notice that "howdy" appears on your screen. Figure 8-6 shows the complete script and its execution.

6. Close the window, and then log out.

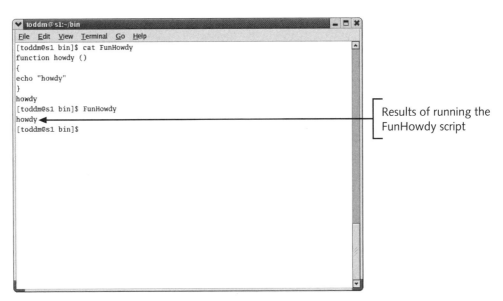

Figure 8-6   A script using a simple function named howdy

You can create a function that the shell can use without creating a script. To do this with the code used in the FunHowdy script, you enter the code at the command line. The shell prompts you with an arrow after each line of text. The right arrow symbol is used by the shell to indicate it is awaiting more commands. You can call the function directly within the shell by typing its name at the command line, in this case, howdy. When creating a function directly within the shell, it is not saved permanently as it is with a file. The shell temporarily saves the function in memory. When you log out, the function no longer exists.

Figure 8-7 shows the creation of the howdy function and the results of the function call performed at the command line. Notice that Figures 8-6 and 8-7 are similar. However in Figure 8-7, you can tell that the function is not a part of a script, but is defined at the command line as indicated by the arrow symbols.

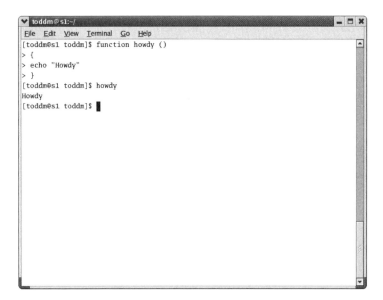

Figure 8-7   Creating a function directly in the shell

Passing Values to Functions

You can make your functions more flexible by allowing the script to give the function different values. When you give a value to a function, it is termed "**passing**." The value of the variable is passed to the function. Once the function has the value, the function can perform calculations or comparisons on the value. Passing values to functions is similar to passing values to shell scripts on the command line. They are both positional. To pass values to a function, you place the values, separated by spaces, immediately after the function name. The general format of passing a value to a function is:

```
Function-name value1 value2 …valueN
```

For example, say you are calculating payroll in a script for La Tasha Trevor's Travel Agency, Inc. You could pass a positional parameter to the CalculatePay function as follows:

```
CalculatePay $1 $2 $3
```

Or you could pass the contents of variables such as Employee, Rate, and Hours as demonstrated in the following code:

```
# In the function call, the first value is $Employee, the
  second is $Rate, and the third is # $Hours.
CalculatePay $Employee $Rate $Hours
```

Next you will write a script that passes values using positional parameters to a function. The script will accept two positional parameters, $1 and $2. The function call will also use an `if` statement with the `elif` clause to determine if the first number is equal to, less than, or greater than the second number. By allowing you to pass any two values to the script and having the function compare them, this exercise demonstrates the flexibility of using a function.

To create a script that passes positional parameter values to a function:

1. Log in to the Linux system as a user, and then open a Terminal emulation window.

2. Create a script named **CompareTwo** in the **$HOME/bin** directory.

3. Insert the following lines to create a function called compare that compares the values of the positional parameters that are passed to it using an `if` statement:

```
compare ()
{
if [[ $1 -eq $2 ]]
then
        echo $1 "equals" $2
elif [[ $1 -gt $2 ]]
then
        echo $1 "is greater than " $2
else
        echo $1 "is less than " $2
fi
}
```

4. Insert the following lines of code to create the comment line and then call the function:

```
# The compare function call:
compare $1 $2
```

5. Save the script, and then close the editor.

6. Make the script executable, and then to execute the script type **CompareTwo 4 4**. A message is displayed indicating the two parameters are equal.

7. Execute the script again. This time, type **CompareTwo 4 6**. A message is displayed indicating that 4 is less than 6.

8. Execute the script one last time. This time, type **CompareTwo 4 2**. A message is displayed indicating that 4 is greater than 2.

9. Close your window, and then log out.

Next you will create a script that uses variable names in a function. Note that only the content, or the data, is passed to the function, not the name of the variable itself. You will use the **read** command to accept the values from the keyboard. The values will then be passed to the function and multiplied. The goal of this exercise is to help you understand how to read data and pass it to a function for processing.

To create a script that passes the variable values to a function:

1. Log in to the Linux system as a user, and then open a Terminal emulation window.

2. Create a script named **ProductPriceCalculation** in the **$HOME/bin** directory.

3. Insert the following lines of code to create the function named Multiply. The function accepts two parameters and calculates their product. The product is stored in the variable named Mult.

```
function Multiply
{
((Mult = $1 * $2))
}
```

4. Insert the following lines of code to read the price and quantity from the keyboard:

```
read -p "Enter Product Price: " Price
read -p "Enter Product Quantity: " Quantity
```

5. Insert the following statement to call the function named Multiply with the variables Price and Quantity:

```
Multiply $Price $Quantity
```

6. Insert the following statement to display the variable named Mult:

```
echo "The total is $Mult"
```

7. Save the script, and then close the editor.

8. Make the script executable, execute the script, and when prompted, input **10** for the Price and **100** for the Quantity. The product of 1000 is displayed on the screen.

9. Close your window, and then log out.

Function Scope

Variables have a scope associated with them. The **scope** of a variable is the set of boundaries that establishes from where the variable's contents can be accessed. There are two attributes of variables scopes:

- global
- local

A variable is considered to have **global scope** if it can be accessed anywhere within the script. All functions have access to global variables and can change the value of the global variable.

A variable is considered to have **local scope** if it is defined within a function. The local variable can only be accessed and changed by the function where it is defined. You cannot change a local variable in a function where it is not defined. For example, you cannot change a local variable outside the function in the main part of the script. You use the `local` statement to declare a local variable.

For instance, you create and set a local variable with the statement `local "PayDay=Y"` in a function named Payroll. You can only read and set PayDay within Payroll. You cannot read or set this variable anywhere else. Now, what if you have another function that uses the same variable name, PayDay. Although this is not recommended, it does occur in the programming industry. If you do have another function, named Paycheck, that has a local variable with the same name, PayDay, the shell treats each as local to the function where they are defined. Think of the variable names as being Payroll's PayDay variable and Paycheck's PayDay variable. They have the same name, PayDay, but are actually unique because they are in separate functions. It is like having two people with the same last name, but different first names. What makes them unique is their first name. To the shell, a global variable and a local variable with the same name are treated as different variables because of where they are created.

 You can only use the `local` statement within a function. If you use it outside a function, you receive an error from the shell indicating that it can only be used in a function.

Consider this example. In the FunScope script shown in Figure 8-8, you see that the variable "x" is defined and set local to the function using the `local "x=5"` statement. Also, "x" is set globally with `((x=10))`. So, to what is "x" really set? This is where the importance of scope takes effect. If you access the locally set "x" within the function, then you are accessing the value "5." If you access the globally set "x" anywhere within the script, then you are accessing the value "10." Figure 8-9 shows the output of the FunScope script, which reinforces the concept of variable scope. By locally defining a variable, you don't have to be concerned with overriding its contents outside of the function.

 Although duplicate variable names can be defined within different functions, their use is not recommended due to the confusion that arises.

```
toddm@s1:~/bin                                          _ □ ✕
File  Edit  View  Terminal  Go  Help
[toddm@s1 bin]$ cat FunScope
function function1
{
    local "x=5"
    echo "Within function1:" $x
}
((x = 10))
echo "Outside function1:" $x
function1
echo "Outside function1:" $x
[toddm@s1 bin]$ ▊
```

Figure 8-8   The FunScope script that sets the variable "x" both globally and locally

You can define a global variable anywhere in the script, including within a function. As long as you don't precede the variable name with the `local` keyword, the variable is considered global and it can be changed in any function or in the main portion of the script. Next you will create a script, similar to the FunScope script, which will include two functions, function1 and function2. The variable "x" will not be defined using the `local` keyword—hence it will be a global variable and able to be changed anywhere.

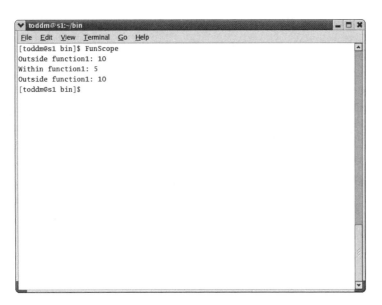

Figure 8-9   Results of FunScope script

To create a script that demonstrates the use of setting and displaying a global variable:

1. Log in to the Linux system as a user, and then open a Terminal emulation window.

2. Create a script named **FunScopeA** in the **$HOME/bin** directory.

3. Insert the following lines of code to create function1. Notice that the variable "x" is set to 5 in this function.

```
function function1
{
    ((x=5))
    echo "Within function1:" $x
}
```

4. Insert the following lines of code to create function2. Notice that the variable "x" is set to 6 in this function.

```
function function2
{
    ((x=6))
    echo "Within function2:" $x
}
```

5. Insert the following lines of code to set "x" to 10, display "x," and call the other functions.

```
((x = 10))
echo "Outside function1:" $x
function1
echo "Outside function1:" $x
function2
echo "Outside function2:" $x
```

6. Save the script, and then close the editor.

7. Make the script executable, and then execute the script. The value of "x" is displayed on the screen. Because "x" is a global variable, the contents of "x" can be set anywhere. Refer to Figure 8-10 for the output. Compare this to Figure 8-9. In Figure 8-9, the global variable "x" is not changed in function1, and the original value 5 remains.

8. Close your window, and then log out.

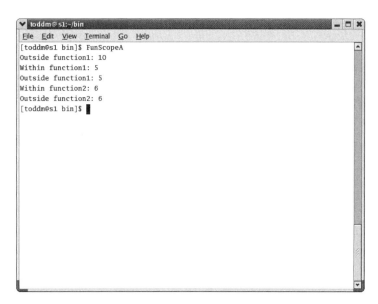

Figure 8-10   The FunScopeA script setting the global variable "x"

Understanding the Return Status of a Function

If you want to test whether a function resulted in an error, you can have the function return an exit status using the **return** keyword. The **return** statement returns the exit status of a function to the shell, much like an exit status is returned for success or failure of a script or command. The general format of the **return** statement is as follows:

```
return n
```

This is where *n* is the return status you specify. You can then test for the return status in an **if** statement. If the function completes successfully, then the function returns with a completion status of zero (true). If the function does not complete successfully, then the function returns a completion status of one (false). Note that the coding of the function and whether or not the return status is zero for a true condition and one is for a false condition is up to the programmer. However, the standard is to use a return value of zero for true (success) and a return value of one for false (failure). You need to plan ahead when writing scripts. If you reverse the order of the **return** statements within the function, any statement may end up executing statements you did not intend for it to execute.

In the following example, a script includes a function that is used to determine if a directory exists. The name of the directory is passed to the script on the command line, and the script calls the function using the positional parameter, **$1**. If the directory exists, then the script changes to the directory, displays the current directory, and displays a listing of the directory's contents. If the directory does not exist, an appropriate message is displayed indicating the directory does not exist. The function returns a status of zero for success and a status of one for failure. Then, the script tests the value of the return status using an **if...then...else** statement. Figure 8-11 shows the contents of the DirExistsA script and the DirExists function. Notice the use of the list command with the statement **(cd $1; pwd; ls | more)**. Although you are not required to use a **(list)** command here, it is done here so you can see variations in the way you can write commands.

 Refer to Chapter 3 for complete coverage of the list commands.

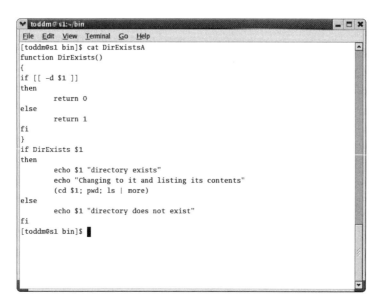

Figure 8-11 The DirExistsA script including the DirExists function

In Figure 8-12, the DirExistsA script is executed twice. Once with /tmp as a positional parameter and the second time with a directory that does not exist. Notice the differences in messages.

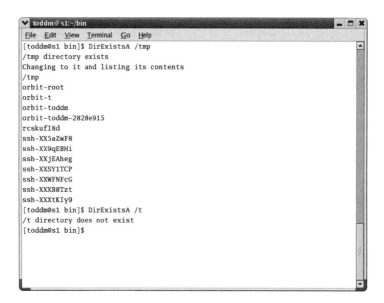

Figure 8-12 Results of the DirExistsA script run twice

Next you will use a function to determine if a file exists. If the file exists, the script removes it and displays a message indicating that it has been removed. The filename is passed to the script and function as a positional parameter. The function returns a status of zero for success or one for failure. Then the script tests the value of the return status of the function using an **if...then...else** statement.

To create a script that tests the return status of a function:

1. Log in to the Linux system as a user, and then open a Terminal emulation window.

2. Create a script named **TestReturn** in the **$HOME/bin** directory.

3. Insert the following lines of code to create the function named FileExist. It accepts a positional parameter and tests for its existence.

```
function FileExist()
{
if [[ -a $1 ]]
then
        return 0
else
        return 1
fi
}
```

4. Insert the following lines of code to test the function. Note the **if FileExist $1** statement has the affect of calling the function and testing its return status. If zero is returned, the **if FileExist $1** condition is true and the file is removed. If the file does not exist, the return status of the function is one and the **else** clause causes a message to be displayed indicating the file is not present. Thus, the file won't be removed.

```
if FileExist $1
then
        rm $1
echo $1 "File removed!"
else
        echo $1 "File is not present"
fi
```

5. Save the script, close the editor, and then make the script executable.

6. Create a file named **file4.txt** so you can see what happens when you run the script with a file that does exist.

7. Type **TestReturn file4.txt**, and then press **Enter**. The file named file4.txt is removed. See Figure 8-13. A message appears indicating the file has been removed.

8

8 Type **TestReturn file4000.txt**, and then press **Enter**. See Figure 8-13. A message appears indicating the file is not present.

9. Close your window, and then log out.

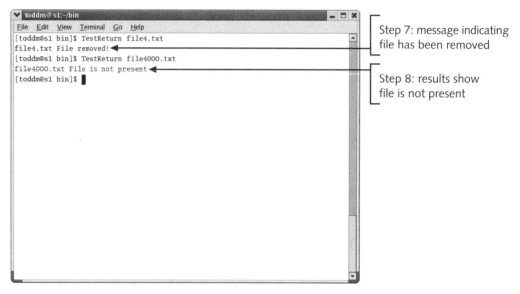

Step 7: message indicating
file has been removed

Step 8: results show
file is not present

Figure 8-13   Running the TestReturn script twice

Exporting Functions

You can export a function to shells created by the current shell. You would do this to use the functions in any subshell spawned from the current shell. To do this, you use the **export** statement with the **-f** option. The **export** statement allows functions and variables to be used by subshells. The **-f** option is required when exporting a function. If you omit it, your function is not exported. To export the function, you run this command:

```
export -f function-name
```

This is where *function-name* is the name of a function that already exists.

In Figure 8-14, the first statement creates a function named **hi** at the command line. Next, a subshell of bash is spawned using the **bash** statement. Then comes the test. The third statement in Figure 8-14 calls the hi function. However, because you are in a subshell and the function has not been exported, the function call to hi fails; the function does not exist in the subshell. In the next sequence of statements, the subshell is exited, the function is exported, another subshell is created; this time, the function call to hi succeeds.

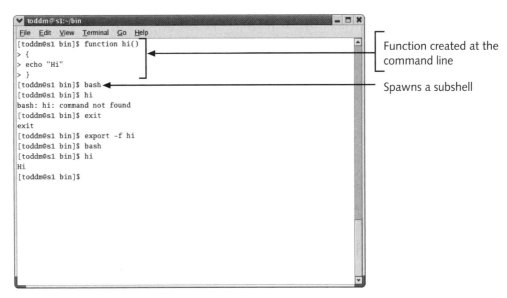

```
toddm@s1:~/bin                                          _  □  ✕
File  Edit  View  Terminal  Go  Help
[toddm@s1 bin]$ function hi()                              ▲
> {
> echo "Hi"
> }
[toddm@s1 bin]$ bash
[toddm@s1 bin]$ hi
bash: hi: command not found
[toddm@s1 bin]$ exit
exit
[toddm@s1 bin]$ export -f hi
[toddm@s1 bin]$ bash
[toddm@s1 bin]$ hi
Hi
[toddm@s1 bin]$
                                                          ▼
```

Function created at the command line

Spawns a subshell

Figure 8-14   Execution of a function in a subshell with and without exporting the function from the parent shell

IMPLEMENTING A FUNCTION LIBRARY

The shell allows you to create a **function library**, which is a file that contains the functions you want to make available to scripts for yourself and others. The benefit of a function library is that you create the function in the library only once. Any modifications to the function affect all the scripts that use it. Also, if there is a problem with a function, you only have to make corrections in one place—the library file. Generally, you place functions that are frequently used in the function library. This enhances the programming effort involved for all.

Here are the recommended steps that allow you to create and implement a function library:

1. Create a file containing your functions.

2. Place the file in the `$HOME/bin` directory. If you have access to user passwords, you can place the file for all users in /usr/local/bin.

3. Use the `source` command in a script. The `source` command reads and executes a script when you enter `source script-name`. If the script contains a function definition, you can then call the function in the script. Note that you must run the `source` command prior to calling a function it contains.

There are numerous uses for a function library. For instance, say you work as a System Administrator and script programmer for Giant Top Circus Performers, Inc. You interview the users, and it has been determined that certain processes need to be automated due to their frequent use. You decide the best way to do this is to create the following functions:

- A function named goto which includes these commands: `cd`, `ls`, and `pwd`.

- A function named WhoProc which includes these commands: `who` and `ps`.

- A function named Prompt, which changes the prompt to include the date and the full path of the present working directory.

Next you will create a function library containing the functions for Giant Top Circus. You will also use these functions with the **source** command.

To create a function library file and use its functions:

1. Log in to the Linux system as a user, and then open a Terminal emulation window.

2. Create a file named **FunLibA** in your **$HOME/bin** directory.

3. Insert the following lines of code to create the three functions to be used by the shell:

```
function goto ()
{
    cd $1
    ls $1
    pwd
}
function WhoProc ()
{
    who
    ps
}
function Prompt ()
{
    PS1='`date` `pwd` ->' # PS1 is the variable for the
prompt.
}
```

4. To utilize the functions in the function library named FunLibA, type **source FunLibA**, and then press **Enter**.

5. To show that the functions are created, type **typeset -f | more**, and then press **Enter**. You want to use the **typeset -f** command, because the **-f** option is used to display only functions. If you leave the **-f** option off, the **typeset** command displays variables that are set, too. See the functions displayed in Figure 8-15.

Recall that the set and `declare` commands display all variables, including functions, too.

6. To use the WhoProc function, type **WhoProc**, and then press **Enter**. See Figure 8-15. A list of users and processes is displayed.

7. To use the Prompt function, type **Prompt**. See Figure 8-15. Your prompt changes.

8. Close your window, and then log out.

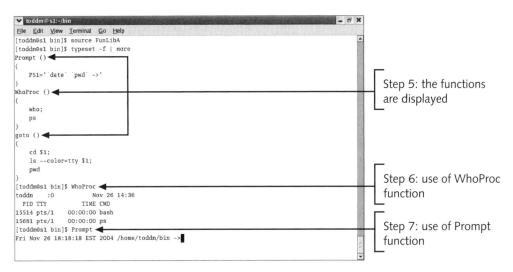

Figure 8-15   Utilizing functions in a function library

Unsetting a Function

You can remove a function from use with the **unset** command. You do this if you no longer need the function. For example, **unset WhoProc** removes WhoProc from memory and no longer allows you to use the function. However, this does not remove it from the FunLibA script. If you wanted to remove the function from the function library, you edit the function library file and delete the lines associated with the function.

UNDERSTANDING ARRAYS

An **array** is a variable that contains a series or list of elements. An array refers to the elements in its list using an integer starting from zero; this number is called a **subscript** or an **index**. The subscript begins at zero and there is no maximum number limiting the size of the array. When the array is created, the subscripts are created automatically; they cannot be changed or deleted. You use an array when you have a group of variables that contain data values that are similar in nature. Instead of creating a variable for each value, you create a single variable name and then place all of the values in this array variable.

You can then refer to either all of the data by referencing the whole array variable, or you can refer to just one specific item in the variable by referencing a single element (using the subscript) in the array.

 You can think of an array as a variable even though it differs from a variable in that a variable has only one value. An array can contain multiple values identified by the subscript. They both store data that can be changed and accessed. Arrays and variables are stored temporarily in memory unless written to disk.

Data can be placed in an array from the keyboard or with positional parameters. Once the data is in the array, the data can be processed as needed. An advantage of using an array is that you can process large amounts of data in memory by just using the array's name.

Processing data in memory is much faster than processing data on the hard disk. This makes arrays suitable for sorting a large amount of data. You have a script or a function read all the records to an array, process the array, then rewrite the data to either the same file or a new file. To complete the same task on a hard disk would prove much more time consuming. An example of processing data in an array in memory is sorting and searching. You will learn about sorting and searching data in an array in Chapter 9.

The items in an array are stored and accessed using their subscripts. Accessing items in an array is much like going to the back of your textbook and looking up a term in the index. You know the term you want to locate in the book, but you need the page reference. The page reference is like the subscript—both are numerical references to the item you need.

In Figure 8-16, you see what an array looks like from a user's standpoint. In the figure, there are 10 items that are all related—they are all animals. (The decision to place just 10 items is arbitrary.) Although the programmer may have input from users, the programmer of the script typically decides how much data to place in the array. Look at some of the items in the array. Subscript number 3 in the animal array refers to Zebra. Subscript number 0 refers to Cat.

You could create 100 different variables and name them something like Animal1, Animal2, Animal3, all the way to Animal100. Set up as variables, you could only access each item as shown in the following example:

```
echo $Animal1
echo $Animal2
echo $Animal3 …
```

With 100 items, this would not be a very efficient approach. Using an array is more efficient because you can use other programming structures to easily loop through the array and assign and access values within it. Then, you could turn your list of animals into the following statement:

```
for ((num=0; num<=100; num++))
do
    echo ${animal[num]}   # Display one element, or animal, in the array.
done
```

Element subscript	Data value
0	Cat
1	Dog
2	Elephant
3	Zebra
4	Octopus
5	Lion
6	Kangaroo
7	Gorilla
8	Seal
9	Tortoise

Figure 8-16   Animal array

DECLARING AN ARRAY AND ASSIGNING ARRAY VALUES

If you want to create an array and not put any data in it immediately, you declare the array with the `declare -a` or `typeset -a` commands; they are synonymous and are shell builtin commands. These commands are used to simply create an empty array. If you want to create an array and immediately place data in it, you assign a data value to a location in the array, using the array name and a subscript.

Declaring an Array

You can create an empty array that can later be used to hold data with the `declare -a` statement. Because the `declare` statement can be used to create variables, integers, or functions, you are required to specify the `-a` option in order to create an array. You use this approach if you want to allow users to input data from the keyboard or if you want to read data in from another file. Because you don't know the exact data the array will contain, it makes sense to simply declare it. Once declared, you can use the `read` command to allow a user to place data in the array. The general format of the `declare -a` statement is:

```
declare -a array-name
```

This is where *array-name* is a user-defined name. For example, in order to create an array named car which can hold various car types, you enter:

```
declare -a car
```

Once you've created the array, you need to assign values to it.

Assigning Values to the Array

Once the array is declared, you can input values into it using the subscript. You use the following method to assign values to elements in the array. If the array is not created, you can use this method to both create the array and assign values to it.

```
array-name[subscript-number]=value
```

This is where *array-name* is a user-defined name for the array. The square brackets are required, and they surround the *subscript-number*. The equal sign is required to assign the element in *array-name*. The element referenced by *subscript* is assigned to the item specified by *value*.

> Place quotes around data that contains text or spaces; otherwise, the shell cannot interpret them properly. Do not put quotes around numeric values.

Consider the following example:

```
product[0]= "Tire"
```

This creates an array named product and places the data value "Tire" in the first, subscript, which is 0.

You can specify any value to be referenced by any subscript in any order. The following example places the data "The Hardware Store" in the array named Store using the subscript 5. (Note that it becomes the sixth element because subscripts begin with 0.) The data referenced by subscript 2 in the array is "The Craft Store" (it becomes the third element). Note the use of quotes around the data because the data contains spaces. If you leave off the quotes, you encounter an error from the shell.

```
Store[5]="The Hardware Store"
Store[2]="The Craft Store"
```

If you know what the data is that you want assigned to your array, you can assign values to the multiple elements in the array on a single line using the following syntax:

```
array-name= (value1 value2 value3…valueN)
```

Notice that this format uses parentheses to surround the values, not brackets. Also, each item between the parentheses is separated by using a space as the delimiter. Each of the values is stored in the array and given a subscript beginning with 0. Look at an example:

```
grade=(100 99 85 88 97)
```

In this example, 100 is assigned `grade[0]`, 99 to `grade[1]`, 85 to `grade[2]`, 88 to `grade[3]`, and 97 to `grade[4]`.

If you want to assign elements to specific subscripts, you can use the following method:

```
grade[0]=100
grade[1]=99
grade[2]=85
grade[3]=88
grade[4]=97
```

ACCESSING AND CLEARING VALUES IN AN ARRAY

Once you create an array and assign values to it, at some point in time, you need to access the data within it. To reference or access an element in an array, you must use the correct subscript associated with it. Here is the syntax:

```
${array-name[subscript]}
```

To display the sixth element (subscript 5) in an array named food, you enter `echo ${food[5]}`.

You can also assign a variable to an array element. In the following statement, the variable fooditem is assigned to the sixth element in the array. You could then use `echo $fooditem` to display the contents of fooditem. In this example, fooditem is not an array but a variable that contains a single value from the array.

```
fooditem=${food[5]}
```

Next you will create a script named Tools that creates an array and assigns and accesses values in the array.

To declare an array and assign and access values in the array:

1. Log in to the Linux system as a user, and then open a Terminal emulation window.

2. Create a script named **Tools** in the `$HOME/bin` directory.

3. Insert the following lines of code to create the array and assign values to the first three elements:

```
declare -a Tool
Tool[0]="Wrench"
Tool[1]="Hammer"
Tool[2]="Saw"
```

4. Now insert the following lines of code to display the values you've just assigned:

```
echo ${Tool[0]}
echo ${Tool[1]}
echo ${Tool[2]}
```

8

5. Save the script, and then close the editor.

6. Make the script executable, and execute the script. Figure 8-17 shows the output of the execution of the Tools script. In this case, the values for the Tool array are listed: "Wrench," Hammer," and "Saw."

7. Close your window, and then log out.

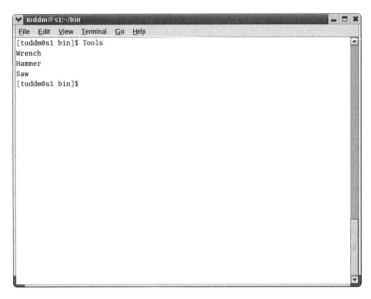

Figure 8-17   Output of the Tools script

You could rewrite the last three **echo** statements of the previous exercise using a looping structure. The advantage of using a looping structure is that you save keystrokes if you have many array elements to display. Examine the following Tools script that has been revised to replace the last three **echo** statements with one **echo** statement using a **for** loop.

```
declare -a Tool
Tool[0]="Wrench"
Tool[1]="Hammer"
Tool[2]="Saw"
for num in 0 1 2
do
        echo ${Tool[num]}
done
```

At first glance, it does not appear that you have saved very much in the way of entering text in the script. After all, you had three **echo** statements and now you have four statements to replace those three. However, if you had 100 array elements to display, then using the **for** statement is more productive.

Importance of Using Braces

The braces, { } in ${array-name[subscript]} are required to avoid conflicts. The use of braces serves to protect the square brackets when referencing an element in an array. Remember in Chapter 4 that the use of braces, as in ${x}, refers to the contents of "x." Without the braces, the square brackets, ([ ]), are displayed on the screen along with inaccurate results. Figure 8-18 shows an array named food being assigned six values in the first statement. Next, the sixth element is accessed using the statement echo ${food[5]}. You can see that the correct text "apple" is displayed on the screen. In the last statement, echo $food[5], the braces are left off. Notice that the text "sandwich[5]" is displayed, which is not the correct result. The first element in the array, "sandwich," is displayed as well as the literal meaning of the square brackets and the subscript, instead of using the bracket's meaning to access a data value in an array.

8

Figure 8-18   The importance of using braces when accessing an element in an array

Another reason to use braces is to avoid conflicts with pattern-matching expansion. You can use pattern-matching symbols, [...], to match a range of characters when using pathname expansion. (This topic was discussed in Chapter 4). Because you use square brackets in pathname expansion and in array substitution, you need a way to protect the meaning of the square brackets when referencing an array element.

Arithmetic Operations and Variable Name Substitution

You can use arithmetic operations and variable name substitution to determine a subscript number. In Figure 8-19, the contents of the food array are displayed using a variety of methods including name substitution and arithmetic operations. Although this is not necessarily a practical implementation of arithmetic operations, when you get to Chapter 9, which deals with sorting and searching, you will need to have an understanding of these concepts.

The statement, echo ${food[1+2]} is equivalent to echo ${food[3]} due to the addition operation, thus "lettuce" is displayed. The statement, echo ${food[6-1]} is equivalent to echo ${food[5]}, again due to the arithmetic operation of subtraction, and "apple" is displayed. You can also see that a variable named "T" is set to 4. So, the statement, echo ${food[T]} using name substitution is equivalent to echo ${food[4]} and "carrots" is displayed. Finally, a division operation, echo ${food[4 / 2]}, results in "spinach" being displayed.

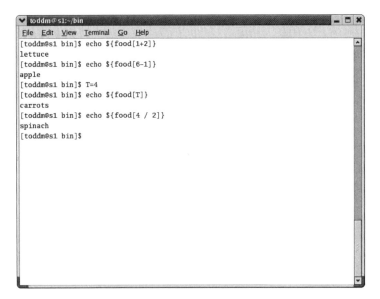

Figure 8-19   Examples of variable name substitution and arithmetic operations in an array

Referencing all the Elements in an Array

You can reference all of the elements in an array by using the asterisk symbol enclosed in the square brackets. This is useful when you want to display the contents of the entire array. The echo ${food[*]} statement displays all of the elements in the array.

To help you remember that the asterisk allows you to reference all the elements in an array, think back to Chapter 4 and the use of the asterisk symbol to expand to all characters. So, simply equate * with "all."

Determining the Number of Elements in an Array

You can determine the number of elements in the array by placing the number sign, #, immediately before the array's name, as in the following statement:

```
echo ${#food[*]}
```

This is useful for determining how large the array is, at least in terms of the number of elements.

You can use a looping structure, such as the **for** statement, to loop through the elements in an array and process each element. For example, look at the code shown in Figure 8-20. In the **for** statement, the variable num is compared to the number of elements in the array, specified by `echo ${#food[*]}` which has a value of 5 (remember it starts with 0) because there are six elements in the array. As long as num is less than the number of elements in the array, then num is incremented until it reaches the number of elements. Using the number of elements in the array in this manner is very flexible because it displays all of the elements in the array regardless of the amount of data.

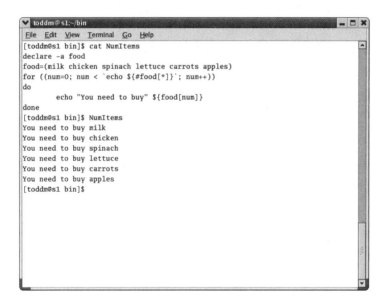

Figure 8-20   Using the number of elements in an array in a looping structure

Determining the Length of an Element in an Array

You can display the length of one data value in the array if you replace the asterisk in the preceding example with the subscript number of the element. So, if the third element in the array is "spinach," then the echo ${#food[2]} statement will display the number 7, because "spinach" is seven characters long.

This is useful for determining if an element is of a minimum or maximum length. One reason you might want to use this is to make sure a user has entered an element. For example, you could test this statement to determine whether a user entered a value or not. In the following code segment, the length of the third element is tested for a length of zero. If the length is zero, then the contents of subscript 2 in the food array is empty, and thus, an appropriate message is displayed indicating so. If the length is nonzero, then the contents of subscript 2 do indeed contain data and an appropriate message is displayed indicating there is data. You could use this code segment in a script to test whether or not an array item contains data or not.

```
if [[ `echo $#{food[2]}` -eq 0 ]]
then
      echo "Element referenced by subscript 2 is empty."
else
      echo "Element referenced by subscript 2 contains data."
fi
```

The read Statement and Arrays

You can use the read statement to enter data into an array from the keyboard. This allows greater flexibility by allowing users to enter data. All you need to do is write the script to manipulate the data.

Next you will create a script named ArrayRead that accepts text you enter from the keyboard and displays your data.

To create a script that reads data from the keyboard and displays the data:

1. Log in to the Linux system as a user, and then open a Terminal emulation window.

2. Create a script named **ArrayRead** in the **$HOME/bin** directory.

3. Insert the following lines to read the data from the keyboard:

```
read -p "Enter total number of entries: " total
for ((n=0; n < $total; n++))
do
      read -p "Enter value: " entries[$n]
done
```

4. Insert the following lines of code to display the data previously read from the keyboard:

```
for ((n=0; n < $total; n++))
do
      echo "Value $n is  ${entries[n]}"
done
```

5. Save the script, and then close the editor.

6. Make the script executable, execute the script, and then enter **3** when prompted for the number of entries, and enter **1**, **2**, and **3** when prompted for the values. Be sure to press Enter after each entry. See Figure 8-21. The array items are displayed on the screen.

7. Execute the script again, and then enter **5** when prompted for the number of entries, and enter **100**, **90**, **99**, **80**, and **87** when prompted for values. Be sure to press Enter after each entry. These array items are displayed on the screen. See Figure 8-21. Notice how easy it is to allow a user to enter data into an array.

8. Close your window, and then log out.

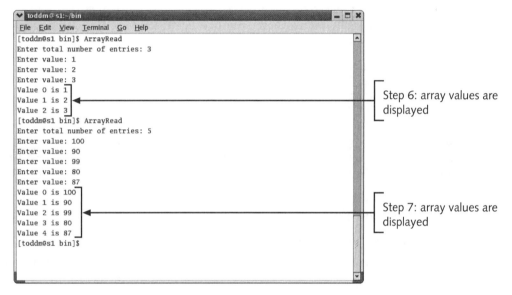

Figure 8-21   Reading data into an array using a looping structure

CREATING RECORDS USING ARRAYS

As you know, you can use arrays to store variables, but it's important to note that these variables can also be complete records. Recall that an array is stored temporarily in memory. By placing records into an array, you are accessing the data much faster than if you were to access them from disk. This is because memory access is faster than disk access.

For example, say that Denise Chyan-McConnell's drywall business has several employees working for it. Each employee record consists of the following fields:

- Identification number
- Name
- Salary

Each record is a data element in the array. A subscript references one record. Here is what two sample records look like:

```
100:"DuJuan Sing":56000
101:"Mary-Lou Buttercup":50000
```

In these records, the colon has been chosen to act as the field separator. You cannot use a space because the space is used to delimit the elements in an array. The use of quotes surrounding the name allows spaces to exist in the name; otherwise, the shell assumes they are separate array elements.

Assume that the data for subscript 0 is `100:"DuJuan Sing":56000` and the data for subscript 1 is `101:"Mary-Lou Buttercup":50000`. Here's how the records appear in the emp array (Remember, there are three fields per record, and one record is referenced by one subscript.):

```
emp=(100:"DuJuan Sing":56000   101:"Mary-Lou Buttercup":50000 )
```

Although the fields in each record are arranged in one order, you might want to display them in a different order, for example, the name followed by the salary and then the identification number. Or, you could just display the name and the salary. To accommodate this, you need to separate each field within each record. You can use the **cut** command to get each field from a record. Because the colon symbol is used to separate individual fields in the array, the **cut** command can be used to separate fields delimited by the colon.

Look at the identification number field as an example.

```
id=`echo ${emp[$count]} | cut -d: -f1`
```

The identification number, or id, is the first field of each record. You need to first echo the contents of an element (a record in this case), then use the pipe operator to send the data to the **cut** command to cut the first field, and then use the colon as a delimiter to separate the fields. In the following statement, the contents of an array element for a subscript named count is echoed to the **cut** command. The **-d:** option for **cut** means to delimit the fields using a colon. The **-f1** option for **cut** cuts the first field, which is id. Thus, this command takes the record contained in the array named emp at subscript position count, cuts the first field using the delimited colon, and places the contents in the variable named id. The name and salary are cut similarly.

Next you will create an array of records, and then cut the fields within each record. Each record occupies one subscript position in the array.

To create a script that displays fields from records in an array:

1. Log in to the Linux system as a user, and then open a Terminal emulation window.

2. Create a script named **ArrayRecords** in the **$HOME/bin** directory.

3. Insert the following lines of code to create the array and set the variable max to the total number of elements in the array:

```
# The array emp holds the records
emp=(100:"DuJuan Sing":56000 101:"Mary-
  Lou Buttercup":50000 103:"Joe Brown":45000
  104:"Mary Seoul":67000 )
max=${#emp[*]}  # Max equals the total number of elements
```

4. Insert the following lines of code to create the loop to process all the records in the array. The variable count is used to increment the items in the array. It begins at 0 and is incremented until it reaches the variable named max.

```
for (( count=0; $count < $max ; count++ ))  # Count is the subscript
do
```

5. Insert the following lines of code to set each of the fields to variable names that can be used:

```
id=`echo ${emp[$count]} | cut -d: -f1`      # Field 1
name=`echo ${emp[$count]} | cut -d: -f2`   # Field 2
salary=`echo ${emp[$count]} | cut -d: -f3` # Field 3
```

6. Insert the following lines of code to display all of the fields and terminate the loop:

```
     echo "The id of $name is $id and the salary is $salary."
done
```

7. Save the script, and then close the editor.

8. Make the script executable, and execute the script. See Figure 8-22. All of the records in the array are displayed. You could modify the script to include additional records and rerun it without changing anything else. Because the variable max contains the maximum number of array elements, it always reflects the correct number.

9. Close your window, and then log out.

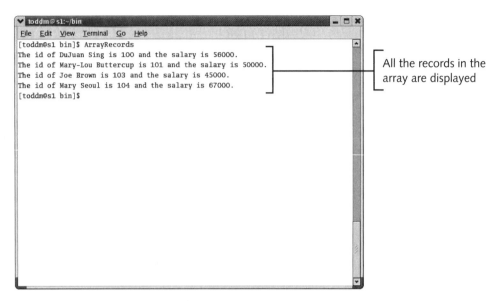

Figure 8-22   Processing records in an array

CHAPTER SUMMARY

❑ Functions are miniprograms that can be executed from a shell or from within a script. They allow you to reuse program code and they reduce redundancy because they can be called multiple times. Because functions are modular, you can troubleshoot a program quickly.

❑ The parts of a function include the name of the function and the list of the commands the function performs. When creating a function, you must precede the function name with either the text "function" or follow it with left and right parentheses. You must also use a left brace, ({), and a right brace, (}), to begin and end the function.

❑ A function is called in a script by placing the name of the function where you want it used. Functions are flexible because they allow you to pass data to them during the function call. Variables defined in functions can be either local or global. A local variable can only be defined within a function. A local variable can only be changed within the function—hence it is local to the function. A global variable can be changed anywhere in the script. You can determine whether or not a function succeeded by using the **return** keyword. You can export a function so it can be used in a subshell.

❑ You can place functions that are frequently used in a function library. A function library is a file that contains functions. By creating a function library, you allow other users to utilize the functions. You use the **source** command to access the function library. If the script only contains functions, then running the `source` command makes the functions available to users.

❑ An array is a variable that holds data as a series of elements. The data is accessed using a subscript which is an integer. Subscripts start numbering at zero; there can be an unlimited number of subscripts in any given array. You can refer to all the data or individual data elements by using a subscript. The advantage of an array is that it can be held in memory.

❑ Arrays can be created with the `declare -a` statement. An array is also created when assigning a value to a subscript, as in *array-name*[*subscript*]=*value* or *array-name*=(*value1 value2...valueN*). You can access individual items by referencing the subscript number that corresponds to the array element, as in `echo` *$array-name*[*subscript*].

❑ You can create and access records within an array. You need to use a separator such as the colon to delimit the fields. When using an array this way, the elements in the array represent an entire record. The advantage of accessing records in an array is improved performance because the records are held in memory until written to disk.

8

REVIEW QUESTIONS

1. A _____ is a set of statements that is considered a miniprogram.

   a. function

   b. array

   c. function library

   d. block

2. Which of the following commands is used to create an array?

   a. `create`

   b. `declare`

   c. `function`

   d. `source`

3. You use the _____ command to call a function library file.

   a. `create`

   b. `declare`

   c. `function`

   d. `source`

4. Which of the following commands is used to display all variables?

   a. `create`

   b. `typeset`

   c. `function`

   d. `source`

5. You use the _____ command to create a function named Goals.

   a. `unset Goals`

   b. `declare -a Goals`

   c. `function Goals ()`

   d. `source Goals`

6. Which of the following commands is used to remove a function named Goals?

   a. `unset Goals`

   b. `declare -a Goals`

   c. `function Goals ()`

   d. `source Goals`

7. You use the _____ statement to display all the values in an array named Beaches.

   a. `echo ${Beaches[0]}`

   b. `echo ${Beaches[*])[`

   c. `echo ${Beaches[#]}`

   d. `echo ${Beaches[*]}`

8. A _____ refers to the element number in an array.

   a. call

   b. data value

   c. subscript

   d. return value

9. _____ is the process of breaking a programming task into smaller pieces.

   a. Function calling

   b. Subscripting

   c. Indexing

   d. Modularization

10. A _____ activates a function.

   a. function call

   b. return value

   c. subscript

   d. function module

11. Which of the following commands is used to display the length of the data value located at subscript 5 in the array named Beaches?

   a. `echo ${Beaches[5]}`

   b. `echo ${#Beaches[4]}[`

   c. `echo ${#Beaches[5]}`

   d. `echo ${@Beaches[*]}`

12. Which of the following commands is used to display the first value in the array named Beaches?

   a. `echo ${Beaches[0]}`

   b. `echo ${Beaches[1]}[`

   c. `echo ${Beaches[2]}`

   d. `echo ${Beaches[*]}`

13. You use the _____ command to declare a variable so it can only be used in a function.

   a. `global`

   b. `function`

   c. `declare -a`

   d. `source`

14. A value is _____ to a function when the function is given the value to process.

   a. called

   b. returned

   c. passed

   d. evaluated

15. Which of the following commands is used to display the total number of data values in the array named Beaches?

   a. `echo ${Beaches[]}`

   b. `echo ${*Beaches[#]}[`

   c. `echo ${#Beaches[*]}`

   d. `echo ${@Beaches[*]}`

8

16. Which of the following declares an array named States with the elements Florida, Georgia, Maine, Montana, and Alabama?

    a. `states=( Florida Georgia Maine Montana Alabama )`

    b. `states[]=( Florida Georgia Maine Montana Alabama )`

    c. `states[01234]=( Florida Georgia Maine Montana )Alabama`

    d. `function()=( Florida Georgia Maine Montana Alabama )`

17. What is the result when the following function is executed?

    ```
    Function airplane{}
    (
    echo "Airplane"
    )
    airplane $1
    ```

    a. a syntax error

    b. The first positional parameter is displayed.

    c. The text "Airplane" is displayed.

    d. The text "Airplane $1" is displayed.

18. What is the result when the following function is executed?

    ```
    Function airplane()
    {
    echo $1
    }
    airplane $1
    ```

    a. a syntax error

    b. The first positional parameter is displayed.

    c. The text "Airplane" is displayed.

    d. The text "$1" is displayed.

19. What is the result when the following script is executed?

    ```
    array1=(a b c d e)
    echo ${array1[3+1]}
    ```

    a. a syntax error

    b. The letter "b" is displayed.

    c. The letter "d" is displayed.

    d. The letter "e" is displayed.

20. What is the result when the following script is executed?

```
array1=(a b c d e)
echo $[array1{0}]
```

a. a syntax error

b. The letter "a" is displayed.

c. The letter "d" is displayed.

d. The letter "e" is displayed.

HANDS-ON PROJECTS

Project 8-1

In this project, you will create an array and manipulate data within the array.

1. Log in to the Linux system as a user, and then open a Terminal emulation window.

2. Create a shell script named **Project8-1** in the **$HOME/bin** directory.

3. At the command line, enter the following statements:

```
Array[0]=5
Array[1]=10
Array[4]=2
Array[2]=100
Array[3]=7
```

4. Display all the elements in the array using one **echo** command, and then record the command that you used.

5. What is different about the order of the items entered compared to the order in which they are displayed?

6. Insert the following lines of code to use calculations and variables to determine the subscript value:

```
((t=3))
echo ${Array[t]}
echo ${Array[(t + 1) / 2]}
echo ${Array[${Array[4]}]}
Array[5]=`expr ${Array[1]} + ${Array[3]} `
echo ${Array[5]}
```

7. Save the script, close the editor, make the script executable, and then execute the script.

8. Record the results.

9. Give an explanation why each value was displayed.

10. Close your window, and then log out.

8

Project 8-2

In this project, you will create a function to display whether a profit, loss, or breakeven occurs when entering Sales and Costs. A function is also used to read the Sales and Costs amounts by quantity.

1. Log in to the Linux system as a user, and then open a Terminal emulation window.

2. Create a shell script named **Project8-2** in the **$HOME/bin** directory.

3. Insert the following lines of code:

```
function GetData ()
{
read -p "Enter Sales Amount: " Sales
read -p "Enter Costs: " Costs
}
function BELP ()
{
((Sales=$1))
((Costs=$2))
((Net=$Sales - $Costs))
if [[ $Net -eq "0" ]]
then
        echo "Profits and Costs are equal - breakeven"
elif [[ $Net -gt "0" ]]
  then
        echo "Profit of: " $Net
  elif [[ $Net -lt 0 ]]
        then
        echo "Loss of " $Net
fi
}
GetData
BELP $Sales $Costs  # Call the BELP (BreakEvenLossProfit)
    function
```

4. Save the script, close the editor, and then make the script executable.

5. Execute the script, input **1000** for Sales and **2000** for Costs when prompted, and then record the output.

6. Run the script, input **80000** for Sales and **27000** for Costs when prompted, and then record the output.

7. Run the script, input **50000** for Sales and **50000** for Costs when prompted, and then record the output.

8. Close your window, and then log out.

Project 8-3

In this project, you will display a message if a value entered into the array is blank. Two functions will be called, one to read the data and another to check the data. The goal of this project is to help you implement functions and arrays and test the length of data elements.

1. Log in to the Linux system as a user, and then open a Terminal emulation window.

2. Create a shell script named **Project 8-3** in the **$HOME/bin** directory.

3. Insert the following lines of code:

```
ReadEntries ()
{
read -p "Enter total number of entries " tot  # Read
  total values.
for ((n=0; n < $tot; n++))  # Loop and read values.
do
    read -p "Enter value " entries[$n]
done
}
CheckForBlanks()
{
for ((n=0; n < $tot; n++))
do
    if [[ `echo ${#entries[n]}` eq 0 ]]  # If
        element length 0, assume blank.
    then
        echo "Value" $n "is blank"
    else
        echo "Value" $n "is" ${entries[n]}
    fi
done
}
ReadEntries
CheckForBlanks
```

4. Save the file, close the editor, and then make the script executable.

5. Run the script and enter **4** as the number of entries, and then insert the following four values when prompted: **frog**, **dog**, press **Enter** for the third value, and **400**.

6. Record the output.

7. Rerun with different values, and then record your findings.

8. Close your window, and then log out.

Project 8-4

In this project, you will use an array to hold directory names. You will test whether each directory exists and if so, a tree listing of the directory is displayed. This project reinforces the use of arrays.

1. Log in to the Linux system as a user, and then open a Terminal emulation window.

2. Create a shell script named **Project8-4** in the **$HOME/bin** directory.

3. Insert the following lines of code:

```
declare -a dir
```

```
dir=( cats dogs birds snakes cats/large cats/small )
   # The directories.
max=${#dir[*]}
for (( num=0; num < $max; num++ ))
do
   if [[ ! -d ${dir[num]} ]]  # If
      directory does not exist create and perform a tree
      listing.
   then
      echo "Creating directory " ${dir[num]}
      mkdir ${dir[num]}
   fi
done
```

4. Save the script, close the editor, and then make the script executable.

5. Execute the script, and then record the output.

6. Close your window, and then log out.

Project 8-5

In this project, you will work with the scope of variables. You will create a function with a locally defined array and a globally defined array. You will then attempt to access the contents of the arrays inside and outside the function.

1. Log in to the Linux system as a user, and then open a Terminal emulation window.

2. Create a shell script named **Project8-5** in the **$HOME/bin** directory.

3. Insert the following lines of code:

```
function Arrays()
{
local -a LocalArray       # Locally defined array.
LocalArray[0]=0           # Set local array values.
LocalArray[1]=1
LocalArray[2]=2
echo "Local inside function" ${LocalArray[*]}
echo "Global inside function"  ${GlobalArray[*]}
}
GlobalArray[0]=100 # Set global array values.
GlobalArray[1]=101
GlobalArray[2]=102
Arrays # Function call
echo "Local outside function" ${LocalArray[*]}
echo "Global outside function"  ${GlobalArray[*]}
```

4. Save the script, close the editor, make the script executable, and then execute the script.

5. Record the output. Why can't you see the contents of the local array outside of the function?

6. Close your window, and then log out.

Project 8-6

In this project, you will populate an array with as many positional parameters as the user enters on the command line.

1. Log in to the Linux system as a user, and then open a Terminal emulation window.

2. Create a shell script named **Project8-6** in the **$HOME/bin** directory.

3. Insert the following lines of code:

```
PopulateArray()
{
max=$#  # Max equals total number of positional parameters.
for ((i=0; i < $max; i++))# Loop through
  array for all parameters.
  do
    values[$i]=$1  # Array element equals positional
      parameter.
    shift 1 # Shift the parameters to get the next
      parameter.
done
}
ListArray()
{
echo ${values[*]}  # Display all elements in the array.
}
PopulateArray $*  # Function Call with all positional
  parameters.
ListArray  # Function Call to display array contents.
```

4. Save the script, and then close the editor.

5. Make the script executable, execute the script, and then input the following positional parameters: **4**, **1**, **50**, **11**, **200**, and **The End!**.

6. Record the output.

7. Execute the script again, this time passing no positional parameters.

8. Execute the script one last time, and then input the following positional parameters: **cars**, **plane**, **trucks**, **fences**, and **plants**.

9. Record the output.

10. Close your window, and then log out.

Project 8-7

In this project, you will create a function that uses the `date` command to display the date in either Julian format (numeric day), the date in MM/DD/YYYY format, or the time in H:M:S (hours, minutes, and seconds) format. A positional parameter ("J" or "j" for Julian, "T" or "t" for Time format, and "M" or "m" for MM/DD/YYYY format) is passed to the function.

1. Log in to the Linux system as a user, and then open a Terminal emulation window.
2. Create a shell script named **Project8-7** in the **$HOME/bin** directory.
3. Insert the following lines of code:

```
function DateFun()
{
if [[ $# -eq 1 ]]
then
  case "$1" in
    J|j) echo "The Julian date including the
         year is:" `date +%Y%j`
        ;;
    T|t) echo "The time is:" `date +%X`
        ;;
    M|m) echo "The date in MM/DD/YYYY
         format is:" `date +%x`
        ;;
     * ) echo "Invalid date format.  Use J, T or M"
    esac
else
  echo "Invalid number of parameters.  Use J, T or M"
fi
}
DateFun $1
```

4. Save the script, and then close the editor.
5. Make the script executable, execute the script, pass **M** as the positional parameter when prompted, and then record the output.
6. Execute the script, pass **t** as the positional parameter when prompted, and then record the output.
7. Execute the script, pass **J** as the positional parameter when prompted, and then record the output.
8. Execute the script, pass **a** as the positional parameter when prompted, and then record the output.
9. Execute the script, and then pass no positional parameter when prompted. What happens when you do not pass a positional parameter to the script?
10. Close your window, and then log out.

Project 8-8

In this project, you will create a menu in which you can enter grades to be averaged. The grades are to be placed in an array.

1. Log in to the Linux system as a user, and then open a Terminal emulation window.
2. Create a shell script, named **Project8-8** in the **$HOME/bin** directory.
3. Insert the following lines of code:

```
declare -a grade
Ans="Y"
```

```
while [[ $Ans = "Y" ]]
do
 read -p "Enter number of grades " Max
 for ((num=0; num < $Max; num++))
 do
    read -p "Enter value" grade[$num]
    ((tot=$tot+${grade[$num]}))
 done
 ((avg=$tot/$Max))
 echo "The average is " $avg
 read -p "Do you want to continue? Y/N" Ans
 ((avg=0))
 ((tot=0))
done
```

4. Save the script, and then close the editor.

5. Make the script executable, execute the script, and when prompted, input **3** for the maximum number of grades followed by the grades: **100**, **100,** and **90**.

6. Record the result.

7. Press **Y** to continue.

8. Rerun the script, input **4** for the maximum number of grades followed by the grades: **80**, **88**, **90**, and **77**.

9. Record the result.

10. Press **Y** to continue.

11. Rerun the script, and when prompted, input **2** for the maximum number of grades followed by the grades: **80** and **88**.

12. Record the result.

13. Press **N** to stop.

14. Close your window, and then log out.

Project 8-9

In this project, you will create an array of records and manipulate the fields contained in a record. You will also perform calculations based upon two fields, then accumulate totals and display the results.

1. Log in to the Linux system as a user, and then open a Terminal emulation window.

2. Create a shell script, named **Project8-9** in the **$HOME/bin** directory.

3. Insert the following lines of code:

```
prod=(Hammers:10:20 Saws:12:5 Nails:100:2 Drills:75:3 )
max=${#prod[*]}
for (( count=0; $count < $max ; count++ ))
do
```

```
product=`echo ${prod[$count]} | cut -d: -f1`
price=`echo ${prod[$count]} | cut -d: -f2`
quantity=`echo ${prod[$count]} | cut -d: -f3`
((total = $price * $quantity))
echo "Total for \$$product is \$$total"
((GrandTotal = $GrandTotal + $total))
done
echo "Grand Total is \$$GrandTotal for $max items. "
```

4. Save the script, close the editor, and then make the script executable.

5. Execute the script, and then record the output.

6. Close your window, and then log out.

CASE PROJECTS

Case 8-1

You are asked to implement the TMI menu script that you created in Case 1 of Chapter 7, but this time you are to use functions. Also, create the functions in a function library file, and place it in an appropriate directory.

Case 8-2

In this case, you will use functions, looping structures, arrays, decision statements, calculations, and other commands necessary to complete the following tasks:

1. Use an array to hold a student record with a name and three grades, for example: "Maude Tedders":100:88:90.

2. Use the necessary commands to cut the fields into the name and grades fields.

3. Use another array to contain the three grades. For example:

   ```
   Grade[1]=necessary statements to get the first grade
   Grade[2]=necessary statements to get the second grade
   Grade[3]=necessary statements to get the third grade
   ```

4. Take a numeric average of the three grades.

5. Convert the numeric average to a letter grade using this scale:

   A is 90 to 100

   B is 80 to 89

   C is 70 to 79

   D is 65 to 69

   F is 0 to 64

6. For each student record, display the student name, numeric average, and letter grade.

7. You must implement at least one function within the script.

# CHAPTER 9

ADVANCED SHELL PROGRAMMING

In this chapter, you will:

♦ Implement a bubble sort

♦ Implement a Shell sort

♦ Compare the bubble sort and Shell sort

♦ Implement sequential search techniques

♦ Implement binary search techniques

♦ Understand the here document

♦ Understand file access

♦ Validate data

This chapter focuses on advanced shell programming concepts. You will expand your knowledge of arrays and functions by implementing sort and search techniques. At the heart of processing data is accessing records on disk. You will be able to read records from a file and write records to a file. Finally, you will learn how to perform data validation techniques so that improper data is not processed.

IMPLEMENTING A BUBBLE SORT

You learned in Chapter 2 that you can use the **sort** command to organize data. Understanding how to implement your own sorting mechanism can also provide a practical application of arrays and functions.

There are a variety of techniques used to sort data. The two discussed in this chapter are the bubble sort and the Shell sort. The **bubble sort** uses an algorithm to sort the data. An **algorithm** is a method or formula used to solve a problem. The bubble sort algorithm compares adjacent elements in an array and sorts them in either ascending or descending sort order. With an ascending sort, items are sorted from lower to higher. With a descending sort, they are sorted from higher to lower. For example, the numbers 1, 2, 3, 4, 5 are sorted in ascending order, while 5, 4, 3, 2, 1 are sorted in descending order. The term "bubble" in bubble sort comes from the fact that in an ascending sort, the low order values in sequence "bubble" to the top of the array. In a descending sort, the high order values in sequence "bubble" to the top. Once the bubble sort completes, all of the data is sorted.

The bubble sort can be used to sort numbers or characters. **Adjacent elements** are separated by a subscript value of 1. So, $a[1] and $a[2] would be considered adjacent elements because their subscripts values, 1 and 2, differ by 1. If you are implementing an ascending sort and $a[1] equals the number 4 and $a[2] equals the number 3, they are swapped so they can be in the correct sort order. Consider the following overview of the pseudocode for the bubble sort algorithm:

While there are elements in the array

Do

> *Compare N and (N + 1) data elements*
>
> *If N > N + 1 THEN*
>
> > *Swap N and N + 1*
>
> *End-if*
>
> *Increment N*

Done

While you can use the bubble sort to sort data elements in an array in descending order, in this section you will focus on sorting data in ascending order with the bubble sort. The bubble sort uses two loops, an outer loop and an inner loop; an **if** statement to compare the elements; and a function named **swap** to swap the two elements if they are out of sort order. These two loops are shown in Figure 9-1.

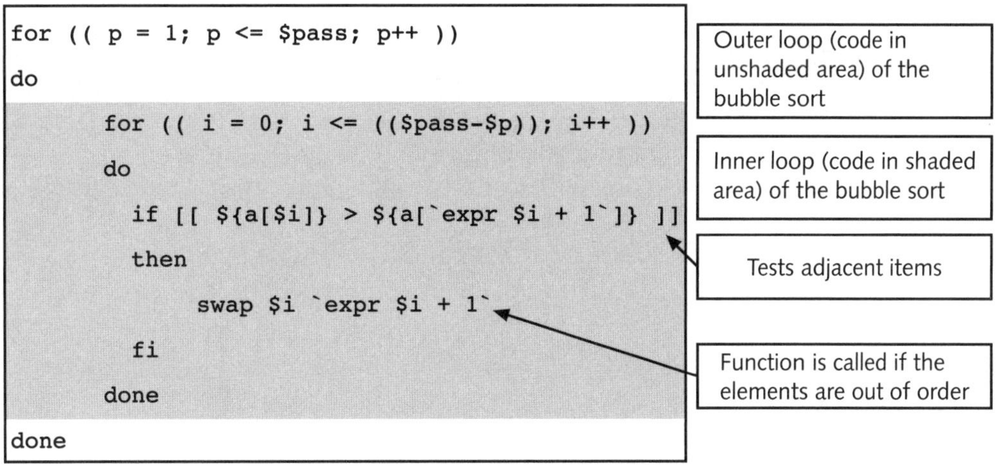

```
for (( p = 1; p <= $pass; p++ ))
do
        for (( i = 0; i <= (($pass-$p)); i++ ))
        do
            if [[ ${a[$i]} > ${a[`expr $i + 1`]} ]]
            then
                  swap $i `expr $i + 1`
            fi
        done
done
```

	Outer loop (code in unshaded area) of the bubble sort
	Inner loop (code in shaded area) of the bubble sort
	Tests adjacent items
	Function is called if the elements are out of order

Figure 9-1   Loops used by the bubble sort

The term **pass** is used to describe the comparison of the elements within the loop from the beginning of the array to the end. The data is not necessarily sorted on a single pass. It may take several passes to sort all the data. A pass is comprised of multiple iterations using the **for** statement. The bubble sort cannot possibly sort all adjacent items on a single pass. So, it makes multiple passes adjusting which adjacent elements to compare and swapping them accordingly.

The outer loop shown in Figure 9-1, **for ((p = 1; p <= $pass; p++))**, controls the overall number of passes through the array. The outer loop is performed for the number of elements in the array less one. This is because on the first pass, the largest valued element is in its proper position—last. So, there is no need to compare the last element in subsequent passes. In Figure 9-1, the variable "p" controls the overall number of loop passes. It is always set to one.

For every outer loop pass, the inner loop is performed "pass minus p" times. This is accomplished in the **for** statement: **for ((i = 0; i <= (($pass-$p)); i++))**. Here, the variable "p" is subtracted from **pass** because the inner loop has to do one less comparison on the current pass because the previous pass placed the highest value in its proper place; thus, it is left with "last minus one."

The inner loop is used to perform the iterations of a pass. It includes the **if [[${a[$i]} > ${a[`expr $i + 1`]]}** statement to compare two adjacent items. This is where the bubbling effect occurs. If the contents of "i" are greater than the contents of "i" plus one, then the function named swap is called with the two values in the statement: **swap $i `expr $i + 1`**. The heart of the bubble sort is the swap function. The swap function accepts the two elements as positional parameters and uses a temporary holding variable name "T" to arrange the elements so that "i" is now less than "i" plus one. At the completion of an inner loop pass, the greater of the two numbers is in its correct position.

Figure 9-2 shows a screenshot of the bubble sort in action. First, the unsorted array is displayed, and then the bubble sort passes are displayed to show you what occurs at each pass. Finally, the sorted array is displayed. You can see that in each pass the largest value is moved to its proper place. In Pass 1, the number 9 is moved to the last position. In Pass 2, the number 8 is moved to its proper position. In Pass 3, the number 7 is moved to its proper position, and so on. In the last pass, all the numbers are in their correct sort order.

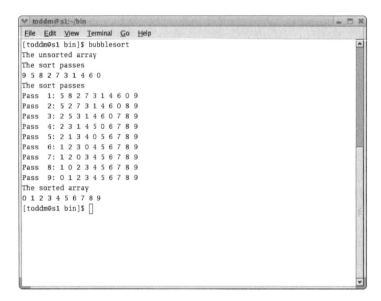

Figure 9-2   Bubble sorting 10 numbers

In the next example, the bubble sort is used to sort the letters of the alphabet. Letters are sorted using their ASCII sequence number. This is called the **collating sequence**. In the ASCII collating sequence, the letter "a" is assigned a lower valued number than the letter "z" which is why the letters can be sorted. So, you can say that "a" is lower than "z" or that "z" is higher than "a." The sort actually occurs on the number representing the letter rather than on the letter itself.

In Figure 9-3, the 26 letters of the alphabet are sorted. You can really see the bubbling effect here. Notice the letter "a" in each pass. From one pass to the next, you can watch the letter "a" move towards the left or "up" in the array, or closer to subscript zero. Also, at each pass, the "highest" letter moves towards the right, or bottom, of the array. Notice the number of passes, 25; this is equal to the number of values minus one.

Next you will implement the bubble sort to sort a list of items you could purchase at a clothing store.

Figure 9-3   Bubble sorting of the 26 letters of the alphabet

To create the bubble sort:

1. Log in to the Linux system as a user, and then open a Terminal emulation window.

2. Create a file named **BubbleSortClothes** in your **$HOME/bin** directory.

3. Insert the following lines of code to create the swap function:

```
# The Bubble Sort
swap()
{
        local T=${a[$1]}
        a[$1]=${a[$2]}
        a[$2]=$T
}
```

4. Insert the following lines to assign elements to the array, display various output, and set necessary variables:

```
a=( shirt belt shoes hat socks tie dress )  # The items
    to be sorted.
echo "The unsorted array"
echo ${a[@]}    # Display all the items in the array.
echo "The sort passes"
```

```
n=${#a[@]}   # The variable "n" equals the
   maximum number of elements in the array.
((pass=$n - 1))  #  The variable "pass" equals one less
      than the total number of elements used in the outer loop.
```

5. Insert the following lines to create the outer and inner loops:

```
for (( p = 1; p <= $pass; p++ ))
do
   for (( i = 0; i <= (($pass-$p)); i++ ))
   do
         if [[ ${a[$i]} > ${a[$(expr $i + 1)]} ]   ] # Compare
            two adjacent items.
         then
         swap $i $(expr $i + 1)      # If unsorted,
            swap the two adjacent items.
         fi
   done
  echo "Pass " $p":" ${a[@]}  # Display the array at each pass.
done
```

6. Insert the following lines to display the sorted array:

```
echo "The sorted array"
echo ${a[@]}
```

7. Save the script, and then close the editor.

8. Make the script executable, and then execute the script. The array of clothes is displayed in sorted order.

9. Close your window, and then log out.

IMPLEMENTING A SHELL SORT

The bubble sort is efficient for small amounts of data. However, for larger amounts of unsorted data, say over 25 data elements, the Shell sort is more efficient. The Shell sort, named for its developer David Shell, uses a value called a **gap** to compare array elements. As part of the Shell sort, the gap is halved using the formula, ((gap=$gap/2)) to determine which elements to compare. Instead of always comparing two adjacent elements as in the bubble sort, the Shell sort algorithm starts off comparing two elements that are distant from one another and ends up comparing two adjacent elements by minimizing the gap interval. **Distant elements** are two values in the array that are separated by a gap interval of more than one. In the Shell sort algorithm, as in the bubble sort, adjacent elements are separated by a gap interval of one. So, $a[1] and $a[3] would be considered distant elements while $a[1]$ and $a[2]$ would be considered adjacent elements. Consider the pseudocode for the Shell sort algorithm:

The Gap is initialized to half the number of elements.

While Gap >=1

Do

> *Until no more swaps exist for the current Gap*
>
> *Do*
>
> > *Compare N and (N + Gap) data elements.*
> >
> > *If N > (N + Gap) Then*
> >
> > > *Swap N and (N + Gap).*
> > >
> > > *Set Swapped variable to "Y."*
> >
> > *End-if*
>
> *Done*
>
> *Gap is halved.*

Done

The Shell sort has three loops. The goal of the Shell sort is to "close the gap" on unsorted items, in this case, N and (N + Gap). Once this is done, the array is sorted. Figure 9-4 shows the Shell sort script.

Like the bubble sort, the Shell sort uses the outer loop to control the number of array passes. Once the gap is zero, this loop terminates. In Loop 2, the until [$Swapped = N] statement tests if a swap has occurred on this pass. The term **pass** applies to the Shell sort as it does in the bubble sort. If there is nothing to swap because the most distant elements are sorted for this pass, then gap is halved again. If there is something to swap, it uses the current gap because distant elements are unsorted for this pass. As the gap reaches zero, the elements tested for swapping are closer together.

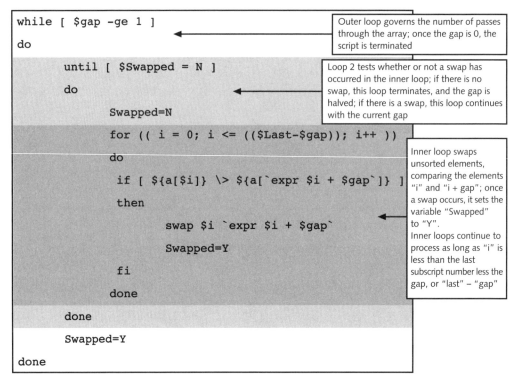

Figure 9-4   Loops used by the Shell sort script

The inner loop for ((i = 0; i <= (($Last-$gap)); i++)), controls the number of iterations in each pass. Inside this loop is the decision statement, if [[${a[$i]} > ${a[`expr $i + $gap`]}], which is used to compare items, "i" and "i" plus gap. It is similar to the decision statement used in the bubble sort but differs in that it compares elements *separated* by the gap. If elements are unsorted, the items are swapped, and the variable named Swapped is set to "Y," indicating a swap occurred.

Both sorts use the same swap function. On the very last pass, the Shell sort functions like the bubble sort because adjacent items are being tested.

Figure 9-5 shows the Shell sort algorithm sorting the letters of the alphabet. These letters are in the same unsorted order as they are in the bubble sort in Figure 9-3. Notice that the number of passes for the Shell sort is only four. Recall that it took 25 passes to accomplish the sort in the bubble sort shown in Figure 9-3.

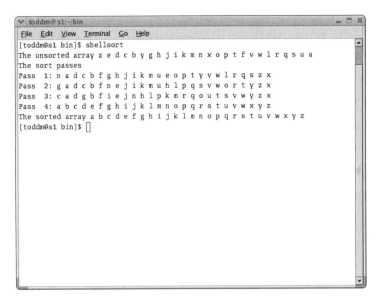

Figure 9-5   Shell sort used to sort 26 letters of the alphabet

Next you will implement the Shell sort to sort a list of items. You will allow the user to enter the maximum number of elements to sort. Then the user will enter the elements in random order. Finally, the Shell sort will be used to sort the items in descending order.

To implement the Shell sort:

1. Log in to the Linux system as a user, and then open a Terminal emulation window.

2. Create a file named **ShellSort** in your **$HOME/bin** directory.

3. Insert the following lines of code to create the functions to get the data and swap the data:

```
GetData()
{
read -p "Enter the number of elements to sort: " max
for ((items=0; items <= $max-1; items++))
do
      read -p "Enter element number $items: " a[$items]
done
}
swap()
{
      local T=${a[$1]}
      a[$1]=${a[$2]}
      a[$2]=$T
}
```

4. Insert the following lines of code to create the function called GetStarted to initialize necessary variables and display messages:

```
GetStarted()
{
First=0
echo "The unsorted array"
echo ${a[@]}
n=${#a[@]}
((Last=$n - 1))
((gap=$Last/2))
((swapnum=0))
Swapped=Y
}
```

5. Insert the following lines of code to create the function called ShellSort that performs the Shell sort:

```
ShellSort()
{
while [ $gap -ge 1 ]
do
    until [ $Swapped = N ]
    do
       Swapped=N
       for (( i = 0; i <= (($Last-$gap)); i++ ))
       do
       if [[ ${a[$i]} < ${a[`expr $i + $gap`]} ]]
          # Descending order swap
       then
                swap $i `expr $i + $gap`
                Swapped=Y
       fi
       done
    done
Swapped=Y
((gap=$gap/2))
done
}
```

6. Insert the following lines of code for the main section of the script that calls the functions and displays the sorted array:

```
# Main section of the script
GetData
GetStarted
ShellSort
echo "The sorted array"
echo ${a[@]}    # Display the sorted array.
```

7. Save the script, and then close the editor.

8. Make the script executable, and then execute the script. Enter **4** for the number of elements to sort, and then press **Enter**. Next, enter these elements: **hammer**, **wrench**, **jigsaw**, and **toolkit**. Be sure to press Enter after you enter each item. See Figure 9-6. The items are shown in both unsorted order and in descending sort order.

9. Run the script again. Enter **6** for the number of elements to sort, and then press **Enter**. Next, enter these elements: **1**, **2**, **3**, **4**, **5**, and **6**. Be sure to press Enter after you enter each number. See Figure 9-6. The items are shown in both unsorted order and in descending sort order.

10. Close your window, and then log out.

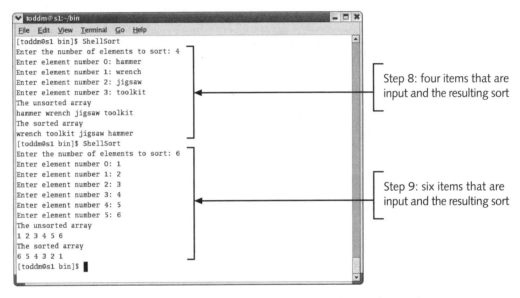

Figure 9-6   Output of the Shell sort used to sort items in descending order

COMPARING THE BUBBLE SORT AND SHELL SORT

Even though the Shell sort only took four passes to sort the 26 letters in Figure 9-6, for a smaller number of elements in an array the bubble sort performs a smaller number of comparisons than the Shell sort. This is because for a small unsorted array, it is more efficient to compare every adjacent item, as done by the bubble sort, than to compare distant items (and ultimately adjacent), as done by the Shell sort.

Although small is a relative number, in this case, small is typically under 25 unsorted elements. Look at a modification of the two previous scripts with an added variable that displays the number of actual comparisons performed inside the decision statement of each algorithm. This variable is used because a comparison, done with the **if** statement, is a processor intensive activity and translates to more time needed for each sorting algorithm. By comparing these two elements you can see how much work each algorithm must perform.

Look at Figure 9-7 and notice that for an unsorted array containing seven elements—zucchini, pear, orange, banana, carrot, peach, and apple—that the bubble sort only performs 21 comparisons while the Shell sort performs 30. In this case, the bubble sort is more efficient.

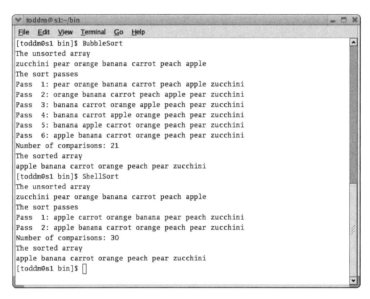

Figure 9-7   Comparison of the bubble sort and Shell sort for a small number of unsorted elements

Now, if you look at Figure 9-8, you notice that the bubble sort performs 325 comparisons for 26 unsorted items and the Shell sort performs 271 comparisons for the same 26 unsorted items. Here, the Shell sort is more efficient.

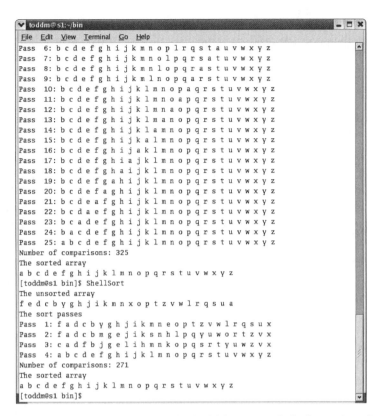

Figure 9-8   Comparison of the bubble sort and Shell sort for a larger number of unsorted elements

The bubble sort compares adjacent items, whether sorted or not, on every pass and it always makes N - 1 passes. The Shell sort starts out comparing distant items first until it finally compares adjacent values—it does not always compare adjacent items as the bubble sort does.

Table 9-1 shows a summary of the number of comparisons of running both sorting algorithms with varying amounts of data on the same computer.

Table 9-1   Number of comparisons for different input for the Shell sort and the bubble sort

Amount of Data Elements	The Shell Sort	The Bubble Sort
5	17	10
7	30	21
26	271	325
58	960	1,653
106	2,462	5,565
208	7,708	21,528

What you should understand after looking at the table is that each sorting algorithm can be more or less advantageous depending upon the amount of data you want to sort.

IMPLEMENTING SEQUENTIAL SEARCH TECHNIQUES

There may be times when you need to search for data in an array. You can employ two different search techniques—sequential search or binary search—when you want to find one piece of data in a small or large array.

The simplest search you can perform in an array is the sequential search. The **sequential search** starts with the first array element and increments the subscript until the data item you are searching for is found or there are no more data elements in the array. If the item is found, it is displayed. If the item is not found, then a message is displayed indicating the item was not found. The logic of the sequential search script is straightforward. The sequential search does not require its data to be sorted in primary key field order because it inspects each array element anyway. Consider the pseudocode logic of the sequential search:

Set Found variable to N.

Read ID to search.

Set the array's subscript to 0.

While array items exist

Do

> *Compare item in array to item searching for.*

> *If there is a match*

>> *Display the record.*

>> *Set Found to "Y".*

>> *Break out of the loop.*

> *End-if*

> *Increment subscript by 1.*

Done

If not found

> *Display "Not Found" Message.*

End-if

Next you will implement a sequential search to search for one of five animal records in an array. Each animal record is composed of an ID and the animal name and is stored in the array, using a colon as a delimiter.

To create the sequential search:

1. Log in to the Linux system as a user, and then open a Terminal emulation window.

2. Create a file named **AnimalSearch** in your **$HOME/bin** directory.

3. Insert the following lines of code to create the array or records, read in the ID number to search, and set two variables. Note the variable "n" equals the maximum number of elements in the array.

```
a=( 1:"King Pup" 2:"Fritz" 3:"Princess" 4:"Molly Cat"
   5:"Ginger" )
read -p "Enter animal identification number: " tid
n=${#a[@]}
Found="N"
```

4. Insert the following lines of code to initiate the search loop:

```
for (( count=0; $count <=n ; count++ ))
do
```

5. Insert the following lines of code to cut the id field from the record and to compare the ID that is read in with the id in the array:

```
id=`echo ${a[count]} | cut -d: -f1`
if [[ $tid = $id ]]
then
```

6. Insert the following lines of code to display the matched record, set Found to "Y," and break out of the loop read:

```
echo ${a[count]}
Found="Y"
break
```

7. Insert the following lines of code to terminate the decision statement and loop:

```
        fi
done
```

8. Insert the following lines of code to test the Found variable. If Found is never set to "Y," then the record was not found and an appropriate message should be displayed:

```
if [ $Found = "N" ]
then
    echo "Animal record not found!"
fi
```

9. Save the script, quit the editor, make the script executable, and then execute the script.

10. Enter **1** when prompted for input, and then press **Enter**. See Figure 9-9. The record for King Pup is displayed.

9

11. Execute the script again, enter **3** when prompted for the animal identification number, and then press **Enter**. See Figure 9-9. The record for Princess is displayed.

12. Execute the script again, enter **5** when prompted for the animal identification number, and then press **Enter**. See Figure 9-9. The record for Ginger is displayed.

13. Execute the script again, and then enter **9** when prompted for the animal identification number. See Figure 9-9. A message is displayed indicating that the record was not found.

14. Close your window, and then log out.

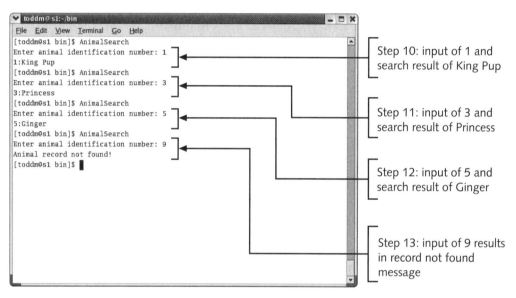

Figure 9-9   Search results for the AnimalSearch script

IMPLEMENTING BINARY SEARCH TECHNIQUES

A sequential search is fine for small amounts of data, but it is not very efficient for large amounts because each element in the array is compared. There is a much faster search algorithm—the binary search algorithm. One major difference between the sequential search and the binary search is that the binary search requires its data to be sorted before searching. The binary search uses a "divide and conquer" method to locate a data item much more quickly than the sequential search. The expression, "divide and conquer" in this case means that the script divides the data into more manageable pieces in order to conquer the problem of searching for an item. Assume you have over 5,000 data items and you want to search for just one. If it just so happens that you needed to find item number 5,000 out of all 5,000 data items, finding it would take quite some time using the sequential search method. The binary search works by continually dividing the array into sections. Then the value you seek is compared to an element in the array.

The binary search uses a variable named Middle to locate the item for which you are searching. If the element located at Middle is equal to the value you seek, then you've found your item, and the search completes. If the item you seek is less than the element, then the array is divided, and the top half of it is searched. If the item you seek is greater than the element, then the bottom half of the array is searched. The binary search continually searches for the element by performing successive cuts until the item is found. If the item is never found, it is a good idea to have a message displayed in your script indicating this.

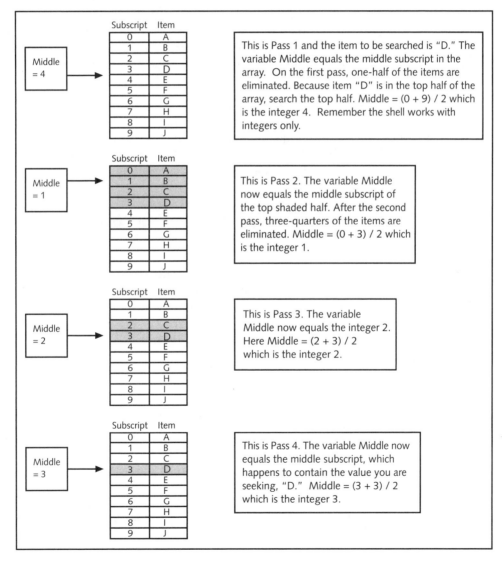

Figure 9-10   Understanding the binary search

Take a look at an example that can help you understand how the binary search works. Say you have an array of sorted letters as shown in Figure 9-10 and you want to search for letter "D" in the array. In the figure, you can see how the array is halved each time the item that you are seeking, in this case "D," is not equal to the variable named Middle. In Pass 1, the Middle variable equals the middle subscript in the array, which in this case is 4. During the first pass, one half of the items are eliminated.

The items are eliminated using a decision statement. The `if` statement is used to compare items in the array. If the item you are seeking is equal to the item for subscript Middle, then a match has occurred and the binary search terminates. If the item for subscript Middle is less than the item you are seeking, the top half of the array is searched. The bottom half is not searched because the items are sorted and compared. If the item for subscript Middle is greater than the item you are seeking, the bottom half of the array is searched. In this case, the top half is not searched because the items are sorted and compared. This is repeated until either the item you seek matches the item for subscript Middle or the record is not found.

Because item "D" is in the top half of the array, the top half is searched instead of the lower half. In Pass 2, the Middle variable now equals the middle subscript of the top shaded half. By the end of this pass, three-quarters of the items are eliminated from comparison. In Pass 3 the Middle variable now equals 2. Notice the search is closing in on the targeted item. Finally, in Pass 4 the Middle variable equals the subscript you are seeking.

Just remember, the binary search divides the array into two ("bi" in the term binary) on each pass. Because it works by comparing items, the binary search requires the data to be sorted.

Next you will implement a binary search to locate an employee record for George Patel's Computer Shop. A record contains two fields—Employee Name and the Shift (e.g., 1, 2, or 3) they work—separated by a colon. You will search using Employee Name as the primary key field. The goal is to locate the shift the employee works using the Employee Name.

To create a binary search to locate a field within a record:

1. Log in to the Linux system as a user, and then open a Terminal emulation window.

2. Create a file named **ShiftSearch** in your **$HOME/bin** directory.

3. Insert the following line of code to create the array that holds the employee records:

    ```
    emp=( Adam:3 Bob:1 Carlon:2 Dijon:2 Eve:1 Fritz:2 Gunter:3 )
    ```

4. Insert the following lines of code to read in the name to search:

    ```
    read -p "Enter name to search: " TempName
    ```

5. Insert the following lines of code to set up the initial variables:

```
First=0
n=${#emp[*]}
((Last=$n - 1))
Found="N"
```

6. Insert the following lines of code to begin the loop for the binary search:

```
while [ $First -le $Last ]
do
```

7. Insert the following lines of code to calculate the variable Middle:

```
((Middle=($First + $Last) / 2))
```

8. Insert the following lines of code to cut the record into fields:

```
Name=`echo ${emp[$Middle]} | cut -d: -f1`
Shift=`echo ${emp[$Middle]} | cut -d: -f2`
```

9. Insert the following lines of code to test for a match:

```
if [[ $TempName = $Name ]]
then
        echo "Employee $Name works Shift $Shift "
        Found="Y"
        break
fi
```

10. Insert the following lines of code to set Middle so the top half of the array is searched on the next iteration:

```
if [[ $Name > $TempName ]]    # Set up for searching top half
   on next iteration.
then
        ((Last=$Middle - 1))
fi
```

11. Insert the following lines of code to set Middle so the bottom half of the array is searched on the next iteration:

```
if [[ $Name < $TempName ]]    # Set up for searching bottom
   half on next iteration.
then
        ((First=$Middle + 1))
fi
done
```

12. Insert the following lines of code to display a message if there is no match:

```
if [ $Found != "Y" ]
then
        echo "Record not found"
fi
```

13. Save the script, quit the editor, make the script executable, execute the script, enter **Adam** when prompted for the name, and then press **Enter**. See Figure 9-11. Notice that the search returns the shift as number 3.

14. Execute the script again, and then enter **Eve** when prompted for the name. See Figure 9-11. Here the search returns the shift worked as number 1.

15. Execute the script again, and then enter **Carlon** when prompted for the name. See Figure 9-11. Notice that the search returns 2 as the shift he works.

16. Execute the script again, and then enter **Lin** when prompted for the name. See Figure 9-11. Notice the message "Record not found" is returned because Lin doesn't exist in the array.

17. Close your window, and then log out.

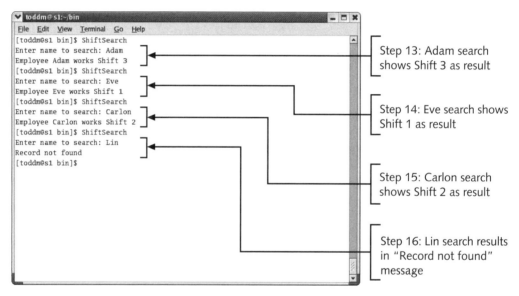

Figure 9-11   Search results of the ShiftSearch script

UNDERSTANDING THE HERE DOCUMENT

A here document is not really a document file at all. It is simply used to signify the beginning and ending of commands or text that can be collectively used in a command. A **here document** allows you to enter text on multiple lines to be used as input into a program. The benefit of using a here document is that it is efficient. You do not need an editor such as **vi** as you do when you create a regular file, and the here document is temporarily stored in memory when the script containing it executes. So, access to it is faster than dealing with a file on disk. You use the here document when you want to enter a small amount of data at the command line to be processed by a program but do not want to use an editor. You would typically use this with the `cat`, `mail`, or `sort` commands to read a body of text at the command line. The format of a here document is as follows:

```
Command << here-document-name
Text line 1
Text line 2
Text line 3
...
here-document-name
```

Note that the *Command* can be any Linux command that allows you to redirect input. The two less-than symbols are required and are used to redirect the text lines into the *Command*. You cannot use a single less-than symbol because it is used to redirect input from an actual file. The text lines are delimited by the name of the here document, specified in the above code as *here-document-name*. The first occurrence of the document name marks the beginning of the here document. The second and last occurrence of the document name on a line by itself identifies the end of the here document—it is like an end-of-file (EOF) symbol to a file. The first and second document name must be identical. Note the *here-document-name* is user-defined. Also note that a right arrow symbol, >, appears after you enter the first line and disappears after you terminate the here document. This is the prompt for the here document.

Look at an example. In the following code, the `cat` command is used to help you understand how to implement a here document.

```
cat << Here
Today is `date`.
The stock price of the company rose 4 points yesterday.
Have a wonderful day!
Here
```

In this example, the first line, `cat << Here`, indicates to the shell that the `cat` command is using a here document as input. The next three lines are the actual data or text of the here document. The final line, `Here`, terminates the here document.

 A here document gets it name because the data is literally "here" on the command line for the program using it—instead of within an actual file.

Next you will create a here document.

To create a script that uses a here document:

1. Log in to the Linux system as a user, and then open a Terminal emulation window.

2. Insert the following lines of code to create a here document that you can e-mail to yourself. Be sure to replace *username* with your own username.

```
mail username << MailDoc
Today is `date`.
A meeting will be held in room B11 at 2 pm.
It will cover the production reports for last week.
Please be prompt.
Thanks,
MailDoc
```

3. Wait a few minutes for the mail daemon to send the mail.

4. Type **mail** to receive your e-mail, and then press **Enter**. A list of e-mail messages appears with message numbers to the left of each line in the list.

5. Type *number* where *number* is one of the numbers in the e-mail message list, and then press **Enter**.

6. Repeat Step 5 until you see the contents of the here document you created in Step 2.

7. Close your window, and then log out.

UNDERSTANDING FILE ACCESS

In this section, you will learn how to process records within files. **File access** is the act of accessing records within files that are stored on disk. There are two components to file access—reading records and writing records. Using files allows you to read and write records to and from a file on disk, which is a permanent computer storage medium. Until now in this book, most of the data you have been dealing with has not been stored permanently. You need to know how to access records in files because almost all organizations today process data that is either saved to or retrieved from disk.

To process records within files, you need to use the redirection symbols and file descriptors you learned about in Chapter 4. Although file descriptor 0 is reserved for standard input, file descriptor 1 is reserved for standard output, and file descriptor 2 is reserved for standard error, you can use other file descriptor numbers to refer to files that you create. To successfully access files you need to understand how to open files, process data within them, and close those files.

Opening the File

To access data within a file, you need to be able to open the file. Here is the general form for opening a file:

```
file-descriptor < filename
```

Where *file-descriptor* is a number between 0 and 9 representing the file descriptor. You must use a file descriptor because the shell uses the file descriptor to refer to the file. The shell does not allow you to substitute a filename for the file descriptor. You should use numbers 3 though 9 when accessing your own files because 0, 1, and 2 are already reserved. It is up to you to decide which file descriptor number to use. The *filename* is simply a user-defined filename. Consider the following example: 3< in.dat. File descriptor 3 is used to refer to a file named in.dat.

> Remember, you refer to the filename in.dat by its file descriptor instead of the filename with the script.

Process the Data—Reading Records from a File

Once the file is open, you can read and process the records within it. Note a record here is considered to be one line of text. Reading a record involves placing the record in a variable for later processing. Once you have the record in the variable you can use the **cut** command to split the record into fields. Processing includes tasks such as displaying fields, totaling fields, counting the number of records or performing decision logic on fields. Here is the general format for reading a record within a file after it has been opened.

```
read variable-name <& file-descriptor
```

This is where *variable-name* equals the contents of a line of text within the file. The **read** statement is used and is modified to read one line of the file into the variable. The symbols, <&, are required. Again, *file-descriptor* is the number representing the file. Consider the following example: **read InRecord <&3**. The variable, InRecord, contains a record. Notice the file descriptor, 3, is used in the opening of the file. Remember, file descriptor 3 refers to the file named in.dat. So, in this example, you are reading the first line of the in.dat file into the variable named InRecord which can now be cut into fields or manipulated using other programming logic.

Records are processed sequentially from the beginning of a file. Each record must be read using the **read** statement.

Process the Data—Writing Records to a File

Records must first be written to a file in order to be read later. To write a record to a file using the shell, you use the **echo** statement to redirect the fields to a file. Here is the general format:

```
echo ${var1}:${var2}:${var3}... >> filename
```

This is where *var1*, *var2*, and *var3* are variables to be written to a file named *filename*. The output is redirected using the redirect append operator, >>, because using just the redirect operator, >, would overwrite existing records in the file.

Look at an example. Jack McAllister works as a shoe salesman. The company he works for requires him to enter sales for the week into a shell script. The fields for a shoe record are: Model, Manufacturer, Price, and Quantity Sold. Here is the actual code:

```
read -p "Enter Model: " Model
read -p "Enter Manufacturer: " Mfg
read -p "Enter Price: " Price
read -p "Enter Quantity Sold: " Qty
echo ${Model}:${Mfg}:${Price}:${Qty} >> shoe.dat   # Write
    the record to the file named shoe.dat.
```

Notice the last statement lists each field separated by a colon, and then redirects the fields to a file called shoe.dat. After the data is written to a file, the **cut** command can be used to access each field.

Figure 9-12 shows the above code for writing records as part of the Shoe1 script. In the figure, the Shoe1 script's contents are displayed. Within Shoe1, you can see that four variables can be entered from the keyboard, and then the variables are redirected to the shoe.dat file. Next, notice the execution of the script with the data for the Sneaker and Dress Shoe entered. Finally, you can see the contents of the shoe.dat file that are created. The last line of the script creates this file by redirecting the four fields as a record to it.

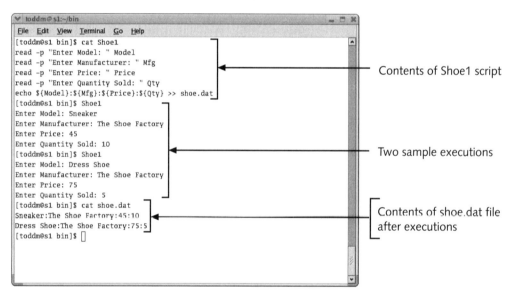

Figure 9-12   Writing records to the shoe.dat file

Closing the File

Once you are finished processing the records within a file, the file needs to be closed. It is good programming practice to close your files to avoid the chance of corruption by other programs. Here is the general form:

```
file-descriptor <&-
```

To close the file named in.dat that was opened and processed previously, you simply enter the code, 3<&-.

Combining Opening, Processing, and Closing a File in a Script

Now that you've seen how to open, process, and close a file, next you will put these steps in a script to process data. This is best done with the following exercise, in which you will process records within files. First, you will create three records in a file, then you will create a script that will process the three records within the file, and finally, you will close the file.

To process three records within a file:

1. Log in to the Linux system as a user, and then open a Terminal emulation window.

2. Create a file named **in.dat** in your **$HOME/bin** directory. This is the data file.

3. Insert the following lines of code to create the three records, one per line. Note that the first field is the ID number, the next is the employee name, and the last is the salary.

```
1:Li Tang:50000
2:Mary Jones:64033
3:Greg Haywood:56444
```

4. Create a script named **ProcessRecsA** in your **$HOME/bin** directory.

5. Insert the following lines of code to open the file using the file descriptor, 3, read and display all the records into the script, and then close the file:

```
3<in.dat
read Record <&3
echo $Record
read Record <&3
echo $Record
read Record <&3
echo $Record
3<&-
```

6. Save the script, close the editor, make the script executable, and then execute the script. The data within the file is displayed on the screen.

7. Close your window, and then log out.

Using Loops to Read in Data

In the previous exercise, you have one **read** statement for each record. What would you do if more records than you thought existed in the file? In that case, any records after the third would not be processed. Normally, files have an undetermined number of records, so it is likely that you would not know how many **read** statements to use. The best approach is to use a looping structure to read and process the records in the file. Using a loop, such as **while** or **until**, allows you to process any number of records within the file without specifically coding for a specific number. In the following code, the file opens and while there are records to be read, they are, and their contents are displayed. Once there are no additional records, the file closes.

```
3< in.dat  # Open the file.
while read Record <&3 # While there are records, read them.
do
        echo $Record # Display the record.
done
3<&- # Close the file.
```

Another approach that accomplishes the same goal is demonstrated in the next script. This script uses a shortened version of the previous script by opening and closing the file in one statement. While you can achieve the same results with either this script or the previous one, it is important to understand alternative approaches provided by the shell. You may come across this technique in system shell scripts. This technique is simpler because you don't have to explicitly refer to file descriptors.

```
while read Record
do
    echo $Record
done < in.dat # Open and close the file in one step.
```

Next you will use the shortened approach with the until statement to read through the records in the file. You are using the until statement instead of the while statement to gain greater familiarity with the different loops available for file access. You will also display a count of the total number of records within the file.

To use a loop to process an undetermined number of records within a file:

1. Log in to the Linux system as a user, and then open a Terminal emulation window.

2. Append the following records to the data file named **in.dat** located in your **$HOME/bin** directory:

   ```
   4:Francis Martel:50440
   5:Gennady Vladosky:45101
   ```

3. Create a script named **ProcessRecsB** in your **$HOME/bin** directory.

4. Insert the following lines of code to read the records until there are no more records to be read, close the file, and then display the number of records that are read:

   ```
   until ! read Record # Until there are no more records,
      read a record.
   do
       echo $Record
       ((RecordCount++))  # Count up the total number.
   done < in.dat
   echo "The number of records is:" $RecordCount
   ```

5. Save the script, close the editor, make the script executable, and then execute the script. See Figure 9-13. Notice that the five records are displayed on the screen followed by the total number of records.

6. Close your window, and then log out.

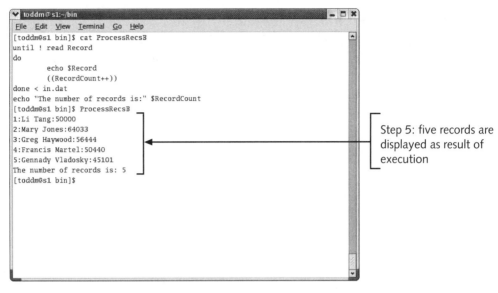

```
[toddm@s1 bin]$ cat ProcessRecsB
until ! read Record
do
        echo $Record
        ((RecordCount++))
done < in.dat
echo "The number of records is:" $RecordCount
[toddm@s1 bin]$ ProcessRecsB
1:Li Tang:50000
2:Mary Jones:64033
3:Greg Haywood:56444
4:Francis Martel:50440
5:Gennady Vladosky:45101
The number of records is: 5
[toddm@s1 bin]$
```

Step 5: five records are displayed as result of execution

Figure 9-13   Using a loop to process files

VALIDATE DATA

It is important to validate your data before it is ever written to the screen or file. There is an expression in the computer industry: Garbage In Garbage Out. If you don't validate your data, it may write invalid data to a file. Invalid data is garbage. If you allow garbage data to go in, you can reasonably expect garbage to come out of your program, hence **Garbage In Garbage Out (GIGO)**. Ultimately, invalid data could be printed on a sales report or an incorrect grade could be printed on a student's transcript. So, to prevent GIGO, you should validate your data. Generally, users don't consciously put invalid data into fields. For the most part, it is an honest mistake. For example, accidentally placing a character in a field that is supposed to be numeric happens frequently. Can you imagine how you would feel if your paycheck was not processed because someone entered "AA" instead of "45" in the hours field for the number of hours you worked?

There are several data validation techniques you can use to help remove the probability of invalid data. These can be implemented using shell script techniques and can be placed in a function library for all scripts to use. The techniques are listed below:

- Empty
- Length
- Numeric
- Range

Testing for an Empty Variable

Many times a user may not enter anything and simply press the Enter key on a field by mistake. They may be caught up in the business of the day and accidentally leave a field empty. In order to test for this, you can use a decision construct. Figure 9-14 shows the code to determine if a variable is empty or not.

```
read ans

if [[ $ans = "" ]]   # Is the variable empty?
then
      echo "Variable is Empty"
else
      echo $ans
fi
```

Figure 9-14   Testing for an empty variable

In the figure, the contents of a variable named ans are tested for an empty value. If ans is empty, a message is displayed that it is empty; otherwise, the contents of the variable are displayed.

Next you will create a function that tests whether a variable is empty. The benefit of setting this up as a function is that you can place the code in a function library, and then call the function from the shell or from within a script.

To create a function that allows you to test for an empty variable:

1. Log in to the Linux system as a user, and then open a Terminal emulation window.

2. Create a file named **EmptyTest** in your **$HOME/bin** directory.

3. Insert the following lines of code to create the function named empty:

   ```
   empty()
   {
   if [[ $1 = "" ]]
   then
      return 1 # If the parameter is empty, then return 1.
   else
      return 0 # If the parameter is not empty, then return 0.
   fi
   }
   ```

4. Insert the following lines of code to get the data from the keyboard, place it in the variable named ans, and call the function with the contents of the variable named ans:

   ```
   read -p "Enter value: " ans
   empty $ans
   ```

5. Insert the following lines of code to determine whether the function returned a 1 (empty) or 0 (not empty):

```
if [[ $? -eq 1 ]]  # Check the return value of the
   function, either 0 or 1.
then
    echo "Field is empty."
else
    echo "Field is not empty."
fi
```

6. Save the script, close the editor, make the script executable, execute the script, when prompted, type **5**, and then press **Enter**. A message indicating the field is not empty is displayed.

7. Run the script again, when prompted, type **abc123**, and then press **Enter**. A message indicating the field is not empty is displayed.

8. Run the script one final time, and then press **Enter**. A message indicating the field is empty is displayed.

9. Close your window, and then log out.

Testing for Length

Many times you may need to make sure that a minimum number of characters are entered into a field. For example, you know that a Social Security number (SSN) is exactly nine digits. So, you may want to test to ensure that a user enters nine digits. To do this, you use $\{#var\}$ to test for a specific length. In this case, *var* is the variable name.

Take a look at an example of testing to ensure that the SSN of an employee is nine digits. The following code displays a message if the SSN is not exactly nine digits.

```
read -p "Enter: " SSN
len=`echo ${#SSN}`
if [[ $len != 9 ]]
then
    echo "SSN length is not 9 digits"
else
    echo $SSN
fi
```

Next you will create a script with a length test function. In this function, you will make sure the two-digit state code for a state is in fact only two digits. For example, the two-digit state code for Georgia is GA and the two-digit state code for Massachusetts is MA. Also, if the state code is exactly two character positions, they will be translated into uppercase.

To create a function that allows you to perform a length test:

1. Log in to the Linux system as a user, and then open a Terminal emulation window.

2. Create a file named **LengthTest** in your **$HOME/bin** directory.

3. Insert the following lines of code to create the LenTest function:

```
LenTest()
{
SCLength=`echo ${#SC}`  # SC = State Code
if [[ $SCLength = 2 ]]
then
     return 0
else
     return 1
fi
}
```

4. Insert the following lines of code to get the data from the keyboard, place it into the variable named SC, and call the function with the contents of the variable named SC:

```
read -p "Enter State Code: " SC
LenTest SC
```

5. Insert the following lines of code to determine whether the function returned a 1 (empty) or 0 (not empty):

```
if [[ $? -eq 1 ]]
then
     echo "State code invalid length"
else
```

6. Insert the following lines of code to display the contents of the variable in uppercase and terminate the decision statement:

```
     echo $SC | tr [:lower:] [:upper:]    # Display in uppercase.
fi
```

7. Save the script, close the editor, make the script executable, execute the script, when prompted type **nc** for North Carolina, and then press **Enter**. See Figure 9-15. The letters NC for the state code of North Carolina are displayed.

8. Run the script again, when prompted type **zzz**, and then press **Enter**. See Figure 9-15. A message indicating the length is invalid is displayed.

9. Run the script again, when prompted, type **GA**, and then press **Enter**. See Figure 9-15. The letters "GA" for the state code of Georgia are displayed.

10. Close your window, and then log out.

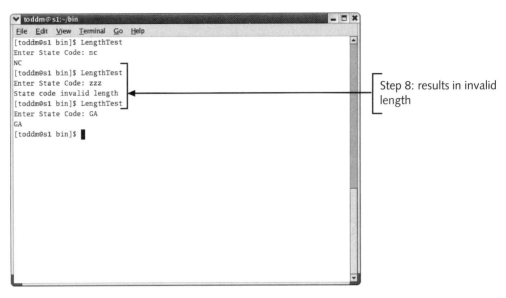

Step 8: results in invalid length

Figure 9-15   The length test

Testing for Numeric Values

You may also want to test to ensure that a field contains only numeric values. For example, you may have an amount field within an application. If a user places nonnumeric data within the field, errors in calculation may result. In order to test for numeric values, you could use pattern-matching techniques along with the **grep** command. In the script shown in Figure 9-16, a **for** statement checks each position of a value to determine if the position is numeric or not. A variable "i" in the **for** loop is set to 0, compared to the length of the variable called ans, and incremented by one. Each position of ans is then tested and if the position is not a digit, then the script sets the variable named Numeric to "N" and breaks out of the **for** loop. You break the loop because you have found at least one digit to be nonnumeric and that is all that is needed to make the overall value nonnumeric.

The key to this script is the statement `val=`echo ${ans:$i:1}``. You saw this used in Chapter 4; with this statement you can inspect each position of a variable. By embedding this statement inside the **for** loop, each position of the variable named ans is set to val for each of the loop's iterations.

Consider the following example to help clarify this concept. If ans equals "4T," then the **for** loop executes twice at most, or the length of the variable. On the first iteration, "i" is set to zero and `${ans:0:1}` is equal to the first position of "4T" which is "4." It is numeric so the **for** loop increments "i". Now "i" is set to one causing the zero to change to a one. This is the middle variable in the statement `${ans:1:1}`. So, position 1 of "4T" equals "T."

Now "T" is not numeric; this causes the `echo $val | grep ^[0-9] > /dev/null` test to fail and return a status of one. By the way, the output of the `grep` command is being redirected to /dev/null because `grep` is not displayed on the screen. Because you don't need the output, only the return status of `grep` is needed.

```
Numeric="Y"
read -p "Enter: " ans
len=`echo ${#ans}`
for ((i=0; i<$len; i++)) # Use a loop to inspect each position of the vari-
able named ans.
        val=`echo ${ans:$i:1}`
        echo $val | grep ^[0-9] > /dev/null  # Is the first character a digit?
        RetVal=$?        # Save the return value.
        if [[ $RetVal -eq 1 ]]     # Test RetVal (0=numeric; 1=non-numeric)
        then
                Numeric="N"
                break
        fi
done
if [[ $Numeric = "Y" ]]
then
        echo "Value is numeric"
else
        echo "Value is not numeric"
fi
```

Figure 9-16   The script for testing numeric values

 You can set up the function shown in the previous script in a function library so that it can be used by multiple scripts.

In Figure 9-17, you can see the output resulting from several executions of NTest2, the script from Figure 9-16. Notice when 45412 is entered, that the script displays a message indicating it is numeric. However, when 4545455T is entered, the script displays a message indicating the value is not numeric—this is due to the "T" in the value. The last value, 56000%#@&@@*(), is a nonnumeric value as well.

Figure 9-17   Numeric test and results of execution given various data

Range Checks

There may be times where you want to perform a test to ensure that a field is within a proper range of values. For example, you need to enter an hourly rate for an employee. The range may be from $20 to $99 for the hourly rate. You could enforce a range test to ensure no values outside this range are entered. This does not test the accuracy of the rate for an individual that has been entered—no script or program can do that—but it validates that the amount is within the specified range. The following example script is named Range1. The user enters name and hourly rate data, if the amount is not within the range of 20 to 99, then an error message is displayed; otherwise, a record is written to the payroll.dat file.

```
read -p "Enter Name: " Name
read -p "Enter hours: " amt
if [[ $amt -ge 20 && $amt -le 99 ]]
then
     echo ${Name}:${amt} >> payroll.dat
else
     echo "The amount is out of range"
fi
```

Figure 9-18 shows the execution of the script named Range1. Notice in the figure that the amount for both Dexter Hudlen and Marge LaRue are out of range. This is because their hourly amounts are outside of the range (20 to 99). The last line shows the contents of the payroll.dat file. Notice that only records for Mike McMasterston and Mindy Hallstein appear. This is because their hourly amounts are within the range (20 to 99). You can see how the use of the **if** test eliminated the garbage data by not allowing it into the file.

Figure 9-18   Execution of the Range1 script

Next you will perform a range test to validate a grade.

To create a script using the range test:

1. Log in to the Linux system as a user, and then open a Terminal emulation window.

2. Create a file named **RangeTest** in your **$HOME/bin** directory.

3. Insert the following lines of code to create the function to test for data with a range of 0 to 100:

```
RangeCheckIt( )
{
if [[ $1 -ge 0 && $1 -le 100 ]]
then
    return 0    # 0=Within range
else
    return 1    # 1=Out of range
fi
}
```

4. Insert the following lines to create a function to read data from the keyboard:

```
ReadVar( )
{
read -p "Enter grade: " Var1
}
```

5. Insert the following lines of code to call the ReadVar function and the RangeCheckIt function with the contents of Var1, and set its exit status to the variable named RetVal:

```
ReadVar
RangeCheckIt Var1
RetVal=$?
```

6. Insert the following lines of code to test RetVal. If the return status equals one, the data is not within the range. If it equals zero, the data is within the range.

```
if [[ $RetVal -eq 1 ]]
then
     echo "Out of range!"
else
     echo $Var1
fi
```

7. Save the script, close the editor, make the script executable, execute the script, when prompted, type **0**, and then press **Enter**. See Figure 9-19. The value is displayed because it is within range.

8. Run the script again, when prompted type **50**, and then press **Enter**. See Figure 9-19. The value is displayed because it is within range.

9. Run the script again, when prompted type **100**, and then press **Enter**. See Figure 9-19. The value is displayed because it is within range.

10. Run the script again, when prompted type **400**, and then press **Enter**. See Figure 9-19. A message indicating the data is out of range is displayed.

11. Run the script again, when prompted type **–1**, and then press **Enter**. See Figure 9-19. A message indicating the data is out of range is displayed.

12. Close your window, and then log out.

9

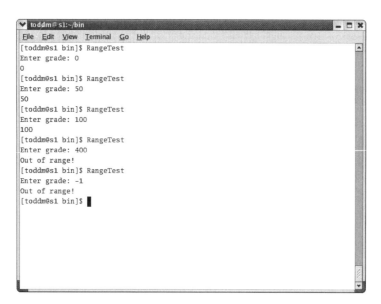

Figure 9-19 Several runs of the RangeTest script

CHAPTER SUMMARY

❑ Both the bubble sort and Shell sort algorithms swap elements that are unsorted in an array. The bubble sort always sorts adjacent elements. The Shell sort algorithm begins by sorting distant elements and then finishes by sorting adjacent elements. The Shell sort uses a gap interval to control the distance between elements. The bubble sort is more efficient for 25 or fewer unsorted elements; a Shell sort is more efficient for more than 25 unsorted elements.

❑ The sequential search algorithm searches an array from the first to the last element unless it finds a match. Once a match is found, the search stops. If the search reaches the last element and there is no match, then it is determined that the element is not in the array. The binary search uses a "divide and conquer" technique to successively split the array in half and compare the searched value to an element in the array. The binary search is more efficient than the sequential search for a large amount of data because it does not compare each element in the array to the searched value. However, the data must be sorted before the binary search can be used.

❑ A here document is text embedded within the body of a script. It is generally used instead of an editor when the amount of text is small.

❑ Records can be read from a disk file or written to a disk file. Files need to be opened prior to processing the data. Processing involves reading or writing the records. Files should be closed when they are no longer needed. Files are opened, processed, and closed with the same file descriptor throughout a script.

❐ Data needs to be validated in order to prevent Garbage In Garbage Out (GIGO). There are a variety of data validation techniques including empty, length, numeric, and range.

REVIEW QUESTIONS

1. _____ uses a "divide and conquer" technique to locate records.
   a. Collating sequence
   b. Shell sort
   c. Sequential search
   d. Binary search

2. If you have fewer than 10 records to be sorted in descending order, which technique should be used?
   a. bubble sort
   b. Shell sort
   c. sequential search
   d. binary search

3. If you have more than 100 records to be sorted in descending order, which technique should be used?
   a. bubble sort
   b. Shell sort
   c. sequential search
   d. collating sequence

4. A(n) _____ is a formula or process to accomplish a specific set of steps.
   a. algorithm
   b. here document
   c. invalid data
   d. gap in the Shell sort

5. A _____ should be performed to ensure a field contains data.
   a. Shell sort
   b. numeric test
   c. sequential search
   d. blank test

9

6. Prior to processing a record, you should _____ the file.

   a. sequentially search

   b. close

   c. read the records from

   d. open

7. After processing a record, you should _____ the file.

   a. sequentially search

   b. close

   c. read the records from

   d. use the collating sequence on

8. If you have over 50,000 items to search, which technique is most efficient?

   a. bubble sort

   b. Shell sort

   c. sequential search

   d. binary search

9. A(n) _____ is used for adding text to a command and uses the << operator.

   a. bubble sort

   b. numeric test

   c. algorithm

   d. here document

10. A _____ only compares adjacent values.

    a. bubble sort

    b. collating sequence

    c. Shell sort

    d. blank test

11. A field or variable that is empty is considered _____.

    a. collated

    b. sorted

    c. searched

    d. null

12. A _____ compares distant values and then adjacent values.

    a. bubble sort

    b. numeric test

    c. Shell sort

    d. blank test

13. The _____ facilitates character sorting.

   a. bubble sort

   b. collating sequence

   c. algorithm

   d. here document

14. Values in out-of-sort order in the bubble sort are _____.

   a. collated

   b. swapped

   c. written to a file

   d. closed

15. A _____ can be used to ensure a field contains a specified number of character or numbers.

   a. collating sequence

   b. swap function

   c. length test

   d. range test

16. A _____ can be used to ensure the contents of a field falls within a specific minimum and maximum number.

   a. collating sequence

   b. swap function

   c. length test

   d. range test

17. Which of the following closes file descriptor 4 for the file named inputfile.dat?

   a. `4 < inputfile.dat`

   b. `4<&-`

   c. `4>&-`

   d. `4 > inputfile.dat`

18. Which of the following opens file descriptor 4 for the file named inputfile.dat?

   a. `4 < inputfile.dat`

   b. `4<&-`

   c. `4>&-`

   d. `4 > inputfile.dat`

19. Which of the following writes the fields, EmpName, EmpStatus, EmpSalary to the file named payroll.dat, in the order shown and separated by a colon?

    a. `echo ${EmpName}:${EmpSalary};${EmpStatus} < payroll.dat`

    b. `echo ${EmpName};${EmpSalary};${EmpStatus} > payroll.dat`

    c. `echo ${EmpName}:${EmpStatus}:${EmpSalary} >> payroll.dat`

    d. `echo ${EmpSalary}:${EmpStatus}:${EmpName} < payroll.dat`

20. What is the result of the following script?

    ```
    while read SalesRecord
    do
         echo $SalesRecord
    done < sales.dat
    ```

    a. It fails due to a syntax error.

    b. It writes records to the sales.dat file.

    c. It sorts the records.

    d. It reads records in the sales.dat file.

HANDS-ON PROJECTS

Project 9-1

In this project, you will create a script that can use a here document. The **read** statement will be used to accept input. The goal of this project is to help you understand how to create a script that can use a here document.

1. Log in to the Linux system as a user, and then open a Terminal emulation window.

2. Create a shell script named **Project9-1** in the **$HOME/bin** directory.

3. Add the following lines of code:

   ```
   for ((c=0; c<=5; c++))
   do
       read a
       echo $a
   done
   ```

4. Save the script, close the editor, and then make the script executable.

5. Type the following at the command line:

   ```
   $HOME/bin/Project9-1 << Animals
   Cat
   Dog
   Mouse
   Parrot
   Lion
   Animals
   ```

6. Record the result.

7. Close your window, and then log out.

Project 9-2

In this project, you will implement the bubble sort as a function to help you understand how the bubble sort works. This project will further your knowledge of arrays and functions.

1. Log in to the Linux system as a user, and then open a Terminal emulation window.

2. Copy the **BubbleSortClothes** script you created earlier in this chapter to a new shell script named **Project9-2** in the **$HOME/bin** directory.

3. Convert the bubble sort in the new script to a function, and then call it within the script.

4. Record your results.

5. Close your window, and then log out.

Project 9-3

9

In this project, you will implement the Shell sort to sort the data in ascending order. You will place the Shell sort in a function library to be used in the shell or within other scripts. This project will reinforce your understanding of the Shell sort, arrays, and functions.

1. Log in to the Linux system as a user, and then open a Terminal emulation window.

2. Copy the **ShellSort** script from the earlier exercise to a new shell script named **Project9-3** in the **$HOME/bin** directory.

3. Make the necessary code changes to sort the data in ascending order.

4. Place the new script in a function library file in the **$HOME/bin** directory named **Project9-3a**.

5. Use the **source** command to read and execute **Project9-3**.

6. Make both scripts executable.

7. Execute **Project9-3a**.

8. Record the result.

9. Close your window, and then log out.

Project 9-4

In this project, you will implement the bubble sort algorithm to sort elements in descending order. The goal of this project is to help reinforce the concept of arrays, functions, and the logic intrinsic to the bubble sorting algorithm.

1. Log in to the Linux system as a user, and then open a Terminal emulation window.

2. Create a shell script named **Project9-4** in the **$HOME/bin** directory.

3. Use the bubble sort to sort the following items in descending order:

```
farm ranch brook stream tree shrub bush lagoon archipelago island zoo
```

4. Save the script, quit the editor, make the script executable, and then execute it.

5. Print your script.

6. Close your window, and then log out.

Project 9-5

In this project, you will test fields before you write them as a record to a file. You will also perform a blank data validation test and use a decision statement to determine if the data is correct before writing a record to the file. A loop will be used to allow the user to continue entering records.

1. Log in to the Linux system as a user, and then open a Terminal emulation window.

2. Create a shell script named **Project9-5** in the **$HOME/bin** directory.

3. Create a function, named **EmptyTest**, to test for empty variables. Note that 0 is not empty and 1 is empty.

4. Insert the following lines of code to create a loop that reads data from the keyboard, to call the function named EmptyTest, and then save the return status:

```
YesNo="Y"
while [[ $YesNo = "Y" ]]
do
    clear
    read -p "Enter Part Number: " PartNo
    EmptyTest $PartNo
    Ret1=$?
    read -p "Enter Part Name: " PartName
    EmptyTest $PartName
    Ret2=$?
    read -p "Enter Part Price: " PartPrice
    EmptyTest $PartPrice
    Ret3=$?
```

5. Insert the following lines of code to test the return status of each value passed to EmtpyTest. If the data is empty, display a message indicating so. If the data is not empty, write it to the parts.dat file.

```
if [[ $Ret1 -eq 1 || $Ret2 -eq 1 || $Ret3 = 1]]
then
    echo "Field(s) blank"
    echo "Re-enter, record not written"
else
    read -p "Correct (Y/N) ?" Correct
    Correct=`echo $Correct | tr [:lower:] [:upper:]`
    if [[ $Correct = "Y" ]]
    then
        echo ${PartNo}:${PartName}:${PartPrice} >> parts.dat
```

```
                echo "Record written"
        else
                echo "Not writing record"
        fi
    fi
```

6. Insert the following lines of code to ask users whether or not they want to continue, change their answer to uppercase, and terminate the loop:

```
    read -p "Continue (Y/N) ?" YesNo
    YesNo=`echo $YesNo | tr [:lower:] [:upper:]`
done
```

7. Save the script, and then quit the editor.

8. Make the script executable, and then execute the script using various data.

9. Record your results, and if possible, print your script.

10. Close your window, and then log out.

Project 9-6

9

In this project, you will read the records entered in Project 9-5. The goal of this project is to help you understand how to read records from a file using a loop structure.

1. Log in to the Linux system as a user, and then open a Terminal emulation window.

2. Create a shell script named **Project9-6** in the **$HOME/bin** directory.

3. Write the appropriate code to read the records created in Project 9-5 using a loop structure.

4. Print the script.

5. Save the script, close the editor, make the script executable, execute the script, and then record the output.

6. Close your window, and then log out.

Project 9-7

In this project, you will modify the Project9-5 script to include a numeric test for the Part Price.

1. Log in to the Linux system as a user, and then open a Terminal emulation window.

2. Copy **Project9-5** to **Project9-7** in the **$HOME/bin** directory.

3. Modify the script to include a numeric test for the Part Price.

4. Print the script.

5. Execute the script with various data, and then record the result.

6. Close your window, and then log out.

Project 9-8

In this project, you will implement the bubble sort and the binary search in one script. You will also implement the bubble sort and binary search as separate functions. The goal of this lab is to help you understand how to implement sorting and searching into a single script as functions.

1. Log in to the Linux system as a user, and then open a Terminal emulation window.

2. Create a shell script named **Project9-8** in the **$HOME/bin** directory.

3. Write a script that implements both the bubble sort and binary search as functions. The array to sort and search contains an employee record that includes an employee number followed by the employee's name. The contents of the unsorted array are as follows:

```
a=( 9:Joe 5:Mike 8:Marge 2:Sue 7:Chandra 3:Tian 1:Vien
    4:Lars 6:Ivan 0:Edward )
```

4. Allow the user to search for an employee ID. If the record is found, display the employee ID and the employee's name. Otherwise, display a message indicating the record is not found.

5. Execute the script with various data, and then record the result.

6. Close the window, and then log out.

CASE PROJECTS

Case 9-1

You have been hired by TMI to help their payroll department write a sorting algorithm and a searching algorithm in one script. A record consists of an employee's name and his or her salary. The company has approximately 22 employees and is expected to add five employees each year for the next three years, based upon projected growth rates for their company. Write the script for the type of sorting algorithm and searching algorithm you suggest. Allow the user to search by entering an employee name, and then display the salary given the search results. Finally, discuss in writing why you suggest this type of sorting algorithm and why you believe it is best to implement it now and over the next three years. Also, discuss the type of searching algorithm you suggest and why they should implement it now and over the next three years. Defend your response.

Case 9-2

Pan-Pacific Vegetable Corporation needs a few scripts to be created to handle their vegetable orders. You have been hired as a consultant to assist. Here are their requirements:

1. Create a script for adding records given the fields below. You are to ensure the numeric fields are numeric and the other field is not empty before writing a record to the veg.dat file.

   Vegetable Product ID

   Vegetable Name

   Vegetable Quantity

   Vegetable Price

2. Create a script for reading the records from the file. In the same script, fill an array with the records. Then, use one of the searching algorithms to allow a user to locate a record based on the ID. Once found, display all fields; otherwise, indicate the record is not in the file.

3. Run the script to create the records. Use these eight records with the fields in the order of Vegetable Product ID, Vegetable Name, Vegetable Price, Vegetable Quantity:

Table 9-2   Pan-Pacific vegetables

Vegetable Product ID	Vegetable Name	Vegetable Price	Vegetable Quantity
401	Broccoli	4	1
402	Asparagus	6	2
403	Kale	2	1
404	Zucchini	3	8
405	Portobellos	9	2
406	Onions	1	7
407	Peppers	4	5
408	Spinach	2	4

4. Run the script to search and enter various data.

5. Print all scripts.

INCORPORATING ADDITIONAL TECHNIQUES AND TOOLS

In this chapter, you will:

♦ Use the arbitrary precision calculator to perform arithmetic operations
♦ Search for text using the grep command
♦ Understand the stream editor
♦ Understand sed commands
♦ Create sed scripts
♦ Understand signals

In this chapter, you will learn how to use additional shell techniques and tools. Specifically, you will learn how to use the precision calculator to perform arithmetic on numbers that contain decimals, as well as how to search for text within files using the grep command. You will learn the sed command which provides text-processing capabilities at the shell command prompt. Finally, you will learn how to send and catch signals.

USING THE ARBITRARY PRECISION CALCULATOR TO PERFORM ARITHMETIC OPERATIONS

As you know, you can only perform integer-based arithmetic using builtin operations for the bash shell. To perform arithmetic operations on numbers containing decimals, you can use the bc command. One important aspect about the bc command is the ability of the user to arbitrarily set the precision of the calculations that are performed—hence the phrase "arbitrary precision" in its name. This is accomplished with the `scale` command within bc. If you try to accomplish the same calculations strictly within the shell, you receive an error.

There are several options available with the bc command. A few of them are listed in Table 10-1.

Table 10-1   A few of the bc options

Option	Description	Example
-h	The help option displays the usage for bc when executed	bc -h
-l	The math library option allows the use of the standard math library with access to additional mathematical functions such as sine, cosine, and tangent	bc -l
-q	The quiet option does not display the normal welcome message	bc -q
-v	The version option gives you version information	bc -v

The bc command has its own set of language statements that work similarly to the ones you find in the bash shell. For example, the bc command has builtin if, for, and while statements. It also includes mathematical functions such as sine, cosine, and square root. These tools are especially useful when the Linux operating system is used in an engineering environment.

To give you a sense of the bc command's capabilities, Table 10-2 provides you with some of the commands available with bc. Some of them you are sure to recognize because a similar shell command has been covered in an earlier chapter. If you would like to know more about the bc command, you can refer to its man pages.

Table 10-2   A few of the bc commands

Option	Description	Example
length	Is a function that returns the length of a variable	length (pay_rate)
print	Is a function that allows you to print text or the contents of a variable	print "Enter value: "
read ()	Is a function that allows you to read data from the keyboard	sales=read()

Table 10-2   A few of the bc commands (continued)

Option	Description	Example
scale	Allows you to set the decimal precision	scale=3
s	Is a mathematical function that allows you to perform the trigonometric sine function on a variable	s(3)
c	Is a mathematical function that allows you to perform the trigonometric cosine function on a variable	c(1/3)
sqrt ()	Returns the square root of a function	sqrt (4)
if (expression) statement1 else statement2	Allows you to perform decisions; note the else portion is optional	if (hours>=40) print "Overtime Pay" else print "Regular Pay"
for (expression1; expression2; expression3)	Allows you to perform loops; this follows a syntax similar to the shell's for statement	for (var1=1; var1 <=5; var1++) print var1

10

Next, you learn how to work with the bc command. You can execute bc commands in one of three ways:

- Interactively

- In a script

- In a pipeline command

Running bc Interactively

Understanding how to run bc interactively makes learning how to execute the commands in a script and a pipeline easier. The quickest way to become familiar with the bc command is through an exercise. Next you will enter commands to learn how to run bc commands effectively. You will also examine the arithmetic precision that bc offers over the bash shell.

To use bc interactively and set the precision with the scale command:

1. Log in to the Linux system as a user, and then open a Terminal emulation window.

2. To use the **bc** command interactively, type **bc** at the shell prompt, and then press **Enter**. As you can see, the **bc** prompt is different from the shell's prompt. See Figure 10-1. The prompt is simply a flashing cursor. Notice above the flashing cursor you have a few lines indicating the version of **bc** and the copyright information. This is called the welcome message. Examine what it looks like so you can be familiar with default behavior.

3. To help you understand the precision of **bc**, set the variable "x" to 15 by typing **x=15**, and then press **Enter**. The prompt returns to the next line.

4. To set the variable "y" to 7, type **y=7**, and then press **Enter**. The prompt returns to the next line.

5. To divide "x" by "y," type **x/y**, and then press **Enter**. The answer 2 appears, and the prompt returns to the next line. Notice that there are no decimal places in the answer by default.

6. To arbitrarily change the precision using the **scale** command and set the number of decimal places to two, type **scale=2**, and then press **Enter**. The prompt returns to the next line.

7. Type **x/y** again, and then press **Enter**. The answer of 2.14 appears, and the prompt returns to the next line. See Figure 10-1. Notice that there are two decimal places in the answer.

8. To arbitrarily set the precision to four decimal places, type the following lines of code:

```
scale=4
x/y
```

See Figure 10-1. Notice the answer of 2.1428 is displayed on the screen, and then the prompt returns to the next line. You can see that the division problem has been carried out to four decimal places.

9. Arbitrarily set the precision to 10 decimal places to help you understand its precision further. Type the following lines of code:

```
scale=10
x/y
```

See Figure 10-1. Notice the answer of 2.1428571428 is displayed on the screen, and then the prompt returns to the next line. You can see that the division problem has been carried out to 10 decimal places.

10. To quit, type **quit**, and then press **Enter**. This statement is required to exit **bc**.

11. Close your window, and then log out.

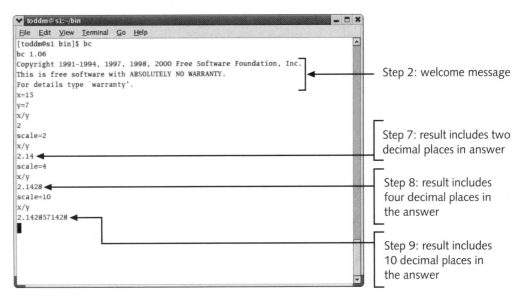

Figure 10-1   Using the bc command to perform arbitrary precision

Adding User Input with bc

10

You can use the **bc** command to prompt a user to enter a value in a variable. To do this, you need to use the **read** function within **bc**. Using the **read** function is useful for making **bc** flexible because you can get data for your script from the keyboard. This application of **bc** is similar to the shell's **read** command. For example, to display a prompt that reads a person's age from the keyboard in **bc**, you enter the following:

```
print "Enter age: " ; age=read()
```

The **bc** command also allows you to perform calculations using the various operations such as multiply, add, divide, and subtract, as you've seen in the shell. You can also use parentheses to change the order of operation. You need to understand how to use these operations in **bc** in case you need to use its arbitrary precision capabilities. Next you will turn off the welcome message, prompt the user for data, and read the data from the keyboard to perform some mathematical operations.

To use bc to prompt the user for data and perform mathematical operations on the data:

1. Log in to the Linux system as a user, and then open a Terminal emulation window.

2. To remove the welcome message, type **bc −q**, and then press **Enter**. Recall from Table 10-1 that **−q** is the quiet mode of **bc** and now only the prompt is displayed.

3. To set the decimal precision to two decimal positions, enter **scale=2**.

4. To read a variable from the keyboard, type **print "Enter value: " ; val1=read( )**, and then press **Enter**. See Figure 10-2. The prompt "Enter value: " appears on the screen. Note that the semicolon is required to separate the text from the variable statement.

5. Type **50**, and then press **Enter**.

6. To read another variable from the keyboard, type **print "Enter value: " ; val2=read( )**, and then press **Enter**. See Figure 10-2. The prompt "Enter value: " appears on the screen.

7. Type **6.67**, and then press **Enter**.

8. To add the two values, type **print "Sum is " ; val1 + val2**, and then press **Enter**. See Figure 10-2. The sum of 56.67 is displayed.

9. To multiply the two values together, type **print "Product is " ; val1 * val2**, and then press **Enter**. See Figure 10-2. The product of 333.50 is displayed.

10. To subtract one value from the other, type **print "Difference is " ; val1 – val2**, and then press **Enter**. See Figure 10-2. The difference of 43.33 is displayed.

11. To take the square root of each of the two values, type **print "Square Root is " ; sqrt(val1); sqrt(val2)**, and then press **Enter**. See Figure 10-2. The square root answers of 7.07 and 2.58 are displayed. The **sqrt( )** statement performs a function on the value between the parentheses.

12. To quit, type **quit**. This statement is required to exit **bc**.

13. Close your window, and then log out.

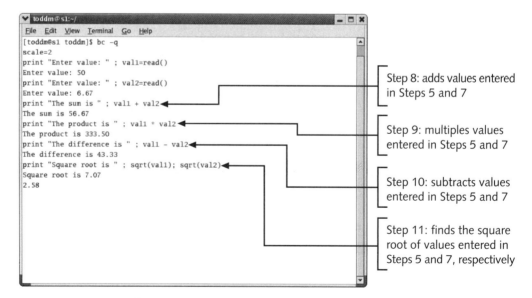

Figure 10-2   Using the bc command to prompt the user to enter data from the keyboard and perform mathematical operations

Running bc in a Script

When you place **bc** in a script, you must run the script as follows:

```
bc script
```

The **bc** command also allows you to create arrays. These work in much the same way as they do in the shell. For example, in **bc**, to set the value of subscript 3 to 42 in an array named array1, and then display the value on the screen, you enter:

```
array1[3]=42
print array1[3]
```

Next you will run **bc** commands in a script. For example, say you want to calculate the average of several grades to two decimal places. You have performed averages in an earlier chapter, but you were only able to work with whole numbers. In this next exercise, you will the use the **bc** command with a **for** loop, an array, and an average calculation to determine an average to two decimal places.

To use bc to determine an average to two decimal places:

1. Log in to the Linux system as a user, and then open a Terminal emulation window.

2. Create a script named **bc5** in your **$HOME/bin** directory.

3. Insert the following lines of code to set the scale to two decimal positions and to set a variable named max to 3. The variable named max contains the maximum number of grades that can be entered.

```
scale=2
max=3
```

4. Insert the following lines of code to create the loop, read a value in the array named grade, and accumulate a total. Note the variable named tot is the accumulated total. Notice the **for** statement uses left and right curly brackets, {...}, instead of a **do...done** pair that the **bash** shell uses. These are required when you have several statements that are part of the iteration. All of the statements are performed for each iteration of the loop.

```
for (i=1 ; i<=max ; i++) {
print "Enter value: "; grade[i]=read()
tot=tot+ grade[i]
}
```

5. Insert the following lines of code to compute the average, display the average, and quit **bc** when the script completes. The \n in the **print "\nAverage is: "; avg** statement causes a newline to be generated before the average is printed.

```
avg = tot / max
print "\nAverage is: " ; avg
quit
```

6. Save the script, close the editor, and then make the script executable.

7. To run the script, type **bc –q bc5**, and then press **Enter**. The script prompts you to enter values.

8. Enter these three values when prompted: **100**, **88**, and **68**. See Figure 10-3. The average, 85.33, is displayed.

9. Rerun the script. And then enter these three values when prompted: **98.50**, **100.50**, and **75.33**. See Figure 10-3. The average, 91.44, is displayed.

10. Rerun the script, and then enter these three values when prompted: **5**, **10**, and **15**. See Figure 10-3. The average, 10.00, is displayed

11. Close your window, and then log out.

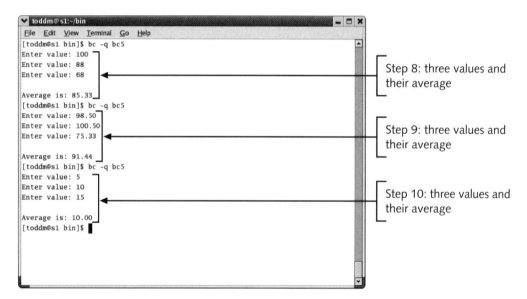

Figure 10-3 Using the bc command with a script

When using the bc command and specifying the subscript in an array, you don't need to precede the subscript name with a dollar sign as you do when you refer to a subscript in the bash shell. For example, *arrayname*[*var*] is correct, but *arrayname*[*$var*] generates a syntax error in bc.

Running bc in a Pipeline Command

The **bc** command can be used in a pipeline command that pipes regular shell variables to **bc**. Typically, you should run **bc** this way instead of in a script for greater convenience. For example, if you have a script that is written in the shell and you want to pipe variables to **bc** when you need arithmetic precision, you use the following syntax:

```
echo "(var1 operation var2)" | bc -l
```

This is where *var1* and *var2* are shell variables that are passed to bc. The *operation* is a bc operation such as multiply, divide, add, or subtract. The bc command uses the same arithmetic operators as the **bash** shell. Everything between parentheses is considered a bc command and must adhere to its syntax—not the shell's syntax. Also, the **-l** ("l" as in "library") option tells bc to use the math library files and is required when piping data to bc.

Next you will pipe shell variables to bc so bc can perform operations not offered by other commands.

To pipe shell variables to bc:

1. Log in to the Linux system as a user, and then open a Terminal emulation window.

2. Create a data file named **ScriptBC** in your **$HOME/bin** directory.

3. Insert the following lines of code to establish the values, create the pipeline using bc, and display the result of the pipeline on the screen:

   ```
   value1=10.50
   value2=10.70
   answer=`echo "($value1 + $value2)" | bc -l`
   echo $answer
   ```

4. Save the script, quit the editor, make the script executable, and then execute the script. Notice that the resulting value 21.20 is displayed on the screen.

5. Close your window, and then log out.

SEARCHING FOR TEXT USING THE grep COMMAND

The Linux operating system allows you to search for text within a file using the **grep** command. The **grep** command prints matching patterns in a file. For example, if you could not remember the name of a file that contained a piece of data but you remember the actual data, you would use the **grep** command. The general syntax is:

> grep *options pattern filename*

As with many Linux commands, the **grep** command has numerous options. One useful option is **-i** which ignores the case you are matching. Because the shell is case sensitive, if you search for "Smith," but it is entered as "SMITH" in the file, **grep** without the **-i** option will not find it. If you use the **-i** option to ignore the case, then **grep** will find "Smith" or "SMITH" in this example. The *pattern* can be any character string or a regular expression. The *filename* is the file in which you are attempting to locate the pattern. For example, to locate the name Smith in the file sort.dat, you enter **grep** **"Smith" sort.dat**. The **grep** command displays the whole line containing the text Smith, or it displays nothing if a match is not found.

10

The `grep` program uses regular expressions for matching lines. A **regular expression** is a metacharacter used to match a particular pattern that describes a set of strings. You use a regular expression operator to construct a regular expression. Table 10-3 lists the metacharacters that are used to construct regular expression operators and their meanings.

Table 10-3   The regular expressions operators used by the `grep` command

Metacharacter	Description
^	Matches characters at the beginning of a line
$	Matches characters at the end of a line
.	Matches a single character
*	Matches all characters
[characters]	Matches any characters between brackets
\[characters]	Removes the meaning of a metacharacter

Next you will use `grep` to search for text within a file.

To use `grep` commands:

1. Log in to the Linux system as a user, and then open a Terminal emulation window.

2. Create a data file named **parts.dat** in your **$HOME/bin** directory.

3. Insert the following lines of code to create records. Each line is a record with the Part Number, Name, and Quantity as fields, and colon delimited.

   ```
   100:Saw:120
   101:Hammer:102
   102:Wrench:10
   ```

4. To display matching lines containing "101," type **grep 101 parts.dat**, and then press **Enter**. See Figure 10-4. The record for the Hammer is displayed. Note the entire line is displayed by default.

5. To display matching lines containing "102," type **grep 102 parts.dat**, and then press **Enter**. See Figure 10-4. This time, the records for Hammer and Wrench are displayed because both match.

6. To display matching lines containing the number "102" when it appears at the beginning of a line in the first field, type **grep ^102: parts.dat**, and then press **Enter**. See Figure 10-4. The record for Wrench is displayed because it is the only record with "102" at the beginning of the line. The use of the caret assures a match at the beginning of the line. Note the use of the colon following the number. This is used to make sure that a match occurs exactly for "102" as the first field. If you left it off, a number such as 1022 or 1023 could appear in the output.

7. To display matching lines containing either "S" or "H," type **grep [SH] parts.dat**, and then press **Enter**. See Figure 10-4. The records for Hammer and Saw are displayed because both of these lines match.

8. Close your window, and then log out.

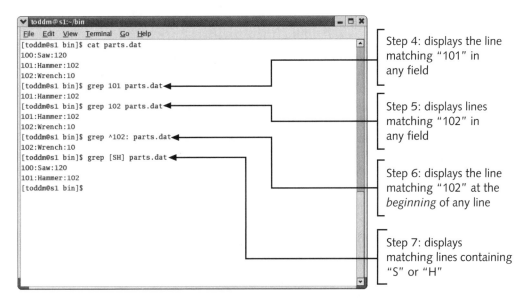

Step 4: displays the line matching "101" in any field

Step 5: displays lines matching "102" in any field

Step 6: displays the line matching "102" at the *beginning* of any line

Step 7: displays matching lines containing "S" or "H"

Figure 10-4   Displaying matching lines with the grep command

UNDERSTANDING THE STREAM EDITOR

Linux provides a command, called **sed**, that allows you to perform editing tasks similar to **vi** at the command line. The **sed** command literally means "stream editor." The command reads a stream of input from a file and processes it using text-editing commands. The **sed** command operates on characters in a file and uses regular expressions. Unlike the **vi** editor, with the **sed** command, you can automate processes that you might need to perform on a text file.

For instance, say that everyday you receive a file electronically from another company that is then processed by your company, and then some of the processed data is sent out to your customers. The daily electronic file has state codes abbreviated using two characters. Susie Weatherstone, the vice president of marketing, wants the full state name spelled out for your customers. For example, "CA" needs to be replaced with "California" and "TN" needs to be replaced with "Tennessee." Unfortunately, you don't receive the daily file until around 6 p.m. when most users have left for the day. What do you do? You can write a program in C or COBOL which handles this situation, but it will also take a while to complete. Or, you can use the **sed** command to search for the two-character state codes and replace them with the state names. Because you can run this program in the background, you can log out and go home. When you return to your office the next morning, the process of changing the two-character state codes to full state names will have completed.

As you've already seen with the **bc** command, the **sed** command has its own set of commands and syntax. The **sed** command takes care of opening the file, reading the input stream, and closing the file for you. It completes the entire process in only one pass, making it very efficient. First, the **sed** command reads characters in a file and places them in a temporary memory buffer. This buffer is called the **pattern space** because it is the area, or space, that holds the text that is currently being processed. Once **sed** is through processing the characters in the pattern space, the characters are removed from the pattern space, but not from the file. Then, **sed** reads the next line of characters into the pattern space, and processing resumes with the new characters. It repeats this process until there are no more lines in the file.

Because the pattern space holds a line of text from the file, you can think of each line as a record. In essence, the pattern space is like a variable that contains a whole record.

Generally, you run the **sed** program as follows:

```
sed options filename
```

Using sed Options

By default, **sed** prints all the lines in the file. When you use the **-n** option, **sed** only prints matches. The **-f** *filename* option runs **sed** commands in a *filename*. This is useful for automating **sed** commands that are done routinely. For example, in the previous state code example, you could write a **sed** script that performs this. Then, a user could simply run the script to update the state names. The **-e** option allows you to perform multiple edits on a single line of text. The advantage here is speed because the **sed** command has to make fewer passes in the file if you combine edits in a single line.

You are required to give **sed** either a command or the name of a script file for options. Leaving either off results in a syntax error.

As previously mentioned, the **sed** command has a set of its own commands, and they are listed in Table 10-4. You can also use these commands with redirection operators to create a new file.

Table 10-4 A few of the sed commands

Command	Purpose
p	Prints the current pattern space to the screen
d	Deletes the current pattern space
s/regular-expression/ replacement/g	Matches regular-expression to characters in the pattern space; if there is a match, then it replaces the regular-expression with replacement. The letter "s" represents substitute and the letter "g" means to make the change globally to all lines.
a\ text	Appends text
c\ text	Replaces, or changes, lines with text
i\ text	Inserts text
r filename	Reads text from filename
w filename	Writes the pattern space to filename
b label	Branches, or transfers execution, to a label
t label	Tests for a successful substitution and branches to a label if successful
: label	Defines the label for the b and the t commands
{ }	Begins and ends a block of commands
# comment	Indicates a comment

The **sed** command uses the following structure for matching regular expressions and establishing the corresponding command action to be taken:

        /pattern/ command-action

The forward slashes surrounding **pattern** serve as a delimiter and indicate where the pattern begins and ends.

UNDERSTANDING sed COMMANDS

Because the **sed** command has its own set of commands, it's a good idea to become familiar with how the commands are used. A strong understanding of the various **sed** commands allows you to create more powerful scripts and streamline your development time. In this section, you will look at some examples using the **sed** command. For instance, a store named The Hardware Supply Store has a supplies file that contains part records. The records include the following fields that are colon delimited: Part Number, Supplier, Part Name, Price, and Quantity. The **sed** command can be used to modify the text within the supplies file. Figure 10-5 shows the contents of the supplies file.

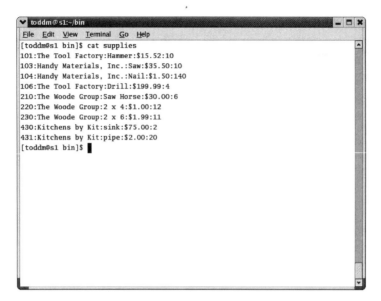

Figure 10-5   The supplies data file content

The Print Command

The simplest and most useful of the **sed** commands is the print command. It allows you to print characters from the current pattern space. For instance, if you wanted to print all the records in the supplies data file, you enter the following:

```
sed -n p supplies
```

Note there is a space between the **-n** option and the **p** command. There is a hyphen prior to the n option but not prior to the p command. The **-n** option, which allows the **sed** command to print only matched lines, is necessary because the default behavior of **sed** is to print every line of input. In this example, the p command for print is specified; without this option, each line is printed twice—once for the default behavior and once for the specified p option. It is the **-n** option that causes the lines to be displayed only once. This behavior is atypical when compared to other Linux commands, however it is how **sed** works. Now, look at the following example, where the **-n** option is omitted:

```
sed  p supplies
```

Figure 10-6 shows the running of the **sed p supplies** command. Figure 10-7 shows the running of the **sed -n p supplies** command. Compare these two figures. Notice in Figure 10-6 that the command, **sed p supplies** displays each line twice. In Figure 10-7, the command **sed -n p supplies** displays matched lines only once.

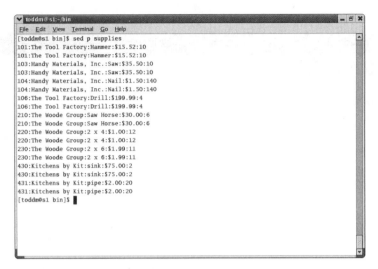

Figure 10-6   Supplies data file displayed with the sed p supplies command

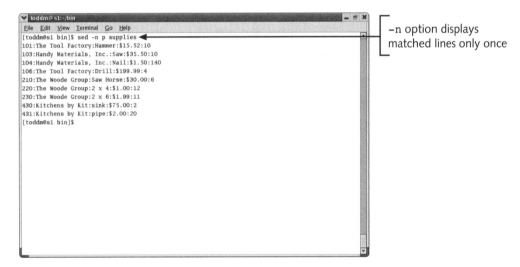

Figure 10-7   Supplies data file displayed with the sed -n p supplies command

It's important that you fully understand how the **sed** command works with the default behavior as well as with the required command or script that you must specify for **sed**. If you are still a little uncertain about how the **sed** commands operate, your understanding will become more fully evolved as you learn about additional commands for **sed**.

The **sed** command also allows you to pick and choose which text lines of a file to process. Table 10-5 includes a few examples of printing specific lines using variations of the print command for **sed**.

Table 10-5   A few sed print examples

Examples	Description
1p	Prints the first line
$p	Prints the last line
1,5p	Prints lines 1 through 5
8,12p	Prints lines 8 through 12
/The*/p	Prints lines that have the text "The" followed by any characters; the asterisk serves as a wildcard
/^T/p	Prints lines that have a "T" as the very first character on the line
/[2-4]/p	Prints lines that have a "2" or "4" in them
/^[2-4]/p	Print lines that begin with a "2" or "4"
/V. /p	Prints lines that contain a "V" followed by any single character and a space

Although the p option is used to print the lines, you could easily replace p with another option such as d for delete.

Here are a few more examples to consider. Each of the following examples and its results are shown in Figure 10-8. To print the first three lines of the supplies file, you enter:

```
sed  -n 1,3p supplies
```

If you leave off the –n option, it prints the first three lines twice and each of the remaining lines once because of the default print behavior.

To print all lines containing the text "Handy," followed by any characters, you enter:

```
sed  -n '/Handy*/p' supplies
```

The asterisk, or wildcard symbol, means to search for any characters subsequent to "Handy."

To print all lines with a Part Number beginning with "2" or "4" in the supplies file, you enter:

```
sed  -n '/^[2-4]/p' supplies
```

The caret, ^, indicates that the match is made at the beginning of the line.

To print all lines with amounts between one and two dollars, you enter:

```
sed  -n '/\$1\./p' supplies
```

Note there is a period, or dot, after the second backslash, \. In this case, the $ sign is preceded with a backslash so it is not used as the metacharacter listed in Table 10-3. The dot is preceded with a backslash for the same reason. So, this literally lists all lines containing "$1.".

To print all lines that have a "43," followed by a single character, enter:

```
sed  -n '/43./p' supplies
```

Here, the dot *is* the metacharacter listed in Table 10-5 and matches a single character.

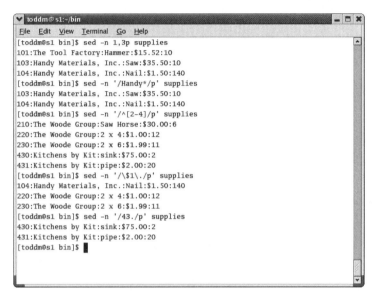

Figure 10-8   Execution of several `sed` print commands

You can also read data into a variable and perform matches with the **sed** command based upon the variable's contents. This gives you the flexibility of allowing the user to enter data from the keyboard. In the next statements, variables are read from the keyboard, and then the variables are used to match characters with a **sed** command.

```
read -p "Enter part number to view record: " PartNo
sed -n "/$PartNo/p" supplies
read -p "Enter part name to view record: " PartName
sed -n "/$PartName/p" supplies
```

Figure 10-9 displays the script named sedB. It uses the **read** command just shown to obtain input from the keyboard. It also uses the **sed** command to demonstrate how **sed** can use the data entered from the keyboard.

Figure 10-9   The sedB script which matches characters using values entered from the keyboard

It is a good idea to surround your patterns with single quotes or double quotes. Without them, you may get unexpected results.

Next you will execute various **sed** print commands.

To use sed commands:

1. Log in to the Linux system as a user, and then open a Terminal emulation window.

2. Create a data file named **employeesA** in your **$HOME/bin** directory.

3. Insert the following lines of code. Each line is a record with Employee ID, Name, and Salary as fields, and colon delimited. Be sure to save the file, and then close the editor.

   ```
   1:Marge Hammer:100000
   2:Doug Allister:45000
   3:Vu Louis:40000
   ```

4. To understand what happens when you do not issue a valid command, type **sed employeesA**, and then press **Enter**. See Figure 10-10. An error is generated because you are required to enter either a command or a script name.

5. To understand the default behavior and display the employeesA file, type **sed p employeesA**, and then press **Enter**. See Figure 10-10. Notice that each employee record in the file is listed twice due to the default behavior.

6. To suppress the default behavior with the **–n** option, type **sed –n p employeesA**, and then press **Enter**. See Figure 10-10. This time, each employee is listed once because the **–n** option only prints those lines explicitly indicated by the print command.

7. To print the last two lines, type **sed –n 2,3p employeesA**, and then press **Enter**. See Figure 10-10. The last two lines are displayed.

8. To print the last line, type **sed –n '$p' employeesA**. See Figure 10-10. The last line is displayed.

9. Close your window, and then log out.

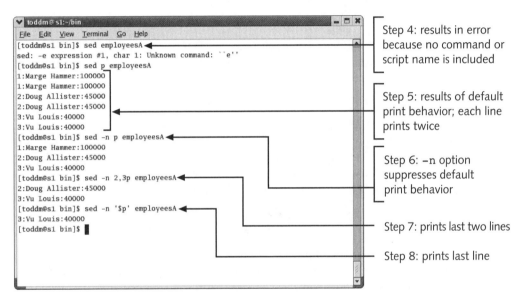

Figure 10-10   Executing sed commands on the employeesA file

The Delete Command

You can use the **sed** delete command (**d**) to delete lines of text within a file. You don't use the **–n** option with the delete command. You only need to use the **–n** option when you are printing. Think back to The Hardware Supply Store example. This store no longer sells part number 220, which you may recall is 2x6s, as one of its supplies. To delete this supply from the supplies file, you enter:

```
sed  '/^220:/d' supplies
```

Note the use of the caret before the number 220 and the colon after the number 220. These are used to make sure the first field is matched exactly. You can see in Figure 10-11 the supplies file before part number 220 is deleted and then after it is deleted. Notice in Figure 10-11 that the other remaining records are displayed.

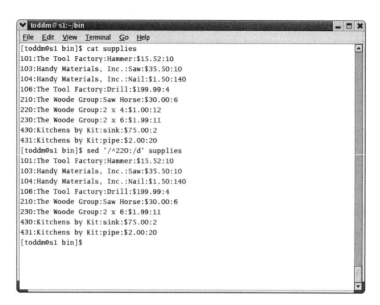

```
[toddm@s1 bin]$ cat supplies
101:The Tool Factory:Hammer:$15.52:10
103:Handy Materials, Inc.:Saw:$35.50:10
104:Handy Materials, Inc.:Nail:$1.50:140
106:The Tool Factory:Drill:$199.99:4
210:The Woode Group:Saw Horse:$30.00:6
220:The Woode Group:2 x 4:$1.00:12
230:The Woode Group:2 x 6:$1.99:11
430:Kitchens by Kit:sink:$75.00:2
431:Kitchens by Kit:pipe:$2.00:20
[toddm@s1 bin]$ sed '/^220:/d' supplies
101:The Tool Factory:Hammer:$15.52:10
103:Handy Materials, Inc.:Saw:$35.50:10
104:Handy Materials, Inc.:Nail:$1.50:140
106:The Tool Factory:Drill:$199.99:4
210:The Woode Group:Saw Horse:$30.00:6
230:The Woode Group:2 x 6:$1.99:11
430:Kitchens by Kit:sink:$75.00:2
431:Kitchens by Kit:pipe:$2.00:20
[toddm@s1 bin]$
```

Figure 10-11   Deleting text from a file

Actually, the part number is not physically deleted from the original file. To effectively delete the text, you have to redirect the output to another file, and then copy the output file back to the supplies original file as shown in the following code:

```
cp supplies supplies.old
sed '/^220:/d' supplies.old > supplies
```

In the previous code, supplies is copied to supplies.old. The file, supplies.old, becomes the one on which the **sed** delete command is operating. That result is then redirected back to supplies, which then has all the records except the one that has been deleted.

The Substitute Command

The **sed** substitute command (**s**) is useful for making changes to text. Remember the earlier state code-to-state name conversion example. The substitute command could have been used to substitute the two-letter code for the state's name. Here's another example to consider. The supplier by the name of The Tool Shop changed its name to The Tool Factory. To make that change using the **sed** substitute command, you enter the following:

```
sed 's/The Tool Shop/The Tool Factory/' supplies
```

As with the delete command, the substitute command does not modify the contents of the original file, in this case the supplies file. To physically substitute the data, you have to perform two commands as follows:

```
cp supplies supplies.old
sed 's/The Tool Shop/The Tool Factory/' supplies.old >
    supplies
```

These two commands are executed in Figure 10-12. The contents of the supplies file is displayed with the **cat** command before and after the two commands are executed. Notice that before the **cp** and **sed** commands are executed, the supplier The Tool Shop still exists, and after the commands are executed, the name has been changed to The Tool Factory. The use of redirection is carried out in the same way as it is done when you perform a deletion using **sed**.

```
toddm@s1:~/bin                                                       _ □ ×
File  Edit  View  Terminal  Go  Help
[toddm@s1 bin]$ cat supplies
101:The Tool Shop:Hammer:$15.52:10
103:Handy Materials, Inc.:Saw:$35.50:10
104:Handy Materials, Inc.:Nail:$1.50:140
106:The Tool Shop:Drill:$199.99:4
210:The Woode Group:Saw Horse:$30.00:6
220:The Woode Group:2 x 4:$1.00:12
230:The Woode Group:2 x 6:$1.99:11
430:Kitchens by Kit:sink:$75.00:2
431:Kitchens by Kit:pipe:$2.00:20
[toddm@s1 bin]$ cp supplies supplies.old
[toddm@s1 bin]$ sed 's/The Tool Shop/The Tool Factory/' supplies.old > supplies
[toddm@s1 bin]$ cat supplies
101:The Tool Factory:Hammer:$15.52:10
103:Handy Materials, Inc.:Saw:$35.50:10
104:Handy Materials, Inc.:Nail:$1.50:140
106:The Tool Factory:Drill:$199.99:4
210:The Woode Group:Saw Horse:$30.00:6
220:The Woode Group:2 x 4:$1.00:12
230:The Woode Group:2 x 6:$1.99:11
430:Kitchens by Kit:sink:$75.00:2
431:Kitchens by Kit:pipe:$2.00:20
[toddm@s1 bin]$
```

Figure 10-12   The sed substitute command

The Append Command

The **sed** command also allows you to append text below any line with the append command, (**a**). For example, if you want to display a message indicating saws are 10% off, you enter:

```
sed  '/:Saw:/a\
* Saws 10% off this week *' supplies
```

 Technically, the above code is one command, but you must place the text on a second line, otherwise you receive an error. Single quotes surround the text starting with "/:Saw:..." and ending with "...this week*". Also, notice that asterisks are used to visually call attention to the sale and not as metacharacters. Figure 10-13 shows the sed append command. The append command always places text below the line that is matched.

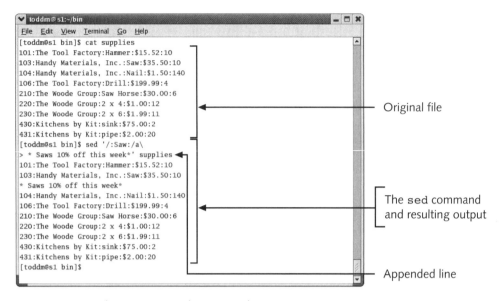

Figure 10-13 The sed append command

Notice the text "*Saws 10% off this week*" immediately following the line with the text :Saw:. The original file is left intact.

The Insert Command

You can insert text using the **sed** insert command (i). The insert command places text above the line that it matches. Recall that the append command places text below the line that it matches. For example, if you wanted to insert text indicating that the supplier named Kit is planning to raise prices, you enter:

```
sed  '/Kitchens by Kit/i\
* Kit will raise prices soon *' supplies
```

Like the append command, you must place the text on a second line, otherwise you receive an error. Figure 10-14 shows the **sed** insert command. Also like the append command, the insert command does not change the original file's contents.

Next you will execute the sed delete, substitute, append, and insert commands. In this exercise, you will make a copy of the employeesA file to employees.old. Then, you will work with the employees.old file and as necessary, redirect output to the original employeesA file, thus incorporating the changes into the original file.

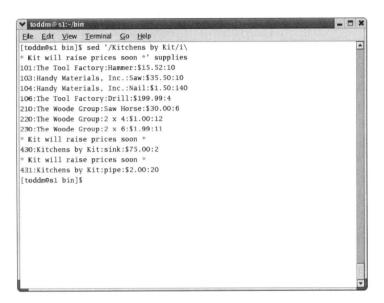

Figure 10-14   The sed insert command

To use sed delete, substitute, insert and append commands:

1. Log in to the Linux system as a user, and then open a Terminal emulation window.

2. Copy the **employeesA** file to a new file named **employees.old**.

3. To delete Doug Allister's record and redirect the results to the employeesA file, type **sed '/Doug Allister/d' employees.old > employeesA**, and then press **Enter**. The prompt returns. Because the output of the command is redirected to a file, there is no output displayed.

4. Display the contents of the **employeesA** file. Doug Allister's record does not appear.

5. Copy the **employeesA** file to the **employees.old** file again.

6. To change Marge Hammer's name to Marge Stevens using substitution, and then redirect the results to the employeeA file, type **sed 's/Marge Hammer/Marge Stevens/' employees.old > employeesA**, and then press **Enter**.

7. Display the contents of the **employeesA** file. Notice that Marge's name has changed.

8. Copy the **employeesA** file to **employees.old** again.

9. To add a new hire to the employees file as the last record in the file, and then redirect the results to the employeesA file, type the following lines of code.

```
sed '$a \
5:Lin Tuan:75000' employees.old > employeesA
```

10. Display the contents of the **employeesA** file. Notice that the record for Lin Tuan has been added.

11. Copy the **employeesA** file to the **employees.old** file again.

12. To add another hire to the employees file, insert it before the record with Employee ID 5, and then redirect the results to the employeesA file, type the following lines of code. Note that you must type the new record following the right arrow prompt.

```
sed '/5/i \
4:Jenny Santiago:85040' employees.old > employeesA
```

13. Display the contents of the **employeesA** file. See Figure 10-15. The record for Jenny Santiago has been inserted.

14. Close your window, and then log out

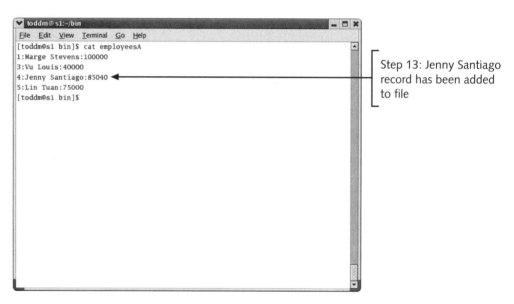

Figure 10-15   Final result of the employeesA file

CREATING sed SCRIPTS

You might consider setting up a script when you have a set of **sed** commands that you want to run automatically with a text file. Or, you might want to place commands in a script file that generate a report. When placing **sed** commands in a script file, you have to run the commands using the following format:

```
sed -f script-name data-filename
```

The **-f** option indicates that a **sed** script name follows. The *script-name* is the name of the **sed** script. The *data-filename* is the name of the data file. Look at the script shown in Figure 10-16. The Hardware Supply Store wants a simple report written from the supplies data file.

```
# Report Title
1i\
    Transaction Report\
    --------------------
# Insert a blank line between records
/:/i\
      \
# Replace all colons with a space
s/:/ /g
# Append to the end of the file
$a\
   *** End of Report ***
```

Figure 10-16   Transaction Report script

In this script, any line preceded by a # sign is a comment. The first **sed** command 1i\ inserts the lines, "Transaction Report\" and the separator line, "--------------------," one line above. The backslash is required at the end of each line in a multiple line **sed** command. Leaving it out results in an error. The next **sed** command, /:/i\ , inserts a blank line between records; this is specified by the single backslash on the line by itself. The **s/:/ /g** command globally searches for all colons and replaces them with a space or blank. This is done for readability.

Another way to achieve greater readability is with the Tab key. You can press the Tab key to cause tabs to be placed between fields. You press the Tab key in the replacement field between the second and third forward slashes which results in: s/:/   /g.

The last command, $a\, appends the line, "*** End of Report ***," after the last line in the file, which is represented by the dollar sign.

Next you will create a **sed** script to become more familiar with these concepts.

To create a sed script file that will be used to generate a report from a data file:

1. Log in to the Linux system as a user, and then open a Terminal emulation window.

2. Create a file named **SedEmp** in your **$HOME/bin** directory.

10

3. Insert the following lines of code to create the report title lines:

```
# Insert the report lines above the first line.
1i\
   \
          Employee Report\
     --------\
ID            Name              Salary\
--            ----              ------\
```

4. Insert the following lines of code to indicate a name change for Marge:

```
# Indicate that Marge Stevens had a name change.
/^1:/a\
      * Recent name change *
```

5. Insert the following lines of code to indicate a promotion and phone number change for Lin Tuan:

```
# Indicate Lin Tuan's promotion and new number.
/Lin Tuan/ a\
      * Recently promoted to Manager  \
      Her new extension is X1173   *
```

6. Insert the following lines of code to place a blank line and replace the colon with two tabs. These are for making the report more visually appealing. Note that there is a blank line after the /:/a\ line.

```
/:/a\


# Search for a colon and globally replace it with two tabs.
s/:/       /g
```

7. Insert the following lines of code to indicate the report's end:

```
# Indicate the report's end after the last line.
$a\
   \
         *** Report End ***
```

8. Save the script, and then close the editor.

9. To run the script, type **sed −f SedEmp employeesA**, and then press **Enter**. The results of the SedEmp script are shown in Figure 10-17.

10. Close your window, and then log out.

A sed script is not the same thing as a shell script. A sed script only contains sed commands.

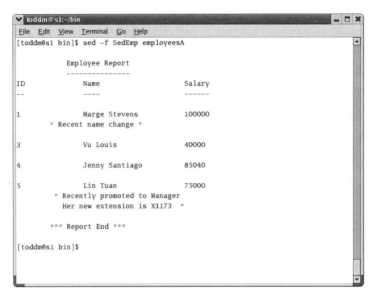

Figure 10-17   The employee report file generated using the SedEmp script

Using sed Commands in Shell Scripts

You can also integrate **sed** commands with other Linux operating system commands within shell scripts. This allows you to take advantage of the features of **sed** that are not provided by other commands. Probably the most powerful use of the **sed** command is that it can be used as a pipeline command. Although you can perform editing techniques with **vi**, you cannot use **vi** commands in a shell script, nor can you use it as a pipeline command.

Take a look at one of the script statements of a script called sed6 shown in Figure 10-18 that uses the **sed** command as a pipeline.

```
price=$(echo $tprice | sed 's/\$//g')
```

This statement uses command substitution to set the variable named price. The variable named tprice, for temporary price, is echoed and piped to the **sed** command.

In the second part of the pipeline statement, **sed 's/\$//g'**, the **sed** command globally substitutes a dollar sign and replaces it with nothing. This is so a calculation can be done. You cannot perform calculations on a variable containing a dollar sign. Hence, the result of the statement is the variable price containing a number without a dollar sign that can now be used in calculating the total.

The next statement in Figure 10-18, **subtotal=`echo "($price * $qty)" | bc -l`**, sets the variable subtotal to be the price times the quantity. This product is echoed and piped to the **bc** command. Because the **bc** command works with decimal numbers, you get a more precise value than if you just performed multiplication within the shell itself.

The statement `total=`echo "scale=2; ($subtotal * $tax)" | bc -l`` performs the final calculation for the variable named total. The portion of the statement `scale=2` sets the decimal places to two digits.

```
tax=1.06
read -p "Enter Part Number: " PartNo
        # Rec contains the line which matches the Part Number entered.
Rec=`echo $PartNo | sed -n /^$PartNo:/p supplies`
if [[ $Rec != "" ]]
then
tprice=`echo $Rec | cut -d: -f4`
        qty=`echo $Rec | cut -d: -f5`
        price=$(echo $tprice | sed 's/\$//g')   # Search for $ and replace with space.
        subtotal=`echo "($price * $qty)" | bc -l`
        total=`echo "scale=2; ($subtotal * $tax)" | bc -l`
        echo "The total is: " '$'$total
else
            echo "Record not on file"
fi
```

Figure 10-18   Shell script with `sed` commands

Figure 10-19 shows the contents of the shell script named sed6 from Figure 10-18, as well as the results of various runs of the sed6 script. You can compare the contents of records in the file to the output. For example, for Part Number 101, the price is $15.52 and the quantity is 10. With a 6% tax, the total is $164.51 as shown in the figure. Also, notice that the script uses a decision statement to determine whether or not the Part Number is in the file. If not, then a message is displayed.

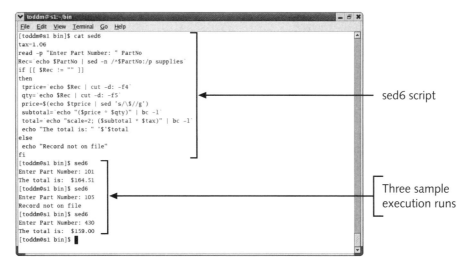

Figure 10-19   sed6 script and output of three sample executions

Next you will incorporate **sed** commands into a shell script. Each employee in the employeesA file is to receive a 4% raise. You want to open the employeesA file, and read each line as a record into EmpRec. Then, you want each of the three fields, EmpID, Name, and Salary, to be cut and placed into variables.

To create a shell script that incorporates sed statements:

1. Log in to the Linux system as a user, and then open a Terminal emulation window.

2. Create a script named **SalaryRaise** in your **$HOME/bin** directory.

3. Insert the following lines of code to begin a **while** statement that reads information into the EmpRec file:

```
while read EmpRec
do
```

4. Insert the following lines of code to cut the individual fields from the record:

```
EmpID=`echo $EmpRec | cut -d: -f1`        # Field 1
Name=`echo $EmpRec | cut -d: -f2`         # Field 2
Salary=`echo $EmpRec | cut -d: -f3`       # Field 3
```

5. Insert the following line of code to increase the salary by four percent. Notice that the scale is set to allow for two decimal places.

```
NewSal=`echo "scale=2; ($Salary * 1.04)" | bc  -l`
    # Give a 4% raise.
```

6. Insert the following lines of code to append the employee ID, Name, and New Salary to the employee.new file, and then complete the **while** statement.

```
echo ${EmpID}:${Name}:${NewSal}>> employee.new
    # Rewrite to a new file.
done < employeesA
```

7. Save the script, close the editor, and then make the script executable.

8. Execute the script.

9. Display the contents of the employee.new file. The contents of the file appear with the new salary amounts.

10. Close your window, and then log out.

Using sed to Modify Command Output

One of the greatest advantages of **sed** is the ability to use its commands on the output of other Linux commands. For instance, a group of users have a difficult time discerning a directory from a file. The goal is to make the output of the **ls -l** command a little more user-friendly. To accomplish this, a directory can be indicated for the **ls -l** by having the text "Directory" replace the letter "d" that exists at the far left of a long listing. A file can be indicated by replacing the dash with the text "File." The output of the `ls -l` command can be piped to the **sed** command which modifies the output. This can all be achieved using the following code:

```
ls -l | sed -e 's/^d/Directory /' -e 's/^-/File /'
```

Figure 10-20 shows a regular run of the `ls -l` command, and the results after making the above changes using the **sed** command in a script named sed101. The letter "d" is replaced by the text "Directory" as long as "d" is the first letter (this is determined by using the caret ^) of a line of text. The character "-" is replaced by the text "File." Note that the home directory for user toddm is shown. The directories and files in your home directory may be different, but the output of the command will be similar.

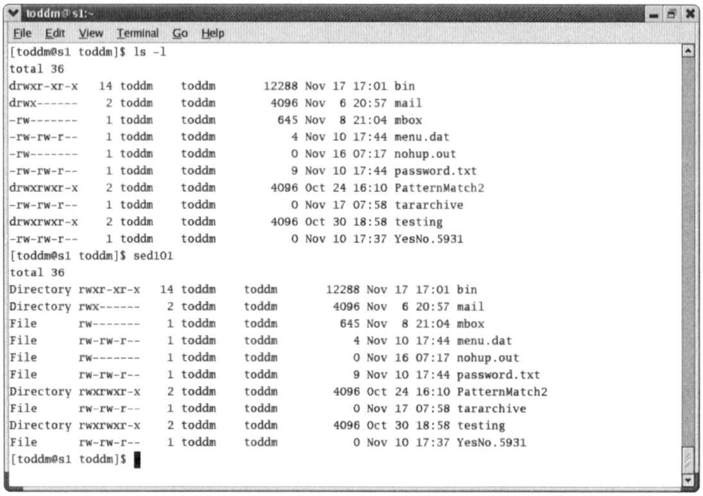

Figure 10-20 Output of the `ls -l` command and its output modified with sed

Next you will place the text "Employee logged in:" to the left of the logged-in user-name. The output of the **who** command is piped as input to the **sed** command.

To use sed to modify the output of other commands:

1. Log in to the Linux system as a user, and then open a Terminal emulation window.

2. To modify the output of the **who** command with **sed**, type **who | sed 's/^/ Employee logged in: /'**, and then press **Enter**. The text "Employee logged in:" appears to the left of the user's name.

3. Close your window, and then log out.

UNDERSTANDING SIGNALS

The shell uses signals to control the processing of jobs. A **signal** is a message sent to a process from another process such as the shell or a program. There are several types of signals. The most important ones are listed in Table 10-6.

Table 10-6   List of important Linux signals

Signal Number	Signal Name	Description
1	SIGHUP	Hangup, such as a user logging out
2	SIGINT	Interrupt from the keyboard
3	SIGQUIT	Quit from the keyboard
9	SIGKILL	Kill signal; you cannot prevent the kill signal from terminating a process
14	SIGALARM	Alarm signal used for timing out a process
15	SIGTERM	Termination

To see all of the signals, you need to view the contents of the file /usr/include/asm/signal.h, or run the `kill –l` command.

10

The two main concepts you need to understand regarding signals are how to send them and how to catch them. Signals are sent using the `kill` command, and they are caught using the `trap` command.

The `kill` Command

The `kill` command can be used to send a signal to a process. There are other ways in which a signal can be sent. For instance, you can press Ctrl+C to quit a process. You can press Ctrl+S to stop a process, or you can press Ctrl+Q to continue the process. All of these actions are signals sent to a process. The `kill` command takes the following general form:

```
kill signal PID
```

This is where *signal* is a signal number and *PID* is the process ID of the process to kill. If you need to find out the PID of a job, you run the **ps** command to display it. Once you know the PID, you can send a signal to it. Next you will use a command named **yes** that displays the text "y" on the screen infinitely. Note that the **yes** command is very CPU intensive. You should run it on a computer system when no other users are on it. Then, you will determine the PID of a process, and finally terminate the process.

To understand how to determine a PID and terminate a process:

1. Log in to the Linux system as a user, and then open a Terminal emulation window.

2. Type **yes**, and then press **Enter**. This command displays the text "y" on the screen infinitely, or until it is killed.

3. Open another Terminal emulation window.

4. Type **ps -a | grep yes**, and then press **Enter**. The **ps** command with the **-a** option displays all processes. This output is piped to the **grep** command which searches for the text **yes** anywhere in the output of the **ps** command. Remember, your other window is still running the **yes** command, so the **ps -a | grep yes** command displays output similar to the following:

```
1671    pts/2    00:01:01   yes
```

The first number is the PID, or 1671 in the example shown. The text "yes" is the command that is continually running.

5. Type **kill *PID***, and then press **Enter**. Be sure to substitute your PID number for *PID*. Now, look at the window that had been running the **yes** command. The command has terminated and the message " Terminated" appears on the screen.

6. Close both windows, and then log out.

The **trap** Command

The **trap** command catches, or traps, a signal to a process. You use this command to intercept a signal. One application is to use the **trap** command to prevent a signal from stopping a running script. You can either display a message or execute a program when the signal is trapped. For example, when a user presses Ctrl+C, signal number 2 is sent to the script, thereby terminating it. You can prevent termination by trapping signal number 2. The **trap** command takes the following general form:

```
trap argument signal
```

This is where *argument* is a command to be executed or a message to be displayed in the event the running script, or job, receives the specified *signal*. Next you will trap a signal.

To understand how to trap a signal:

1. Log in to the Linux system as a user, and then open a Terminal emulation window.

2. Create a script named **TrapIt** in your **$HOME/bin** directory.

3. Insert the following lines of code. The second command traps signal 2 (which is specified at the end of this statement) and displays "Caught Ctrl+C" when it receives this signal number. The command portion of the **trap** command is `"echo Caught Ctrl-C"`. (You must surround the command in quotes because of the quoting rules specified in Chapter 4.)

```
#!/bin/bash
trap "echo Caught Ctrl+C" 2
yes
```

4. Save the script, close the editor, and then make the script executable.

5. Press **Ctrl+C** to quit the process. The message "Caught Ctrl+C" is displayed on the screen.

6. Close your window, and then log out.

CHAPTER SUMMARY

❐ The shell allows you to use the **bc** command to perform precise arithmetic using decimal numbers. You can run **bc** interactively, in a script or in a pipeline.

❐ The **grep** command allows you to display lines in a file that match a pattern. A regular expression uses metacharacters to match at the beginning of a line, the end of a line, or match a character in a range.

❐ The **sed** command is a text-editing tool with **vi** editing capabilities. The benefit of **sed** is that you can use it to perform commands automatically.

❐ The **sed** command has its own command language. You can print, delete, search, substitute, append, or insert text using sed.

❐ The **sed** command can also be combined with scripts. You can create a set of **sed** commands and use the **-f** option to run the **sed** script. You can also use sed commands in scripts as well as in a pipeline process.

❐ Signals are messages the shell uses to manage a script or program. You use the **kill** command to send a signal to a script, and you use the **trap** command to capture a signal and act on it. The SIGKILL signal cannot be caught or ignored. Even if your script is set to trap for this signal, if it receives a SIGKILL, the script will terminate.

REVIEW QUESTIONS

1. The _____ command allows you to perform precise calculations.

   a. sed

   b. readonly

   c. bc

   d. grep

2. The _____ command allows you to only perform searches.

   a. sed

   b. search

   c. bc

   d. grep

3. The _____ metacharacter makes a regular expression that allows you to match at the beginning of a line.

   a. $

   b. >

   c. <

   d. ^

4. The _____ metacharacter makes a regular expression that allows you to match at the end of a line.

   a. $

   b. >

   c. <

   d. ^

5. To set the number of decimal places to two in the precision calculator, use _____ .

   a. precise=4

   b. scale=4

   c. decimal=4

   d. Scale4

6. To set the precision calculator to quiet mode, use _____ .

   a. -q

   b. -1

   c. -scale

   d. -v

7. The _____ command is used to send a signal to a process.

   a. trap

   b. kill

   c. echo

   d. chmod

8. Which command is used to catch a signal sent to a process?

   a. `trap`

   b. `kill`

   c. `shift`

   d. `chmod`

9. What signal cannot be caught?

   a. 9

   b. 1

   c. 2

   d. SIGALARM

10. What signal number is represented by SIGQUIT?

   a. 9

   b. 1

   c. 2

   d. 3

11. The _____ metacharacter makes a regular expression that allows you to match a single character position.

   a. .

   b. *

   c. \

   d. ^

12. The _____ metacharacter makes a regular expression that allows you to match all character positions.

   a. .

   b. *

   c. \

   d. ^

13. To run the precision calculator with the math library, use the _____ option.

   a. `-q`

   b. `-l`

   c. `-scale`

   d. `-v`

10

14. The **sed** command used to delete a line is _____.

    a. d

    b. p

    c. s

    d. i

15. The **sed** command used to print a line is _____.

    a. d

    b. p

    c. s

    d. i

16. The **sed** command used to substitute a line is _____.

    a. d

    b. p

    c. s

    d. i

17. The **sed** command used to insert a line is _____.

    a. d

    b. p

    c. s

    d. i

18. The **sed** command used for a comment is _____.

    a. &

    b. *

    c. #

    d. ^

19. The **sed** option used to run commands in a file is _____.

    a. -l

    b. -q

    c. -s

    d. -f

20. Which command calculates monthly salary from an annual salary amount?

    a. NewSal=`echo "scale=2; ($Salary / 12)" | bc -q`

    b. NewSal=`echo "scale=3; ($Salary / $NumMonths)" | bc -l`

    c. NewSal=`echo "scale=2; ($Salary / 12)" | bc -l`

    d. NewSal=`echo "scale=2; ($Salary ** 12)" | bc -l`

HANDS-ON PROJECTS

Project 10-1

In this project, you will send and catch various signals by creating a script that traps signals. You will use a looping structure to have the script run indefinitely. (This is to give you enough time to send a signal to it.) You will use the `while...do...done` command to structure your loop.

1. Log in to the Linux system as a user, and then open a Terminal emulation window.

2. Create a script named **Project10-1** in the `$HOME/bin` directory.

3. Type the following lines of code to create the infinite loop:

```
while :
do
        trap "echo Got signal 2" 2
        trap "echo Got signal 3" 3
        trap "echo Got signal 9" 9
done
```

4. Save the script, close the editor, and then make the script executable.

5. Type `$HOME/bin/Project10-1 &` to run the job in the background using the `&` symbol, so the job remains available as a process you can signal.

6. Record the output. (*Hint*: The second number is the PID.)

7. Type `kill -2 PID` to send a signal to the PID. (This is where *PID* is the second number you found in Step 6.)

8. Record the output.

9. Send signal 3 to the same PID.

10. Record the output.

11. Send signal 9 to the same PID.

12. Record the output.

13. Close all windows, and then log out.

Project 10-2

In this project, you will pipe values to the `bc` command to keep track of patients and their temperatures.

1. Log in to the Linux system as a user, and then open a Terminal emulation window.

2. Create a script named **Project10-2** in the `$HOME/bin` directory

3. Add the necessary code to allow a user to enter patient names and patient temperatures for five days. Use the shell's `read` command for data input. See Table 10-7 for a list of patients and their temperatures taken over the five day period.

10

Table 10-7 Patient temperatures

Patient Name	Day 1	Day 2	Day 3	Day 4	Day 5
Joe Antigua	100.2	99	102.5	98.6	99.1
Sandy Broughton	99.5	98.7	102.2	99.9	98.6
Amy Brock	98.6	99.6	100.5	100.2	101.1
Mary Walsch	99.9	102.2	103.50	102.75	101.00

4. Average the five temperatures using **bc**.

5. Write each patient's name, the five temperatures, and the average to a file named **Patients.dat**.

6. Save the script, close the editor, make the script executable, and then execute your script.

7. Close your window, and then log out.

Project 10-3

In this project, you will perform pattern-matching techniques using the **grep** command.

1. Log in to the Linux system as a user, and then open a Terminal emulation window.

2. Create a data file named **Project10-3.dat** in the **$HOME/bin** directory.

3. Place the following three records in the file (the fields for these records are: Employee ID:Department:Name:Salary):

   ```
   100:MIS:Micki McSunday:45000.50
   103:ENG:Zachary Scott:40122.44
   104:ACC:Jessie Garcia:50000.01
   ```

4. Create a script named **Project10-3** in the **$HOME/bin** directory.

5. Write the code needed to perform the following. Use the **case** statement to create a menu. Users should be able to enter "1" to search for a name, "2" to search for an Employee ID, "3" to search for a department, and "4" to exit the script. Use **grep** to perform the pattern matching. You may need to use double quotes when searching on the variable names.

6. Save the script, close the editor, make the script executable, and then execute your script.

7. Close your window, and then log out.

Project 10-4

In this project, you will perform text-processing techniques using the **sed** command. You will use the data file created in Project 10-3.

1. Log in to the Linux system as a user, and then open a Terminal emulation window.

2. Create a script named **Project10-4** in the **$HOME/bin** directory.

3. Create a menu-based script using the **case** statement. Option "C" or "c" allows users to perform a name change. Option "D" or "d" allows users to delete a record. Option "S" or "s" (for Show Records) shows all records in the file. Option "X" or "x" exits the menu. You need to update the files, so make copies of the file and redirect output as necessary.

4. Save the script, close the editor, make the script executable, and then execute your script.

5. Close your window, and then log out.

Project 10-5

In this project, you will use file processing and precision calculations using the **bc** command. You will use the data file created in Project 10-3.

1. Log in to the Linux system as a user, and then open a Terminal emulation window.

2. Create a script named **Project10-5** in the **$HOME/bin** directory.

3. Create a script that reads the records in the file created in Project 10-3 and writes records to a new file. A record in the new file needs to contain these fields: Employee ID and a new amount for the Salary. The new salary amount needs to be the salary plus a five percent raise. For example, if the salary is $60,000, then the new amount written would include the five percent raise bringing the salary to $63,000.

4. Save the script, close the editor, make the script executable, and then execute your script.

5. Close your window, and then log out.

Project 10-6

In this project, you will create a report using the **sed** command. You will use the data file created in Project 10-3. You may have to recreate the file if you deleted records containing the data in Project 10-4. You will also create a **sed** script file and execute it using the **-f** option.

1. Log in to the Linux system as a user, and then open a Terminal emulation window.

2. Create a script named **Project10-6** in the **$HOME/bin** directory.

3. Create a Personnel Report using the features of **sed**. Create an appropriate report heading and end line. Important facts to indicate in your report: the MIS department is only a month old. If employees are in the MIS department, indicate they are newly hired. Jessie in accounting just got a promotion to the Phoenix office. Zachary in engineering just had his 15th year anniversary with the company.

4. Save the script, close the editor, make your script executable, and then execute your script.

5. Close your window, and then log out.

Project 10-7

In this project, you will use the **bc** command to perform calculations for a new mall store called It's Your Clothing Store.

1. Log in to the Linux system as a user, and then open a Terminal emulation window.

2. Create a script named **Project10-7** in the **$HOME/bin** directory.

3. Create a script composed completely of **bc** statements. The script needs to use a looping structure. Allow the user to enter the number of times to loop. Allow the user to enter a tax amount. Allow the user to enter the price and quantity for apparel. Use two decimal places. Calculate the subtotal as price multiplied by quantity. Include the tax in the total. When data is entered, the script needs to display the subtotal, tax, and total for each iteration.

4. Save the script, close the editor, make your script executable, and then execute your script.

5. Close your window, and then log out.

Project 10-8

In this project, you will read a record from a file containing payroll data. You will then use the **bc** command to perform pay calculations.

1. Log in to the Linux system as a user, and then open a Terminal emulation window.

2. Create a script named **Project10-8** in the **$HOME/bin** directory. The script needs to read in five employee records using a loop. (*Hint:* You might need to refer to Chapter 9 for more information regarding file processing.) Refer to Table 10-8 for a table of the employee records to use. Notice that the fields are comma delimited. For each record, calculate gross pay. You are to account for regular pay and overtime pay in your calculations. Use the **bc** command to perform the calculations. Set the scale to two decimal positions. Here is the code you will need to calculate the gross pay for regular pay calculations:

```
gp=`echo "scale=2; ($rate * 40)" | bc -l`
```

Once the gross pay is calculated, display the Employee ID, Name, Rate, Pay, and Hours.

Table 10-8 Employee records

Employee ID	Name	Rate	Hours
1	Li Tanglees	50.30	41
2	Frank Jones	44.50	43
3	Jay Haywood	50.55	44
4	Fran Martel	40.00	40
5	Jen Vladosk	41.99	10

3. Save the script, close the editor, make your script executable, and then execute your script.

4. Close your window, and then log out.

CASE PROJECTS

Case 10-1

TMI needs help writing a script that calculates net pay. However they need the data to be precisely calculated. Rewrite the script from Case 5-1 in Chapter 5 with these modifications:

1. Prompt for user input.

2. Implement a loop allowing the user to enter records until they no longer want to continue.

3. Don't allow the user to terminate the script if they press Ctrl+C.

4. Calculate the Gross Pay, the Deductions, and the Net Pay amounts to the penny.

5. Display the Employee's ID, the Gross Pay, all of the deductions, and the Net Pay in an appropriate manner.

Case 10-2

Darwood's Doughnut and Bagel Shop needs a menu script that allows the user to:

1. Create a data file with the following records: Product ID, Product Name, Product Price, and Supplier

2. Delete a product based upon Product ID

3. Change a Product Name

4. Display all Product Names

5. Print the data file

10

11

ADVANCED TECHNIQUES
AND TOOLS

In this chapter, you will:

◆ Understand the awk pattern-scanning and processing language program
◆ Learn about awk program execution and command structure
◆ Get data into the awk program
◆ Use awk scripts
◆ Work with the `dialog` command
◆ Implement multiple dialog boxes within a script

In this chapter, you will learn how to use the awk program. The awk program is a complete programming language that allows you to perform tasks that other Linux tools don't provide. The advantage of awk is that you can manipulate fields within a record in a file, and perform decision and looping structures based upon patterns. It combines the features of **sed** and **grep** that allow you to search for patterns, plus it provides programming techniques that the shell offers. Other tools alone cannot support these combined features. You can use awk to modify the output of Linux shell commands allowing you to create custom scripts. In this chapter, you will also learn about the **dialog** command which allows you to create graphical, user-friendly menus that can be incorporated in your scripts.

UNDERSTANDING THE awk PATTERN-SCANNING AND PROCESSING LANGUAGE PROGRAM

The awk command was named after the three developers who wrote it, Alfred Aho, Peter Weinberger, and Brian Kernighan. The **awk program** is a programming language with decision and loop structures similar to what you've already used in the bash shell. In fact, some of the same statements you have used within the shell exist in awk as well.

The awk program allows you to manipulate data within files, extract and compare fields, print reports, and match regular expressions easier than other tools such as grep and sed or even other shell commands. Although bash allows you to perform decision statements, loops, and other programming structures, it relies on other commands to perform file, record, and field manipulation. Because these techniques are built into the awk program, they execute faster than by implementing several different commands to accomplish the same task in the bash shell. Also, the awk program has its own variables that it uses to keep track of the current record number in a line or the number of fields in a record. These variables are used as a record counter and are faster and easier to use than incrementing a variable as you have seen in previous chapters.

Table 11-1 includes some of the Linux programs you've learned about and the techniques they provide. Note the letter "Y" in a column indicates the technique is provided by the program and the letter "N" in a column indicates the technique is not provided by the program. You can refer to this table and quickly decide which program to use based upon what you want to accomplish. For example, if you need to create a report for a data file, you could use either awk or sed because there is a "Y" for both programs in that column. As you can see, awk provides for all the techniques.

Table 11-1   Comparison of the techniques provided by various Linux programs

Linux Utilities	Field Manipulation and Comparison	Report Generation	Decimal Precision	Mathematical Operations	Searching for Data within a File	Decision and Looping Structures	Built-in counters and variables
awk	Y	Y	Y	Y	Y	Y	Y
bash	Y	N	N	Y	N	Y	N
bc	N	N	Y	Y	N	Y	N
grep	N	N	N	N	Y	N	N
sed	N	Y	N	N	Y	N	N

The awk program also allows you to perform numeric operations on real numbers (numbers containing decimal points), and it also has builtin functions, such as calculating the square root. With the awk program you can use such regular expression techniques as those used with grep and sed which you learned about in Chapter 10.

The awk command can be executed the following way:

```
awk option program-text file
```

The awk command allows you to place an *option* after its name which can be any one or a combination of the options listed in Table 11-2. The *program-text* is a set of awk patterns and/or actions. These will be discussed later in this chapter. The *file* is a file containing data that the awk command processes.

Table 11-2   Some of the awk options

Option	Description	Example
`-f program-text file`	Lets you specify a file that contains awk commands to be executed	`awk -f awkscript employees.dat`
`-F fs`	Lets you specify a field separator as *fs*	`awk -F : -f awkscript employees.dat`
`-v variable=value`	Lets you pass values to awk; once passed, awk can manipulate them	`awk -f awkscript -v Amt=5`
`-W options`	Lets you use such options as help or version to print additional information about awk	`awk -W version`

11

LEARNING ABOUT awk PROGRAM EXECUTION AND COMMAND STRUCTURE

The awk command operates similarly to the sed program discussed in Chapter 10. The awk program reads lines of input from the keyboard or a file and matches lines based upon a pattern. It differs from sed in that awk allows you to specify an action that is to be performed on those matched lines.

This section takes a look at some general guidelines governing patterns and actions before discussing each in greater detail. An awk command is composed of a sequence of pattern and action statements. Think of the **pattern statement** as what you want to match a record in the data file with and the **action statements** as what occurs when a pattern is matched in a record in the data file. Here is the general structure for how a pattern and action are formed:

```
pattern_to_match { action_to_take }
```

The syntax of awk requires you to enter at least one pattern or one action when using it. You can enter both on the same line, but when you do, the pattern comes first followed by the action. Action statements are enclosed within a pair of braces, {...}. If you utilize the awk command without the pattern, the action is performed for each line of input. If you don't include the action statements, all input lines matching the pattern are displayed.

Patterns

There are quite a few patterns in the awk language. Only the following three patterns will be discussed here:

- Regular expressions
- BEGIN
- END

The Regular Expression Pattern

The awk program allows you to perform pattern matching using the regular expressions discussed in Chapter 10 for sed. When using regular expressions you need to surround the regular expression with a forward slash, within single quotes, as in '/regular_expression/'.

Next you will learn how to use regular expressions with awk. In this exercise and those to come, you will need to use a file that contains records with these fields: Employee ID, First Name, Last Name, and Annual Salary.

To use regular expressions with awk:

1. Log in to the Linux system as a user, open a Terminal emulation window, and then change to the **$HOME/bin** directory.

2. First, you must create the data file to be used. Create a data file named **employees.dat** in your **$HOME/bin** directory and insert the following lines below. Make sure you leave a space (not a colon) for the field separator between each field. The awk command uses a space as a separator.

   ```
   1 Marge Smith 100000
   2 Vu Lung 40000
   3 Jenny Patel 85040
   4 Lin Liu 45000
   ```

3. Save and close the **employees.dat** file.

4. To display the line containing the Employee ID starting with "1," type **awk '/ ^1/' employees.dat**, and then press **Enter**. Note the caret (^) is used to match at the beginning of the line. Here, it is required to match Employee ID. If you left the caret off, it would display any line with a "1" in it. See Figure 11-1. The record for Marge Smith is displayed.

5. To display the line containing Lin Liu, type **awk '/ Lin Liu /' employees.dat**, and then press **Enter**. Be sure to include a space before the first name and after the last name. See Figure 11-1. The record for Lin Liu is displayed. Note that there is a space before the name Lin and after the name Liu. If you leave them out, the awk statement would display "Lin Liuxyz" if it appeared in the file. By including spaces, you are guaranteed to only get this match for the data in the employees.dat file.

6. To display lines with employees earning a salary between $40,000 and $49,999, type **awk '/ 4..../' employees.dat**, and then press **Enter**. Note there is a space before the number "4." See Figure 11-1. The records for Vu Lung and Lin Liu are displayed.

7. To display lines with employees earning a salary of between $40,000 and $89,999 inclusive, type **awk '/ [48]..../' employees.dat**, and then press **Enter**. Again, there is a space prior to "[48]." See Figure 11-1. The records for Vu Lung, Jenny Patel, and Lin Liu are displayed.

8. Close your window, and then log out.

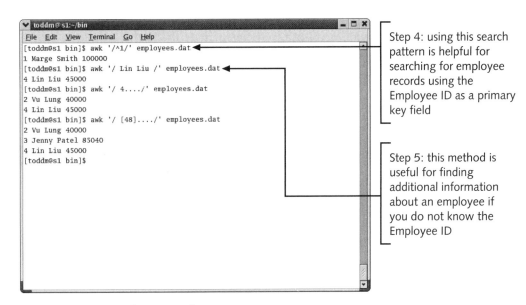

Step 4: using this search pattern is helpful for searching for employee records using the Employee ID as a primary key field

Step 5: this method is useful for finding additional information about an employee if you do not know the Employee ID

Figure 11-1   Use of awk regular expressions

The BEGIN and END Patterns

Although most patterns are compared to a line of input in the data file, the BEGIN and END patterns are not evaluated. They contain statements that are executed. The BEGIN pattern is executed before any input is read. The END pattern is executed after all of the input lines have been read. You can use the BEGIN pattern to display a heading line before all the records are printed, and then you can use the END statement to display an ending after all records have been printed.

Think of the BEGIN pattern as a header and the END pattern as a footer.

You must type BEGIN and END in all uppercase letters.

Next you will work with the BEGIN and END patterns.

To use BEGIN and END pattern-matching statements in the awk program:

1. Log in to the Linux system as a user, open a Terminal emulation window, and then change to the **$HOME/bin** directory.

2. To display a heading line and match the first character in the range of 1 to 4, type **awk 'BEGIN {print "ID First Last Salary"}; /^[1-4]/' employees.dat**, and then press **Enter**. Note the use of the caret in the pattern /^[1-4]/ matches either a 1, 2, 3, or 4 in the first character position. See Figure 11-2. The heading line is displayed followed by the matching records.

3. To first display records then an ending line, type **awk '/^[1-4]/; END {print "*** End of Report ***"}' employees.dat**, and then press **Enter**. See Figure 11-2. The matching records are displayed followed by the ending line you established in the code.

4. To display a heading line, input records followed by an ending line, type **awk 'BEGIN {print "ID First Last Salary"}; /^[1-4]/; END {print "*** End of Report ***"}' employees.dat**, and then press **Enter**. See Figure 11-2. The two heading lines are displayed followed by the matching records and finally the closing line.

5. Close your window, and then log out.

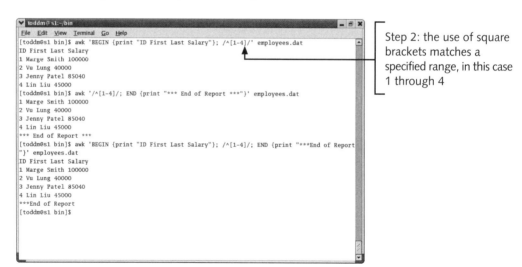

Step 2: the use of square brackets matches a specified range, in this case 1 through 4

Figure 11-2   Use of the awk, BEGIN, and END pattern statements

Actions

In awk, an action must be enclosed in braces and consists of variable assignments, arithmetic and logic operators, decision structures, and/or looping structures. The print statement is an action. Also, the awk command uses statements similar to those used by the shell such as if, while, and for.

Using the print Statement to Extract Fields

As you have already seen in the earlier exercises, the print statement is an action statement that prints fields in an input record. By default, the entire line of input is printed. However, you can control which fields are printed. Next you will learn how to use the print action statement in awk to extract specific fields. In awk, each column of input is referred to as a positional parameter. In other words, the first field is $1, the second field is $2, and so on. The positional parameter $0 represents the entire line of input.

 In awk, as in the bash shell, $1, $2, and so on are called positional parameters.

To use the print action statement in awk:

1. Log in to the Linux system as a user, open a Terminal emulation window, and then change to the **$HOME/bin** directory.

2. To display all fields, type **awk '{print $0}' employees.dat**, and then press **Enter**. See Figure 11-3. All fields of all input lines are printed.

3. To display the First and Last Name fields, type **awk '{print $2, $3}' employees.dat**, and then press **Enter**. See Figure 11-3. The First and Last name of all input lines are displayed.

4. You can also change the display order of the fields. So, to display the Last Name followed by the First Name, reverse the positional parameters by typing **awk '{print $3, $2}' employees.dat**, and then press **Enter**. See Figure 11-3. The Last Name and then the First Name for all input lines are displayed.

5. To display the Last Name first, followed by the Employee ID, and then the Annual Salary, type **awk '{print $3, $1, $4}' employees.dat**, and then press **Enter**. See Figure 11-3. The Last Name, Employee ID, and then the Annual Salary of all input lines are displayed respectively.

6. To embed text within the print statement for use in displaying a user-friendly descriptive statement, type **awk '{print "Employee " $2 " earns "$4 ". "}' employees.dat**, and then press **Enter**. See Figure 11-4. The First Name and Annual Salary, along with descriptive text, are displayed for all lines.

11

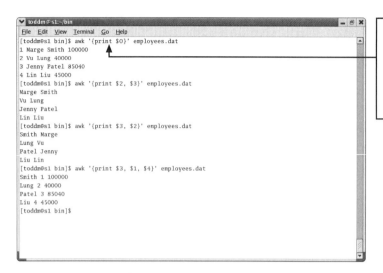

Step 2: because a column represents a field and a line represents a record, you can say that all fields of all records are displayed with the use of print $0

Figure 11-3   Use of awk print statements

7. To place a tab between the First Name and the Annual Salary fields for use in displaying additional space between the fields and text, type **awk '{print "Employee " $2 "\t earns " $4 "."}' employees.dat**, and then press **Enter**. See Figure 11-4. The First Name and Annual Salary along with descriptive text are displayed.

8. To place a new line between the First Name and the Salary fields and text, type **awk '{print "Employee " $2 "\n earns " $4 "."}' employees.dat**, and then press **Enter**. See Figure 11-4. The First Name is displayed on one line, and the Annual Salary is displayed on the next line for each line of input.

9. Close your window, and then log out.

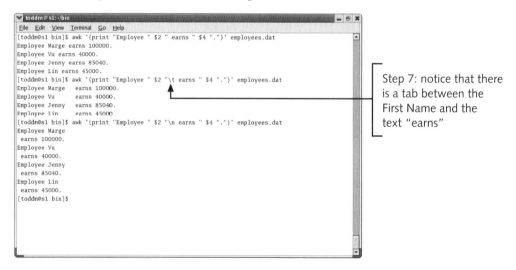

Step 7: notice that there is a tab between the First Name and the text "earns"

Figure 11-4   Use of awk print statement to customize output

The if Statement

The if action statement in awk logically works the same way as in the shell. However, its implementation differs slightly. You use the if decision structure to display lines of input when certain conditions are matched. For example, you have a Sales file, and you want to display the name of all sales people who earned over $250,000 in commissions last year. To do so you use the if statement. Next you will use this decision structure in awk. You will use the employees.dat data file that you created earlier.

To use the if action statement in awk:

1. Log in to the Linux system as a user, open a Terminal emulation window, and then change to the **$HOME/bin** directory.

2. To use the if statement to display the First Name, Last Name, and Salary when the Employee ID equals 3, type **awk '{if ($1 == 3) print $2, $3, $4}' employees.dat**, and then press **Enter**. Note you must surround the condition statement ($1 == 3) with parentheses. Also, two equal signs represent "equal to" in awk. See Figure 11-5. The record for Jenny Patel is displayed.

3. To display the First Name, Last Name, and Salary when the Employee ID equals 1 or 4, type **awk '{if ($1 == 1 || $1 == 4) print $2, $3, $4}' employees.dat**, and then press **Enter**. See Figure 11-5. The records for Marge Smith and Lin Lui are displayed.

4. To display the First Name, Last Name, and Salary when Salary is less than or equal to $42,000, type **awk '{if ($4 <= 42000) print $2, $3, $4}' employees.dat**, and then press **Enter**. See Figure 11-5. The record for Vu Lung is displayed.

5. To display the First Name, Last Name, and Salary when the Last Name contains the letters "Liu," type **awk '{if ($3 ~ "Liu") print $2, $3, $4}' employees.dat**, and then press **Enter**. See Figure 11-5. The record for Lin Liu is displayed.

6. To display a message for employees with a salary over or under a specific amount, in this case $50,000, you can also use an else clause with the if statement. Type **awk '{if ($4 > 50000) print $2 "\t Over**

$50,000"; else print $2 "\t Under $50,000" }'
employees.dat, and then press **Enter**. See Figure 11-5. Each input line
is displayed with an appropriate message depending on whether their
salary is over or under the amount.

7. Close your window, and then log out.

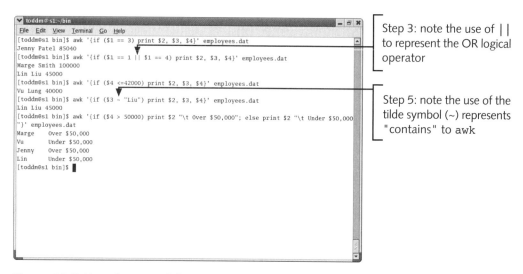

Step 3: note the use of | |
to represent the OR logical
operator

Step 5: note the use of the
tilde symbol (~) represents
"contains" to awk

Figure 11-5 Use of awk and the if statement used to determine employee information

GETTING DATA INTO THE AWK PROGRAM

In general, inputting data makes your **awk** statements more flexible because you can control the data that **awk** uses. The **awk** program allows you to input data using two different
styles. They are as follows:

- Passing data at the command line
- Prompting for user input of data

Passing Data at the Command Line

The **awk** program allows you to assign values to variable names at the command line. The
benefit of this is that these values can then be used by **awk** for displaying, calculating, or
comparing data, for example. Variable assignment is much like using positional parameters
for the shell and makes **awk** very flexible because it can accept any data for manipulation.
Here's the general syntax:

```
awk —v variable-name=value
```

The **-v** option is required and is used to indicate the *variable-name* and *value* assignment. You can assign multiple values but you must use separate **-v** options for each pair. For instance, if you want to assign product to be equal to 50 and price equal to 100, then you must enter this partial code, awk -v product=50 -v price=100, at the command line. You could then use these variable names within the awk statements. Next you will learn how to make variable assignments at the command line.

To use variable assignments in awk:

1. Log in to the Linux system as a user, open a Terminal emulation window, and then change to the **$HOME/bin** directory.

2. To display a message that displays employee names with a salary over or under a determined amount specified at the command line, type
   `awk -v Amt=60000 '{if ($4 >=Amt) print $2 "\t Over/Equal to"; else print $2 "\t Under "}' employees.dat`, and then press **Enter**. See Figure 11-6. Each input line of the employees.dat data file is displayed with an appropriate message whether the salary for the employee is over or under the specified amount.

3. To assign two variables at the command line and compare their values to the contents of the employees.dat file, type `awk -v Amt=60000 -v Name=Marge '{if ($4 >= Amt && $2 ~ Name) print $2 "\t You are eligible to receive the executive bonus. "; else print $2 "\t You are eligible to receive the administrative bonus. " }' employees.dat`, and then press **Enter**. Note, the use of the tilde for "contains." If the second field, $2, contains the Name Marge, then the text "You are eligible to receive the executive bonus." is displayed. See Figure 11-6. Each input line of the employees.dat file is displayed with an appropriate message based on how the salary evaluates against the conditions established in the **if** and **else** statements.

4. To create a report with a report header and footer combined with a variable assignment, type `awk -v Amt=60000 -v Name=Marge 'BEGIN {print "Salaries Over/Equal or Under " Amt} {if ($4 >= Amt) print $2 "\t Over/Equal"; else print $2 "\t Under " } END {print "*** Report End ***"}' employees.dat`, and then press **Enter**. See Figure 11-6. The header is displayed, followed by the records, then the footer.

5. Close your window, and then log out.

11

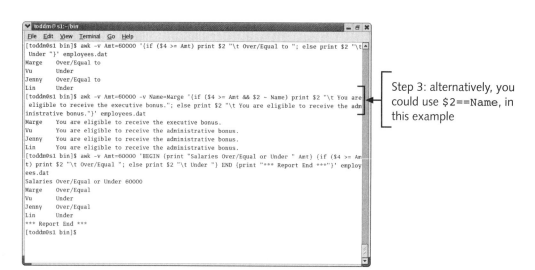

Step 3: alternatively, you could use $2==Name, in this example

Figure 11-6 Use of variable assignments

Prompting for User Input of Data

You can also prompt for user input as you can with the **read** statement in the shell. The **awk** statement that accomplishes this is the **getline** statement. This translates to "get a line" of text from standard input—the keyboard. You use the **getline** statement when you want to prompt a user for input. The prompt method allows you to customize a user-friendly prompt for a user instead of having the user enter positional parameters as with the previous method. Here's the general form:

```
getline variable-name < file
```

This is where **variable-name** is the name of a variable that contains the data that the user enters. The less-than symbol is used to redirect data from a file. The following line of code shows how to place data contents entered by a user into a variable named "pay."

```
getline pay < "-"
```

Note the use of < "-" means to redirect from standard input, which as you recall is your keyboard. Next you will create a script that prompts for user input for an Employee ID. As **awk** processes each line of input, it compares field 1 with the Employee ID that is entered. If what is entered and the Employee ID are equal, then the First Name, Last Name, and Annual Salary are displayed. Note there is a report footer that is also displayed.

To use the prompt for user input in awk:

1. Log in to the Linux system as a user, and then open a Terminal emulation window.

2. Create a script named **awkprompt** in your **$HOME/bin** directory.

3. Insert the following lines of code to set up the prompt, create the condition to be evaluated, and display a report footer. Notice the use of the `printf` command. In `awk`, this command is similar to `print`, but allows you to format the text being printed. In this case, it serves to keep the cursor on the same line as the prompt "Enter ID:." If you had used `print`, the cursor would appear on the line below the prompt "Enter ID:." Using `printf` in this case, is more user-friendly.

```
BEGIN { printf "Enter ID: "; getline ID < "-" }
{
if ($1 == ID)
    {
    print "Employee Data"
    print $2, $3, $4
    }
}
END { print " *** Report End *** " }
```

4. Save the script, close the editor, and then make the script executable.

5. Type **awk -f awkprompt employees.dat** to execute the script, and then press **Enter**.

6. Enter **3** as input when prompted to enter ID, and then press **Enter**. See Figure 11-7. The First Name, Last Name, and Salary fields for employee Jenny Patel are displayed.

7. Rerun the script. This time enter **1** as input when prompted, and then press **Enter**. See Figure 11-7. The First Name, Last Name, and Salary fields for employee Marge Smith are displayed.

8. Execute the script again. This time enter **6** as input when prompted, and then press **Enter**. See Figure 11-7. Because there is no employee with this Employee ID, no record is displayed.

9. Close your window, and then log out.

11

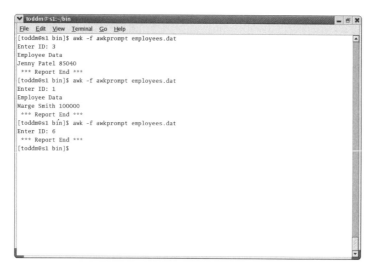

Figure 11-7   The awkprompt script and its execution

USING awk SCRIPTS

As you have seen in the previous exercise, you can place **awk** commands in a script file and then run **awk** with the **-f** option to process the commands within the script file. The main reason you place **awk** commands in a script file is to ensure programmer readability for a large number of commands in need of processing. Just like a shell script, the commands within an **awk** script can be indented or commented to make them easier to view and understand. Any **awk** command can be placed within a file and used as an **awk** script.

Refer to the man pages on **awk** for additional commands.

If you do create an **awk** script, you cannot run the script in the shell without explicitly using **awk**. This is because the **awk** statements are not executable by the shell. Here is the general syntax form for using an **awk** script:

    awk -f *script-name file*

The **-f** option means that you are giving **awk** a script, specified by *script-name*, that contains **awk** commands. The *file* specification is a data file used as input into **awk**. When creating **awk** script files, you use the # character when commenting. You can also place multiple statements on one line, but you need to separate each statement with the semicolon metacharacter, **;** .

Next you will create a script named awkscript1 which uses the employees.dat data file to create an output file named EmpMon.dat and a report that is displayed on the screen. The output file, EmpMon.dat, is created to show you how creating files is done in **awk**. This new file could in turn be processed by yet a different **awk** script for some other purpose—for example, to give employees a raise based on their monthly salary. Also introduced is the use of an **awk** builtin variable named NR. This variable represents the total number of input records **awk** has processed. If you place NR within the END pattern, it can be used to display the total number of records within the file, thus acting as a record counter. Finally, an **awk** builtin numeric function, int(*expression*), is used to turn the monthly salary into an integer value. The employee's monthly salary is calculated using the value for Annual Salary.

To create an awk script:

1. Log in to the Linux system as a user, and then open a Terminal emulation window.

2. Create a script named **awkscript1** in your **$HOME/bin** directory.

3. Insert the following lines of code to display the heading line and begin the awk script:

```
BEGIN { print "ID \t   Name \t\t Monthly Pay" }
{
```

4. Insert the following line of code to calculate the monthly salary as an integer:

```
MonthlySal=int(($4 / 12))
```

5. Insert the following line of code to display the Employee ID, the Last Name, a comma, the First Name, and the Monthly Pay of an employee respectively:

```
print $1 "\t" $3 ",\t" $2 "\t" MonthlySal
```

6. Insert the following line of code to redirect the Employee ID, the First Name, Last Name, and the Monthly Pay to a file named EmpMon.dat. Note the use of the redirection symbol to redirect the output to the file:

```
print $1, $2, $3, MonthlySal > "EmpMon.dat"
```

7. Insert the following lines to display a footer line that is displayed after all input lines, in this case records, are processed. The number of employees is displayed using the **awk** NR builtin variable:

```
}
END { print " " ;print "Number of employees: " NR;
    print "*** End of Report ***" }
```

8. Save the script, and then close the editor.

9. Make the script executable, and then execute the script. Type **awk -f awkscript1 employees.dat** to execute the script, and then press **Enter**.

11

The script runs and displays the report on the screen. Figure 11-8 shows the execution and the resulting report.

10. Display the contents of the EmpMon.dat file. Figure 11-9 shows the contents of this file. Notice the fourth field is the Monthly Pay instead of the Annual Salary.

11. Close your window, and then log out.

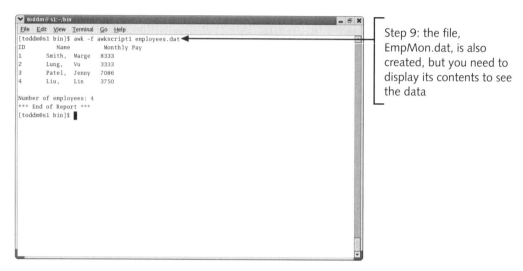

Step 9: the file, EmpMon.dat, is also created, but you need to display its contents to see the data

Figure 11-8 The awkscript1 awk script processing employee records in the employee data file

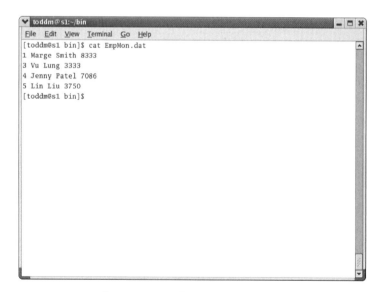

Figure 11-9 The contents of the EmpMon.dat file also created by awkscript1

Creating System Administration Utilities Using awk

One benefit of awk is that you can use it to customize the output of other Linux commands, thus allowing you to create scripts that suit your own needs. To better understand this concept, take a look at a few awk scripts that modify the output of Linux commands. Note that the output of these Linux commands is piped to the awk command for further processing.

You are already familiar with the who command and its output. Suppose you want to customize the output to display text indicating the username and when the user logged in. Because the who command displays text in columns, you could reference these columns by their position using the positional parameters $1, $2, and so on. To display usernames and the times they logged in, you use $1 and $5, respectively. You write the script statement as follows:

```
who | awk '{print $1, $5}'
```

Say you want to display the usernames, the month, and date. You use positions $1, $3, and $4 of the who output listing. The next statement displays these columns along with a footer line indicating the number of users that are currently logged in using NR.

```
who | awk '{print $1, $3, $4} END {print "There are " NR "
    users logged on now."}'
```

If you want to see one column listed before another, you could even alter the order in which the columns are displayed. Suppose your manager wants to see the output of the who command modified so that a header line is displayed followed by the day of the month, then the month name, and finally the user name for each user logged in. You write this script statement as follows:

```
who | awk 'BEGIN {print "Date \t Username"} {print $4, $3,
    "\t", $1}'
```

Figure 11-10 shows the statements and output for these three requirements.

Look at another example. The Linux command df shows you disk space usage and the availability of various file systems. A **file system** is a partition, or portion, of a hard disk drive. Look at Figure 11-11. After the df command is executed, the file system information is shown in six columns of data. The first column represents the file system name. The fifth column displays the usage as a percent. Say you don't want to see all of the output of the df command. Perhaps you only want to see the file system name and the percent used. In this case, you can use awk to display the file system name as $1 and the percent used as $5. Note the awk if statement is used to eliminate the file system labeled "none" from the listing. The use of the {if ($1 !~ "none") { print $1, $5}} statement is to display the first and fifth column *only* if the first column does not contain the text "none" in Figure 11-11.

11

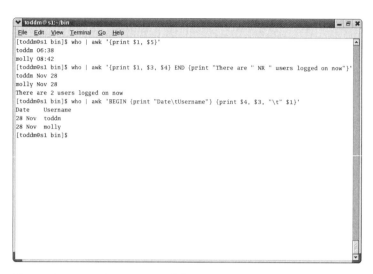

Figure 11-10 The output of the who command using the previous three
who | awk statements

You can also use the awk system(*command*) function to run or call an operating system
command, specified by *command*. The benefit of using the system(*command*) function
is that you can incorporate Linux commands within an awk script. Once the *command*
completes, control returns to the next awk command, which in the example shown in
Figure 11-11 is the if statement. In this script the system("date +%D") command is
used to display the current date in "MM/DD/YY" format.

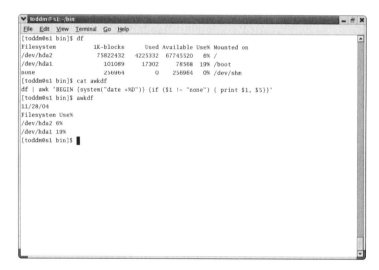

Figure 11-11 The df command, the awkdf script, and the output from executing awkdf

Look at one more example. As you know, the `ls -l` command displays output in columns. Say you want to display the file type, permissions, and the filename, plus show a total count of the number of directories or files in the list. To do so you enter this statement:

```
ls -l | awk '{print $1, $9} END {print "Number of entries: " NR - 1}'
```

Both file type and permissions are located in $1. Note that the END {print "Number of entries: " NR - 1}' statement is displayed last. The use of NR - 1 displays the total number of directories and files in the listing. If you don't subtract one from NR, then awk includes the first line that displays "total" in NR. Figure 11-12 shows the awk script named awkls and the output from executing it. The output of the `ls -l` command is not shown.

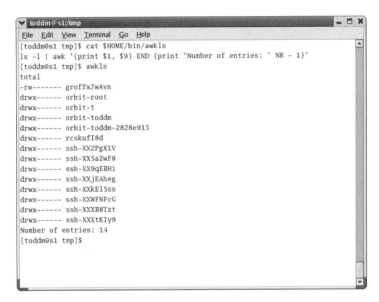

Figure 11-12   The awkls script and its output

WORKING WITH THE dialog COMMAND

The `dialog` command is extremely useful for creating dialog boxes within scripts. A **dialog box** is a window that appears on the screen and establishes user interaction. Dialog boxes allow you to make an extremely user-friendly, screen-oriented script. For example, you can create dialog boxes to list shell commands that users can execute by pressing a specific number or letter on the keyboard. Users could then use this dialog box to execute commands for themselves instead of having to enter the commands directly into the shell. Using dialog boxes reduces the possibility of users encountering errors when entering shell commands. The general syntax of the `dialog` command is:

```
dialog common-options box-options
```

This is where *common-options* are options that apply to all boxes, such as specifying a title or redirecting standard output. The *box-options* options are the types of dialog boxes you can use along with their own specific options. Look at Table 11-3 for a listing of the *common-options* and their purposes. Note that the third column shows only a partial example. You also need to add the correct dialog box statements to the `dialog` command for the commands to work. In other words, you cannot simply use the common options without using a dialog box. However, you can use a dialog box without using a common option.

Table 11-3   A few of the common options used by the `dialog` command

Common Option	Description	Partial Example (requires a dialog box)
`--backtitle` *backtitle*	Specifies the title that is displayed at the top of the screen	`dialog --backtitle "Inventory Screen"`
`--begin y x`	Specifies the position of the upper-left corner of the dialog box on the screen	`dialog --begin 3 4`
`--clear`	Clears the dialog screen	`dialog --clear`
`--shadow`	Draws a shadow to the right and bottom of each dialog box	`dialog --shadow`
`--sleep` *seconds*	After processing a dialog box, delays processing for the amount of seconds specified	`dialog --sleep 15`
`--stderr`	Directs output to standard error; this is the default	`dialog --stderr`
`--stdout`	Directs output to standard output	`dialog --stdout`
`--timeout` *seconds*	Times out if there is no user response for the amount of seconds specified	`dialog --timeout 10`
`--title` *title*	Specifies the title that appears at the top of the dialog box	`dialog --title "Add Record Screen"`

For now, just be aware of these common options that apply to all dialog boxes. In a later section, you will use these options along with dialog boxes.

The Menu Dialog Box

Several dialog box types exist, each with its own purpose. Although each dialog box type can have different parameters, there are certain parameters that are common to all dialog boxes. The common parameters are as follows:

- Text—The contents or caption of the dialog box
- Height—The height in character positions of the dialog box
- Width—The width in character positions of the dialog box

Although quite a few dialog boxes exist, not all of them will be discussed in detail in this chapter. The menu dialog box is very practical because it allows you to present the user with a list of choices in the form of a menu. It takes the following general form:

```
dialog --menu text height width menu-height tag1 item1
     tag2  item2...
```

The first three parameters, *text*, *height*, and *width*, have already been mentioned. The *menu-height* is the height of the menu within the menu dialog box. A menu entry is composed of a *tag* and an *item* pair. The *tag* is a unique entry distinguishing the item from other items in the menu. If the height of the menu is not large enough to display all of the menu choices, then users can scroll up and down within the menu items or they can select the tag representing the item. The user selects an item by highlighting the tag associated with it.

Here is an example to help you understand how this works. In the following code segment, the menu dialog box is used to display a menu. The text is set to display "Menu List," the dialog box's height is set to 15 character positions, the width is set to 60 character positions, and the menu height is set to two character positions. There are two tag/item pairs which allow users to choose tag 1 for "Item 1" or to choose tag 2 for "Item 2." Right now, you are just learning about the syntax of this command. Later, you will add additional code to make your menu more functional.

```
dialog --menu "Menu List" 15 60 2 1 "Item 1" 2 "Item 2"
```

11

Note that the tag a user enters is written to standard error. So, if users enter "1," for selection 1, the number 1 is written to standard error. If they enter "2," the number 2 is written to standard error instead. Using this knowledge, a script can be created to perform a task in the event users make one choice and another task if users make a different choice.

Figure 11-13 shows the menu dialog box that is displayed as a result of entering the previous command. Users can press Tab to move between the menu items. They can press the OK and Cancel buttons that appear on the screen as well. Note if users press the OK button, then the menu dialog box exits with a status of zero, and if users press the Cancel button, then the menu dialog box exits with an exit status of one. This is true for most of the other dialog boxes that exist as well. Users can select a menu item by pressing the number to the left of the item they want. Or, users can press the up and down arrows to scroll up and down within the menu list, and then press Enter to make a selection.

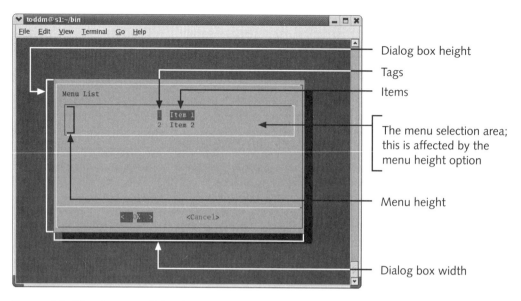

Figure 11-13   A menu dialog box

Modifying a Menu Dialog Box

Next, you change a few things so you can see what happens to the dialog box. First, two common options are added, the `--title` and `--backtitle` options. Also, the menu height is changed from 2 to 1, so you can see how scrolling within the menu works. Here is the menu dialog box with revisions to the code:

```
dialog --title "Main Menu List" --backtitle "THE MENU" --
    menu "Menu List"15 60 1 1 "Item 1" 2 "Item 2"
```

Figure 11-14 shows the resulting menu dialog box of the previous statement. You can use the common options to modify the output appearing on your screen. This allows you to customize all dialog boxes for your users. Notice the changes. A backtitle appears in the Terminal emulation window, and a title appears at the top of the menu dialog box. Also, the menu height has been changed to 1. This demonstrates what happens when you have more tag/item pairs than allowed for by the menu height. Also, in Figure 11-14, a little green "V (+)" appears below the menu indicating there are more options from which to choose. To go to Item 2, you scroll down using the down arrow key. If you do this, then "^ (+)" appears indicating you need to scroll up using the up arrow key to go back to Item 1. You can scroll up and down as needed to see any choice in the list.

Next you will create a practical system administration script using a menu dialog box that allows users to press the number "1" for the `ls` command to execute and the number "2" for the `who` command to execute. If users press Cancel, the exit status of the menu dialog box is one. If they press OK, the exit status is zero. The exit status is tested so that if the user decides to cancel the dialog box, the script exits instead of running the commands.

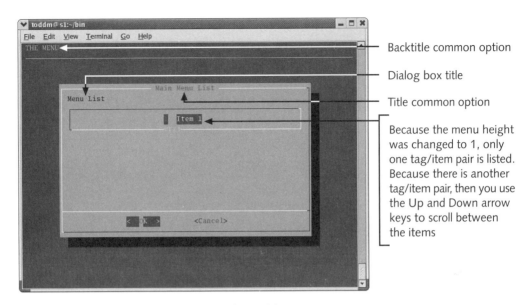

Figure 11-14   A menu dialog box with modifications

Once the user chooses an item, its corresponding tag is redirected to standard error. Standard error is then redirected to a file so you can keep track of the choices and later test them. However, you only want to keep the choice that was made for the duration of the script, so the file is removed afterwards. You use the shell's special parameter, $, which expands to the PID of the current shell to name the file. The name of the file is $HOME/menu.$$. By using $$, you are guaranteed to get a unique filename because the PID is different each time the shell is run. This way, you won't accidentally name it a filename used by another script. This is a standard way to name files that contain temporary data.

You also use command substitution to save the contents of the temporary file to a variable. The shell's **case** statement is used to establish the value of the variable. If the variable is a "1," then the user selected item 1, and this indicates he or she wants the **ls** command to run. If the variable is a "2," then the user selected item 2, and this indicates he or she wants the **who** command to run.

To create a menu using the dialog command:

1. Log in to the Linux system as a user, and then open a Terminal emulation window.

2. Create a script named **dialogmenuA** in your **$HOME/bin** directory.

3. Insert the following line of code to display the menu dialog box and redirect the tag entered by the user from standard error to a temporary file named $HOME/menu.$$:

```
dialog --
menu "Menu List" 10 60 5 1 pwd 2 who 2>$HOME/menu.$$
```

4. Insert the following line of code to maintain the exit status of the `dialog` `--menu` command:

```
Status=$?
```

5. Insert the following lines of code to create the decision structure to test whether OK or Cancel has been entered by the user:

```
if [[ $Status —eq 0 ]] # OK was pressed.
then
```

6. Insert the following line of code to retrieve the tag from the file and store it in a variable named ans:

```
ans=`cat $HOME/menu.$$`
```

7. Insert the following lines of code to test for the possible choices and execute the appropriate command:

```
case $ans in
        "1") pwd
        ;;
        "2") who
        ;;
esac
```

8. Insert the following line of code to remove the temporary file:

```
rm $HOME/menu.$$
```

9. Insert the following line of code to test whether Cancel has been entered:

```
else # Cancel was pressed.
```

10. Insert the following line of code to display an exit message because Cancel has been pressed:

```
echo "Exiting..."
```

11. Insert the following line of code to terminate the decision structure:

```
fi
```

12. Save the script, and then close the editor.

    Make the script executable, execute the script, and then select choice **1** to run the **pwd** command. See Figure 11-15. The output of the **pwd** command appears on the screen. Note the output could appear anywhere on the screen.

To clear the screen of the menu dialog box, you could insert the `clear` command immediately prior to the `case` statement.

13. Rerun the script, and then select choice **2** to run the **who** command. The output of the **who** command appears on the screen.

14. Rerun the script, and then press **Cancel**. The message "Exiting…" appears on the screen.

15. Close your window, and then log out.

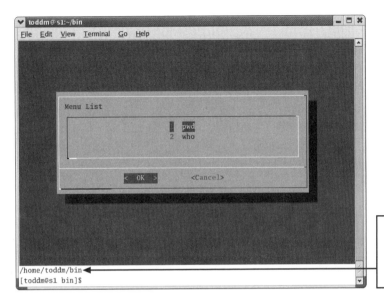

The result of selecting tag number 1; the present, or current, working directory is displayed

Figure 11-15   Using a menu script in conjunction with Linux operating system commands

Other Dialog Boxes Supported by the `dialog` Command

The `dialog` command supports a number of other dialog boxes. They work similarly to the menu dialog box. A few are listed in Table 11-4.

Table 11-4   A few of the dialog boxes used by the `dialog` command

Dialog Box	Description	Example
`--checklist` *text* *height width* *list-height tag* *item status*	Similar to the menu dialog box; instead of choosing one entry from the list, a user can choose from several items; you can also set the status of a tag/item pair to either "on" or "off"	`dialog --checklist` `"Check List"` `10 60 5 1 pwd 2` `who off`
`--fselect` *path* *height width*	Allows you to display a text-oriented window showing directories and files beginning at a specified path	`dialog --fselect` `$HOME 10 50`
`--inputbox` *text* *height width* *initial-value*	Allows you to prompt users for input; users can enter any characters or numbers; you can set an initial value using the *initial-value* option	`dialog --inputbox` `"Enter value to` `display" 10 50`

Table 11-4 A few of the dialog boxes used by the `dialog` command (continued)

Dialog Box	Description	Example
`--msgbox` *text* *height* *width*	Allows you to display text followed by an OK button; users can read the message, and then press OK. This is useful for displaying informational messages to users.	`dialog --msgbox "File deleted" 10 50`
`--passwordbox` *text height width initial- value*	Allows you to prompt a user for a password; the password is not displayed as the user enters it on the screen	`dialog --passwordbox "Enter password" 9 60`
`--radiolist` *text height width list-height tag item status*	Similar to a menu dialog box; however, you can indicate which entry is selected by setting the status to either "on" or "off" for a tag/item. The user can select only one item. On exit, the tag is sent to standard error.	`dialog --radiolist "Radio List" 10 60 5 1 pwd 2 on who off`
`--textbox` *file* *height* *width*	Allows you to display the contents of a file as a simple text viewer	`dialog --textbox file4.txt 15 50`
`--yesno` *text* *height* *width*	Allows the user to select from either a "Yes" button or a "No" button; the text displays the message to which the user needs to respond. This box is used for prompting a user for responses that can only be answered in either the affirmative or negative	`dialog --yesno "Enter value" 7 50`

IMPLEMENTING MULTIPLE DIALOG BOXES WITHIN A SCRIPT

Now that you have seen some of the `dialog` commands, it is important to understand how to combine multiple commands within a single script. Suppose you work for Rockets Red Glare Inc., a manufacturer of model rockets. They use the Linux operating system, and the manager wants you to create a script that displays the directories and files in a user's home directory, allows the user to select a file, and then display the contents of the file. To complete this request, you need to use several `dialog` commands.

The File Selection, Text Box, and Message Dialog Boxes

Next you will create a script that uses the file selection dialog box, using the `dialog --fselect` command, to display a list of directories and files in the user's home directory. If the user selects a file and then presses OK, a text box dialog box using the `dialog --textbox` command is used to display the contents of a file. Like the menu dialog box, standard error is redirected to a file, and then the contents of that file are held in a variable named filename. Also, a function named **msg** is used to display a message box and clear the screen when the user presses Cancel or EXIT. A function is used here because the same steps are performed in several places within the script.

To create a script that selects files using multiple dialog boxes:

1. Log in to the Linux system as a user, and then open a Terminal emulation window.

2. Create a script named **dialogfileview** in your **$HOME/bin** directory.

3. Insert the following lines of code to create the message box function and clear the screen:

```
function msg  ()
{
dialog --msgbox "Exiting" 5 40
clear
}
```

4. Insert the following line of code to display the file selection dialog box and redirect the filename chosen to a temporary file:

```
dialog --fselect $HOME/bin/dialogmenuA 5 50 2>$HOME/fs.$$
```

Note

$HOME/bin/dialogmenuA (this is used in the previous exercise so it should be present) is the file that appears by default unless the user chooses another filename. If the user presses OK, then this is the file that is selected. This is an example of setting a default value. The name of the file is sent to standard error. In this example, standard error is redirected to a file named $HOME/fs.$$. It contains the name of the file the user selected.

5. Insert the following lines of code to keep the exit status and test it. If the user presses OK, then the exit status is zero. If the user presses Cancel, the exit status is one.

```
Status=$?
if [[ $Status -eq 0 ]]
then
```

6. Insert the following line of code so the variable named filename contains the name of the file selected:

```
filename=`cat $HOME/fs.$$`
```

7. Insert the following line of code to display the file selected using $filename:

```
dialog --textbox $filename 15 50
```

8. Insert the following line of code to call the function named msg:

```
msg
```

11

9. Insert the following line of code to remove the temporary file:

```
rm $HOME/fs.$$
```

10. Insert the following lines of code for the remaining **if** condition. Again, the steps here are done if the user presses Cancel in the **dialog --fselect** dialog box:

```
else
      msg
fi
```

11. Save the script, and then close the editor.

12. Make the script executable, and then execute the script. See Figure 11-16. The initial file selection dialog box appears. Depending upon the directories and files within your current directory, your screen may differ from Figure 11-16.

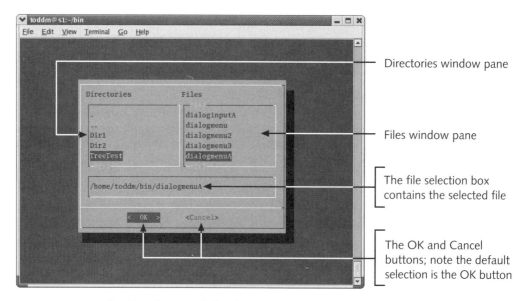

Figure 11-16 The file selection dialog box

13. Press **OK**. See Figure 11-17. The contents of the dialogmenuA script file are displayed in the text box dialog box. You can use the up and down arrow keys or page up and page down keys to scroll through the file.

14. Scroll up and down within the file. When you have viewed everything, press the **EXIT** button to exit the textbox dialog box. See Figure 11-18. The final message dialog box screen appears and displays the text "Exiting."

15. Press **OK** to close the last dialog box and exit the script.

16. To get familiar with the file selection dialog box, rerun the script. When the file selection dialog box appears, press Tab as many times as necessary to move through the Directories window pane on the left side, the Files window pane on the right side, the file selection box in the bottom pane, and the OK and Cancel buttons.

17. To select a new file to view, press **Tab** until the cursor blinks in the Files pane. Press the **up** and **down** arrow keys to locate a file of your choosing. The file you choose is highlighted in blue.

18. To select the highlighted file, press the **spacebar**. The path of the file appears in the file selection box.

19. Press the **OK** button to display the contents of the file. The newly selected file is displayed.

20. Press the **EXIT** button to close the text box dialog box. The message dialog box appears displaying the text "Exiting" on the screen.

21. Press the **OK** button to exit. The screen clears and the script terminates.

22. Close your window, and then log out.

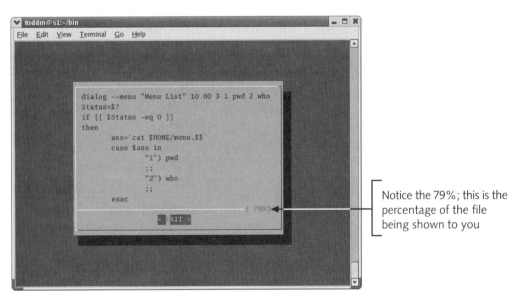

Notice the 79%; this is the percentage of the file being shown to you

Figure 11-17   The text box dialog box displaying the contents of the file

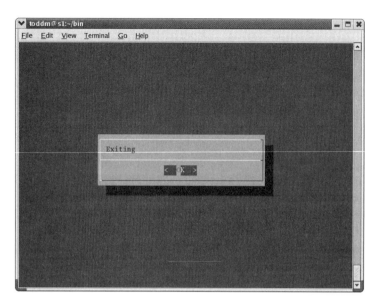

Figure 11-18   The message dialog box

Using the Checklist, Msg, and Calendar Dialog Boxes

If you want to allow your users to select multiple choices, you need to understand how to implement the checklist dialog box. Next you will use a checklist dialog box that allows the user to select from one to three choices. When the user presses OK, the script executes the commands for the choices selected. The choices are sent to standard error and standard error is redirected to checkmenu.$$. Because the user can select any combination of 1, 2 or 3, the **grep** statement is used to search for the existence of a 1, 2, or 3 in the checkmenu.$$ file. If a "1" exists, then the user selected item 1, and the code for item 1 executes. The same logic exists for the other two options. If a user selects any combination, then all the items selected execute.

To create a script that uses the checklist dialog box:

1. Log in to the Linux system as a user, and then open a Terminal emulation window.

2. Create a script named **dialogcheckA** in your **$HOME/bin** directory.

3. Insert the following lines of code to create the checklist dialog box. The first option, "Display Message," is set to "on," indicating it is the default. If the user presses OK without selecting an option, then the code for item 1 executes. Notice standard error is redirected to a file.

```
dialog --checklist "Checklist" 10 30 5 1 "Display
    Message" on 2 "Display File" off 3 "Display
    Calendar" off 2>$HOME/checkmenu.$$
```

4. Insert the following lines of code to search for the value of "1" in the checkmenu.$$ file. If the user selects 1 in the previous statement, a "1" is redirected to checkmenu.$$.

```
grep 1 $HOME/checkmenu.$$ > /dev/null
```

5. If a "1" is found in the file, the `grep` command completes with an exit status of zero. Insert the following lines of code to test for a successful exit status. If the exit status equals zero, then display a message in a msg box dialog box. The msg box displays the text "Hello" on the screen.

```
if [[ $? -eq 0 ]]
then
    dialog --backtitle "Message Box" --msgbox "Hello" 5 10
fi
```

6. Insert the following lines of code to handle selection 2. Notice this is very similar to the previous few lines for handling selection 1. If the user selected item 2, then a text box dialog box is displayed. The text box displays the contents of a file.

```
grep 2 $HOME/checkmenu.$$ > /dev/null
if [[ $? -eq 0 ]]
then
    dialog --backtitle "Text Box" --textbox
        $HOME/bin/dialogmenuA 10 30
fi
```

7. Insert the following lines of code to handle selection 3. Again, this is very similar to the previous few lines for handling selection 1 and 2 above. If the user selected item 3, then a calendar dialog box is displayed.

```
grep 3 $HOME/checkmenu.$$ > /dev/null
if [[ $? -eq 0 ]]
then
    dialog --backtitle "Calendar" --calendar
        "Current Month" 5 30
fi
```

8. Insert the following lines of code to remove the temporary file named checkmenu.$$ and clear the screen:

```
rm $HOME/checkmenu.$$
clear
```

9. Save the script, and then close the editor.

10. Make the script executable, and then execute the script. See Figure 11-19. The checklist dialog box displays.

11. To display the calendar, use the down arrow to move your cursor to item 3. When item 3 is highlighted, press the **spacebar** to select it. An "X" appears to the left of item 3. At this point, the first and third items are selected.

12. Press **Enter**. Because item 1 has been selected, the message "Hello" appears on the screen.

11

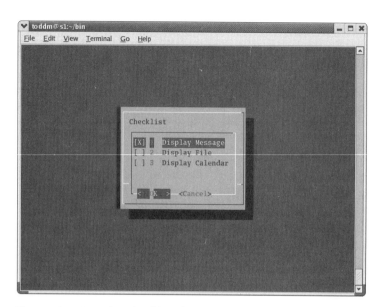

Figure 11-19   The checklist dialog box for the dialogcheckA script

13. Press the **OK** button. Because item 3 has also been selected, the current calendar appears on the screen. See Figure 11–20.

14. Press the **OK** button to exit. The screen clears and the script terminates.

15. Close your window, and then log out.

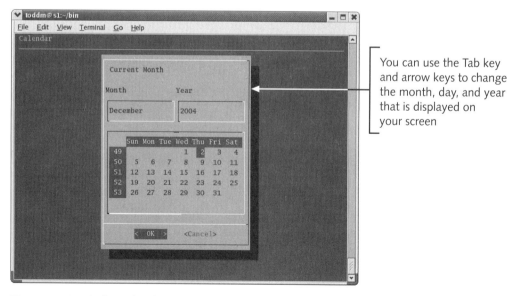

You can use the Tab key and arrow keys to change the month, day, and year that is displayed on your screen

Figure 11-20   The calendar dialog box displaying the current month's calendar

Creating a Simple Application

You can also use the dialog box to create a simple application to insert and delete records within a file and to display the file with the text box dialog box. The manager at Rockets Red Glare, Inc., now wants a simple application that allows a user to enter an employee's name, hours worked, and pay rate. Next you will create an application comprised of three scripts. The main script is called dialogmenuB. It allows the user to insert an employee's name, hours, and pay; delete an employee record, using name as input; and view the contents of the pay.dat file. The data to be entered is employee name, hours, and pay. A script named dialinsA is used to insert the record into the pay.dat file. A script named dialdelA is used to delete a record from the pay.dat file.

To create a simple application that uses dialog boxes:

1. Log in to the Linux system as a user, and then open a Terminal emulation window.

2. Create a script named **dialogmenuB** in your **$HOME/bin** directory.

3. Insert the following lines of code to create the dialmenuA script:

```
dialog --menu "Payroll Menu" 10 60 5 1 "Insert Employee"
   2 "Delete Employee" 3 "View Payroll File"
   9 "Exit" 2>$HOME/menu.dat
Num=`cat $HOME/menu.dat`
case $Num in
     1) dialinsA ;;     # The insert script.
     2) dialdelA ;;     # The delete script.
     3) dialog --textbox $HOME/bin/pay.dat 10 30  ;;
     9) dialog --msgbox "Exiting" 10 20 ;;
     *) echo "Invalid" ;;
esac
```

4. Save the script, and then close the editor.

5. Make the script executable.

6. Create a script named **dialinsA** in your **$HOME/bin** directory.

7. In this script, the user is presented with three dialog boxes allowing him or her to enter the name, hours, and pay. This data is added as a record to a data file named pay.dat. Because each field needs to be written and separated by a colon, each field is written to a temporary file. Then, command substitution is used to set three variables, Name, Hours, and Pay to the contents of those files. Finally, each field is written, separated by a colon, to pay.dat. You have seen all of these techniques before. To create three input dialog boxes to allow the user to enter the name, hours, and pay, enter the following:

```
dialog --title "Input Box" --backtitle "Scripting"
   --inputbox "Enter Name" 9 50 2>>$HOME/name.$$
```

11

```
dialog --title "Input Box" --backtitle "Scripting"
    --inputbox "Enter Hours" 9 50 2>>$HOME/hours.$$
dialog --title "Input Box" --backtitle "Scripting"
    --inputbox "Enter Pay" 9 50 2>>$HOME/pay.$$
```

8. Insert the following lines of code to set the fields to the contents of the files:

```
Name=`cat $HOME/name.$$`
Hours=`cat $HOME/hours.$$`
Pay=`cat $HOME/pay.$$`
```

9. Insert the following line of code to send the fields, separated by a colon, to the file named pay.dat:

```
echo ${Name}:${Hours}:${Pay} >> pay.dat
```

10. Insert the following lines of code to remove the temporary files:

```
rm $HOME/name.$$
rm $HOME/hours.$$
rm $HOME/pay.$$
```

11. Save the script, close the editor, and then make the script executable.

12. Create a script named **dialdelA** in your **$HOME/bin** directory.

13. The explanation of deleting a record is explained here but implemented in the next few steps. The user is allowed to enter the name of the employee to delete. The grep command is used to search for the employee in the file. The −v option is used to select nonmatching items; what you have left is all the records but the deleted one. These are rewritten to a new file that is copied back to pay.dat. The command grep −i −v ^$NAME: pay.dat > newpay.dat accomplishes this. Note ^$NAME: is used to select characters at the beginning of the file followed by a colon. This ensures selection based on the name, which is the first field. The grep −i option is used to ignore the case. First, insert the following lines of code to display the input dialog box and redirect the selection to a temporary file:

```
dialog --title "Input Box" --backtitle "Scripting"
    --inputbox "Enter Name to delete" 9 50 2>>$HOME/name.$$
```

14. Now, insert the following line of code that uses command substitution to set the variable Name to the contents of the temporary file:

```
Name=`cat $HOME/name.$$`
```

15. Insert the following line to search for nonmatching lines. Then, redirect those remaining records (the ones you want to keep) to another file, newpay.dat:

```
grep -i -v ^$Name: pay.dat > newpay.dat
```

16. Insert the following lines of code to copy newpay.dat to pay.dat and remove the temporary file $HOME/name.$$ and newpay.dat:

```
cp newpay.dat pay.dat
rm $HOME/name.$$
rm newpay.dat
```

17. Save the script, close the editor, and then make the script executable.

18. Execute the script named **dialogmenuB**. See Figure 11-21. The dialog menu appears.

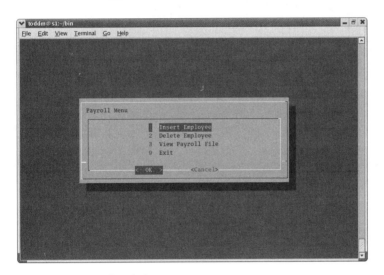

Figure 11-21   The dialogmenuB script

19. Press **1**, and then press **Enter** to insert an employee. The dialinsA script executes and displays an input box for you to enter an employee's name.

20. Enter **Ralph**, and then press the **OK** button. An input box is displayed allowing you to enter the hours.

21. Enter **40**, and then press the **OK** button. An input box is displayed allowing you to enter the pay.

22. Enter **35**, and then press the **OK** button. The shell prompt is returned.

23. Run the **dialogmenuB** script again. This time, press **3** to view the payroll file, and then press the **OK** button. See Figure 11-22. A text box appears with the data.

24. Press the **EXIT** button to exit the script. The shell prompt returns.

25. Run the **dialogmenuB** script again. This time, press **2** to delete a record, and then press the **OK** button. An input dialog box appears allowing you to enter a name.

26. Enter **Ralph**, and then press the **OK** button. The record for Ralph is deleted. You can rerun the script and view the file to make sure.

27. Close your window, and then log out.

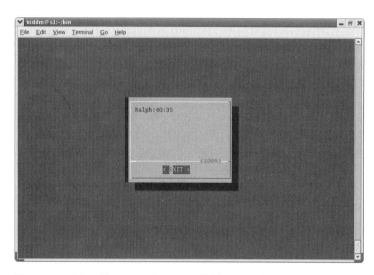

Figure 11-22   Viewing the payroll file

CHAPTER SUMMARY

❐ The awk program is a complete programming language allowing you to implement decision statements, calculations, and looping structures. It also allows you to manipulate data within files and has builtin variables. The awk program offers the use of several options.

❐ The awk program lets you use patterns and actions. A pattern is a set of characters that can be matched. An action is what occurs once a pattern has been matched. At least a pattern or an action is required. If you leave the pattern off, the action is performed on the input lines. If you leave the action off, all input lines matching the pattern are displayed.

❐ There are two methods you can use in order to get data into your awk script. You can either pass values to awk or you can prompt users for data. Either method allows for a flexible script because any data can be input into the awk script.

❏ You can place `awk` statements in a script that can be executed by `awk`. You must use the `-f` option when using statements in an `awk` script. Also, the shell cannot be used to execute `awk` scripts because the syntax is different. You can use the `awk` builtin variable `NR` to display the number of records; this is a form of record counting. You can modify the output of shell commands with `awk` in order to create a customized command.

❏ The `dialog` command is used to create interactive windows that are displayed on the screen. The benefit of using the `dialog` command to create windows-based screens is that you can build a user-friendly script that meets the needs of the users, and at the same time reduce the need for the users to learn operating system commands. There are certain parameters common to all dialog boxes. They are text, height, and width.

❏ There are various types of dialog boxes with different purposes. You can use dialog boxes to display messages, create menus for item selection, or allow user entry. You can combine dialog boxes into a single script to build a powerful script.

REVIEW QUESTIONS

1. A(n) _____ in `awk` is what is performed when a data matches a specific set of characters.

   a. action

   b. pattern

   c. decision statement

   d. script

2. A(n) _____ in `awk` is the term used to describe matching a specific set of characters.

   a. action

   b. pattern

   c. decision statement

   d. script

3. You can use `awk` _____ to display the version of `awk`.

   a. `-V version`

   b. `-F version`

   c. `-f version`

   d. `-W version`

4. The `awk` pattern that contains statements that are performed before input lines are read is:

   a. `BEGIN`

   b. `END`

   c. `int`

   d. `print`

5. The `awk` _____ option is used to indicate a specific field separator.

   a. `-V`

   b. `-F`

   c. `-f`

   d. `-W`

6. The `awk` builtin variable that equals the total number of input lines is _____.

   a. `int`

   b. `getline`

   c. `NR`

   d. `BEGIN`

7. The `awk` symbol that means "contains" is _____.

   a. `= =`

   b. `-`

   c. `~`

   d. `<<`

8. The `awk` command that allows you to read data from the keyboard is _____.

   a. `int`

   b. `getline`

   c. `NR`

   d. `END`

9. The `awk` _____ option is used to pass data to `awk`.

   a. `-v`

   b. `-F`

   c. `-f`

   d. `-W`

10. The `awk` pattern that contains statements that are performed after input lines are read is _____.

    a. `BEGIN`

    b. `END`

    c. `int`

    d. `getline`

11. The dialog box common option that specifies the title displayed at the top of the screen is _____.

    a. `BEGIN`

    b. `backtitle`

    c. `clear`

    d. `shadow`

12. Which of the following dialog boxes allow you to display a message on the screen?

    a. `messbox`

    b. `mbox`

    c. `msgbox`

    d. `message`

13. Which of the following dialog boxes can you use to present the user with a list of choices from which to select?

    a. `msgbox`

    b. `password`

    c. `textbox`

    d. `menu`

14. The dialog box allowing the user to select only one item from several items listed is the _____ dialog box.

    a. `radiolist`

    b. `infobox`

    c. `textbox`

    d. `checklist`

15. Which of the following dialog boxes allows the user to select several items from a list?

    a. `radiolist`

    b. `infobox`

    c. `textbox`

    d. `checklist`

11

16. The dialog box that allows you to display the contents of a file is _____.

    a. `radiolist`

    b. `infobox`

    c. `textbox`

    d. `checklist`

17. Which of the following can properly execute an **awk** script named script1 using the suppliers data file?

    a. `awk —v script1=suppliers`

    b. `awk —W script1 suppliers`

    c. `awk —f script1 suppliers`

    d. `awk —f suppliers script1`

18. Which of the following statements indicates to use the colon as a delimiter in **awk** when executing an **awk** script named awkit on the production data file?

    a. `awk —f —v awkit production`

    b. `awk —W: -f awkit production`

    c. `awk —f: -F awkit production`

    d. `awk —F: -f awkit production`

19. Which of the following statements creates a dialog box with a height of 10 and a width of 20 that displays text indicating the deletion of a file?

    a. `dialog --messagebox "File created" 10 20`

    b. `dialog --msgbox "File deleted" 20 10`

    c. `dialog --textbox "File deleted" 10 20`

    d. `dialog --msgbox "File deleted" 10 20`

20. Which of the following statements creates a dialog box, with a height of 10, a width of 50, and displays the contents of a file named `$HOME/payroll.dat`?

    a. `dialog --msgbox $HOME/payroll.dat 10 50`

    b. `dialog --textbox $HOME/payroll.dat 10 50`

    c. `dialog --textbox $home/payroll.dat 10 50`

    d. `dialog --fselect $HOME/payroll.dat 10 50 2>payroll.dat`

HANDS-ON PROJECTS

Project 11-1

In this project, you will use the **awk** command to create a script allowing you to terminate a process by name.

1. Log in to the Linux system as a user, and then open a Terminal emulation window.
2. Create a script named **Project11-1** in the **HOME/bin** directory.
3. Insert the following line of code using `kill`, `grep`, `awk`, command substitution, piping, and positional parameters to terminate a process by name:

```
kill -9 $(ps -e | grep $1 | awk '{print $1}')
```

4. Save the script, and then close the editor.
5. Make the script executable.
6. Open another Terminal emulation window.
7. In the second window, run the **yes** command.
8. In the first window, type **Project11-1 yes**.
9. Record your results.

Project 11-2

In this project, you will create a script that uses the checklist dialog box to allow a user to enter a menu selection to execute a shell command.

1. Log in to the Linux system as a user, and then open a Terminal emulation window.
2. Create a script named **Project11-2** in the **HOME/bin** directory.
3. Use the checklist dialog box to allow the user to enter a "1" to display the current working directory or to enter a "2" to display a listing of the current user's directory. If both "1" and "2" are entered, the working directory followed by the current user's directory should be displayed.
4. Save the script, close the editor, and then make the script executable.
5. Close your window, and then log out.

Project 11-3

In this project, you will create a script that uses the awkprompt script created in an earlier exercise and that requires the user to enter both the ID and the name to display the name and salary.

1. Log in to the Linux system as a user, and then open a Terminal emulation window.
2. Copy **awkprompt** to **$HOME/bin/Project11-3**.
3. Make the appropriate code change to require the user to enter both the ID and the name before displaying the employee's name and salary.
4. Run the script using the employees.dat file which was created in an earlier exercise.
5. Enter **1** and **Smith** for the ID and Name, and then record the result.
6. Enter **1** and **Liu** for the ID and Name, and then record the result.
7. Close your window, and then log out.

11

Project 11-4

In this project, you will create a script that uses the radio list dialog box. The goal of this project is to help you understand how to implement a radio list dialog box.

1. Log in to the Linux system as a user, and then open a Terminal emulation window.

2. Create a script named **Project11-4** in the **$HOME/bin** directory.

3. Insert the following lines of code to create a radio list dialog box.

```
dialog --radiolist "Radio List" 10 30 5 1 pwd on 2 who off
    2>$HOME/menu.dat
CheckStatus=$?
ans=`cat $HOME/menu.dat`
res=`echo $ans | sed 's/"//g'`
case $res in
    "1") pwd
    ;;
    "2") who
    ;;
    "1 2") pwd; who
    ;;
esac
```

4. Save the script, and then close the editor.

5. Make the script executable, and then execute the script

6. Rerun the script. This time select both commands.

7. Close your window, and then log out.

Project 11-5

In this project, you will create a script that uses the password dialog box. The goal of this project is to help you understand how to implement a password dialog box and further your knowledge of dialog boxes.

1. Log in to the Linux system as a user, and then open a Terminal emulation window.

2. Create a script named **Project11-5** in the **$HOME/bin** directory.

3. Insert the following lines of code to create a password dialog box.

```
dialog --passwordbox "Enter value" 9 62 2>$HOME/password.$$
PWStatus=$?
if [[ $PWStatus -ne 0 ]]
then
    echo "Exiting..."
    exit
fi
ans=`cat $HOME/password.$$`
if [[ $ans = "cactus214" ]] # The password.
```

```
then
    echo "Correct password"
else
    echo "Incorrect password"
fi
rm $HOME/password.$$
```

4. Save the script, and then close the editor.

5. Make the script executable, execute the script, and then enter **fun100** as the password.

6. Press the **OK** button, and then record the results.

7. Run the script again, and then enter **cactus214** as the password.

8. Press the **OK** button, and then record the results.

9. Close your window, and then log out.

Project 11-6

In this project, you will create a script that uses awk and an if statement to determine if employees are due a raise. The script allows the user to enter a raise threshold amount. If the employee earns less than the amount entered, he or she will receive a three percent raise; otherwise, he or she will earn a five percent raise. Also, appropriate headers and footers are displayed along with record counters. A message is displayed indicating if the salaries are over or under the amount entered. Finally, the new amount is written to a new file named newemp.dat.

1. Log in to the Linux system as a user, and then open a Terminal emulation window.

2. Create a script named **Project11-6** in the **$HOME/bin** directory.

3. Insert the following lines of code:

```
BEGIN { print "Id\t Name\t\tSalary  New Salary\n" }
{
{if ($4 >= Amt)
        {
         NS=$4 * 1.03
         MSG="Over"
         lo++
        }
else
        {
        NS=$4 * 1.05
        MSG="Under "
        hi++
        }
}
printf ("%s:%s:%s:%d\n", $1, $2, $3, int(NS)) > "newemp.dat"
print  $1"\t", $2"\t", $3"\t", $4"\t", int(NS)"\t", MSG
```

11

```
print "\n"
}
END { print "Number of employees: " NR "\n\nNumber low: "
    lo "\n\nNumber hi: " hi}
```

4. Save the script, and then close the editor.

5. Make the script executable.

6. Run the script as follows:

```
awk -v Amt=60000 -f Project11-6 employees.dat.
```

7. View the output file, and then record the result.

8. Close your window, and then log out.

Project 11-7

In this project, you will create a script that uses the input dialog box to delete a file. The goal of this project is to further your knowledge of dialog boxes.

1. Log in to the Linux system as a user, and then open a Terminal emulation window.

2. Create a script named **Project11-7** in the **$HOME/bin** directory.

3. The script needs to allow users to delete a file if it indeed exists. If the file exists, use a yes/no dialog box to ask users if they are sure they want to delete the file. If they are indeed sure, then delete it, and display a msg dialog box indicating the file has been deleted. If the file exists and the user decides not to delete it, exit the script. If the file does not exist, then display a message box indicating it does not exist, and then exit the script.

4. Save the script, and then close the editor.

5. Make the script executable.

6. Close your window, and then log out.

Project 11-8

In this project, you will create a script that copies a file. You will use two input boxes—one for users to enter the source file to copy and one for users to enter the destination filename. The goal of this project is to further your understanding of dialog boxes.

1. Log in to the Linux system as a user, and then open a Terminal emulation window.

2. Create a script named **Project11-8** in the **$HOME/bin** directory.

3. The script needs to allow users to enter the filename to copy and a destination filename. If the file exists, copy it, and then display a message indicating it has been copied. If the file does not exist, indicate that the file is not present. Use the msg box for displaying all messages to users.

4. Save the script, and then close the editor.

5. Make the script executable.

6. Close your window, and then log out.

CASE PROJECTS

Case 11-1

TMI wants you to write a script application that allows the user to run operating system commands by selecting menu items. You may have to create multiple scripts and use multiple dialog boxes. However, the user must enter the correct password, banana5, before the operating system command menu appears. If a correct password is entered, allow the user to select from the following menu items:

1. Display the amount of disk free space.

2. Enter an IP address to ping, and then ping the IP address.

3. Display the current number of users on the system.

4. Delete a file if present.

5. Copy a file to another if the source file is present.

Case 11-2

Basic Manufacturing Corporation has hired you to write a small menu-based dialog script that does the following:

1. Allows a user to add fields into a file, named parts.dat. The fields are: Part ID, Part Name, Price, and Quantity.

2. Deletes a record based upon Part ID.

3. Displays the file on the screen without the colon separators.

4. Allows the user to press Y, for Yes, to continually display the menu on the screen.

11

CHAPTER
12

SCRIPT DESIGN AND MANAGEMENT ISSUES

In this chapter, you will:

- ◆ Design and create Web page scripts
- ◆ Understand MySQL
- ◆ Create scripts that interface with MySQL
- ◆ Enhance menu-based scripts
- ◆ Understand the Revision Control System
- ◆ Add a script as a launchable application from the GUI desktop
- ◆ Understand additional management techniques
- ◆ Create custom manual pages

In this chapter, you will learn how to manage and design your shells using various techniques. You will learn how to design and create Web page scripts that include system commands. These Web page scripts can be executed over a network using a Web browser that allows remote access to shell commands. You will learn how to design scripts that interface with the MySQL database management system. This will allow you to take advantage of database technology for writing records instead of having to use text files.

It is important to know how to manage your scripts in an environment where a team of programmers can access the same set of scripts at the same time. You will learn to manage multiple accesses of a single script by different programmers through the Revision Control System. Additionally, you will learn how to execute your script as an application that can be launched from your desktop. Once your shell scripts have been written, you need to create documentation so users can understand how to utilize your scripts. So, you can learn how to create man pages for the scripts you design and create.

Designing and Creating Web Page Scripts

Any computer that provides Web page access over the Internet or an intranet is called a **Web server**. The computer accessing the Web server is called the **Web client**. A user sits at a client computer and uses a Web browser to connect to the Web server. The user enters either the IP address or DNS name of the server within the browser. The Web client and Web server use a protocol to request and send Web pages over a network. This protocol, **Hypertext Transfer Protocol (HTTP)**, is part of TCP/IP. The connection to the server must be available and accessible in order for the Web server to send the Web pages to the Web client once they are requested.

A **Web page** is a file that is made up of ASCII text containing special codes that describe the page layout. These special codes are called HTML tags and will be discussed later. A Web page may have a set of supporting files that contain images and sounds. The server reads the Web page file, sends it to the browser over the network as well as any supporting files for the page at the request of the browser.

You can design a Web page that incorporates the output of operating system commands in a script; this is termed a Web page script. This is advantageous because Web page scripts allow users access to the Linux computer via a Web browser over the Internet or an intranet, resulting in a more flexible work environment

 Linux can use any compatible Web server software, but Red Hat Linux comes packaged with the Apache Web server software. Any Linux computer running Apache is considered a Web server. Apache software can be installed during the installation of the operating system or after the installation using the Red Hat Package Manager program or the `rpm` command. Refer to its `man` pages for how to run this command. Although you can run other Web servers on Linux, this chapter assumes the use of the Apache Web server.

When a client computer requests Web pages via the Apache Web server, the server sends Web pages from the directory /var/www. Recall that the directory /var is one of the system directories discussed in Chapter 2. By default, Apache uses a subdirectory, named cgi-bin, for storing executable scripts. This is where you will place your Web page scripts when you create them. The "www" in /var/www, stands for World Wide Web. You need root user account access in order to copy scripts to the /var/www/cgi-bin directory. The **Common Gateway Interface (CGI)** is a protocol used for Web servers to be able to work with scripts. As you know, the Web client uses a Web browser to access the Web pages. The Web pages must be written in **Hypertext Markup Language**, or **HTML**, a language the Web browser understands. Although fully learning how to write HTML language code statements, called **tags**, is beyond the scope of this book, you will learn the HTML statements necessary to interface Linux scripts with the Web browser. Table 12-1 presents a listing of a few of the HTML tags with which you need to be familiar to create Web page scripts.

Most HTML tags have a corresponding closing tag. The use of a forward slash in front of a tag name makes the tag a closing tag. There must be a closing tag for each opening tag. Although the normal coding convention is to enter tags in uppercase, it is not a requirement.

Table 12-1   A few HTML tags

HTML Tag	Description	Example
`<B>` and `</B>`	Bolds characters	`<B>This text will be bold.</B>`
`<CENTER>` and `</CENTER>`	Centers characters	`<CENTER>Payroll Employee List</CENTER>`
`<HTML>` and `</HTML>`	Identifies the beginning and ending of an HTML document	`<HTML>...</HTML>`
`<HEAD>` and `</HEAD>`	Identifies the beginning and ending of a document header	`<HEAD>System Administration Utilities Screen</HEAD>`
`<TITLE>` and `</TITLE>`	Identifies the beginning and ending of a title on the Title bar	`<TITLE>System Tools </TITLE>`
`<Hn>` and `</Hn>`	Controls the size of the header font; the *n* represents a number from 1 to 6, with 1 being the largest font size and 6 being the smallest	`<H2>Application Utilities</H2>`
`<HR>` and `</HR>`	Used to display a horizontal line	`<HR></HR>`
`<PRE>` and `</PRE>`	Preserves the preformatted output, tabs, spaces, and new lines of commands	`<PRE></PRE>`

12

You can create your Web page scripts as a standard user. Once they are complete, you need to ask your instructor to copy these to the /var/www/cgi-bin directory as the root user. If you have root access, you can perform this operation.

Next you will create a script that includes the basic HTML code to allow you to create and view a Web page with a Web browser. You will then copy the script, or have your instructor copy it, as the root user, to the /var/www/cgi-bin directory. Note that the use of the shell's `echo` statement is used to interface a script with the browser. When the script is executed, the output of the `echo` statement, as in `echo "<HTML>"`, is used to literally send the text "<HTML>" to the Web browser for processing.

To create a simple Web page script that displays the date:

1. Log in to the Linux system as a user, and then open a Terminal emulation window.

2. Create a script named **webscript1** in your **$HOME/bin** directory.

3. Insert the following required line of code to indicate which shell is to be used when accessing the script.

   `#!/bin/bash`

4. Insert the following line of code to indicate to the Web server the content type of the script. It is called the header line and indicates to the Web browser the type of content the file contains. Because this script contains text or HTML code, you must include this line. It is typically placed at the beginning of an HTML document so the Web server software knows how to process the data.

   `echo "Content-type: text/html"`

5. Insert the following line of code to display a blank line. The output of the script is not displayed unless there is a blank line after the header line. This is required for your Web page script to work correctly.

   `echo ""`

6. Insert the following line of code to indicate that this is the start of the HTML section. In Step 8 you will add the corresponding closing tag, `</HTML>` which terminates the HTML code section. Any code between the opening and closing tags is treated as HTML code.

   `echo "<HTML>"`

7. Insert the following line of code to display the current date. Note the use of command substitution is required here to replace the actual command with its date-formatted output.

   `echo "Today is " $(date)`

8. Insert the following line of code to indicate that this is the end of the HTML section.

   `echo "</HTML>"`

9. Save the file, close the editor, and then make the script executable.

To complete the rest of this exercise, you must be logged in as the root user. If you do not have access to the root user password, then have your instructor log in as the root user.

10. Copy the **webscript1** file to the **/var/www/cgi-bin** directory.

11. On the Linux desktop, double-click the **world icon** on the task bar. The Web browser window appears on your screen. If your desktop doesn't include the world icon, then start your Web browser of choice.

All Web-related exercises in this chapter assume you are using the Gnome desktop with the world icon on the task bar.

12. In the Address bar, type **http://*Web-server*/cgi-bin/webscript1**, and then press **Enter**. Insert the IP address or DNS name of your Web server for *Web-server*. See Figure 12-1.

13. Close your windows, and then log out.

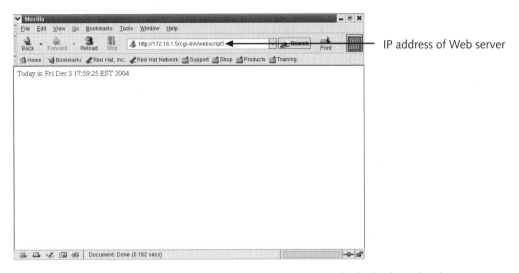

Figure 12-1   Accessing the webscript1 Web page script which displays the date

You can use this exercise as a model to create other simple Web pages. All you have to do is to modify Step 7 to include the Linux command you want. To enhance this simple Web page script, you can include multiple commands, on separate lines, as well.

Preserving Preformatted Output in a Web Page

Linux commands use preformatted output so it is displayed in a user-friendly manner. Preformatted output includes characters such as tabs, spaces, and new lines which are used to make the output more readable. The Web server software does not preserve this preformatted output by default. So, if the output of a command contains preformats, these formats disappear when the command executes within a Web page script. In the previous exercise, the format of the output of the **date** command was not preserved by the Web server software.

In order to preserve the output of preformatted tabs, spaces, and new lines, the HTML tag named **<PRE>** is used. Next you will display the output of the **who** command in a manner you are accustomed to seeing in the shell. You will use the **<PRE>** HTML tag to accomplish this. Before you perform this exercise, it may be helpful to see the output of a Web page script using the **who** command without the **<PRE>** HTML tag. Figure 12-2 shows the results of the upcoming exercise without the **<PRE>** and **</PRE>** HTML tags surrounding the **who** command. Notice how the output of **who** is not formatted as you are accustomed to seeing it.

The users logged on are: toddm :0 Dec 5 16:58 molly pts/1 Dec 5 17:03 (172.16.1.10) bob pts/2 Dec 5 17:04 (172.16.1.10)

Figure 12-2   A Web page script that does not preserve the output of a command

To create a simple Web page script that uses the <PRE> tag to preserve the preformatted output of Linux commands:

1. Log in to the Linux system as a user, and then open a Terminal emulation window.

2. Create a script named **webscript2** in your **$HOME/bin** directory.

3. Insert the following lines of code to reference the shell, indicate the content type, and display a blank line after the header:

   ```
   #!/bin/bash
   echo "Content-type: text/html"
   echo ""
   ```

4. Insert the following line of code to indicate HTML code is to come:

   ```
   echo "<HTML>"
   ```

5. Insert the following line of code to preserve the output of Linux commands:

   ```
   echo "<PRE>"
   ```

6. Insert the following lines of code to display a message line and execute the who command:

   ```
   echo "The users logged on are: "
   who
   ```

7. Insert the following line of code to close the preservation of preformatted output:

   ```
   echo "</PRE>"
   ```

8. Insert the following line of code to terminate the HTML code:

   ```
   echo "</HTML>"
   ```

9. Save the file, and then close the editor.

10. Make the script executable.

11. Properly gain root user access either on your own or through your instructor.

12. Copy the **webscript2** file to the **/var/www/cgi-bin** directory.

13. Open your Web browser.

14. In the Address bar, type **http://*Web-server*/cgi-bin/webscript2**, and then press **Enter**. Again supply the correct IP address or DNS name of your Web server. Figure 12-3 shows the results of this exercise. Your output may differ. Because you used the HTML tags, the output appears the same as if you entered the **who** command at the shell prompt. Compare Figure 12-2 and Figure 12-3 and notice how the output differs when the **<PRE>** tag is used.

15. Close your windows, and then log out.

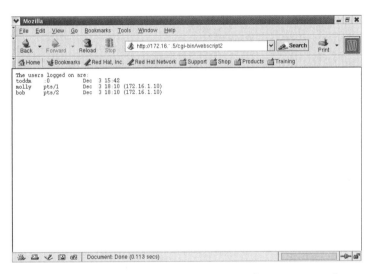

Figure 12-3   Accessing the webscript2 Web page script that uses a preformatted output tag

Customizing Web Page Scripts with Additional HTML Tags

You can include additional HTML tags from Table 12-1 in order to customize your Web page. You add these HTML tags to make the Web page script more visually appealing or to have specific text stand out on your Web page. For example, to center text, you use the following statement:

```
echo "<CENTER>"
echo "The users logged on are:"
echo "</CENTER>"
```

The text that you want to center follows the initial HTML statement, and then you terminate the centering tag with the matching HTML closing tag. You can have multiple HTML tags in sequence. For example, in the code that follows, the text "The users logged on are:" is centered, bolded, and displayed with heading level 1.

```
echo "<CENTER>"
echo "<B>"
echo "<H1>"
echo "The users logged on are: "
echo "</H1>"
echo "</B>"
echo "</CENTER>"
```

 You can also place the opening and closing HTML tags on a single line as in this example of the opening tags shown to center, use heading level 1, and bold, echo "<CENTER><B> <H1> "

Next you will create a Web page script that includes additional HTML tags to show you how to add these tags to customize your Web page. Performing this exercise will help you understand how to use these additional tags in a Web page script.

To create a Web page script that uses additional HTML tags:

1. Log in to the Linux system as a user, and then open a Terminal emulation window.

2. Create a script named **webscript3** in your **$HOME/bin** directory.

3. Insert the following lines of code to reference the shell, indicate the content type, place a blank line after the header, use the preformatted output tag, and indicate that HTML code will follow:

```
#!/bin/bash
echo "Content-type: text/html"
echo ""
echo "<HTML>"
echo "<PRE>"
```

4. Insert the following lines of code to center, bold, and use heading level 1 for text that is displayed on the screen. Notice each opening tag has a corresponding closing tag.

```
echo "<CENTER>"
echo "<B>"
echo "<H1>"
echo "The users logged on are: "
echo "</H1>"
echo "</B>"
echo "</CENTER>"
```

5. Insert the following lines of code to use heading level 2 and display the output of the who command on the screen:

```
echo "<H2>"
who
echo "</H2>"
```

6. Insert the following lines of code to close the preformatted output tag and close the HTML text tag:

```
echo "</PRE>"
echo "</HTML>"
```

7. Save the file, and then close the editor.

8. Make the script executable.

9. Properly gain root user access either on your own or through your instructor.

10. Copy the **webscript3** file to the **/var/www/cgi-bin** directory.

11. Open your Web browser.

12. In the Address bar, type **http://*Web-server*/cgi-bin/webscript3**, and then press **Enter**. Again supply the correct IP address or DNS name of your Web server. Figure 12-4 shows the results of this exercise.

13. Close your windows, and then log out.

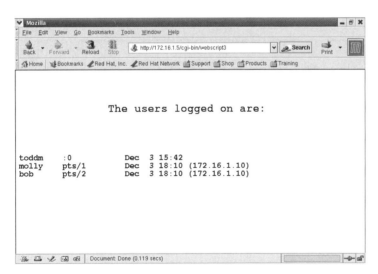

Figure 12-4   Accessing the webscript3 Web page script that uses additional HTML tags to customize scripts

Just remember when you have opening and closing tags that everything between the tag pairs is subject to what those tags do. Also, make sure that each opening tag has a corresponding closing tag.

Adding Web Server Variables to a Web Page Script

You can further enhance your Web page script by incorporating Web server variables. Typically you do this to customize your Web page with additional information about the Web server such as the Web server name, the server protocol and version, and the Web server software the server is running. Table 12-2 provides a listing of a few of the Web server variables that can be used in a Web page script.

Table 12-2   A few web server variables

Variable	Description	Example
DOCUMENT_ROOT	Directory where Web pages are stored and loaded	echo "The directory containing Web pages is $DOCUMENT_ROOT"
SCRIPT_FILENAME	Path name of the script that is executing	echo "The script name is $SCRIPT_FILENAME"
SERVER_ADMIN	E-mail address of the Web server administrator	echo "Contact the Web master: $SERVER_ADMIN"
SERVER_NAME	Server's IP address or DNS name	echo "The server address is $SERVER_NAME"
SERVER_PROTOCOL	Protocol and version used by the Web server	echo "The protocol is $SERVER_PROTOCOL"
SERVER_SOFTWARE	Web server software the Web server is running	echo "The Web software running on this Web server is: $SERVER_SOFTWARE"

A practical use of adding Web server variables is to display information about the Web server in a Web page script that deals with server utilities. Figure 12-5 shows a Web page script that includes many of the variables shown in Table 12-2. Figure 12-6 displays the script shown in Figure 12-5. Notice that in Figure 12-6 you can see the server's address, name, software and version, and protocol and version.

Also, in the script in Figure 12-5, see the **who** command using the pipe symbol to pass its output to the **awk** command to display only two fields. This demonstrates how you can put more complex commands within your Web page script.

```
#!/bin/bash
echo "Content-type: text/html
echo ""
echo "<PRE>"
echo "<HTML>"
echo "<HEAD>"
echo "<H2>"
echo "<HR>"
echo "<CENTER>"
echo "<System Utilities"
echo "</CENTER>"
echo "</HEAD>"
echo "</H2>"
echo "<Server Name: $SERVER_NAME"
echo "Script Name: $SCRIPT_NAME"
echo "Server Software: $SERVER_SOFTWARE"
echo "Server Protocol": $SERVER_PROTOCOL"
echo "<TITLE>"
echo "System Admin Web Page"
echo "</TITLE>"
echo "<B>"
echo "The file system usage: "
echo "</B>"
df
echo "<B>"
echo "The users logged on:"
echo "</B>
who|awk '{print $1 " at " $5}'
echo "</PRE>"
echo "<HR>"
echo "</HTML>"
```

Figure 12-5   A Web page script that uses Web server variables to enhance a system
utilities script

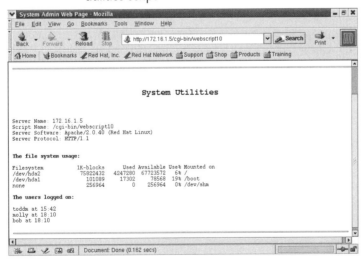

Figure 12-6   Results of a Web page script which uses additional HTML tags to
customize scripts

Using Other Commands in Web Page Scripts

You can place other commands, such as decisions, in your Web script. This allows you to customize your Web pages for certain conditions you may want to test. For example, say you want to implement a decision structure to display a message based upon how many users are logged in to the Linux computer system. In the code shown in Figure 12-7, you can see a modification to Figure 12-5 which uses an `if` statement to determine how many users are logged in.

Notice in Figure 12-7 that the number of users on the system is held in a variable named num. Next the variable num is tested using the shell's `if` statement. If its contents are greater than zero, then a message is displayed along with the output of the `who` command. If num is less than or equal to zero, then a message indicating that no users are logged in is displayed. Notice the use of the HTML tag `<B>` surrounding only the messages for each of the two conditions in the decision structure.

```
num=$(who|awk 'END {print NR}')
if [[$num -gt 0]]
then
        echo "<B>"
        echo "These are the users logged on:"
        echo "</B>"
        who
else
        echo "<B>"
        echo "No users logged on now."
        echo "</B>"
fi
```

Figure 12-7   A partial Web page script which uses additional shell logic to customize scripts

You could substitute the first statement in the partial script shown in Figure 12-7, with the `wc -1` statement which counts the lines piped to it by the `who` command. (Note that the option is "l" as in "line" on the `wc` command.)

UNDERSTANDING MYSQL

MySQL (My Structured Query Language) is a relational database management system that allows you to store data in database tables within database files. You can also query the data with MySQL statements. The term "relational" means there is a relationship between the fields stored in a table. You can incorporate MySQL code to access a database within a shell script. You use MySQL because it provides much greater control, efficiency, and management of data than processing data in a text file as you've done in Chapter 9. MySQL allows other programming languages such as C, C++, Java, and COBOL to interact with it. Like learning HTML, completely learning MySQL is beyond the scope of this book. However, you will learn the necessary MySQL code statements to perform basic tasks such as selecting, inserting, updating, and deleting data within a database. The main focus, however, will be on how you can integrate the technology of MySQL within shell scripts.

Red Hat Linux comes with database management software named MySQL. However, you may need to install it, and if you do, you must be logged in as the root user. If it is already installed and running, there is a `mysqld` daemon running in the process tree. You can use either the `ps —elf | grep mysqld` command to check to see if the daemon is running, or you can execute the `service mysqld status` command as the root user. If you don't have access to the root user account, ask your instructor for assistance.

First, you need to understand database terminology in order to be able to write MySQL code in a shell script. A **database management system (DBMS)** is software that allows you to manage and access data. MySQL is an example of a DBMS. When you reference a field within a database it is called a **column**, and a record is called a **row**. A **table** is a collection of related columns and rows. A **database file** consists of one or more tables that contain the data. You write data to the table that is contained within the database file. A **query** is the term used to describe a DBMS statement that retrieves or manipulates data within a table.

The basic tasks that you will integrate within shell scripts are listed in Table 12-3.

Table 12-3   A few MySQL statements

Action Statement	Description	Example
insert	Allows insertion of data into a database table	insert into paydb.paytable(name, rate, hours) values ('Jan Banel','43','38')
select	Allows selection of data from a database table	select name, rate, hours from paydb.paytable
delete	Allows deletion of data from a database table	delete from paydb.paytable where name='Mike Brownlee'
update	Allows update of data into a database table	update paydb.paytable set hours='40'

12

Selecting Data

One of the most useful MySQL statements is the `select` statement. You use this to view a portion or all of the data within a database table. It takes the following basic form:

```
select columns from database.table where column='data'
```

This is where *columns* is one or more columns separated by a comma. The term *database* is the name of the database and *table* is the table within the database file.

Farmers, Inc. is a company that sells farm equipment. They use MySQL on a Linux computer and have a database file named farms. The farms database only has one table in it right now. The table is named products. The products table contains these columns: ID, Name, Price, and Quantity. In this case, ID is the primary key. Recall the concept of a primary key is discussed in Chapter 1. Look at an example of how the `select` action statement might work.

To display the ID and Price columns within the products table of the farms database, you enter `select ID, Price from farms.products`. You can also use a `where` clause with MySQL statements as a decision statement. This is useful for selecting columns matching a specific condition. For example, to select the Name column and Price column of the product matching an ID of "101," you enter `select Name, Price from farms.products where ID = "101"`. You can select all the columns within the farms.products database by using the asterisk symbol, as in this example: `select * from farms.products`.

Inserting Data

You use `insert` for inserting or adding new data to a table. It takes the following basic form:

```
insert into database.table(columns) values('data')
```

This is where *columns* are equal to the values specified by *data*. If Farmers, Inc. wants to add a new product to the products table such as a new tractor, with an ID of 102 and a Price of $50,000, they enter:

```
insert into farms.products(ID, Name, Price)
    values ('102', 'Big Tractor 1000XL', '50000')
```

Data is assigned, by position, to the columns using the `values` reserved word. So, `... farms.products(ID, Name, Price) values ('102', 'Big Tractor 1000XL', '50000')`, is similar to saying `ID='102'`, `Name='Big Tractor 1000XL'`, and `Price='50000'` in the products table of the farms database.

Deleting Data

The `delete` statement is used for deleting data within a table. It takes the following basic form:

```
delete from database.table where column='data'
```

In this case, the row is deleted where the *column* is equal to the value specified by *data*. If Farmers, Inc. decides they no longer need the tractor with an ID of 100, they enter a statement such as: `delete from farms.products where ID= '100'`.

Updating Data

When you want to modify current data without having to completely delete the old row and insert a new one, you use the **update** statement. It takes the following basic form:

```
update database.table set column1='data1' where column2='data2'
```

In this case, you set *column1* to equal *data1* where *column2* matches *data2*. For example, the newest tractor for Farmers, Inc. has sold so well that the company has decided to raise the price. They want to increase the price by 500 dollars to $50,500. The **update** statement appears as follows:

```
update farms.products set Price='50500' where ID='102'
```

Setting Access to MySQL

Like most SQL-based products, MySQL allows you to control access to what a user can do within the database. Before a user can use the statements shown in Table 12-3 within MySQL or a shell script, the user must be authorized to do so. Failure to authorize a user to use the MySQL statement results in an error.

Before you get started with MySQL, you need to set the root user's password within MySQL. This root user is the Database Administrator (DBA). A DBA is a person responsible for managing a DBMS. This password is different from the Linux root user's password. However, you must be logged in as the Linux root user to set the MySQL user password. Here the statement only needs to be run once at the Linux command line as the Linux root user. If you don't have access to the Linux root user account, ask your instructor for assistance. The code to set the DBA (root) user's password to "cactus100" follows. Note the **-u** option, which stands for "user," precedes the DBA root username. The **-password** option precedes the actual password you want to assign.

```
mysqladmin —u root password cactus100
```

MySQL contains a default system database file called mysql, which contains several tables to store database system-related data. It stores data including the type of access a user has to a table and what host names the users can use. MySQL comes installed assuming only the DBA has unrestricted access to all database files from any computer. Thus, to manipulate these tables you must be acting as the DBA root user. The tables you need to use to allow users access to your database, are **db** and **users**. Note that this is not done strictly for allowing scripts to interact with your database; it is done to allow users access to your database regardless of the programming language used to access the DBMS. You need to insert data into these tables for the user to access the database file you create. Additionally, you need to set MySQL access for users from the localhost. The term **localhost** is a DNS name that denotes the computer to which a user is logged in.

To set a user's access to MySQL from the Linux computer he or she is logged in to, or the localhost, you need to insert a row within the mysql system database. The following MySQL statement shows you how to insert a user named "molly" to the `user` table for access to MySQL from the localhost.

```
mysql -uroot -pcactus100 —e "insert into user (host,
    user)values ('localhost', 'molly')" mysql
```

Note that there is no space between the **-p** option and the actual password of "cactus100." It is important to understand that you must set the privileges for each user so he or she can select, insert, update, and delete data from the database. Once the following statement is executed, Molly has the ability to select, insert, update, and delete data within the farms database from the localhost.

```
mysql -uroot -pcactus100 —e "insert into db (host, db,
    user, select_priv, insert_priv, update_priv, delete_priv)
    values('localhost', 'farms', 'molly', 'Y', 'Y', 'Y',
    'Y' )" mysql
```

The column **host** is set to localhost. The column **db** is set to farms and the column **user** is set to Molly. Note the last four columns are used to assign privilege to use one of the statements listed in Table 12-3. You can see that columns **select_priv**, **insert_priv**, **update_priv**, and **delete_priv** are set to "Y," giving the user the privilege to select, insert, update, and delete.

 When making changes to the mysql database you may need to reload the MySQL tables so the changes take place. To do this given the previous example, you enter `mysqladmin -uroot —pcactus100 reload`.

Some of the MySQL options that are used in previous statements are listed in Table 12-4. Become familiar with these statements because you will use them in shell scripts.

Table 12-4 A few MySQL options

Action Statement Option	Description	Example
-e	Allows you to give MySQL executable code to run	`mysql -e "insert into mytable(name, number) values('Vien', '111')" mydb`
-u	Allows you to log in to MySQL with a username	`mysql —u bob`
-p	Allows you to give a password to MySQL	`mysql —u bob —p bobspassword`

Creating MySQL Databases and Tables

Before you can manipulate data in MySQL, you must create the database and at least one table to store the data. This is a requirement of most database management software, including MySQL. The command to create a database is as follows:

```
create database database
```

This is where *database* is the name of the database you want to create. To create the farms database for Farmers, Inc. and log in to the MySQL software as the root user with a password of cactus100, you enter: `mysql —uroot —pcactus100 —e"create database farms"`.

Another requirement of most database management software is the need to create a table within the database file. The general format is as follows:

```
create table table(column column-definition…); database
```

This is where *table* is the name of the table to create within the *database*. Note that you are creating the column names and definitions too.

In the following code, the products table is created within the farms database. Note the variable ID is defined as an integer of two integer positions. Name is defined as 20 characters, and both Price and Quantity are defined as integers of two positions.

```
mysql -uroot -pcactus100 -e"create table products (
ID int(2),
Name char(20),
Price int(2),
Quantity int(2)
);" farms
```

12

 You must create the database file before you create any tables within it.

Next you will set the user's access to MySQL and create the MySQL database and tables. You will allow your Linux user name access to insert, delete, update, and select data for the farms database. You will also create the farms database and the products table within farms. The steps in this exercise need to be performed only once to set up access and must be done prior to the inserting, deleting, selecting, and updating of the data within the database table.

To set user access and to create a database and a table:

1. Log in to the Linux system as a user, and then open a Terminal emulation window.

2. To add your user account so you can access MySQL from your Linux computer, enter the following line of code. Be sure to use *your-username* for your Linux user account name.

```
mysql -uroot -pcactus100 —e "insert into user (host,
    user) values ('localhost', 'your-username')" mysql
```

3. To give your Linux user account the ability to select, insert, update, and delete data within the farms database, enter the following line of code. Again, replace *your-username* with your Linux user account name.

```
mysql -uroot -pcactus100 —e "insert into db (host, db,
    user, select_priv, insert_priv, update_priv,
    delete_priv) values('localhost', 'farms', 'your-
    username', 'Y', 'Y', 'Y', 'Y' )" mysql
```

4. To create the MySQL database named farms, enter the following line of code:

```
mysql -uroot -pcactus100 —e"create database farms"
```

5. To create the products table within the farms database enter the following lines of code:

```
mysql -uroot -pcactus100 -e"create table products (
ID int(2),
Name char(20),
Price int(2),
Quantity int(2)
);" farms
```

6. To reload MySQL, enter the following line of code:

```
mysqladmin -uroot -pcactus100 reload
```

7. Close your window, and then log out.

CREATING SCRIPTS THAT INTERFACE WITH MYSQL

Now that you've had the chance to learn about the basics of MySQL, you will learn how to create scripts that use MySQL code statements. In this section, you will create a shell script for each of the four MySQL statements that allows you to insert, select, delete, and update data within the farms database and products table.

Creating a Script to Insert Data

Next you will create a shell script to insert data into the products table within the farms database. You use the **read** command to accept the data from the keyboard. The data is then inserted into the table.

To create a script that allows you to insert a row in a database:

1. Log in to the Linux system as a user, and then open a Terminal emulation window.

2. Create a script named **sqlfarmsins** in your **$HOME/bin** directory.

3. Insert the following lines of code to accept data from the keyboard. Notice the number of variables matches the number of columns in the database file.

```
read -p "Enter ID: " ID
```

```
read -p "Enter name: " Name
read -p "Enter price: " Price
read -p "Enter quantity: " Quantity
```

4. Insert the following line of code to execute the MySQL `insert` statement. The columns in the farms.products database table are set with the `values` clause. The variables that were entered in the previous step are used because they will be read in when the script executes. Note a dollar sign precedes each variable name in order to refer to the contents of the variable.

```
mysql -e"insert into farms.products (ID, Name, Price,
    Quantity) values ('$ID', '$Name', '$Price',
    '$Quantity')"
```

5. Save the file, and then close the editor.

6. Make the script executable.

7. Run the script using the following data. For the ID, enter **1**. For the name, enter **Big Rig Tractor**. For the price, enter **12000**, and for the quantity, enter **4**. The fields are inserted in the database, and the prompt returns. See Figure 12-8.

8. Rerun the script with this data. For the ID, enter **2**. For the name, enter **Little Rig Trailer**. For the price, enter **7500**, and for the quantity, enter **8**. The fields are inserted in the database, and the prompt returns. See Figure 12-8.

9. Rerun the script with the following data. For the ID, enter **3**. For the name, enter **Big Top Silo**. For the price, enter **25000**, and for the quantity, enter **2**. The fields are inserted in the database, and the prompt returns. See Figure 12-8.

10. Close your window, and then log out.

12

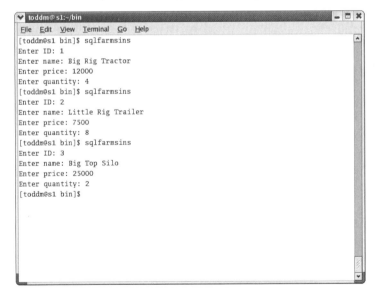

Figure 12-8   Various results of the sqlfarmsins

Creating a Script to Select Data

Next you will create a shell script to select data from the products table within the farms database. The script allows the user to enter an ID from the keyboard. Then, the MySQL `select` statement selects the rows in the database matching the ID that is entered. If there is a match, the row is displayed. You make the script flexible by allowing the user to simply press Enter to select all of the rows within the farms database. This is done with the shell's `if` statement.

To create a script that allows you to select a row in a database:

1. Log in to the Linux system as a user, and then open a Terminal emulation window.

2. Create a script named **sqlfarmssel** in your **$HOME/bin** directory.

3. Insert the following lines of code to accept the ID from the keyboard and create the decision statement that allows the user to enter either an ID or press Enter to select all rows in the database. Note that if the ID is empty, then all of the rows are displayed.

```
read -p "Enter ID to select: " ID
if [[ $ID = "" ]]
then
    mysql -e"select * from farms.products"
else
    mysql -e"select * from farms.products where ID = '$ID'"
fi
```

4. Save the file, and then close the editor.

5. Make the script executable.

6. Run the script, and then press **Enter** at the prompt. See Figure 12-9. All of the rows are displayed.

7. Run the script again, enter **2** for the ID, and then press **Enter**. See Figure 12-9. The data for Little Rig Trailer is displayed.

8. Run the script one last time, enter **3** for the ID, and then press **Enter**. See Figure 12-9. The data for Big Top Silo is displayed.

9. Close your window, and then log out.

Creating a Script to Delete Data

Next you will create a shell script to delete data from the products table within the farms database. The script allows the user to enter an ID from the keyboard.

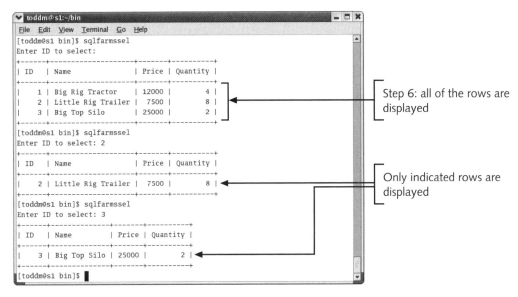

Figure 12-9   The output of multiple executions of the sqlfarmssel script

To create a script that allows you to delete columns in a database:

1. Log in to the Linux system as a user, and then open a Terminal emulation window.

2. Create a script named **sqlfarmsdel** in your **$HOME/bin** directory.

3. Insert the following lines of code to accept the ID from the keyboard and to create the statement to delete the row in the database matching the ID.

   ```
   read -p "Enter ID to delete: " ID
   mysql -e"delete from farms.products where ID='$ID'"
   ```

4. Save the file, and then close the editor.

5. Make the script executable.

6. Run the script, enter **2** for the ID, and then press **Enter**. The data for Little Rig Trailer is deleted.

7. Run the **sqlfarmssel** script to verify that the row with an ID of 2 has been deleted, and then press **Enter** to display all of the rows. See Figure 12-10. All rows except the one with an ID of 2 are displayed.

8. Close your window, and then log out.

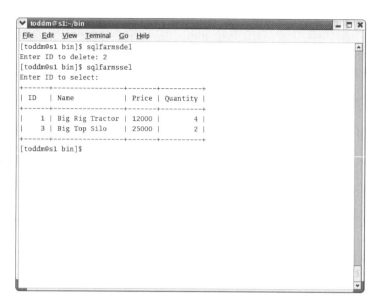

Figure 12-10 The output of the sqlfarmsdel script execution

Creating a Script to Update Columns in a Row

Next you will create a shell script to update a column in a row within the products table in the farms database. The script allows the user to enter an ID from the keyboard. If a matching ID is found in the database, then the price is updated.

To create a script that allows you to update a column in a database:

1. Log in to the Linux system as a user, and then open a Terminal emulation window.

2. Create a script named **sqlfarmsupdate** in your **$HOME/bin** directory.

3. Insert the following lines of code to accept the ID and price from the keyboard and create the statement to update the Price column in the database matching the ID.

```
read -p "Enter ID: " ID
read -p "Enter new price: " Price
mysql -e "update farms.products set Price='$Price' where
    ID='$ID'"
```

4. Save the file, and then close the editor.

5. Make the script executable.

6. Run the script, and then enter **1** for the ID and **13000** for price. The price is updated.

7. Run the **sqlfarmssel** script to verify the price update, and then press **Enter** to display all of the rows. See Figure 12-11. All the rows are displayed. The price is updated for the ID of 1.

8. Close your window, and then log out.

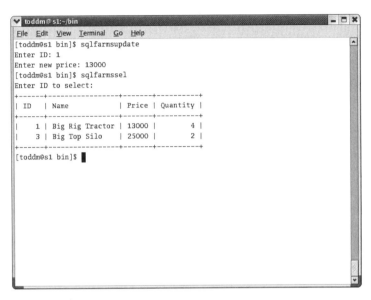

Figure 12-11   The result of the execution of the sqlfarmsupdate script

You can perform calculations on columns in a table. For example, if you wanted to calculate the price multiplied by the quantity in the farms database and create a new heading named Total to display the result, you enter the following: mysql -e "select ID, Name, Price, Quantity, Price*Quantity Total from farms.prod ucts where ID='$ID'".

ENHANCING MENU-BASED SCRIPTS

There are several commands that can be used to create a custom design for your menu-based scripts to make the script more user-friendly. Keep in mind that the term "user-friendly" is relative—what one user may like, another may dislike; so you should carefully moderate your customized changes.

Some of the types of custom changes you can make to enhance your scripts include customizing one of the shell's prompts in a script that displays menus to employ a user-friendly prompt for users indicating what they are supposed to enter; another example is bolding and underlining text or changing the color of the letters that appear on the screen and thus allowing a user to highlight important information on the screen. You can also cause a beep to sound in the event the user selects an invalid menu item. This alerts users that they've pressed an invalid key.

12

The two commands that assist in enhancing menu-based scripts are:

- The `select` command
- The `tput` command

Creating Menus with the `select` Command

The `select` command can be used to customize a menu. This command is similar to creating menus using the `case` statement with loops in a script. However the `select` command differs because the concept of looping is included within its structure. The `select` command was specifically developed to make it easier to code a menu in a script. It takes the following general form:

```
select name in word1 word2…
do
        list
done
```

The `select` command lists each **word** on the screen in a column format. A number, starting with one and corresponding to the word's position in the list, precedes each item; this is done automatically by the `select` command. The user can enter a number in the list. When the number is selected, then the value of *name* equals the word selected. This is like coding `case  name  in` when using the `case` command. Once the number is entered, the command for the number in *list* executes.

The Linux prompt, `PS3`, is used by the `select` command to set the text to prompt the user. If the user simply presses Enter at the prompt, then the list of words, along with the prompt, are displayed once more. The shell automatically places the line that is selected in the shell variable named `REPLY`.

Think of the `select` command as a combination of the `case` statement and a looping structure such as `while`.

Look at an example that uses the `select` command. A list of commands is displayed preceded by a number. The user presses the number, and the corresponding command executes. In the following code for a script named selA, the shell's `select` prompt, `PS3`, is set. The `select` command displays items for the user to select. If the user presses 1, then the variable named cmd contains the `who` command. Next, the `do $cmd done` statement causes the `who` command to execute. If the user presses 2, then the variable named cmd contains the `pwd` command, and the `pwd` command executes. Likewise, if the user presses 3, the `date` command executes.

```
PS3="Enter Command: "
select cmd in who pwd date
do
     $cmd
done
```

Figure 12-12 shows the contents of selA and the output of executing it four times. For the first three times selA is executed, the numbers 1, 2, and 3 are entered, and the associated command is executed. In the fourth and last execution of selA, the Enter key is pressed. Notice that the items are displayed again.

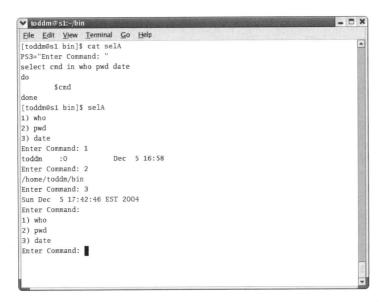

Figure 12-12   The contents of the selA script and the output of several executions

A shortcoming of the **select** command is that both the name in the word list and the command that is executed when its corresponding number is selected must be named the same. Based on the previous example, if you want to use the **select** command to insert a row in the MySQL farms database using the script sqlfarmsins, you would need to use "sqlfarmsins" for both the name in the word list and the name of the script that is executed if a user chooses to insert a row in the farms database. To some people this may not be very user-friendly. So, to create a user-friendly name in the word list that is different from the actual script being executed, you can use the **case** statement.

Next you will create a main menu using the MySQL farms script and database you created in the previous section and incorporate the **select** and **case** statements.

To create a script using the select and case statements:

1. Log in to the Linux system as a user, and then open a Terminal emulation window.

2. Create a script named **sqlfarmsmenu** in your **$HOME/bin** directory.

3. Insert the following line of code to set the prompt for the **select** statement:

   ```
   PS3="Enter choice: "
   ```

4. Insert the following lines of code to create the `select` word list:

```
select ans in Insert Delete Select Update Quit
do
```

5. Insert the following lines of code for the `case` statement. Notice the names in the word list are different than the actual script being executed. If you compare this to the script named selA, you can see the difference. The `select` statement displays "1) Insert" for the first menu item, "2) Delete" for the second menu item, and so on until it finally displays "5) Quit." When the user presses 1, the sqlfarmsins script executes. When the user presses 2, the sqlfarmsdel script executes. This same pattern occurs for the items 3 and 4 as well. If the user presses 5, then the code to break out of the `select` statement executes.

```
case $ans in
    Insert) sqlfarmsins ;;
    Delete) sqlfarmsdel ;;
    Select) sqlfarmssel ;;
    Update) sqlfarmsupdate ;;
    Quit) echo "Quitting"
     break ;;
    *) echo "Invalid Choice!" ;;
esac
```

6. Insert the following line of code to terminate the `select` statement:

```
done
```

7. Save the file, and then close the editor.

8. Make the script executable.

9. Run the script. See Figure 12-13. The menu is displayed showing the Enter choice prompt.

10. Enter **1** to insert a row in the farms database, and then press **Enter**. See Figure 12-13. The sqlfarmsins script executes prompting you to enter the ID, name, price, and quantity for a row.

11. Enter the following data: **4** for the ID, **Mobile Water System** for the name, **15000** for the price, and **3** for the quantity. See Figure 12-13. Once all the data is entered, the sqlfarmsmenu script displays the Enter choice prompt again.

12. At the menu prompt, enter a **3** to verify the data has been entered.

13. Now enter **4** to display the previously entered data. See Figure 12-13. The sqlfarmssel script executes and displays the data.

14. Press **5** to quit the sqlfarmsmenu script.

15. Close your window, and then log out.

 The `select` statement is a builtin shell command. To view additional information about it, refer to the man pages on `bash`.

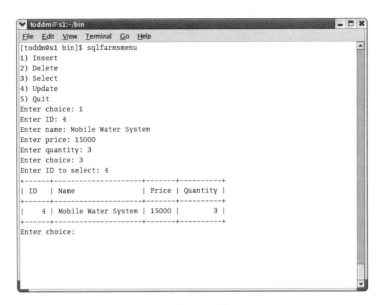

Figure 12-13   The output of the sqlfarmsmenu script

Customizing with the `tput` Command

You can use the **tput** command to customize the output of your terminal. Thus, you can customize your scripts and customize the output for your users. You use this command to initialize a terminal or query the information database about a terminal's capabilities. The **terminal capabilities information database** is a database that contains entries about a terminal and its characteristics. The database contains characteristics for each terminal that is used on the Linux operating system. The characteristics are defined in the database with various escape sequences specific to each terminal. They are called escape sequences because they begin with the Esc key. Among other characteristics, a terminal entry usually includes key sequences for bolding, underlining, carriage returns, ringing the keyboard bell, and the function keys. Generally, the format of an entry is as follows:

> *variable-name=escape-sequence*

Understanding the background behind the *variable-names* and *escape-sequences* gives you a better understanding of the **tput** command.

Take a look at an example. When you run the graphical portion of the Linux operating system, the system defaults to using the terminal type named xterm for an X Windows terminal. Depending on how you access the Linux computer system, your terminal type may be different. This value is stored in an environment variable named **TERM**. If you run **echo $TERM**, your terminal type is displayed. Figure 12-14 shows the information capabilities for the xterm terminal type.

Examine a few of the information capabilities in the figure. Notice the variable named clear on the screen. It has an escape sequence of \E[H\E[2J. Note that each \E represents the Esc key (or escape sequence) and is used to protect the escape sequence from being literally interpreted as [H[2J. When the terminal receives this escape sequence, the screen is cleared. Also, notice the escape sequence for ringing the keyboard bell is ^G for the variable named bel. The caret (^) indicates the Ctrl key. If you press Ctrl+G, then the keyboard bell rings. Finally notice that the carriage return variable named cr is equal to ^M. If you press Ctrl+M, it has the same effect as pressing Enter.

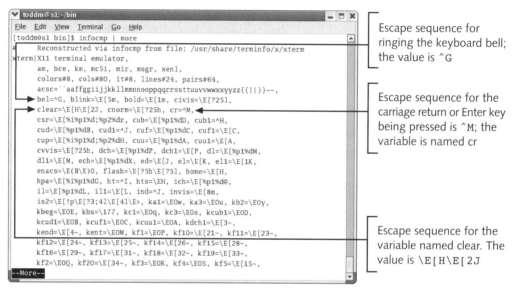

Figure 12-14   The information capabilities of the xterm terminal type

You can utilize these terminal attributes with the **tput** command to do things such as clear the screen, hide the cursor, place text in specific positions on the screen, and underline or bold text. There are several ways to run the **tput** command, but here is the form used in this text:

```
tput capname
```

This is where **capname** is a terminal capability attribute similar to the ones found in Table 12-5.

Table 12-5   Some common terminal attributes

Attribute	Description	Example
clear	Clears the screen	tput clear
bel	Rings the keyboard bell	tput bel
civis	Hides the cursor	tput civis

Table 12-5 Some common terminal attributes (continued)

Attribute	Description	Example
cnorm	Makes the cursor appear as normal	tput cnorm
cupxy	Places the cursor on the screen at a row specified by x-, and column specified by y- coordinates starting at the home position in the upper-left corner of the screen	tput cup 1 10
smso	Bolds text	tput smso
rmso	Turns off bolding of text	tput rmso
smul	Underlines text	tput smul
rmul	Turns off underlining of text	tput rmul
sgr0	Returns the screen to a normal screen (without bolding, underlining, etc.)	tput sgr0

Next you will create a script that contains a partial menu, but is not completely functional as a menu script. It is not completely functional because the script only focuses on how you can design a menu using the **tput** command. For example, when you press 1, there is no code for this menu selection. The coding is left for a later Hands-on Project.

To create a partial menu script that uses the tput command to set terminal attributes:

1. Log in to the Linux system as a user, and then open a Terminal emulation window.

2. Create a script named **tputA** in your **$HOME/bin** directory.

3. Insert the following lines of code to clear the screen and turn on bolding for text:

```
tput clear
tput smso
```

4. Insert the following line of code to place the output of the next statement at row 1 and column 0 on the screen. Note that row 0, column 0, is considered the upper-left corner of the screen, commonly called the home cursor position.

```
tput cup 1 0
```

5. Insert the following line of code to display a message on the screen at position row 1, column 0, on the screen:

```
echo "User $LOGNAME logged on `who | awk '{print $5}'`"
```

6. Insert the following lines of code to place the resulting output of the **date +%D** command at row 1, column 70:

```
tput cup 1 70
date +%D
```

7. Insert the following lines of code to turn off bolding and place the output of the next statement at row 4, column 23:

```
tput rmso
tput cup 4 23
```

8. Insert the following line of code to display the title of the menu at position row 4, column 23, on the screen:

```
echo "The Main Menu"
```

9. Insert the following lines of code to place the output of the next statement at row 7 and column 20 on the screen. This is the first menu item.

```
tput cup 7 20
echo "1.  Employee Information"
```

10. Insert the following lines of code to place the output of the next statement at row 8 and column 20 on the screen. This is the second menu item.

```
tput cup 8 20
echo "2.  System Functions"
```

11. Insert the following lines of code to place the output of the next statement at row 9 and column 20 on the screen. This is the last menu item.

```
tput cup 9 20
echo "9.  Exit"
```

12. Insert the following lines of code to place the output of the next statement at row 13 and column 20 on the screen and underline the text. This is the prompt.

```
tput cup 13 20
tput smul
read -p "Enter Selection: " ans
```

13. Insert the following lines of code to turn off underlining of text and reset the terminal to a normal screen upon exiting the script:

```
tput rmul
Ztput sgr0
```

14. Save the file, and then close the editor.

15. Make the script executable.

16. Run the script. See Figure 12-15.

17. Press **Enter** to reset the terminal and exit the script.

18. Close your window, and then log out.

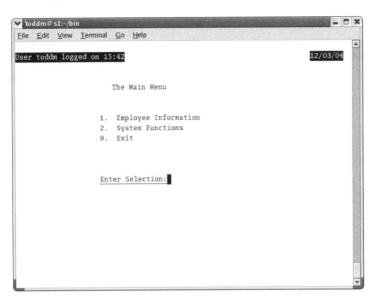

Figure 12-15   The output of the tputA script

UNDERSTANDING THE REVISION CONTROL SYSTEM

In a typical programming environment there may be a team of programmers working on the same project. The potential for problems to arise when changes are made by different programmers to the same scripts at the same time is a reality. For example, a programmer named Molly makes a change to a script named finance. At the same time, another programmer named Charmita also makes a change to the same script. Whose changes take effect? If they are using the **vi** editor, then the last programmer who saved the file and quits the editor has her changes written; any previous changes are overwritten. Note that this is not a **vi**-related problem. This could occur with any editor. So, if Molly and Charmita both work on the same script concurrently, and they both make changes, but Molly saves and exits after Charmita does, then Molly's changes overwrite Charmita's. All of Charmita's work is lost.

To handle this situation, the Linux operating system uses the Revision Control System. The **Revision Control System (RCS)** stores and retrieves multiple revisions of a script and resolves conflicts if multiple programmers access the same script concurrently. There are several commands that allow you to manage the changes that occur in a multiple-access environment such as Linux. They are listed in Table 12-6.

12

Table 12-6   A few of the RCS commands

Command	Description
rcs	Changes the RCS file attributes
ci	Checks in, or stores new revisions into RCS
co	Checks out, or retrieves a revision from RCS
rlog	Displays information about an RCS file
rcsdiff	Compares RCS revisions
rcsmerge	Merges RCS revisions

Look at an example using the `ci` and `co` commands from Table 12-6. The `ci` command allows you to check in a script and place it under the control of RCS. It takes this general form:

```
ci options filename
```

This is where *options* augment the command in some way, and *filename* is the name of the script you want to add to RCS. So, to check in the script named selA created earlier, you enter:

```
ci selA
```

Once you executed this command, `ci` generates a new file that includes the filename you checked in appended by the suffix ",v." When you run the `ci` command, the original file no longer exists. It is not deleted, but it is converted into the RCS version. Once a file has been checked in, it must be checked out before it can be used.

Figure 12-16 shows the `ci` command used to check in the selA script. In the figure, the `ls -l selA*` command is executed before and after the `ci` command to show you that the selA file existed previously and that selA,v exists after the `ci` command execution. Also, notice in the figure, an initial revision of 1.1. A revision number is similar to a version number for an operating system. There are two main parts to a revision in RCS. They are the release number and the version, in the format "r.v." So, revision 1.2 is the first release, second version. In general, revision 1.2 would have more changes than revision 1.1 or 1.0 of a script.

You can use the `-r` option, followed by the release number, to check in a specific revision number of your script. You can use the `-l` (as in lock) option to lock the script so other programmers cannot make changes to it. When locking an RCS file, RCS generates a copy of the script that can be edited. The `-u` option unlocks the script so other programmers can make changes to the script. The `co` command is used to check out an RCS file.

Next you will use the RCS commands to work with scripts you created earlier in this chapter.

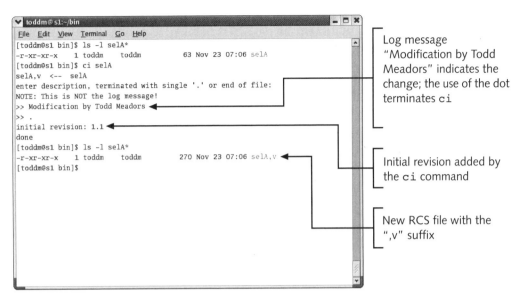

Figure 12-16   The ci command

To use RCS commands:

1. Log in to the Linux system as a user, and then open a Terminal emulation window.

2. Change to the **$HOME/bin** directory, and then copy **sqlfarmsmenu** to **selD** to use a new copy of the script.

3. To check in and lock the script named selD, type **ci -l selD**, and then press **Enter**. See Figure 12-17. Notice that three lines are displayed. The ">>" is the **ci** prompt.

4. To enter a description, type **Initial Check In by *Your Name***, and then press **Enter**. The **ci** prompt is displayed again.

5. Type **.** (the period symbol), and then press **Enter**. See Figure 12-17. The initial revision of 1.1 is displayed, then the text "done," indicating that the command completed, followed by the shell prompt.

6. To check the file out, and lock it for a revision change, type **co -l selD**, and then press **Enter**. See Figure 12-17. A message indicating the file is locked is displayed. Because the file has been checked out using the lock option, the selD file remains. A prompt also asks if you want to overwrite the file.

7. To make a change to the file and overwrite selD, type **y** and press **Enter**. Note that the text "done" appears, indicating that the command completed, followed by the prompt.

12

8. Open **selD** with **vi**, and then add these two comment lines as the first two lines. Be sure to substitute your name and today's date where indicated.

   ```
   # Author: Your Name
   # Date: today's date
   ```

9. Save the file, and then close the editor.

10. To check in the file, lock it, and set the release to 1.2, type **ci −r1.2 −l selD**, and then press **Enter**. See Figure 12-17. The **ci** prompt is displayed indicating a new version is being checked in.

11. At the **ci** prompt, type **Added Comments**, and then press **Enter**. See Figure 12-17. The **ci** prompt is displayed again.

12. Type **.** (the period symbol), and then press **Enter**. See Figure 12-17. The text "done" appears, indicating the command completed. Also, the shell prompt returns.

13. Close your window, and then log out.

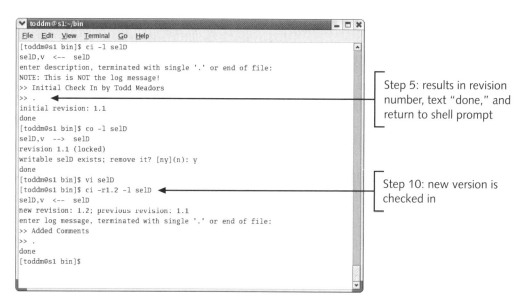

Figure 12-17   Checking in a file, checking out a file, modifying it, and checking it back into RCS

ADDING A SCRIPT AS A LAUNCHABLE APPLICATION FROM THE GUI DESKTOP

Linux allows you to run a script from the graphical user interface desktop. The benefit is that the users do not have to access the shell prompt. Instead, you create a script within the shell, and then configure the script to run when a user double-clicks an icon on the desktop. Next you will create a script that can be run from the GUI desktop simply by double-clicking an icon.

To create a script that can be executed from the GUI desktop:

1. Log in to the Linux system as a user, and then open a Terminal emulation window.

2. Right-click a blank area of your GUI desktop, and then point to **New Launcher**. See Figure 12-18.

Figure 12-18   Launching a new application

3. Click **New Launcher**. The Create Launcher dialog box is displayed as shown in Figure 12-19. Notice there are two tabs and several text fields where you can enter data.

4. Type **Farmers Menu** in the Name text field, and then press **Tab**.

5. Type **Farmers** in the Generic name text field, and then press **Tab**.

6. Type **The Farmers Main Menu** in the Comment text field, and then press **Tab**.

7. Type **bin/selD** in the Command text field, and then press **Tab** several times until Run in Terminal is highlighted. Note that you are using the selD script used earlier for the Farmers main menu script. For a launchable application, the command's path begins in your home directory, so you only need to type bin/selD.

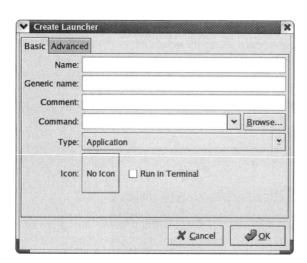

Figure 12-19 The Create Launcher dialog box

8. Click **Run in Terminal** to select it. Figure 12-20 shows the completed Create Launcher dialog box.

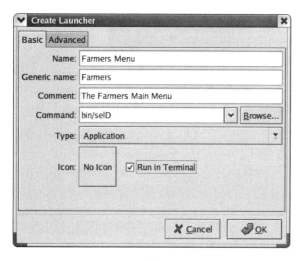

Figure 12-20 Completed Create Launcher dialog box

9. Click the **OK** button. An icon named Farmers Menu appears on your desktop.

10. Double-click the **Farmers Menu** icon. A terminal window opens with the script ready for execution.

11. To run the script, type **3**, and then press **Enter**. See Figure 12-21. A prompt appears indicating that you can enter an ID to select. This is the sqlfarmsupdate script executing. Remember, this script is coded so if you press Enter, then all of the records are displayed.

12. Press **Enter** to display all the records. See Figure 12-21. The records from the MySQL database are displayed.

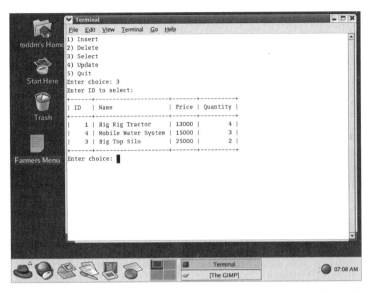

Figure 12-21   The Farmers Menu icon and the Terminal window

13. Close your window, and then log out.

UNDERSTANDING ADDITIONAL MANAGEMENT TECHNIQUES

In this section, you will learn additional techniques for script management. These include the following:

- Back up and restore
- Compression and uncompression

Back up and Restore

Because your scripts are stored in a directory on disk and disk failures do occur, you need to know how to back up and restore your scripts. **Backing up** is the process of copying your files to an alternate location. For example, if your files are stored in one directory on the hard disk drive, you should consider backing them up to another directory on another disk. **Restoring** is the process of bringing the files that have been backed up from their backed up location to their original location. Although there are several backup utilities available in the Linux operating system, here you learn about only one of them—the `tar` command. When you use a backup utility such as `tar`, the files cannot be utilized until they are restored. The `tar` command places them in a format that only it can interpret—not the shell.

The `tar` command comes from the term Tape Archive. It was originally intended to be used with sequential tape methods.

The `tar` command takes the following general form:

```
tar options filename1, filename2,…
```

Although the `tar` command has many options, only a few are discussed here. Table 12-7 shows a description of some of the options.

Table 12-7 A few `tar` command options

Option	Description
-c	Creates a `tar` archive file
-v	Displays more information as `tar` executes (the "v" stands for verbose)
-f filename	Specifies the `tar` backup file name
-t	Shows a table of contents for the files in the `tar` archive file
-r	Restores files within the `tar` archive file

Next you will use the `tar` command to back up the sqlfarmsdel, sqlfarmsins, sqlfarmssel, and sqlfarmsupdate scripts created for Farmers, Inc.

To run the `tar` command to backup, verify, and restore files:

1. Log in to the Linux system as a user, and then open a Terminal emulation window.

2. Change to the **bin** directory.

3. To back up the scripts using the `tar` command, type **tar -cvf farmbackup.tar sqlfarms***, and then press **Enter**. The command displays the files that are backed up. Note that the name "farmbackup.tar" is the name of the file containing the backed up script files. Although not required, the tar extension indicates the file is a tar backup. The use of the asterisk as a wildcard symbol in sqlfarms* causes all files beginning with sqlfarms to be backed up.

The tar backup file is sometimes called a tar archive or a "tarball" because all of the files are rolled up inside of one file.

4. To verify that the `tar` command worked correctly, type **tar -tvf farmbackup.tar**, and then press **Enter**. The files in the tar file are displayed. See Figure 12-22.

5. Remove the four script files.

6. To restore the four script files, type **tar —xvf farmbackup.tar**, and then press **Enter**.

7. List the files to prove they have been restored. See Figure 12-22.

8. Close your window, and then log out.

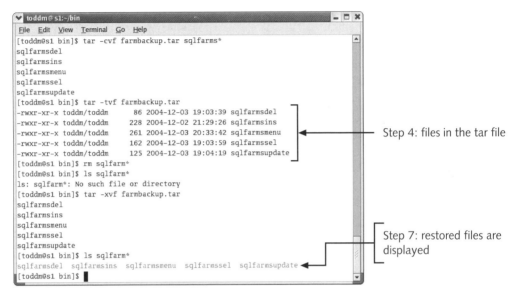

```
[toddm@s1 bin]$ tar -cvf farmbackup.tar sqlfarms*
sqlfarmsdel
sqlfarmsins
sqlfarmsmenu
sqlfarmssel
sqlfarmsupdate
[toddm@s1 bin]$ tar -tvf farmbackup.tar
-rwxr-xr-x toddm/toddm      86 2004-12-03 19:03:39 sqlfarmsdel
-rwxr-xr-x toddm/toddm     228 2004-12-02 21:29:26 sqlfarmsins
-rwxr-xr-x toddm/toddm     261 2004-12-03 20:33:42 sqlfarmsmenu
-rwxr-xr-x toddm/toddm     162 2004-12-03 19:03:59 sqlfarmssel
-rwxr-xr-x toddm/toddm     125 2004-12-03 19:04:19 sqlfarmsupdate
[toddm@s1 bin]$ rm sqlfarm*
[toddm@s1 bin]$ ls sqlfarm*
ls: sqlfarm*: No such file or directory
[toddm@s1 bin]$ tar -xvf farmbackup.tar
sqlfarmsdel
sqlfarmsins
sqlfarmsmenu
sqlfarmssel
sqlfarmsupdate
[toddm@s1 bin]$ ls sqlfarm*
sqlfarmsdel  sqlfarmsins  sqlfarmsmenu  sqlfarmssel  sqlfarmsupdate
[toddm@s1 bin]$
```

Step 4: files in the tar file

Step 7: restored files are displayed

Figure 12-22   Demonstrating the use of the `tar` command to back up, verify, and restore

Tip: Although in these exercises you are backing up to a file on disk, typically you back up and restore much larger amounts of data and use some type of removable media such as magnetic tape, external hard drives, or CD-ROMs.

Compression and Uncompression

Compression is the process of saving disk space by removing the repeating portions of a file in order to make it smaller. You cannot use a file when the file is compressed because a compressed file is in a special format. In order to work with a compressed file, the compressed file must be uncompressed. **Uncompression** is the process of returning a compressed file into its original state. Compression varies based on the amount of data that is duplicated and the compression algorithm used. At times, compression can yield between a 75% to 90% savings. You generally compress a file that is to be downloaded over the Internet. Because it is smaller, it takes less time to download a compressed file. However, in order to utilize the file, you must uncompress it. In Linux, you can use the `gzip` command to compress a file and the `gunzip` command to uncompress a file. Next you will explore how to compress and uncompress files using the sqlfarmsins file for Farmers, Inc.

12

To compress and uncompress a script:

1. Log in to the Linux system as a user, and then open a Terminal emulation window.

2. Change to the **bin** directory.

3. To list the sqlfarmsins file, type **ls −l sqlfarmsins**, and then press **Enter**. This step is done so you can compare the uncompressed and compressed forms of the file.

4. To compress the file named sqlfarmsins, type **gzip sqlfarmsins**, and then press **Enter**. See Figure 12-23.

5. To list all the files beginning with "sqlfarmsins," type **ls −l sqlfarmsins***, and then press **Enter**. The original file has been removed. In order to utilize the original file, the .gz file must be uncompressed.

6. To uncompress the file named **sqlfarmsins**, type **gunzip sqlfarmsins.gz**, and then press **Enter**. See Figure 12-23.

7. To list all the files beginning with "sqlfarmsins," type **ls −l sqlfarmsins***, and then press **Enter**. Notice the original filename appears.

8. Close your window, and then log out.

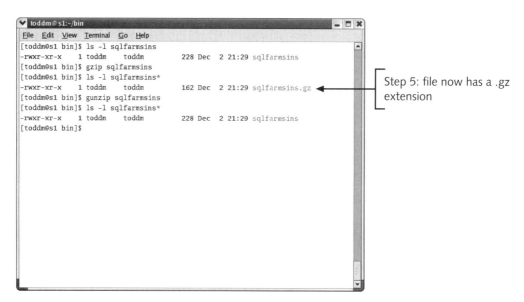

Figure 12-23 The use of compression and uncompression

You can use the -z option on the tar command to compress the tar backup file. For example, to compress and back up all of the sqlfarms scripts to a backup file named farmbackup.gz using tar, you use tar -czvf farmbackup.gz sqlfarm*. To verify the compressed tar file you use tar -tzvf farmbackup.gz. To restore the compressed tar file, you use tar -xzvf farmbackup.gz.

CREATING CUSTOM MANUAL PAGES

After you create your scripts, you should create manual pages for them. This way users can review the manual pages for your application just as they can review the manual pages for an operating system command. When you create manual pages, a decrease in support time by the computer staff most likely results, thereby allowing the staff time for other duties. The manual pages use a document-formatting command named groff.

When creating a manual page for your script, you can use an editor such as vi, but you must write the manual page using the groff language statements. A manual page is typically composed of a preamble followed by sections. A **preamble** is the first line of text prior to the sections; it is like a header line presenting general information about the manual page. The groff command used to identify the preamble is .TH. It takes the following general form:

    .TH *title section date source manual*

The *title* is the title of the manual page, the *section* is the category number of the manual page to which the command belongs, the *date* is the revision date, the *source* is from where the manual page originated, and the *manual* is the title of the manual page. Note that *section* here is a number that represents the type of manual. Most user commands are in section number 1.

A **section** of the manual page is a body of text identifying a specific area of the manual page such as the NAME, SYNOPSIS, DESCRIPTION, OPTIONS, FILES, SEE ALSO, DIAGNOSTICS, BUGS, and AUTHOR. This differs from *section* in the previous syntax, which is a category number. Note that the NAME section is required; you need to follow it with a one-line description. You have seen these sections when you have executed the man pages for an operating system command. The groff command to create a section in a manual page is .SH. It takes the following general form:

    .SH *name*

When creating a manual page for a script, you need to append ".1" to the end of the filename. For example, Menu.1 works; Menu doesn't.

Next you will create a manual page for the Farmers Main Menu that you created earlier in this chapter.

12

To create a manual page for the Farmers Main Menu:

1. Log in to the Linux system as a user, and then open a Terminal emulation window.

2. To create the manual pages, create a file named **Farmers.1**.

3. To create the preamble, insert the following line of code:

```
.TH Farmers "1" "November 2004" "Farmers 1.0"
```

4. To create the NAME section, insert the following lines of code:

```
.SH NAME
Farmers - The Farmers Main Menu
```

5. To create the SYNOPSIS section, insert the following lines of code. Note the `.B` command is used to bold the text following it. The synopsis is "sqlfarmsmenu"; this indicates how you run the command associated with this manual page. In this case, to run the command you simply enter `sqlfarmsmenu` at the shell prompt.

```
.SH SYNOPSIS
.B sqlfarmsmenu
```

6. To create the DESCRIPTION section, insert the following lines of code. Note the `.PP` command is used to begin a new paragraph.

```
.SH DESCRIPTION
The Farmers main menu consists of the following menus
.PP
1) Insert a record in the database
.PP
2) Delete a record from the database
.PP
3) Select records from the database
.PP
4) Update a record from the database
.PP
5) Quit the Farmers Main Menu
```

7. To create the AUTHOR section, insert the following lines of code. Make sure you substitute your own name.

```
.SH AUTHOR
Written by Your Name.
```

8. Save the file, and then quit the editor.

9. To view your manual page for Farmers, Inc., type **groff —Tascii —man Farmers.1 | more**, and then press **Enter**. Note the **—Tascii** option means to display the text in ASCII. The **—man** option means to display the page named Farmers.1. Figure 12-24 shows this command executing.

10. Close your window, and then log out.

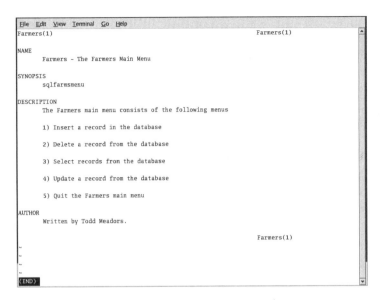

Figure 12-24   Manual pages you just created

 In order to view your manual pages using the `man` command, you should copy your manual page in compressed format to the /usr/share/man/man1 directory. You must have root access to place your manual pages in this directory. If you do, compress Farmers.1, and then copy Farmers.1.gz to /usr/share/man/man1. To view your manual pages as part of the `man` command, you type man `Farmers`.

CHAPTER SUMMARY

❑ You can use a Web browser to access Web page scripts over an intranet or the Internet. A Web client requests Web pages from a Web server. The Web client and Web server transfer Web pages using the HTTP protocol. A Web server is a computer system running Web hosting software such as Apache. Web page scripts are stored and executed in the /var/www/cgi-bin directory.

❑ The Linux operating system uses the MySQL software to manage databases. A database consists of one or more tables for storing data. A table consists of data stored in rows and columns. A row is similar to a record and a column is similar to a field. Database management software provides greater control of the data than simply accessing the data within a text file.

❑ You can create scripts that interface with MySQL. The basic MySQL statements are insert, delete, select, and update. Insert allows you to add data into a row. Delete allows you to remove data from a row. Select allows you to list data in a row. Update allows you to modify data within a row.

❏ You can enhance your menu-based scripts by using the `tput` and `select` commands. The `tput` command allows you to configure the characteristics of the display terminal. For example, you can bold or underline text in a script using this command. The `select` command is explicitly written to create menus. It is similar to a `case` statement with a looping mechanism.

❏ Because Linux is a multiuser operating system, multiple programmers can modify the same script at the same time. Any changes made by the programmer who saves the script first can be lost by the programmer who saves the script last. To rectify this problem, Linux uses the Revision Control System (RCS) to keep track of changes made by programmers. RCS uses the `ci` command to check in a script revision and the `co` command to check out a script revision.

❏ You can create a script that can be launched from the desktop allowing users to avoid going to the shell prompt to run a command. Users can simply double-click an icon on their desktops. Once clicked, the script associated with the icon executes in a separate terminal window.

❏ Your scripts are stored in a directory on a hard disk drive. Because hard disk drives occasionally malfunction, you should consider backing up your script to another device such as a floppy or tape. Restoring is the counterpart of backing up. You restore your scripts to their original locations if the hard drive does indeed malfunction. The `tar` command can be used to back up and restore scripts or other files. Additionally, you can compress your scripts in order to save disk space. A script, or other file, that is compressed cannot be used unless it is uncompressed. The `gzip` command is used to compress and the `gunzip` command is used to uncompress.

❏ Once your scripts have been created, you should create manual pages for them. This provides the user with the ability to review the documentation at any time resulting in a decrease in the need for technical support. The `groff` command is used to format and process the manual pages. A manual page consists of the preamble and sections. The preamble is the first line before any section. The preamble presents general information about the manual page. Sections identify specific parts of the manual page. The required section is NAME.

Review Questions

1. Which of the following does a Web server use to forward Web pages to a Web client?

   a. IP

   b. DNS

   c. HTTP

   d. CGI

2. A(n) _____ is a code statement used in a Web page.

    a. Web server

    b. HTML tag

    c. IP address

    d. MySQL database

3. A database _____ is like a record in a text file.

    a. row

    b. column

    c. table

    d. tag

4. The following HTML code statement is used to terminate the horizontal line statement in an HTML document.

    a. `</HR>`

    b. `<HR>`

    c. `<\HR>`

    d. `</HR/>`

5. A database _____ is like a field in a text file.

    a. row

    b. column

    c. table

    d. tag

6. The following HTML code statements that are used to identify the beginning and ending of the HTML code within a document are _____.

    a. `<CENTER>` and `</CENTER>`

    b. `<HEAD>` and `</HEAD>`

    c. `<HTML>` and `</HTML>`

    d. `<BEGIN>` and `</END>`

7. The directory location on the Web server where you should place your Web page scripts for execution over a network is _____.

    a. `/www/var/cgi-bin`

    b. `/usr/local/bin`

    c. `$HOME/var/www/cgi-bin`

    d. `/var/www/cgi-bin`

12

522   Chapter 12   Script Design and Management Issues

8. The _____ option is used to create a `tar` archive file.

   a. `-c`

   b. `-x`

   c. `-f`

   d. `-t`

9. The _____ command is used to create the preamble in a manual page.

   a. `.B`

   b. `.SH`

   c. `<PRE>`

   d. `.TH`

10. The _____ command is used to create a section in a manual page.

    a. `.PP`

    b. `.SH`

    c. `<SECTION>`

    d. `.TH`

11. The HTML code to preserve the preformatted output of a command is _____.

    a. `<OUTPUT>`

    b. `<PRE>`

    c. `<POST>`

    d. `.TH`

12. The MySQL statement to add data to a table is _____.

    a. `select`

    b. `put`

    c. `add`

    d. `insert`

13. The command to compress a file is _____.

    a. `gunzip`

    b. `tar -t`

    c. `ci`

    d. `gzip`

14. The command to check a file into RCS is _____.

    a. `tar`

    b. `rlog`

    c. `co`

    d. `ci`

15. The MySQL statement to view data in a table is _____.

    a. `select`

    b. `update`

    c. `show`

    d. `echo`

16. The command to check a file out of RCS is _____.

    a. `tar`

    b. `rlog`

    c. `co`

    d. `ci`

17. The manual page section that is required is _____.

    a. SYNOPSIS

    b. PREAMBLE

    c. SEE ALSO

    d. NAME

18. The command to initialize terminal characteristics is _____.

    a. `select`

    b. `tput`

    c. `ci`

    d. `print`

19. The command to create a menu in the shell is _____.

    a. `select`

    b. `tput`

    c. `for`

    d. `case`

20. The command to modify a column within a database is _____.

    a. `place`

    b. `update`

    c. `modify`

    d. `insert`

12

HANDS-ON PROJECTS

Project 12-1

In this project, you will create a Web page script that displays a list of processes and the date.

1. Log in to the Linux system as a user, and then open a Terminal emulation window.
2. Create a shell script named **Project12-1** in the **HOME/bin** directory.
3. Include the necessary code to create a Web page script that displays a list of processes and the current date. Be sure to include a heading line indicating that the Web page is displaying a list of processes. You also need to bold and center this line as well as use a heading level 1 for it. Use a heading level 2 for the output of the process listing and date. Preserve the preformatted output of the commands.
4. Save the file, and then close the editor.
5. Copy this Web page script or have it copied to the correct directory for viewing in a Web browser.
6. View and print this Web page script in a Web browser.
7. Close your window, and then log out.

Project 12-2

In this project, you will create a Web page script that runs a second script. The second script is used to display the contents of a file. When you access the Web page script, it runs the second script, and the output of the second script appears in the Web browser display area. You need to use the payroll file shown in Table 10-8 from Project 10-8 to complete this project.

1. Log in to the Linux system as a user, and then open a Terminal emulation window.
2. If you have not created the payroll file used in Table 10-8, do so now.
3. Create the shell script that displays the records first. Name this script **Project12-2A**, and place it in the **HOME/bin** directory.
4. Write the necessary code statements to read the contents of the payroll file and display the records on the screen.
5. Save the file, close the editor, make the script executable, and test the script. Be sure the records are displayed before proceeding to the next step.
6. Copy **Project 12-2A** to the **/var/www/cgi-bin** directory.
7. Create the Web page script that executes the script named Project12-2A. Name this script **Project12-2**, and place it in the **HOME/bin** directory.
8. Be sure the Web page script displays the server address and script name within the Web page. For the title of the Web page, use "Employee Report." For the heading, use "Payroll Report." Make sure the heading is centered, and has a heading level of 2. Preserve the preformatted output of the commands. Insert the proper code to execute Project 12-2A. (*Hint:* You may need to give the full path.)

9. Copy **Project 12-2** to the **/var/www/cgi-bin** directory.

10. Copy the **payroll** file to the **/var/www/cgi-bin** directory.

11. View and print this Web page script in a Web browser.

12. Close your window, and then log out.

Project 12-3

In this project, you will work with a partner to practice using the RCS commands. The goal is to help you understand how RCS works.

1. Log in to the Linux system as a user, and then open a Terminal emulation window.

2. Create a directory in root named **RCS**, and assign permissions of read, write, and execute for all users. You may need to have your instructor perform this step.

3. Copy the **sqlfarmsmenu** file to this directory as **sqlfarmsmenu***xxx*. Note *xxx* are your initials for this and subsequent steps. You may need to have your instructor perform this step.

4. Change directory locations to the /RCS directory.

5. To check in the sqlfarmsmenu*xxx* file and lock it, type **ci —l sqlfarmsmenuxxx**, and then press **Enter**.

6. Type **Initial check in by xxx**, and then press **Enter**.

7. To terminate the **ci** command, type **.** (a period), and then press **Enter**.

8. Ask your partner to log in and change to the /RCS directory.

9. To attempt a check out on the locked file, your partner should type this command: **co —l sqlfarmsmenuxxx**. Be sure your partner uses your initials.

10. Record your results.

11. Close your window, and then log out.

Project 12-4

In this project, you will create scripts that access rows in a database.

1. Log in to the Linux system as a user, and then open a Terminal emulation window.

2. Have someone log in as the root user, and then create a database named paydb. Also, have someone create a table named paytable within paydb with the following fields: ID as an integer of two positions, Name with 25 characters, Rate as an integer of two positions, and Hours as an integer of two positions.

3. Have someone log in as the root user to create, and then assign the appropriate MySQL permissions to insert, delete, update, and select data.

4. Have someone log in as the root user to reload MySQL.

5. Create a shell script named **sqlpayins** in the **HOME/bin** directory that allows the user to insert data into the paytable. The user inserts data based upon the ID.

6. Save the file, close the editor, and then make the script executable.

7. Run the script, and then insert the data shown in Table 12-8.

Table 12-8   Employee records

Employee ID	Name	Rate	Hours
1	Liam Montag	30	39
2	Susan Gonzalez	40	40
3	Dave Duststanz	38	33
4	Lou Ellenstein	44	43

8. Create a shell script named **sqlpaydel** in the **HOME/bin** directory that allows the user to delete data in the paytable. The user deletes data based upon the ID.

9. Save the file, close the editor, and then make the script executable.

10. Run the script, and then delete record **4**.

11. Create a shell script named **sqlpaysel** in the **HOME/bin** directory that allows the user to select data in the paytable. The user selects data based upon the ID. Allow the user to press Enter to select all rows.

12. Save the file, close the editor, and then make the script executable.

13. Run the script, and then list all the rows.

14. Create a shell script named **sqlpayupdate** in the **HOME/bin** directory that allows the user to update data into the paytable. The user updates data based upon the ID. Allow the user the ability to update hours only.

15. Save the file, close the editor, and then make the script executable.

16. Run the script for ID **2**, and update the hours to **37**.

17. Verify your findings by running the **sqlpaysel** script.

18. Close your windows, and then log out.

Project 12-5

In this project, you will create a menu for Project 12-4.

1. Log in to the Linux system as a user, and then open a Terminal emulation window.

2. Create a shell script named **sqlpaymenu** in the **HOME/bin** directory.

3. Save the file, close the editor, and then make the script executable.

4. Use the **select** statement to allow the user to press 1 to insert, 2 to delete, 3 to select, and 4 to update rows in the database. If the user presses 5, exit the script.

5. Run the script.

6. Close the window, and then log out.

Project 12-6

In this project, you will create a launchable application for Project 12-5.

1. Log in to the Linux system as a user, and then open a Terminal emulation window.
2. Create a launchable application that can be accessed by double-clicking an icon on the desktop.
3. Complete fields such as Name, Generic Name, Comment, and Command. Also make sure you check the Run in Terminal option. For Name, enter **Payroll**. For Command, enter **bin/Project12-6**.
4. Run the launchable application by double-clicking the icon associated with it.
5. Close the window, and then log out.

Project 12-7

In this project, you will create scripts to back up, restore, and verify the script files you created in Project 12-4 and the menu script you create in Project 12-5.

1. Log in to the Linux system as a user, and then open a Terminal emulation window.
2. Create a shell script named **Project12-7** in the **HOME/bin** directory.
3. Use a `select` statement to allow the user to press 1 to back up the sqlpay* files, 2 to verify the files have been backed up, and 3 to restore the sqlpay* files. If the user presses 4, exit the script.
4. Save the file, close the editor, and then make the script executable.
5. Run the script, and enter **1**, and then press **Enter** to back up the files and record the output.
6. Run the script, enter **2**, and then press **Enter** to verify the files and record the output.
7. Exit the script, and then remove the **sqlpay*** files.
8. Rerun the script, enter **3**, and then press **Enter** to restore the files and record the output.
9. Quit the script, close your window, and then log out.

Project 12-8

In this project, you will create a manual page for the sqlpaymenu script you created in Project 12-5.

1. Log in to the Linux system as a user, and then open a Terminal emulation window.
2. Create a file that contains manual page code named **Project12-8** in the **HOME/bin** directory.
3. Using the Farmers.1 manual page as a guide, create a manual page for the sqlpaymenu script.
4. Save the file, and then close the editor.

5. Display the script using the `groff` command.

6. Compress the script.

7. Copy the file or have someone with root access copy the compressed file (with the .gz extension) to the **/usr/share/man/man1** directory.

8. To run the `man` page command for your script, type **man Project12-8**.

9. Close your window, and then log out.

CASE PROJECTS

Case 12-1

TMI needs help writing an application comprising several scripts. Here are the requirements. You need to complete all the projects in this chapter first.

1. First, a main script is needed that can run the other scripts. On this main menu script, the user needs to be able to enter 1 for accessing Employee Information, 2 for accessing System Functions, and 9 to Exit. Use appropriate heading levels and code at least two terminal characteristic statements. Use the trap command to display a message when the user presses Ctrl+C.

2. For the Employee Information script, run the sqlpaymenu from Project 12-5. Because this is a complete module, it runs as it did in Project 12-5.

3. For the System Functions script, require the user to enter a password. Test for the password of "zorro13." Suppress password entry. If a user enters the correct password, run the script paybackupmenu from Project 12-7. Because this is a complete module, it runs as it did in Project 12-7.

4. Create the script as a launchable application.

Case 12-2

McDoogland's Candy Store needs a menu script that allows the user to:

1. Press 1 and enter a filename to back up.

2. Press 2 to verify the backup.

3. Press 3 to restore the backed up file.

4. Press 4 to enter a filename to compress.

5. Press 5 to enter a filename to uncompress.

6. Press 6 to enter a filename to check in to RCS as locked.

7. Press 7 to enter a filename to check out of RCS as locked.

8. Press 8 to quit.

Also, McDoogland's requires that the script can be accessed by double-clicking an icon on the desktop.

APPENDIX

A

GUIDE TO LINUX COMMANDS

This appendix is a quick reference for essential Linux utilities available on most systems. Table A-1 lists the commands alphabetically, including the command name, its purpose, and any useful options. Table A-2 summarizes the vi editor commands. Table A-3 lists the shell script programming-related commands. Table A-4 lists the special characters used by the shell.

Table A-1 Common Linux commands

Command	Purpose	Useful Options and Examples
alias	Creates an alias for a command; created by editing the .bashrc file	`alias dir='ls -l'`
awk	Invokes a pattern-scanning and processing language operation	-f indicates code is coming from a disk file, not the keyboard; -F specifies the field separator
bc	Runs the arbitrary precision calculator	-l uses the math library; -q executes in quiet mode
cal	Shows the system calendar for a specified year or month	-1 shows a single month; -3 shows three months beginning with the previous month; -j displays the calendar in Julian date format
cat	Concatenates or displays files	-n displays line numbers
cd	Changes directories	cd changes your position within the tree to a specified one. For example, the command cd dirA, changes your position to a directory named dirA. When used by itself, cd changes your position to your home directory.
chmod	Changes security mode of a file or directory (r: read, w: write, x: executable); sets file permissions for specified users (u: user, g: group, o: others, a: all)	chmod a+x sets the execute bit for owner, group, and other
ci	Checks a file into RCS	
clear	Clears the screen	Commonly aliased to cls (see the alias command)
co	Checks a file out of RCS	
cp	Copies files from one directory to another	-i requests confirmation if the target file already exists; -r copies directories to a new directory

Table A-1   Common Linux commands (continued)

Command	Purpose	Useful Options and Examples
`cut`	Selects and extracts columns or fields from a file	`-c` specifies the character position; `-d` specifies the field separator; `-f` specifies the field position
`date`	Displays the system date	`-u` displays Greenwich Mean Time
`dialog`	Creates menu-based scripts	
`diff`	Compares and selects differences in two files or directories	`diff /dir1 /dir2` compares the file entries in both directories and shows only the missing files for each directory
`df`	Displays the amount of free space on file systems	
`. (dot)`	Represents the current directory	Used mostly to specify that something happen in the current directory; for example, `cp /dir/file .` copies the file to the current directory
`.. (dot dot)`	Represents the parent directory	Used for referencing the parent directory of the current directory; for example, `cd ..` changes directory locations up one directory level while `cp file2.txt ..` copies a file named file2.txt to the parent directory of your current directory
`echo`	Displays the specified arguments on the output device	`echo $VAR`, where `VAR` is the variable name; echoes the data from an environmental variable to standard output
`emacs`	Starts the emacs editor	
`exit` or `logout`	Logs out of your current session	Ctrl+D also logs the user out of a session or a subshell and places the user back in the parent shell
`export`	Exports a specified list of variables to other shells; makes a variable an environmental variable	`-f` exports a function
`find`	Locates files that match a given value	`-amin n` finds files accessed more recently than *n* minutes ago; `-atime n` finds files last accessed *n*`*24` hours ago; `-user uname` finds files owned by user matching `uname`
`grep`	Selects lines or rows that match a specified pattern	`-c` displays the count of matching lines; `-i` ignores case; `-l` lists only filenames that contain the pattern; `-L` lists only filenames that do not contain the pattern; `-n` displays line numbers; `-v` displays line numbers of lines in a file that do not match the specified pattern

Table A-1   Common Linux commands (continued)

Command	Purpose	Useful Options and Examples
groff	Processes embedded text-formatting codes	
gunzip	Uncompresses a file	
gzip	Compresses files	
head	Displays the first few lines of a file	Shows the first 10 lines by default; -n *n* displays the first *n* lines of the specified file
history	Lists all the commands contained in the bash history file	Bash history file is .bash_history by default and resides in the user's home directory; default number of last commands kept in the history file is 500
kill	Ends a process	-9 destructively ends a process; -HUP causes the service or daemon to stop (hangup) and restart, which causes the rereading of its configuration files; this option is often used to make changes to a running service
last	Shows the login history of all users on the system	-a displays the host name from which the user connected; -d shows the corresponding IP address for a remote connection
less	Allows you to scroll long files on the screen where the more command only allows advancing down a file	
let	Stores the results of arithmetic operations in a variable	
ln	Creates symbolic or hard links to files	By default, creates a hard link, which is another name for a particular inode; -s creates a symlink to a file, like a shortcut
lpr	Prints a file	-d prints on a specified printer; -n prints a specified number of copies of the file
ls	Lists a directory's contents, including its files and subdirectories	-a lists hidden files; -l lists files in long format, showing detailed information; -r lists files in reverse alphabetic order; -s shows the size of each file
man	Displays the online manual for the specified command	-k searches for a specified pattern in the man pages; -t formats the output for printing using ghostscript
mkdir	Makes a new directory	

Table A-1   Common Linux commands (continued)

Command	Purpose	Useful Options and Examples
more	Displays a long file one screen at a time	Pressing the spacebar advances a screen at a time; pressing Enter advances one line at a time
mv	Moves or renames files	−f never prompts before overwrite of existing files and directories; −I prompts before overwriting files and directories; −u moves only when the source file is newer than the destination file or when the destination file is missing
passwd	Changes your Linux password	User can only change own password; root user can change other's passwords
paste	Pastes multiple files, column by column	
ping	Tests the status of another TCP/IP host	
pr	Formats a specified file before printing or viewing	−a displays output in columns across the page, one line per column; −d double-spaces the output; −h customizes the header line; −l*n* sets the number of lines per page
printenv	Prints a list of environmental variables	
printf	Tells the awk program what action to take	
ps	Shows processes on a system	−a shows all running processes; −u shows associated user for process; −x shows background system processes
pwd	Displays your current path	
read	Reads input from the keyboard	−s suppresses text; −p displays text as a prompt
readonly	Reads input that cannot be changed from the keyboard	
rcs	Manages RCS	
rlog	Displays information about an RCS file	
rm	Removes a file	−I requests confirmation before deleting a file; −r deletes a specified directory and its contents
rmdir	Removes a directory	−i requests confirmation before deleting a file; −r deletes a specified directory and its contents

Table A-1   Common Linux commands (continued)

Command	Purpose	Useful Options and Examples
sed	Specifies a stream editor command	-a \ appends text after a line or a script file containing sed commands; -d deletes specified text; -e specifies multiple commands on one line; -n indicates line numbers; -p displays lines; -s substitutes specified text
sort	Sorts and merges multiple files	.+ designates the position that follows an offset (+) as a character position, not a field position; +n sorts the field specified by n; -b ignores leading blank characters; -d sorts in dictionary order; -f indicates that a specified character separates the fields; -m merges files before sorting; -n sorts numbers arithmetically; -o directs the sorted output to a specified file
tail	Displays the last 10 lines of a file by default	-n n displays the last n lines of the specified file
tar	Backs up and restores files to a tar archive	-v indicates the verbose setting which gives additional information; -t takes a table of contents listing; -f *filename* backs up files to *filename*; -c indicates to create a tar archive; -x indicates to extract files from a tar archive
tee	Clones output stream to one or more files	
telnet	Opens a TCP/IP connection to a host	
test	Compares values and validates	! logical negation; -a logical AND; -b file existence tests if a file exists and is a block special file (which is a block-oriented device, such as a disk or tape drive); -c tests if a file exists and is a character special file (that is, a character-oriented device, such as a terminal or printer); -d tests if a file exists and is a directory; -e tests if a file exists; -eq equal to; -f tests if a file exists and is a regular file; *value1* -ge *value2* tests whether *value1* is greater than or equal to *value2*;

Table A-1 Common Linux commands (continued)

Command	Purpose	Useful Options and Examples
		value1 −gt *value2* tests whether *value1* is greater than *value2*; *value1* −le *value2* tests whether *value1* is less than or equal to *value2*; *value1* −lt *value2* tests whether *value1* is less than *value2*; −n tests for a nonzero string length;
		−ne not equal to; −o logical OR; −r true if a file exists and is readable; −s true if a file exists and its size is greater than zero; *string* tests for a nonzero string length; *string1* = *string2* tests two strings for equality; *string1* != *string2* tests two strings for inequality; −w true if a file exists and is writeable; −x true if a file exists and is executable; −z tests for a zero-length string
top	Displays a list of the most CPU-intensive tasks	−c displays the command that initiated each process; −I ignores any idle processes; −q displays output continually, with no delay between outputs (Use with caution! Try the spacebar for periodic updates); −s causes the top command to run in secure mode, disabling its interactive commands; −S runs top in cumulative mode, which displays the cumulative CPU time used by a process
touch	Changes a file's time and date stamp	−a updates access time only; −c prevents touch from creating a file that does not exist; −m updates the modification time only
tput	Formats screen text	clear clears the screen; cols prints the number of columns on the current terminal; cup moves the screen cursor to a specified row and column; rmso disables boldface output; smso enables boldface output

Table A-1 Common Linux commands (continued)

Command	Purpose	Useful Options and Examples
tr	Translates characters	−d deletes input characters found in *string1* from the output; −s checks for sequences of *string1* repeated consecutive times
trap	Executes a command when a specified signal is received from the operating system	
tty	Displays a terminal pathname	
uniq	Selects unique lines or rows	−d outputs one copy of each line that has a duplicate; −u outputs only the lines of the source file that are not duplicated
yes	Displays a string repeatedly until terminated	
w	Displays users currently on the system	Shows user's originating host, idle time, his or her current command, CPU utilization, and login time
wc	Counts the number of lines, bytes, or words in a file	−c counts the number of bytes or characters; −l counts the number of lines; −w counts the number of words
whatis	Displays a brief description of a command	
whereis	Locates source, binary, and manual	−b only searches for binaries; −m only entries for a specified string or searches for manual entries; −s only searches command for source entries
who	Shows who is currently logged onto a system	−H displays column headings; −i displays session idle times; −q displays a quick list of users

Table A-2 vi editor commands

Command	Purpose
!	Leaves vi temporarily
.	Repeats your most recent change
/	Searches forward for a pattern of characters
D$ or D	Deletes from the cursor to the end of the line
D0	Deletes from the cursor to the start of the line
Dd	Deletes the current line
Dw	Deletes the word above the cursor; if the cursor is in the middle of the word, deletes from the cursor to the end of the line
I	Switches to insert mode
P	Pastes text from the clipboard

Table A-2 `vi` editor commands (continued)

Command	Purpose
Q	Cancels an editing session
R	Reads text from one file and adds it to another
Set	Turns on line numbering
U	Undoes your most recent change
:w	Saves a file and continues working
:wq	Writes changes to disk and exits `vi`
:x	Saves changes and exits `vi`
X	Deletes the character at the cursor location
Yy	Copies (yanks) text to the clipboard
ZZ	Saves changes in command mode and exits `vi`

Table A-3 Shell script programming-related commands

Commands	Purpose
#	Establishes as a comment
`ArrayName[subscript]=value`	Sets a value to an array at a specific subscript location; for example, `GroceryList[10]=strawberry`
`ArrayName=(valuea valueb valuec...valueN)`	Populates an array with values beginning with subscript 0; for example, `GroceryList=(apple pear peach)`
`${array-name[subscript]}`	References an array value when performing an operation on the value; for example, `echo ${GroceryList[i]}`
`${ArrayName[*]}`	References all elements within an array; for example, `echo ${GroceryList[*]}`
`${#ArrayName[*]}`	Determines the number of elements within an array; for example, `echo ${#GroceryList[*]}`

`case word in`
    `Pattern1) statements`
        `;;`
    `Pattern2) statements`
        `;;`
    `PatternN) statements`
        `;;`
`esac`
	Makes a decision when multiple inputs exist for a variable; for example, `case $response in`
	`1) ls`
	   `;;`
	`2) who`
	   `;;`
	`*) echo "Invalid response!"`
	   `;;`
	`esac`

`declare` or `typeset`	Defines variables; –a defines an array; for example, `declare –a array5`

Table A-3 Shell script programming-related commands (continued)

Commands	Purpose

`function function-name ()`
`{`
`  statements`
`}`
	Defines a function; for example,
	`Function Divide ()`
	`{`
	`   Answer=$value1 / $value2`
	`}`
	To call the function from another script or the command line, divide *value1* by *value2*

`if condition`
`then`
`    statements`
`elif`
`    statements`
`else`
`    statements`
`fi`
	Makes decisions for example
	`if [[ $x -gt 5 ]]`
	`then`
	`   echo $x`
	`else`
	`   echo 10`
	`fi`

`for variable in value1`
`value2 value3...`
`do`
`statements`
`done`
	Performs looping constructs when the number of times to loop is known, for example:
	`for tools in hammer wrench saw`
	`do`
	`     echo $tools`
	`done`

`for ((variable=initial value;`
`variable operator value;`
`increment or decrement value))`
`do`
`statements`
`done`
	Performs looping constructs when the number of times to loop is known; this type of looping construct is particularly suited to traversing an array, for example:
	`for ((i=1; i<5; i++))`
	`do`
	`     total=a[$i] + $total`
	`done`

`return n`	Returns a status from a function, for example to return success, `return 0`
`shift`	Shifts positional parameters, for example to shift four positional parameters, `shift 4`

`select name in word1 word2 ...`
`do`
`      list`
`done`
	Creates a menu-based script, for example:
	`select cmd in who pwd date`
	`do`
	`      $cmd`
	`done`

`set`	Turns on debugging with `-xv`; turns off debugging with `+xv`

Table A-3   Shell script programming-related commands (continued)

Commands	Purpose
`source filename`	Reads and executes commands from *filename*; this command is typically used to utilize a function library, for example, `source function27`
`unset name`	Unsets a function that has been created or a variable that has been set, for example, `unset variableA`

`until list`
`do`
`    statements`
`done`
	Performs looping constructs using do statements as long as *list* returns a nonzero (false) exist status; for example:
	`while [[ $YN = "Y" ]]`
	`do`
	`    echo "continuing..."`
	`done`

Table A-4   Special characters

Symbol(s)	Purpose
`>`	Creates a new file by redirecting output
`>>`	Redirects output and appends to a file
`<`	Redirects input
`|`	Pipes output of one command as input into another
`*`	Wildcards all character positions
`?`	Wildcards a single character position
`&`	Runs a job in the background
`[characters]`	Wildcards multiple characters
`;`	Places commands in sequence
`(command)`	Runs a command in a subshell
`{command};`	Executes a command in the current shell
`[Space]`	Separates words
`||`	Executes a command depending upon the failure of another; also used as logical OR
`&&`	Executes a command depending upon the success of another; also used as logical AND
`++`	Increments a variable
`--`	Decrements a variable
`**`	Is used for exponentiation
`*`	Is used for multiplication
`/`	Is used for division

Table A-4   Special characters (continued)

Symbol(s)	Purpose
+	Is used for addition
–	Is used for subtraction
%	Is used for remainder
==	Compares values as equal to one another
!=	Compares values to establish values as not equal to one another
>=	Compares values as greater than or equal to one another
<=	Compares values as less than or equal to one another
>	Compares values to establish a greater than relationship
<	Compares values to establish a less than relationship
\	Protects the character immediately following a symbol
'...'	Protects characters within the single quotes
"..."	Protects all characters except $, ' (single quote), and \
`` `command` ``	Substitutes a command
$(command)	Substitutes a command
${variable }	Allows for the mixing of numbers and characters in the shell
${#variable}	Allows for the mixing of numbers and characters in the shell
$$	Expands to the PID of the shell
$?	Expands to the return status of the previously executed foreground command
$#	Expands to the number of positional parameters
$@	Expands to all of the positional parameters
$0 through $9	Expands to the positional parameters passed to a script
2>filename	Redirects standard error to filename
&>filename	Redirects standard output and standard error to filename

Index